This is the first extensive account of royal propaganda in England between 1689 and 1702. It demonstrates that the regime of William III did not rely upon legal or constitutional rhetoric as it attempted to legitimate itself after the Glorious Revolution, but rather used a protestant, providential, and biblically based language of 'courtly reformation'. This language presented the king as a divinely protected godly magistrate who could both defend the true church against its popish enemies, and restore the original piety and virtue of the elect English nation.

Concentrating upon a range of hitherto understudied sources – especially sermons and public prayers – the book demonstrates the vigour with which the ideal of courtly reformation was broadcast by an imaginative group of propagandists under Bishop Gilbert Burnet; and it demonstrates that this discourse enabled the king to cope with central political difficulties – particularly the royal need to attract support for wars with France (1689–97, and 1701 onwards) and the need to work with parliament.

Cambridge Studies in Early Modern British History

WILLIAM III AND THE GODLY REVOLUTION

Cambridge Studies in Early Modern British History

Series editors

ANTHONY FLETCHER
Professor of History, University of Essex

JOHN GUY
Professor of Modern History, University of St Andrews

and JOHN MORRILL
Reader in Early Modern History, University of Cambridge, and Fellow and Tutor of Selwyn College

This is a series of monographs and studies covering many aspects of the history of the British Isles between the late fifteenth century and the early eighteenth century. It includes the work of established scholars and pioneering work by a new generation of scholars. It includes both reviews and revisions of major topics and books, which open up new historical terrain or which reveal startling new perspectives on familiar subjects. All the volumes set detailed research into our broader perspectives and the books are intended for the use of students as well as of their teachers.

For a list of titles in the series, see end of book.

WILLIAM III
AND THE
GODLY REVOLUTION

TONY CLAYDON

University of Wales, Bangor

Published by the Press Syndicate of the University of Cambridge
The Pitt Building, Trumpington Street, Cambridge CB2 1RP
40 West 20th Street, New York, NY 10011-4211, USA
10 Stamford Road, Oakleigh, Melbourne 3166, Australia

First published 1996

Printed in Great Britain by Redwood Books, Trowbridge, Wiltshire

A catalogue record for this book is available from the British Library

Library of Congress cataloguing in publication data

Claydon, Tony.
William III and the godly revolution / Tony Claydon.
p.   cm. – (Cambridge studies in early modern British history)
Includes bibliographical references and index.
ISBN 0–521–47329–2
1. Great Britain – History – Revolution of 1688 – Propaganda.
2. Great Britain – Politics and government – 1689–1702. 3. Great
Britain – Kings and rulers – Succession. 4. William III, King of
England, 1650–1702. 5. James II, King of England, 1633–1701.
I. Title.   II. Series.
DA452.C63   1996
941.06′8–dc20
95–14567
CT

ISBN 0521 473292 hardback

CONTENTS

ILLUSTRATIONS

ACKNOWLEDGEMENTS

Few first books see the light of day without passing through a long gestation period, in which their authors require considerable intellectual, financial, and emotional support. This volume is no exception. Over the years it has taken for this work to reach its final form, I have been sustained by the generosity and understanding of a great many people. These few paragraphs are an inevitably insufficient attempt to acknowledge some of that sustenance.

My study of this subject began with my PhD thesis, funded by a grant from the British Academy, and continued whilst I was a Scoloudi Research Fellow at the Institute of Historical Research in London (financed by the Twenty Seven Foundation), and a Research Fellow at Fitzwilliam College, Cambridge. All these bodies deserve my thanks, both for keeping me solvent, and for showing more belief in my project than I often felt myself.

Intellectually, my greatest debt has been to my PhD supervisor, Julian Hoppit. As I worked on my thesis, his encouragement, his insight, and the speed and enthusiasm with which he commented upon my work were much appreciated. He has also been an invaluable source of advice since my doctorate has been finished. Others too have helped me, either through broad discussion of the early modern period, or more detailed observations upon specific aspects of my work. Here I would particularly like to thank Toby Barnard, Jeremy Black, Jeremy Gregory, Anne Goldgar, David Hayton, Tim Hitchcock, Joanna Innes, John Morrill, Craig Rose, Bob Shoemaker, John Spurr, Tim Wales, John Walsh, and my PhD examiners, Mark Goldie and John Miller. To these I owe much of what is valuable in the following work; mistakes, of course, are my own. In London, I have benefited hugely from the meetings of Penelope Corfield's 'Long Eighteenth Century' seminar at the Institute of Historical Research; whilst in Cambridge, I have found conversation with members of the History Faculty, and with the fellowship of Fitzwilliam College, extremely useful. In a different, but no less vital way, this project has been aided by the efforts of numerous library staff. Their work is often undervalued, and the appreciation conventionally expressed in acknowledgements of this kind can only ever offer a fragment of the thanks they deserve for their prevailing tolerance, grace, and helpfulness. Notwithstanding the inadequacy of my words however, I would like to express my heartfelt gratitude to the staff of the libraries in which I have worked – especially the British Library, the Library of the Institute of Historical Research in London, Lambeth Palace Library, Dr Williams' Library, the University of London's Senate House Library, the University Library in Cambridge, and the Bodleian Library, Oxford.

Finally, I must thank those who have upheld me in more personal ways. The life of young academics is often lonely and dispiriting, and some of their greatest debts must always be to those whose sympathy, whose faith or whose alcohol were provided at particularly dark moments. Here I would like to mention Andrew de Csilléry, Joy Dixon, Edmund Green, Emma Hughes-Davies, Stephen Jones, Lucy Wooding, my colleagues at Fitzwilliam, my friends from Jesus College, Oxford, and the regulars at the Institute of Historical Research. Above all, I have to thank my mother and my partner. Only they know how much help they have given me over the past years, and perhaps only I know how important that support was. To them this book is dedicated.

ABBREVIATIONS

AHR	*American Historical Review*
BIHR	*Bulletin of the Institute of Historical Research*
BL	British Library
Bodl.	Bodleian Library, Oxford
CJ	*Journals of the House of Commons*
CLRO	City of London Record Office
Cobbett	William Cobbett, ed., *The parliamentary history of England* (36 vols., 1806–20)
CSPD	*Calendar of state papers domestic*
DNB	*Dictionary of national biography* (63 vols., 1865–1900)
EHR	*English Historical Review*
Grey	Anchitel Grey, *Debates of the House of Commons from … 1667 to … 1694, collected by A. Grey* (10 vols., 1769)
HJ	*Historical Journal*
HMC Finch	Historical Manuscripts Commission, *Report on the manuscripts of the late Allan George Finch* (4 vols., 1922)
HMC Lords 1690–1	Historical Manuscripts Commission, *Manuscripts of the House of Lords 1690–1* (1892)
HMC Portland	Historical Manuscripts Commission, *Report on the manuscripts of his grace the duke of Portland, preserved at Welbeck Abbey* (5 vols., 1894)
JBS	*Journal of British Studies*
JEH	*Journal of Ecclesiastical History*
LJ	*Journals of the House of Lords*
Luttrell, *Diary*	Horwitz, Henry, ed., *The parliamentary diary of Narcissus Luttrell, 1691–1693* (Oxford, 1972)
Luttrell, *Relation*	Narcissus Luttrell, *A brief historical relation of state affairs from September 1678 to April 1714* (6 vols., Oxford, 1857)
PP	*Past and Present*
PRO	Public Record Office
TRHS	*Transactions of the Royal Historical Society*

NOTES ON STYLE

Dates are given old style, except where indicated, but the year has been assumed to start on 1 January.

Spelling and capitalisation of seventeenth-century material has been modernised, except in pamphlet titles and block quotations.

The titles of some works have, of necessity, been shortened.

Except where otherwise stated, all books were published in London.

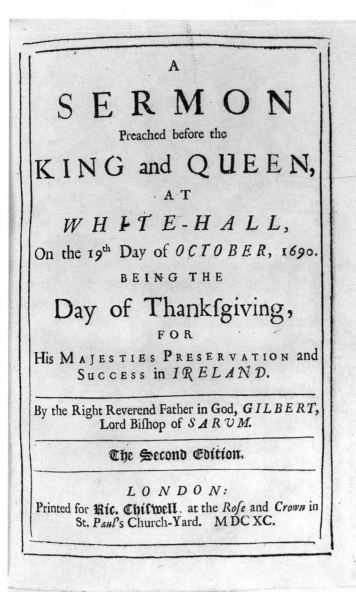

A

SERMON

Preached before the

KING and QUEEN,

AT

WHITE-HALL,

On the 19th Day of *OCTOBER*, 1690.

BEING THE

Day of Thankſgiving,

FOR

His MAJESTIES PRESERVATION and
SUCCESS in *IRELAND.*

By the Right Reverend Father in God, *GILBERT,*
Lord Biſhop of *SARVM.*

The Second Edition.

LONDON:
Printed for Ric. Chiſwell, at the *Roſe* and *Crown* in
St. *Paul's* Church-Yard. MDCXC.

Frontiſpiece to *The new state of England* [1696], showing a regenerated Britannia
enthroned between William III and Bishop Gilbert Burnet (reproduced with
permission of the British Museum)

Title page of Gilbert Burnet's *Sermon preached before the king and queen at Whitehall, 19 October 1690* (1690) as it would have appeared posted in public places (original approx. 8 × 5 inches)

Introduction

Most governments feel a need to advertise themselves to their populations. The regime of William III, king of England at the end of the seventeenth century, must have felt this need more than most. From his accession at the Glorious Revolution, to his death in 1702, this monarch was faced with a series of extraordinary challenges to his authority which demanded an effective propaganda if they were to be overcome. At the most basic level, William had to deal with doubts about his very right to rule. Because he had not inherited the throne in 1689, but had gained it after forcibly invading the country, the king was denied the usual claim of English monarchs to hereditary legitimacy, and had to establish some other justification for his exercise of power. Still more unfortunately, William's predecessor, James II, had not renounced his claims to the throne. Once displaced at the Revolution, the old monarch launched a military and ideological campaign to regain his position, whose arguments, as well as whose arms, had to be rebuffed. Compounding these problems of legitimacy was the need for war propaganda. Soon after becoming king, William took his new realm into a prolonged conflict with France, and consequently had to develop a royal message to preserve his subject's morale during a prolonged, bloody, and frequently discouraging struggle. Finally, the monarch had to find a language which would persuade independently minded legislators of the correctness of his policies. Since the king's war meant endless royal demands for money, he had to call his revenue-granting parliament every winter during his reign, and accordingly became reliant upon the Lords and Commons. Having to cajole cash from the men gathered at Westminster, William found he needed arguments to win over an often stubborn and factious body of people, and became the first monarch whose prime task was the persuasion of a largely autonomous legislature.

Given William's obvious need for effective propaganda, it is remarkable how little study has been made of court ideology in the late Stuart era. A period which has been the object of increasing scholarly attention in recent decades has suffered from a perplexing historical lacuna in this crucial area. Some excellent work on royal propaganda has appeared. However, the studies which have been produced have tended to be brief, and have generally concentrated only on particular aspects of the subject. Thus there have been pieces on Williamite publicity during the invasion of 1688/9, on the regime's organisation of pamphlet campaigns in the early 1690s, on the monarchy's visual and ceremonial propaganda, on the regime's self-presentation in Ireland, and on the role of William's consort, Mary, in the contemporary portrayal of the royal household.[1] Strangely, however, none of these studies has provided a comprehensive examination of the government's publicity campaign, and few have suggested any underlying themes which might have tied the various Williamite messages together. This neglect is doubly surprising, since there has been no lack of interest in either the history of political ideologies in the 1690s, or in the impact of William III's regime upon this field. Over the past few decades, many works have traced such late Stuart developments as the emergence of party philosophies, the impact of John Locke's ideas, and the reconfiguration of constitutional thought after the Revolution; and many of these have recognised that actions by the royal court transformed the content and context of political debates.[2] For example, William's acceptance of the English throne from a parliament-like convention in 1689 is widely thought to have altered perceptions of the relationship between crown and legislature, and to have led to a reconceptualisation of

---

[1] See, for example, Lois G. Schwoerer, 'The Glorious Revolution as spectacle: a new perspective', in Stephen B. Baxter, ed., *England's rise to greatness, 1660–1763* (Los Angeles, 1983), pp. 109–49; Lois G. Schwoerer, 'Images of Queen Mary II, 1689–95', *Renaissance Quarterly*, 42 (1989), 717–48; Lois G. Schwoerer, 'Propaganda in the revolution of 1688–9', *AHR*, 82 (1977), 843–74; Mark Goldie, 'The revolution of 1689 and the structure of political argument: an essay and an annotated bibliography of pamphlets in the allegiance controversy', *Bulletin of Research in the Humanities*, 83 (1980), 473–564; W. A. Speck, 'William – and Mary?', in Lois G. Schwoerer, ed., *The revolution of 1688/9: changing perspectives* (Cambridge, 1991), pp. 131–46; David Hayton, 'The propaganda war', in W. A. Maguire, ed., *Kings in conflict: the revolutionary war in Ireland and its aftermath, 1689–1750* (Belfast, 1990), pp. 106–21.

[2] No footnote of reasonable length could hope to list all the recent work in this area. Perhaps the most influential overviews have been Mark Goldie, 'Tory political thought, 1689–1714' (unpublished PhD dissertation, University of Cambridge, 1977); J. P. Kenyon, *Revolution principles: the politics of party 1689–1720* (Cambridge, 1977); and H. T. Dickinson, *Liberty and property: political ideology in eighteenth-century Britain* (1977), part 1. Many other important studies published before the middle of the 1980s are surveyed in the introduction to Geoffrey Holmes, *British politics in the age of Anne* (revised edn, 1987); whilst more recent works are listed in the bibliography of Tim Harris, *Politics under the later Stuarts: party conflict in a divided society* (Harlow, 1993).

England's mixed monarchy.[3] Similarly, the king's wartime establishment of a large army and of a permanent national debt is believed to have thrown up novel issues in national politics, and to have encouraged new analyses of the decline, corruption, and enslavement of free peoples.[4] Yet what has been missing from all this scholarship is any sense of the court's own ideology. William is acknowledged tó have created the conditions for far-reaching discursive change, but his regime's own contribution to contemporary discussions has been largely ignored. As a result, one of the most innovative regimes ever to have governed England has been left without a recognised voice.

This book will attempt to cure this royal muteness. Through a study of the politics and political languages of the 1690s, it will try to enhance understanding of the late Stuart period with a more complete account of court thought. First, the book will describe the challenges faced by court polemicists at the end of the seventeenth century. It will then demonstrate how these were met by the development of a biblically based discourse which will be labelled 'courtly reformation', and which presented William as a providential ruler who had a divine commission to protect the protestant church in England, and to return the nation to its pristine faith, piety, and virtue. The book will go on to trace the intellectual roots of this ideology; it will assess its strengths as a justification for William's rule; and it will show how it was broadcast through English society. Finally, this volume will describe the flexibility of royal propaganda. Concentrating on particular political difficulties faced by William, the work will show how court propagandists directed their message to deal with these, and will show how they adapted their arguments to appeal to a number of different audiences.

As it lays out its description of Williamite polemic, this book will pursue four further ambitions. The first will be to examine the public presentation of English monarchy at a crucial point in its development. The work will study communication between an English king and his political nation at a time when rulers were being forced to rethink strategies for self-promotion. There were two main reasons for this re-evaluation. First, the traditional point of contact between the monarch and the English elite had fallen into decline. The royal court, which since early Tudor times had encompassed most leading Englishmen, or drawn them into its ambit, had forfeited its central position as it had failed to compete with rival centres of political and social power.

---

[3] Recent discussions of this point are reviewed in Howard Nenner, 'The constitution in retrospect from 1689', in J. R. Jones, ed., *Liberty secured? Britain before and after 1688* (Stanford, 1992), pp. 88–122; and in the introduction to Schwoerer, *Revolution of 1688/9*.

[4] J. G. A. Pocock has done most to describe these new analyses of politics – see below, pp. 217–18; and his classic statement of his case, J. G. A. Pocock, *The Machiavellian moment: Florentine political thought and the Atlantic republican tradition* (Princeton, 1975), part 3.

Financial constraints after 1660 had meant that the royal household could no longer dominate culture or fashion; royal hospitality and patronage had been curtailed as their cost became prohibitive; and the rise of a vigorous public life in London – encompassing coffee-houses, clubs, theatres, and the press – had created influential alternatives for the exercise of political and social leadership. Secondly, the political nation had expanded as the court had lost ground. The number of people whom the monarch had to persuade had grown as parliament and its electorate had taken a more central position within the polity. As a result, effective power had been diffused among a larger number of individuals, and the monarch had had to face a mass public, instead of merely having to deal with the interests and attitudes of a small elite. Taken together, these developments forced a remodelling of the monarch's publicity. Established, court-based methods of propaganda (which have received considerable attention in studies of earlier regimes) became increasingly ineffective because they could no longer reach important audiences. The use of traditional persuaders such as ceremonial, etiquette, visual display, or cultural patronage, had been appropriate when the political elite had crowded round the monarch, but it ceased to be effective once leading politicians stopped coming to court, and once a mass electorate, who could never directly witness royalty, wielded more power.[5] In this situation, new ideas were needed to convince the English of the virtues of their king. This book will examine some of William's experiments in this area and will show how an imaginative English ruler could launch a penetrating propaganda campaign, even within the comparatively limited resources of an early modern state.

This volume's second aspiration will be to contribute to an ongoing reinterpretation of the late Stuart era. Hitherto, most students of the later seventeenth century have assumed that it was a period of steady secularisation. In particular, political and intellectual historians have suggested that the issues discussed in contemporary debates, and the languages in which these debates were couched, became less religious in the decades following the Civil War. The rise of natural philosophy, nervousness about sectarian extremism, and a new emphasis upon 'politeness' have all been held to have replaced theological modes of thought with 'scientific', 'sociological' or 'economic' interpretations of the world.[6] As a result, those historians who have studied ideological developments in the 1690s have played down specifically Christian languages, and have concentrated upon such 'secular' concerns as constitutional debate or contemporary understandings of the relationship between property and power. The study of Williamite

---

[5] For elucidation of all these points, see below, pp. 73–7.

[6] For this historiography, see C. J. Somerville, *The secularization of early modern England: from religious culture to religious faith* (Oxford, 1992); and the works noted below, pp. 42–3.

propaganda which follows will cast doubt on this set of assumptions, and upon this scholarly approach. 'Courtly reformation', the chief language of the royal court, will be revealed as a deeply Christian ideology, which rested upon a set of protestant and biblical idioms first developed during the Reformation of the middle of the sixteenth century. According to the prevailing account of Stuart politics, such religious discourses should have become outmoded by the time of William's accession. If this is wrong, and if theological language remained as crucial in the 1690s as will be argued, then the established view of the later seventeenth century would need considerable revision. As other historians have already begun to argue, protestant beliefs which are believed to have been marginalised would have to be returned to the centre stage, and an era which has been claimed as part of a secularising enlightenment would appear still enmeshed in the spiritual thoughts and concerns of an earlier period.[7]

This book's third objective will be to cast light on the constitutional significance of the Glorious Revolution. This is an area of considerable importance to students of the late Stuart period, which has attracted considerable study in the last few decades. At base, debate has centred on how much damage the events of 1688–9 did to the perceived power of the monarchy within England's fluid and unwritten constitution. Over the past years, an old 'whig' view of this question, which held that the Revolution reasserted traditionally recognised restraints upon the royal prerogative, has been challenged by groups of historians who have either tried to prove that 1688 introduced entirely new limitations upon the court, or have claimed that it actually did very little to reduce the king's majesty.[8] Thus whilst some have argued that the throne was given to William on the understanding that he accept new legal and legislative checks upon his actions, others have denied that this grant was in any way conditional.[9] Similarly, as some scholars have argued that the Revolution brought widespread acceptance of new theories of popular or parliamentary sovereignty, others have stressed that such radical

---

[7] The most aggressive arguments for the survival of earlier seventeenth-century mentalities have been Jonathan Scott, *Algernon Sidney and the Restoration crisis, 1677–1683* (Cambridge, 1991), part 1; Mark Goldie, Tim Harris, and Paul Seaward, eds., *The politics of religion in Restoration England* (Oxford, 1990), introduction by Tim Harris; and Michael Finlayson, *Historians, puritanism and the English revolution: the religious factor in English politics before and after the Interregnum* (Toronto, 1983).

[8] The classic statement of the whig view was T. B. Macaulay, *The History of England to the death of William III* (Heron books edn, 4 vols., 1984), II, 392–8.

[9] For accessible contributions to these debates, see Henry Horwitz, 'Parliament and the Glorious Revolution', *BIHR*, 47 (1974), 36–52; Henry Horwitz, '1689 (and all that)', *Parliamentary History*, 6 (1978), 23–32; Lois G. Schwoerer, *The declaration of rights, 1689* (Baltimore, 1981); Schwoerer, *Revolution of 1688/9*, especially introduction pp. 4–15; Corinne Comstock Weston and Janelle Renfrew Greenburg, *Subjects and sovereigns: the grand controversy over legal sovereignty in Stuart England* (Cambridge, 1981), ch. 8 and appendix.

ideas made little headway, and that strong arguments for the sacredness and absolute power of English rulers survived.[10] This volume will try to shed more light on these disputes by studying what the court itself said about its own position in the 1690s. Whilst demonstrating that the king's rhetoric of 'courtly reformation' was essentially non-constitutional (it deliberately avoided detailed analysis of the king's precise legal status), the volume will show that the discourse did have some implications for contemporary perceptions of royal power, and will examine its rather ambiguous messages in this area.

This book's final, and perhaps most ambitious, aim will be to help explain the extraordinary development of Britain over the centuries which flanked William's reign. Between 1600 and 1800, the British nations were transformed as a remarkable series of events remoulded their internal structures, their mutual relationships, and their wider international positions. Of these changes, two were of particular importance for this study. First, Britain became a major world power. By the early years of the nineteenth century, the relatively weak kingdoms which had been ruled by the Tudors and Stuarts had become united into an impressive military state, which had acquired an extensive empire overseas and had overawed its European rivals. Second, England (and by extension Britain) developed a viable parliamentary system. The repeated constitutional crises of the seventeenth century, in which authoritarian monarchs had become deadlocked with factious and uncooperative parliaments, gave way to a relatively stable political system in which crown and legislature largely accommodated one another's claims, and in which the House of Commons took responsibility for the support and scrutiny of royal government. In these processes, the years of the 1690s were crucial. The decade of William's rule not only saw the first truly successful experiment in parliamentary government, as a king who could not dispense with the legislature found ways to work with that body, but also witnessed the first prolonged commitment by British peoples to the sort of European war which would eventually secure their military dominance. By examining the court's political language in the 1690s, this volume hopes to explain how such things might have been possible. It will describe the ideological contexts in which

[10] Weston and Greenburg, *Subjects and sovereigns*, ch. 8 and appendix; W. A. Speck, *Reluctant revolutionaries: Englishmen and the Revolution of 1688* (Oxford, 1988), ch. 7; Kenyon, *Revolution principles*; Goldie, 'Tory political thought'; Dickinson, *Liberty and property*; Gerald Straka, *Anglican reaction to the Revolution of 1688* (Madison, Wisconsin, 1962); J. C. D. Clark, *English society, 1688–1832* (Cambridge, 1985); Richard Ashcraft, *Revolutionary politics and Locke's 'Two treatises of government'* (Princeton, 1986); Richard Ashcraft and M. M. Goldsmith, 'John Locke, revolution principles and the formation of whig ideology', *HJ*, 26 (1983), 773–800; Martyn P. Thompson, 'The reception of Locke's *Two treatises of government*, 1690–1705', *Political Studies*, 24 (1976), 184–91; Mark Goldie, 'The roots of true whiggism, 1688–94', *History of Political Thought*, 1 (1980), 195–236.

William built his military machine and managed his legislature; and it will argue that government propaganda played an important role in resolving the tensions which these innovatory activities created. Overall, therefore, this book will suggest that the discourse of courtly reformation had a significance far beyond the last years of Stuart rule. The long-neglected propaganda of the Williamite court certainly shaped English political thought between 1689 and 1702. It may also, however, have permitted the vital changes of that period, and in doing this have influenced Britain's development for many subsequent decades.

WILLIAM'S IDEOLOGICAL CHALLENGE:
THE STRUCTURE OF THE STUDY

As suggested in the first section of this introduction, the challenges facing William III as he attempted to construct an effective propaganda can be divided into three broad areas. The first was the doubt about his basic legitimacy; the second was the need to sell his war, and particularly to overcome the suspicion that England was being exploited by her Dutch military allies; and the third was the fact that the king had to govern through parliament. It is worth studying each of these areas in some detail. Once elucidated, they provide both an understanding of the difficulties with which William's publicists had to deal, and a framework for describing the strategies which these men adopted to cope with their situation.

Any account of William's problem with his basic legitimacy has to start with the circumstances of his accession. Explaining these involves some acquaintance with English history before 1688, and in particular with the career of James II – William's predecessor on the English throne. 1673 is a convenient point at which to start, since in that year it became clear that James, who was both heir and brother to the reigning Charles II, had converted to Roman catholicism. No discovery could have worried the English political nation more. For generations, Englishmen had associated the Roman faith with cruel and tyrannous government; and many feared that the advent of a catholic monarch would spell a fanatical persecution of the majority protestant population, a loss of traditional liberties and civil rights, and the subjection of the realm to catholic powers on the continent. The change in James's religion thus sparked nearly three decades of opposition to the man, and became a major cause of instability in English politics.[11]

At first, opposition was expressed in the parliaments of the 1670s. In those assemblies, James's influence at court was heavily criticised as government miscarriages were blamed upon him, and tentative moves were made to bar

---

[11] The best short account of these developments is John Miller, *Popery and politics in England, 1660–1688* (Cambridge, 1973).

him from the throne. In 1679 these currents became a flood when the apparent discovery of a catholic plot to assassinate Charles led to an anti-Roman panic. An exclusion bill was introduced into the Commons to disqualify the king's brother from the crown, and a fierce three-year crisis began in which English opinion polarised, and James's succession appeared to be in great jeopardy. In three successive parliaments, exclusionist majorities promoted their measure, and Charles was forced to exile his heir to protect him from the widely expressed wrath of his subjects. Fortunately for James his position was saved by astute political manoeuvring on the part of the king, and by a gradual, but widespread, reaction against exclusionist tumults. His enemies were defeated, his popular stock rose, and in 1685 he was able to succeed to the throne when his brother died. However, opposition was not over. Within a few weeks of his accession, Scotland and the West Country burst into unsuccessful rebellions, and the new king's actions soon began to alienate those who had supported him in the earlier 1680s. Royal determination to promote fellow catholics led to resentment amongst protestant elites, whilst James's grant of toleration and public office to his co-religionists contravened statute law, and led to new fears that he was bent on tyrannical government. In the three years of his reign James became locked in conflict with much of the political nation as his attempts to emancipate catholics were interpreted as attacks upon his subjects' rights to their property, upon the independence of the legislature and the judiciary, and upon that protestant faith which most of the English viewed as the only true form of Christianity. Relations reached their lowest ebb in the summer of 1688. As the church of England openly defied the regime's religious programme, and local elites protested against royal attempts to pack parliament with court supporters, James announced the birth of his son. The new heir would certainly be raised a catholic, and his arrival horrified a nation who now feared a perpetual Roman monarchy.[12]

In this situation, some began to look towards William. This man, who was both the hereditary prince of Orange, and the elected Stadholder of the United Provinces of the Netherlands, became a focus of hope for protestant Englishmen who believed that he might be persuaded to rescue them from their popish fate. There were several reasons why this was so. First, William was the protestant leader of a neighbouring protestant state. It was therefore possible that he might be persuaded to use the resources at his command to protect his religion in England. Second, William was James's nephew and son-in-law, and so had considerable concern in the future of the English monarchy. Until the birth of the new heir in 1688, his wife, Mary, had been next in line for the English throne and it had been widely expected that he

---

[12] John Miller, *James II: a study in kingship* (1989), pp. 167–88.

would be the effective ruler of England when she succeeded. It was therefore logical to think that William might intervene in English affairs to protect his interests, and this belief was reinforced when rumours began to circulate that James's son was supposititious – a fraud perpetrated by a catholic court to prolong its hold on power. Third, William had long been involved in English politics. Since the early 1670s he had consulted closely with leading Englishmen, and had periodically cultivated a party of supporters within the English elite. From 1687 his activities had become intense as he had communicated with James's opponents, and had built popular support for himself through highly publicised criticism of the king's religious ideals. This behaviour was interpreted as a prelude to intervention, and in June 1688 it encouraged seven English notables to send an 'invitation' to the prince to come to their country and force the king to reverse his policies.[13]

William's response to English hopes was dramatic. In the autumn of 1688 he issued a *Declaration* demanding that James call a free parliament to discuss his recent government and the legitimacy of his son, and then organised a huge invasion force in Holland, which landed at Torbay in Devon on 5 November. Advancing from the West Country, and appealing for English support, he terrified James into fleeing the country, and occupied London as the opposing royal army melted into ineffectiveness. This extraordinary, and perhaps unexpected, success raised the problem of what to do now that the king had left his realm. Over the early winter, consultations between the prince and those peers assembled in the capital led to the calling of a constitutional 'convention', which was empowered to decide what political settlement should be made. Constituted in the same way as a parliament, the convention met at the end of January 1689, and immediately began to discuss whether James could be said to have abdicated his crown, and whether the throne could now be filled by someone else. Debate on these points was intense, but pressure from the prince of Orange, and from his partisans in the convention's two houses, eventually led to an agreement to appoint William as his uncle's successor. On 13 February, in a ceremony at the Guildhall, London, the throne was offered to William and Mary jointly, with the proviso that the prince alone would actually exercise the monarch's power. James was displaced, and the hereditary claims of his son (now dismissed as supposititious) were disregarded.

From the course of events described above, it is fairly clear what William's problems with his legitimacy were to be. He had secured the English throne after his invasion of the country, but had done it in such a way that there were bound to be questions about his right to power. In the first place, real questions could be raised about the authority of the 1689 convention to

---

[13] Stephen B. Baxter, *William III* (1966), pp. 70–242.

bestow the crown. It was widely recognised that an English parliament had the right to deliberate upon, and decide, the royal succession – but the body which had met after William's arrival could not claim to be such a legislature. Any true parliament had to be summoned by royal writ, and had to include a reigning monarch as an integral part of its constitution. The convention had lacked these features, and it was therefore unclear on what grounds it had proceeded. Secondly, the convention's choice of William had violated the hereditary succession of the English crown. This was a problem because most contemporaries accepted direct inheritance as the only legitimate means of acceding to the throne. The history of England since the later middle ages, and vigorous royal propaganda, had persuaded many that heredity was the normal means of transferring sovereign power, and that any other system of succession risked confusion and disorder. In this situation, William's position looked decidedly anomalous. No hereditary account of what had happened in 1688–9 could be constructed to give him a right to the throne. If one accepted that James had abdicated by fleeing the country, then the succession should have passed directly to his infant son. If one thought that this was impossible because the son was fraudulent, then the crown should pass to James's daughter Mary, and William should at most have gained power as his wife's husband. In no circumstances should the prince of Orange have been granted a full monarchical title. Thirdly, and as a consequence of the other two objections, it was quite possible to view what had happened in 1688–9 as a rebellion followed by a usurpation. William had encouraged Englishmen to join him in arms against their monarch, and could be said to have used his force to expel a legitimate king. Such behaviour had always been condemned as sinful and illegal in English constitutional thought, and its heinousness had been particularly stressed after the 'great rebellion' of the English Civil War. As a result of all these doubts, many Englishmen were uneasy about the justice of William's elevation and would need considerable reassurance on this point.[14]

The urgency with which William had to rebut charges of illegitimacy can be gauged by the difficulty he had in persuading his subjects to swear the oaths of loyalty. Despite a careful rewording of the oaths to make them as widely acceptable as possible, large numbers of clergy and several prominent laymen refused them; and a bitter pamphlet controversy erupted over the justice of imposing allegiance to the new monarchs.[15] Even more disturbingly, an appreciable body of Englishmen retained some loyalty to James. The new

---

[14] Accounts of the doubts about William's title can be found in Paul Monod, *Jacobitism and the English people, 1688–1788* (Cambridge, 1989), pp. 15–23; Goldie, 'Tory political thought', pp. 134–44; J. C. Findon, 'The non-jurors and the church of England, 1689–1716' (unpublished DPhil dissertation, University of Oxford, 1979), pp. 126–48.

[15] Goldie, '1689 and the structure of political argument'.

regime's problem here was that the displaced king did not retire into despondency after 1688, but set up court in France, and made a series of attempts to regain his throne. He temporarily reconquered and occupied Ireland between 1689 and 1691; he persuaded the French to amass invasion forces in 1690, 1692, and 1696; and he sponsored a series of English plots against the Williamite regime. A Jacobite restoration did not, therefore, look impossible in the 1690s, and those Englishmen who worried about William's title were consequently encouraged to hope for James's return. Quite how many of the English actively worked for the exiled king under William is uncertain, and has not been made much clearer in a series of historiographical debates on the issue.[16] What is undeniable, however, is that in one field at least Jacobites posed a serious difficulty for the regime. A vigorous underground press, staffed by James's supporters, savaged William's policies and position throughout the reign, and demonstrated a disturbing talent for setting the agenda for public debate. As we shall see, such Jacobite writers as Charlwood Lawton, William Anderton, and James Montgomery set trends with their attacks upon the court's cost and corruption, and forced a desperate government into Draconian policies to control their activities.[17] The Jacobites thus ensured that William's most pressing need was for publicity which could counter questions about his title. Unless he could assert and persuade his subjects of his basic legitimacy, he risked losing ground to an implacable and skilful enemy, and might forfeit his position back to his predecessor.

William's second great reason for requiring an effective propaganda stemmed from his war with France. To understand why William took his new country into battle so soon after gaining the throne, it is again necessary to delve back into history. This time the story must be started at 1672. Then, French forces directed by Louis XIV had launched a massive attack upon the United Provinces of the Netherlands, and in this time of crisis, the Dutch people had turned to William. As prince of Orange, William was head of the family who had led Holland to independence over the previous hundred years, and during the 1672 emergency he came to be regarded as the man most likely to inspire a successful defence of his country. Accordingly he was appointed Stadholder, and masterminded resistance to the French until the peace of Nijmegen in 1678.

The 1672–8 war had been crucial for William's career as it established him

---

[16] Paul Monod describes these feuds, and offers a sensible way out of them, suggesting that arguments over the popularity of Jacobitism cannot be settled, since historians use such widely different definitions of the phenomenon. See Monod, *Jacobitism*, introduction.

[17] Perhaps the biggest success for Jacobite writers came in 1693 when Lawton's pamphlet *A short state of our condition with relation to the present parliament* (popularly known as the 'hush money paper') caused a general outcry with its accusation that ministers were bribing MPs. For more on the Jacobite press, and the Williamite response, see below, pp. 122–5 and Monod, *Jacobitism*, pp. 121–2.

as the chief opponent of France's ambitions in Europe. Both during the conflict, and through the peace which followed, he had portrayed Louis's territorial demands as the greatest contemporary threat to the continental balance of power and had devoted himself to finding a way to contain them. As head of state in the Netherlands, he had emphasised the French threat to his own citizens, and had reminded fellow rulers that seizure of Dutch land by Louis might endanger their own security. As sovereign lord of Orange, the small principality in Provence illegally occupied by French troops in 1682, he had argued that Louis was a threat to every independent state. As a protestant, he had urged more vigorous resistance to a catholic France which was becoming increasingly intolerant of reformed Christianity. From the middle of the 1680s, these arguments began to reap their reward. It became clear that Louis was bent on a new round of expansion, and the other states of Europe started to unite behind William's plan to assemble a grand alliance against the French king. By the end of the decade many of the continental powers, including the Netherlands, several German princes, and the Habsburg Empire, were actively engaged in a war to curtail France.[18]

It is within this historical context that William's actions in 1688–9 must be understood. The introduction of England to the European war against Louis was the primary objective of the prince's intervention in the country. William may have been concerned by the apparent loss of English liberties after James had come to the throne, but the main motivation for his 1688 expedition was his fear that James's religion, and the weakness of his domestic political position, might force him into a dependence on France. If this happened, and England became a French client, it was likely that the country would come into battle on Louis's side: so William had had to invade to prevent this possibility. In a sense, therefore, entry into the war against France was the prince's condition for intervening in England. Given this, it was not surprising that William ordered attacks upon French forces even before he had been offered the crown; nor that he harried parliament for a formal declaration of war as soon as he became king.

In early May 1689 the new monarch achieved his aim and England joined in hostilities against France. Yet once the war had started William was faced with the need to sell it. If he could not produce an effective war propaganda, then there was a risk that English morale might fail, and that the political elite (who had to agree to pay for the conflict through their representatives in parliament) might question whether they should be involved in such a

---

[18] For the European context of William's invasion see John Carswell, *The descent on England: a study of the English revolution of 1688 and its European background* (1969); Jonathan Israel, 'The Dutch role in the Glorious Revolution', in Jonathan Israel, ed., *The Anglo-Dutch moment: essays on the Glorious Revolution and its world impact* (Cambridge, 1991), pp. 105–62.

struggle. Of course, all wars create a need for effective publicity. However, two specific factors ensured William's requirements were particularly urgent. The first was the massive expense involved in the war against France. Over the preceding two centuries, the cost of conflict had escalated tremendously, as military techniques had developed in complexity and sophistication, and as battling states had deployed ever larger forces in the field. By 1689, warfare required the provision of huge, well-drilled armies, and proceeded largely by prolonged and bitter sieges of enemy fortifications.[19] As a result vast sums had to be spent by any nation which wished to retain its military power, and England soon began to reel under the impact of William's war. By the middle of the 1690s, Englishmen complained loudly as their king's actions against France raised the nation's annual tax bill by 150 per cent; as the government's annual deficit leapt from less than £1/4 million to nearly £5 million; and as bullion haemorrhaged from the country to pay for battles abroad. Fears were also raised about economic disruption. William's conflict closed traditional trade routes, created an acute monetary crisis, and transported around 50,000 of the nation's workforce to fight on the fields of Flanders.[20] Some ease came in 1697 when William made peace at the Treaty of Ryswick. However, even after this respite, royal policy still threatened to impose a heavy military burden. The king first requested a large standing army to be kept in readiness for future French aggression; and then, in 1701, led the country back into war to prevent Louis dominating Spain. In the face of this huge cost, persuading the English that their sacrifices were worthwhile was a Herculean task. William needed a brilliant ideological strategy to keep a nation unused to war behind his wearying campaigns.

The king also had to sell his war particularly vigorously because it involved co-operation with the Netherlands. This was a problem, because many late Stuart Englishmen suffered from an inbred suspicion of the Dutch. Despite England's role in securing Holland's independence over the previous hundred years, the two countries had drifted apart in the later seventeenth century as three wars (1652–4, 1665–7, 1672–4), and a bitter trade rivalry, had fostered an intense anti-Dutch xenophobia amongst many Englishmen. After the 1650s, some English commentators had even claimed that the United Provinces aimed at a 'universal monarchy'. Citing that nation's mercantile and colonial aggression, these Englishmen accused Hollanders of being brutal deceivers, who would stop at nothing to engross the world's wealth and

---

[19] For a general account of these changes see Geoffrey Parker, *The military revolution: military innovation and the rise of the West* (Cambridge, 1988).

[20] D. L. Jones, *War and economy in the age of William III and Marlborough* (Oxford, 1988), especially the table on pp. 70–1.

reduce all other nations to dependent status.[21] The war of 1689–97 revealed that such sentiments were widespread amongst the English political classes. At moments of tension they boiled over, as pamphleteers and parliamentarians accused the Dutch of exploiting their country. Dark complaints about William's bias towards Holland led to accusations that the Dutch were not contributing their fair share to the war, and to the suggestion that England had been tricked into a conflict fought solely for the Netherlands' benefit.[22] The king's difficulties with the cost of the war were thus compounded by suspicions about whether it was being fought in the national interest. As a result William's prime task in developing a war propaganda became the elucidation of a rhetoric to counter anti-Dutch sentiment. Unless he could calm English xenophobia, it was unlikely that the king could persuade his subjects to go on supporting his military activities.

William's third reason for developing an effective propaganda was closely linked to his second. Constant conflict with France meant constant demands by the crown for money. Chronic fiscal need involved repeated sessions of parliament. As a result, the legislature became an indispensable part of the English administrative system. Since 1689 it has met every winter for a substantive session, and rulers have had to govern through teams of ministers broadly acceptable to its two houses. William was thus the first English monarch whose essential task was the management of an independent legislature. At least once a year he had to present his case to the Lords, and to the purse-carrying Commons, and secure their support. He therefore faced, not only a general population to be won over to his cause, but a primary audience of parliamentarians, who had to be swayed and convinced on an almost daily basis.[23] Unfortunately for William, his dealings with parliament in the 1690s were to be complicated by the heritage of English history. Unresolved political disputes and ingrained political attitudes ensured that the legislature would not be easily persuaded to rally behind the king. Two problems in particular caused difficulty. The creation of parties in the late seventeenth century, and the tradition of 'country' sentiment, ensured that parliament tended towards contentious and uncooperative behaviour.

The emergence of parties was perhaps the most remarkable development in late Stuart England. Previously there had been factions and temporary alliances between politicians, but these had not dominated politics in the way

---

[21] Steven C. A. Pincus, 'Popery, trade and universal monarchy: the ideological context of the outbreak of the second Anglo-Dutch war', *EHR*, 107 (1992), 1–29.

[22] See below pp. 122–5.

[23] For the shift in the balance of power between executive and legislature see Angus McInnes, 'When was the English revolution?', *History*, 67 (1982), 377–92; Jennifer Carter, 'The Revolution and the constitution', in Geoffrey Holmes, ed., *Britain after the Glorious Revolution* (1979), pp. 39–58; Clayton Roberts, 'The constitutional significance of the financial settlement of 1690', *HJ*, 20 (1977), 59–76.

that the whig and tory camps which had formed under Charles II came to. Although these early groupings had lacked the centralised organisation and tight parliamentary discipline of later political parties, their rivalry had polarised the entire nation in the 1680s, and had filtered almost all contemporary issues through its bifurcating lens. The division between whigs and tories can most safely be dated to the exclusion crisis of 1679–82. As that drama had unfolded, the term 'whig' had been applied to those who attempted to debar the duke of York (the future James II) from the throne; whilst the tag 'tory' had been attached to those who opposed this attempt, and stood by the principle of indefeasible hereditary right.[24] However, although the constitutional issue of exclusion had been the occasion for the crystallisation of parties, religious issues, dating back to the Restoration at least, were perhaps more important in defining the division. When Charles II had returned from exile in 1660, he had come with a scheme to end the confessional quarrels between Englishmen which had contributed to his father's downfall. He had suggested that, whilst the pre-Interregnum church should be re-established, concessions should be made in its government and liturgy to satisfy those who had objected to some of its forms in the 1640s. Unfortunately, the capture of church and parliament by anglican hardliners had meant that such concessions were not to be forthcoming. An act of uniformity in 1662 had led to 'Black Bartholomew's Day', when those parish ministers who had served during the Interregnum, but could not accept the church as reimposed under Charles, were ejected from their livings. These events created a body of 'dissenting' clerics and their followers, who would pose the central political dilemma for Caroline Englishmen. In the early 1680s, debate about how to treat the considerable body of nonconformists helped to define the differences between the emerging political parties. Whilst the tories coalesced around a rigid view, which wanted the schismatic sectarians eliminated and supported a persecuting legislative code to effect this; the whigs drew on dissenting support, and campaigned for toleration of nonconformity. In fact, so strong was the religious polarisation between the two parties, that historians are coming to agree that confessional disagreements were the main cause of partisan division.[25] Matters of faith ensured that the two factions would gain extensive popular support, and fired a bitter, even bloody, power struggle between them, which was played out at both national and local level.[26]

---

[24] See Robert Willman, 'The origins of "whig" and "tory" in English political language', *HJ*, 17 (1974), 247–64.

[25] For a summary of recent discussion between historians about party polarities see Harris, *Politics under the later Stuarts*, ch. 3.

[26] The virulence of party strife in the period is well surveyed in Paul Seaward, *The Restoration, 1660–1688* (1991), pp. 101–42; Harris, *Politics under the later Stuarts*, chs. 4–5; Tim Harris, *London crowds in the reign of Charles II* (Cambridge, 1987).

The development of party posed a severe problem for William. When he came to the throne, he was faced, not only with a nation divided on its interpretation of the constitution, but one deeply fractured into rival religious camps. At the beginning of his reign, the new king hoped that the shock of James II's regime might have united whigs and tories, and he included men from both sides in his first government. The royal dream proved illusory, however, and inherited party hatreds soon burst forth in renewed bouts of political wrangling. These divisions horribly complicated the king's attempts to work with parliament, and ensured that that body was not a helpful partner in William's rule. In the 1690s, the Lords and Commons did not spend their time calmly deliberating on the king's need for money, as the royal court might have hoped; but rather developed into a forum for the factions' endless rivalry, and became a weapon in their mutual struggle. The two sides battled to gain majorities in the two houses; they tried to monopolise the king's government; they pressed for legislation against their opponents' interests; and they attempted to use the judicial authority of parliament to prosecute and destroy their enemies. In this internecine warfare, the monarch's needs were frequently ignored. William was to face a series of political crises as his parliamentary managers lost control of the houses to independent factional leaders – or more frighteningly, as the ministers he had appointed mutated into party politicians and placed the interests of their own faction above those of the ministry to which they belonged.[27]

The king's other great problem in dealing with parliament was the legacy of suspicion of courtiers amongst England's political class. During the seventeenth century, 'country' sentiment – a nagging mistrust of the executive and its ambitions – had become a characteristic element of the national psyche. It had drawn strength from mounting evidence that successive governments had been corrupted by the temptations of power, and had aimed to impose a tyrannical regime. The cumulative experience of Charles I's autocratic proclivities, of the luxury and double-dealing of Charles II's government, and of James II's assault on traditional liberties, had led to the pessimistic conclusion that courts were full of immoral and extravagant men who strove constantly to extend their authority beyond its legitimate bounds. In response to this conviction, a recognisable platform of country policies had been formulated. The crucial period in the process was the 1670s when country-minded politicians in parliament had begun to campaign (against court resistance) for a series of measures to control the damage a corrupt executive might do. These included limits on royal expenditure, better parliamentary scrutiny of

---

[27] The most comprehensive account of parliamentary politics in the 1690s is Henry Horwitz, *Parliament, policy and politics in the reign of William III* (Manchester, 1977).

government, resistance to standing armies, and guarantees against interference in the judiciary and legislature.[28]

Such a tradition of mistrust proved very dangerous for William. When he
came to the throne, he faced a country morbidly sensitive to administrative
corruption and influence. This was not an ideal situation for a monarch
whose bellicose policies would require strong government, and would inevitably extend the state's activities. In the 1690s the war would vastly expand
the armed forces; it would increase the numbers employed in fiscal and
military administration; it would erode civil liberties as ministers tried to
control the actions of enemy agents; and it would create a myriad of new
government creditors as people lent money to finance the conflict. All these
developments could be interpreted as increases in court power, and all would
be opposed by men of 'country' opinions.[29] Equally seriously, 'country'
sentiment promoted ideas about parliament's role which were diametrically
opposed to the royal view of this body. In the eyes of 'country' politicians, the
legislature must never degenerate into a tax-raising department of a military
state. Rather, it must develop its role as a check upon the executive, both
asserting its independence from the court, and developing its power to inquire
into and control the administration. The heritage of political suspicion thus
ensured that William would face a struggle when trying to work with parliament. Throughout his reign he had to appeal for support at Westminster,
whilst enduring a barrage of legislators' attacks upon his prerogative and
administration.[30]

Given all this, William's need for an effective parliamentary propaganda is
clear. He not only had to win over majorities of the two houses in order to
finance his war, but had to deal with specific obstacles to that goal. In the first
place, he required a rhetoric which could address party strife. He had to try to
persuade whigs and tories to moderate their destructive battles, and to
convince them that the national interest must override their private ambitions. Secondly, William needed arguments to calm country suspicions.
Unless he could convince legislators that he was more trustworthy than his
predecessors, he risked total rupture with parliament, or endless attempts to
straitjacket him with limitations and controls. The overall task facing William's propagandists was therefore extraordinarily demanding. A king who
already had to assert his basic right to rule, and counter English xenophobia,

---

[28] See K. H. D. Haley, *The first earl of Shaftesbury* (Oxford, 1968), pp. 348–71; J. R. Jones,
Charles II: royal politician (1987), pp. 65–6; Andrew Browning, *Thomas Osbourne: earl of
Danby and duke of Leeds, 1632–1712* (3 vols., Glasgow, 1951), I, part 2.

[29] The clash between William's war administration and the country party is well described in
John Brewer, *The sinews of power: war, money and the English state* (1989), ch. 5.

[30] For a detailed account of this parliamentary pressure (which unfortunately overstates its
coherence and organisation) see Dennis Rubini, *Court and country, 1688–1702* (1967).

also had to win over an autonomous and fractious legislature on which the success of his reign depended.

The rest of this book will examine how the Williamites met their challenge. Broadly, the work can be divided into three sections, each corresponding to one of the three basic difficulties which the royal propagandists faced. The first section (encompassing chapters 1 to 3) will discuss the fundamental problem of legitimacy. Examining some hitherto understudied sources for 1690s politics, it will suggest that a small coterie of men close to William developed the ideology of courtly reformation and attempted to justify the Orange regime by setting it in a protestant and providential pattern of English history. Over the 1690s, it will be argued, their ideas became the keystone of government propaganda, and were broadcast through a remarkably comprehensive and imaginative publicity machine. After this, the second section (contained in chapter 4) will turn to the problem of anti-Dutch sentiment and the war. It will show how the doctrine of courtly reformation was adapted to drum up support for the military effort against France, and how it attempted to persuade the English to accept the alliance with Holland by manipulating their sense of nationality. Finally, the third section (chapters 5 and 6) will deal with William's difficulties with his legislature. It will demonstrate that courtly reformation could be used in appeals to whig, tory, and 'country' sentiment, and that it helped to moderate the unruliness of late Stuart Westminster.

THE LIMITATIONS OF THE STUDY

Obviously this book has limitations. For a start, its concentration upon one area of government ideology may give a distorted picture of the phenomenon as a whole. Williamite publicists did not devote all their time to the promotion of courtly reformation, and in seeking to explain the centrality of this particular doctrine there is always a danger that the regime's efforts in other fields will receive relatively short shrift. Similarly, Scotland and Ireland are neglected in this study of English politics. Although the 'British' context of William's rule is of crucial importance, and although the king obviously had to sell himself in his other realms as well as England, no study of royal propaganda in these other countries will be attempted here as it would entail descriptions of quite different sets of political circumstances, and would consequently render this work unfeasibly large.[31] Most frustratingly, this study can do little to answer the central question about the Orange

---

[31] Hayton, 'Propaganda war', provides some coverage of William's publicity in Ireland. Williamite propaganda in Scotland is less well served, though P. W. J. Riley, *King William and the Scottish politicians* (Manchester, 1979), provides useful insights into the practice and contexts of Orange government in that country. The use of the term 'British' to cover Ireland as well as England and Scotland in this work is inaccurate, and possibly offensive. No alternative word to describe the three island kingdoms suggests itself, however.

ideological campaign. Despite some attempts to assess the effectiveness of William's rhetoric, this book can offer only unsatisfying claims about the discourse's ability to persuade its audience, or to win support for its sponsor.

At first sight, such reticence over the actual achievements of courtly reformation may seem strange. Superficially, at least, there does seem to be good evidence for the cogency and power of Orange propaganda. Considering the circumstances of the 1690s, the post-Revolution monarchy was remarkably successful, and rose well to the myriad of difficult challenges which faced it. At a very basic level, it contained Jacobitism. Appeals from supporters of the exiled king for the English to rise up against their usurping monarch fell on largely deaf ears, and the various invasion scares and assassination plots seem merely to have strengthened support for the king. Similarly, William managed to involve his new kingdom in war. He proved more adept than his Stuart predecessors in mobilising the realm for armed conflict abroad, and was able to employ considerable English forces in his battles in Ireland and Flanders. Again, William worked surprisingly well with parliament. Despite his foreignness, the strains of war, and the legacy of English political dispute, William's relations with the legislature never reached an *impasse* which interfered with his hold on the country, or the conduct of his struggle with Louis XIV. English legislators were generous and innovative in providing funds for their king's armies; they avoided pushing arguments with him to the point of constitutional crisis; and they rarely subjected him to outright parliamentary defeat.[32] All these political triumphs surely suggest that royal propaganda was doing its job well.

Unfortunately, however, the situation was not as clear as this. Whilst royal polemic may well have won over many of William's subjects, his success cannot be ascribed to his publicity alone, since it is obviously very easy to conceive other possible explanations for English co-operation with the king. People might, for instance, have supported their new regime out of self-interest. Having secured positions of profit or influence after 1688, or merely having accepted the post-Revolutionary government, they may have been frightened of the personal consequences of undermining William. Similarly, William's subjects may have been motivated by ideologies unconnected with reformation propaganda, which were not actively promoted by the court. For example they might have been influenced by the whig discourse of an ancient and free constitution, and might have wanted to co-operate with the king in the belief that William was that constitution's defender.[33] Similarly, the old idea that open opposition to the monarch was treason could have restrained

---

[32] For William's ability to work with parliament, see below, chs. 4–6.
[33] For the adoption of this point of view by men after the Revolution see J. G. A. Pocock, *The ancient constitution and the feudal law: a study of English historical thought in the seventeenth century* (reissue with retrospect, Cambridge, 1987), pp. 229–32.

their behaviour; or alternatively subjects may have been motivated by the various arguments from necessity, conquest, or *de facto* principles, which have been shown to have led to tory acquiescence in the change of ruler.[34]

Isolating the influence of William's propaganda amongst this tangle of potential factors is virtually impossible. For a start it would mean grappling with the intractable problem of making windows into dead men's souls. Historians are rarely, if ever, granted access to the mental states of their subjects, and so cannot ultimately decide which set of beliefs actually control people's attitudes. Because historical evidence is necessarily only of *outward* words or actions, and because it is unusual for historical subjects to explain the ideological roots of their behaviour in any great detail (or to be indubitably sincere when they do so), private opinion has to remain a largely inaccessible world. As a result, historians cannot be sure how influential a set of arguments were at any point in time, and could never state for certain whether they were crucial in persuading their audience. Still more discouragingly, gauging the impact of Orange rhetoric in the 1690s has special difficulties beyond these general methodological problems. Both the thinness of the parliamentary record under William, and the structure of Williamite argument, ensure that it is hard to make any solid claims for the propaganda's achievements.

Obviously any scholar wishing to assess the influence of courtly reformation must concentrate upon parliamentarians. As has already been stressed, the 1690s Lords and Commons were the most important audiences for courtly reformation since these bodies had become indispensable and had to be persuaded to co-operate with the royal government. Unfortunately, however, evidence about reception of the court's case amongst peers and MPs is disappointingly slim. Despite living in a period of intense ideological exchange, William's legislators have left only patchy evidence of their fundamental attitudes, and have provided few hints about their adherence to courtly reformation. The greatest frustration for the historian is the inadequate account which survives of parliamentary proceedings. Debates at Westminster might have provided good clues to legislators' beliefs, if only scholars had a better account of what was actually said. In the 1690s, however, there was no official record of parliamentary speeches; the press was barred from reporting deliberations; and few members of either house made detailed notes of their colleagues' oratory.[35] Whilst the parliamentary diaries of Anchitell Grey, Narcissus Luttrell, and Sir Richard Cocks give some insight into debates in the Commons, they suffer from considerable

---

[34] For tory accommodation with the Revolution, see Goldie, 'Tory political thought'; Dickinson, *Liberty and property*, ch. 1.
[35] For press restrictions, see M. A. Thomson, *A constitutional history of England, 1642–1801* (London, 1938), p. 333.

weaknesses as material for analysis.[36] Not only do they exclude the peers' discussions, and fail to cover a four-year period in the middle of the decade, they consist only of short summaries of speeches which note only the main points made by each MP, along with any oratorical flourishes which caught the diarist's imagination. Such reports reveal a speaker's stance on the topic under discussion, but are usually too abridged and prosaic to allow sustained investigation of the assumptions underlying his position. Records, including such entries as 'Sir John Knight rumbled nothing to the purpose', are hardly a firm foundation for ideological analysis.[37]

Outside parliament, better evidence has survived. Peers and MPs were members of the political and social elite, and were thus the sort of folk who generate archives. Often, therefore, there are useful records of their activities away from Westminster, and something is known about many legislators' social networks, their local influence and behaviour, their membership of political and religious movements, and their economic situation.[38] Also, evidence can be drawn from the vigorous press debates of the 1690s. Some legislators participated in these, publishing full versions of their speeches in parliament, writing their own tracts or pamphlets, or commissioning writers to produce material to advance their political campaigns.[39] However, despite the richness of a few of these sources, most of the material remains too patchy for a proper evaluation of courtly reformation's influence. It is neither extensive enough, nor even enough, for any firm conclusions to be drawn about legislative reactions to executive propaganda. In fact, a good deal of the material could be described as ideologically 'low grade'. It is the sort of evidence which reveals single instances of outward action, but can only give clues to mentality when there is enough of it to establish consistent patterns of thought. More explicit evidence is sufficiently rare that it raises the problem of typicality. Printed polemics by peers or MPs, for example, contain sustained political argument, and so may be very good sources for the thought of those who produced them. Yet since these self-publicists were a small minority of all legislators, historians must be left wondering how representative they were of their silent fellows. Although it could be argued that some of those who organised publications were political leaders, who reflected and influenced the views of a more numerous group of their supporters, political

---

[36] Grey and Luttrell's diaries have been published. Cock's diaries are held in the Bodleian Library as Eng. hist. Ms. B 209–10.

[37] Cobbett, V, 838.

[38] The History of Parliament Trust, currently compiling its volumes for the House of Commons, 1690–1715, has collected much of this kind of information for William III's MPs.

[39] For examples of such activities see J. A. Downie, *Robert Harley and the press: propaganda and public opinion in the age of Swift and Defoe* (Cambridge, 1979); Charles Sedley, *The speech of Sir Charles Sidley in the House of Commons* (1691); John Knight, *The speech of Sir John Knight of Bristol, against the bill for a general naturalisation* [1694].

alignments in the 1690s were too fluid, informal, and transient for anyone to be sure exactly whom a spokesman represented.

Aside from these difficulties of evidence from the 1690s, the structure of William's language provides further problems in assessing its impact. These arise because of the intricate complexity of royal ideology. As will be described, courtly reformation was not a simple idea, whose progress through society could be judged merely by collecting instances of its use. Rather, it was a carefully constructed composite of a number of existing conventions, each of which had an existence outside the doctrine and could consequently be employed by men who had not accepted Orange arguments.[40] For example, William's propagandists made much of God's providence, and of royal campaigns against vice, as part of their legitimation of the new regime. Yet both these notions were traditional commonplaces which could be incorporated into non-Williamite discourses when used in alternative combinations. The idea of providence, for instance, was taken up by Jacobites in the 1690s. They argued that God would ultimately restore England's rightful monarchs, and that the Orange usurpers could not expect to escape divine punishment.[41] Similarly, the concept of a royal campaign against vice was deployed by partisan whigs and tories as well as by William's spokesmen. Party polemicists accused each other of sabotaging the king's moral campaign, and so stoked the political tensions which the court was desperately trying to control.[42] In these circumstances, the real influence of reformation ideals is very hard to judge. Since each element of the rhetoric was polyvalent, and could mean different things in different circumstances, it is not enough to cite the use of these elements as evidence of Williamite beliefs. Late Stuart Englishmen can often be caught expounding one part of the courtly reformation worldview, but unless they can be shown to have combined this with other constituents of the doctrine to produce an explicitly pro-Orange position, they cannot automatically be considered adherents of the king's ideology. Unfortunately records of wholesale rehearsal of courtly reformation are very rare. Without them, historians must be wary of seeing acceptance of Williamite discourse, when all they have is the repetition of very flexible, and widely shared, units of rhetoric.

Given all these difficulties, *proving* the effectiveness of courtly reformation in winning support for William is a virtually hopeless task. In the study which

---

[40] For the construction of Williamite propaganda from existing conventions, see below, pp. 32–52.

[41] Monod, *Jacobitism, passim*, but especially pp. 49–54.

[42] For such an exchange see [Daniel Defoe], 'The legion memorial', in Walter Scott, ed., *A collection of scarce and valuable tracts, on the most interesting and entertaining subjects* (13 vols., 1809–15), XI, 255–9, especially 258; *England's enemies exposed and its true friends and patriots defended* (1701), *A justification of the proceedings of the ... House of Commons in the last sessions of parliament* (1701).

follows, evidence for the influence of the rhetoric will be quoted from sources as diverse as diaries, letters, political pamphlets, parliamentary speeches, and public demonstrations. Yet for all the reasons which have been supplied, the case made must remain partial and circumstantial. In the end, the best indication of the importance of Williamite propaganda is simply the effort invested in it by the court's own spokesmen. As we shall see, the men and women who promoted royal ideology in the 1690s were thoughtful and experienced publicists, who spent much time developing and reviewing their polemical techniques. That such people believed it was worth persisting with courtly reformation as a justification of their king and his policies is the strongest possible signal that it was meeting with success.

Courtly reformation and the revolution of 1688–1689

When William III, prince of Orange, landed at Torbay on 5 November 1688, the opening shot in his propaganda war had already been fired. A month earlier the prince had issued a manifesto, his *Declaration of reasons for appearing in arms in the kingdom of England*, which, as its title suggested, offered a vindication for his bringing a military force across the Channel.[1]

This manifesto was crucial for William during his English expedition. It formed the centrepiece of his entire publicity campaign, and was promoted with an extraordinary care and zeal by his supporters. The importance attached to the document within the Stadholder's circle was evident from the moment William had ordered its preparation. It had, for instance, taken weeks to write. Its author, Gaspar Fagel – the Grand Pensionary of Holland and a seasoned producer of Orange publicity – had completed the work only after an exhaustive process of consultation and redrafting. The manifesto had not emerged until the Pensionary had sought advice about the state of opinion in England, until he had held extensive discussions to decide which were the best arguments to deploy, or until experienced pamphleteers had edited and sharpened his prose. Similar care was shown in the distribution of the manifesto. Once the work was finished, it was broadcast through a sophisticated system of publicity which saturated England with the document. Agents secretly crossed the Channel with bundles of the work before the invasion; and then handed them out to printers, booksellers and leading politicians once William arrived. A press was brought to England to run off more copies of the *Declaration*; William's supporters repeatedly read the piece out in churches and town squares as the prince advanced from Torbay; and other

---

[1] William III, *The declaration of his highness William Henry, prince of Orange, of the reasons inducing him to appear in armes in the kingdom of England* (Hague, 1688). It can be consulted in Cobbett, V, 1–11.

pamphlets were produced to reinforce the manifesto's arguments and direct their readers' attention to that tract. Fagel's essay was publicised further through its use as a badge of allegiance as William marched towards London. Those Englishmen who defected to the prince were asked to endorse the manifesto, and public declarations of its text were made when city corporations or sections of the armed forces came to support the expedition. All this meant that the *Declaration* was highly visible in the winter of 1688–9. In fact Lois Schwoerer, the modern expert on this work, has stated that it was 'everywhere' at the time, and that it so dominated discussions amongst the politically conscious that it must be accounted one of the main reasons for William's eventual success.[2]

Given the attention lavished on the *Declaration*, and its undoubted impact, it would seem natural to root any investigation of Orange propaganda in this text. Here was a hugely successful work, issued right at the beginning of William's English career, which any historian seeking to understand the prince's ideology must surely subject to rigorous analysis. Yet curiously, it would be a mistake to devote too much attention to the 1688 manifesto. The *Declaration* was to prove far less crucial to Orange propaganda during William's reign in England than its original centrality might suggest. Huge effort was certainly put into promoting the document immediately after it had been issued, but this initial publicity campaign had no real sequel. After William's first few weeks in his new country neither the manifesto itself, nor its main arguments, were emphasised within his publicity. Even by January 1689, the prince and his supporters were distancing themselves from the text in which they had set so much store.[3]

To understand why this was so, it is necessary to examine the arguments of the *Declaration*. Broadly, the manifesto took its stand on English constitution. It asserted that William's actions offered the only chance to defeat a conspiracy which, in recent years, had aimed to replace England's free and legal government with an absolutist regime.[4] The first section of the document tried to prove the existence of such a tyrannous plot. It cited a series of high-handed executive actions, which suggested that evil men at court were bent on imposing 'arbitrary' rule.[5] Amongst other worrying developments the manifesto analysed James's notorious suspensions of statute, his 'illegal' establishment of an ecclesiastical commission, his interference with the judiciary, and finally, his attempt to subvert the succession with the dubious claim

---

[2] For the distribution of the *Declaration*, see Schwoerer, 'Propaganda in the revolution'; Schwoerer, *The declaration of rights*, pp. 105–20; Israel, *Anglo-Dutch moment*, pp. 13–22.
[3] The argument in the next paragraphs summarises that of my article, 'William of Orange's *Declaration of reasons*, and the revolution of 1688/9', *HJ* (forthcoming).
[4] Cobbett, V, 1.   [5] *Ibid.* 1–2.

that he had fathered a male heir.[6] Having demonstrated the threat from evil conspirators, the *Declaration* went on to consider possible remedies against them. It acknowledged that the proper safeguard against ambitious government in England was the calling of parliament; but it suggested that creeping tyranny in the past few years had cut off this 'last and great remedy'. The wicked courtiers had prevented the legislature from assembling and had tried to interfere with the free election of the country's representatives.[7] In these circumstances, the *Declaration* argued, more unusual measures were needed. William – who had a family interest in England and who had been asked to intervene by several English notables – had recognised the danger and had 'thought fit to go over to England' to retrieve the situation. His design was to ensure that a 'free and lawful parliament' might assemble, and that all the autocratic actions of the last few years might be referred to it.[8] The *Declaration* therefore dressed William's expedition as a necessary preservative of English rights and freedoms, which all honest and law-abiding subjects must support.

This presentation of the Dutch invasion had great advantages for William in the early autumn of 1688. It avoided alienating potential supporters by eschewing partisan arguments, and by attempting to calm English fears of rebellion. Concentrating upon constitutional improprieties which had worried both whigs and tories, and directing criticism away from the king towards his evil counsellors, it had skirted around controversial arguments and had allowed Englishmen to unite around the prince. However, whilst the *Declaration* was a skilful response to circumstances before William's invasion, developments during that adventure revealed it contained dangerous hostages to fortune, and destroyed its effectiveness as Orange propaganda. As the scale of the prince's military and political success became clear, the manifesto became a serious impediment to William's cause and had to be abandoned by those who had first sponsored it.

The *Declaration*'s fundamental weakness was that it did not advertise William's desire to be king. Written in the autumn of 1688, when any revelation of royal ambitions would certainly have alienated many Englishmen, the document had been punctilious in its respect for James. It had stressed that the king's nephew wanted no more than a free parliament which could address recent grievances, and had scrupulously avoided overt criticism of the head of state. This position was to cause William considerable difficulty. His caution had been entirely appropriate in October, when most of the nation would have feared the revolutionary potential of any direct attack upon a reigning monarch, but it became an embarrassment once that monarch had fled, and William had a realistic chance of replacing him. Since the

---

[6] *Ibid.* 2–7, 9.   [7] *Ibid.* 8.   [8] *Ibid.* 9–10.

Declaration had not stated that the prince of Orange wished to ascend to the throne, the document made it hard for him to campaign for promotion without contradicting his publicly stated objectives. As a result, William was forced into virtual silence on the constitutional position over the winter of 1688–9. The prince might want the crown, and might work for it behind the scenes by privately putting pressure on English politicians, but publicly he could do no more than express support for a free, uncoerced convention.[9] Worse still, the *Declaration*'s lack of reference to William's royal aspirations enabled opponents to accuse him of deceit. Once it became clear what William's aims were, Jacobite pamphleteers showered him in accusations of dishonesty, and claimed that an overweening ambition had been cynically disguised in his appeal to the English people.[10] Some of this rhetoric appears to have hit home. It is noticeable that some politicians (particularly leading tories such as Sir Edward Seymour and the earl of Clarendon) supported William when he first arrived with his *Declaration*, but felt betrayed when he showed a willingness to occupy the throne, and opposed him in the 1689 convention.

Quite apart from this basic defect, William's document had another deficiency which also destroyed its effectiveness as Orange propaganda. Capitalising on contemporary fears of arbitrary government, it suggested that the powers of the English monarch should be tightly controlled. It cited a series of occasions on which the king had overstepped his legal powers, and demanded that the limits of the prerogative be defined and upheld by an independent legislature. Again, the *Declaration*'s position was entirely appropriate in the autumn of 1688 when William was trying to build support against the Jacobite court. Again, however, the document became an embarrassment once that court had collapsed, and William wanted to replace it. The controls on royal power which the *Declaration* had suggested were a popular political programme whilst the old king still ruled, but they would be restrictive limitations once William was on the throne and wished to use his new authority to organise England for war with France. This troublesome contra-

---

[9] No claim to the throne was made in any of the following texts: William's answer to James's delegation during the Hungerford negotiations, 8 December 1688 – *The commissioners' proposals to his royal highness the prince of Orange, with his highness's answer* (1688); William's speech to the lords assembled at St James's, 21 December 1688 – Cobbett, V, 21; William's speech to the assembled members of Charles II's parliaments, 23 December 1688 – *CJ*, 10, 5; William's letter to both houses of the convention, 22 January 1669 – *LJ*, 14, 101–2. For William's private pressure for the throne, see D. W. Jones, *A parliamentary history of the Glorious Revolution* (1988), pp. 36–9.

[10] See, for example, *Some reflections upon his highness the prince of Orange's declaration* (Edinburgh, 1688); *Animadversions upon the declaration of his highness the prince of Orange* (1688); *The prince of Orange his declaration, shewing the reasons why he invades England, with a short preface, and some modest remarks on it* (1688).

diction was fully revealed in the convention of 1689. Then, various members of the lower chamber had suggested that a declaration of subjects' rights should accompany any offer of the throne, and should explicitly bind any new monarch within a tightly defined prerogative. William opposed these moves, but was hamstrung by the fact that those advocating controls cited his manifesto in support of their initiative. He would, therefore, have to repudiate his earlier stated position if he were to pursue his later political goals, and was persuaded, reluctantly, to allow a declaration of rights to go forward with the offer of the throne.[11] The *Declaration* had thus proved a double disaster. It had hugely complicated William's advocacy of his claims to the crown, and had threatened to reduce monarchical power just at the moment he attained it.

Given these problems, it is not surprising that the Orange camp began to distance itself from its original manifesto. Once James had fled, the initial burst of enthusiasm for the *Declaration* faded, and its sponsors abandoned it as soon as decently possible. William referred to the document when organising the convention, but his opening letter to that body on 22 January was the last time he mentioned it publicly, and he was soon wrestling against its implications as the assembly deliberated. In fact by the middle of winter, discussion of the manifesto was led, not by its first advocates, but by those who opposed the prince's elevation and realised they could cite the document to emphasise the shame of his conduct.[12] The *Declaration* had thus been a glorious beginning to the Orange propaganda campaign, but had ultimately led nowhere. If we are to understand how William met his need for effective publicity, we must look beyond his opening essay – and beyond the predominantly secular, legal, and constitutional case that it made.

WILLIAM'S SECOND STRATEGY: GILBERT BURNET AND REFORMATION

The search for more enduring Williamite propaganda should start with a sermon preached at St James's Palace on 23 December 1688.[13] It is easy to

---

[11] Lois Schwoerer has also argued along these lines, see her *Declaration of rights*, especially pp. 125, 236–7.

[12] For example, both loyalist peers in December 1688, and tories in the convention, attempted to block William's path to the throne with his own document. See Robert Beddard 'The Guildhall declaration of 11 December 1688, and the counter-revolution of the loyalists', *HJ*, 11 (1968), 403–20; Lois G. Schwoerer, 'A jornall of the convention at Westminster begun 22 January 1688/9', *BIHR*, 49 (1976), 242–63, especially 247; Schwoerer, *Declaration of rights*, pp. 175–6.

[13] Gilbert Burnet, *A sermon preached in the chappel of St James' before his highness the prince of Orange, 23 December 1688* (1689).

overlook this work in a study of contemporary English politics since it did not address the constitutional issues which were dominating debates during William's invasion, and there is little evidence that it itself was widely discussed. However, both the circumstances in which the sermon was delivered, and the position of the man who preached it, invite a closer study of its text. In the first place, the sermon was given in front of the prince of Orange only five days after he had arrived in London. It thus represented one of the earliest pieces of rhetoric to emerge from the Orange camp after power had definitively shifted away from James. Secondly, and most importantly, the sermon was spoken by Gilbert Burnet. It was, therefore, a statement by a man very close to the heart of Williamite counsels, who was effectively acting as the prince's chief of propaganda during the invasion of England.

Even by 1688, Gilbert Burnet had had one of the most colourful careers of the late seventeenth century. Burnet was an anglican cleric of Scottish origin who had entered English politics in the early 1670s through his association with the earl of Lauderdale. Favoured by King Charles for his anti-catholic writings, he had been suspected by James, and had left England when this man acceded to the throne. Burnet had toured through Europe from 1685 to 1686, and had finally arrived in Holland where, despite protests from the English government, he was received by the Stadholder. Remarkably quickly, he had become very close to the prince of Orange and his wife. He was accepted, particularly by Mary, as a friend and as an intimate spiritual adviser, and was made privy to the royal couple's most personal family problems.[14]

Burnet had also helped to produce Williamite propaganda. By the middle of the 1680s William had effectively established an Orange publicity office under Gaspar Fagel, and when Burnet arrived in the Hague, he was put in touch with this organisation, and urged to co-operate with it.[15] Between 1686 and 1688 he laboured alongside Fagel, benefiting from the Pensionary's network of political informants and the unrivalled power of the Dutch printing industry, to produce a series of works in support of the Orange position.[16] In the first place, he wrote a number of pamphlets to undermine James II. Citing his experiences of catholic bigotry, he questioned the legality of the king's policies in England, and denounced the cruelty and absurdity of

---

[14] Still the best account of Burnet's life is T. E. S. Clarke and H. C. Foxcroft, *A life of Gilbert Burnet, bishop of Salisbury* (Cambridge, 1907).

[15] Burnet reported he 'found the prince was resolved to make use of me' and was recommended to the confidence of Fagel. Gilbert Burnet, *History of his own times* (2nd edn, 6 vols., Oxford, 1833), III, 135.

[16] For Fagel's publicity machine, see Carswell, *Descent on England*, pp. 25–9.

his religion.[17] Secondly, Burnet advised upon other works produced by Fagel's publicity office. As a literary stylist, as a native English speaker, and as a man with first-hand knowledge of English politics, he was greatly valued by the Dutch, and his opinions were often sought when Williamite polemic was being prepared.[18] For example, he took a key role in the production of the *Declaration* in the autumn of 1688. He was consulted on its wording whilst it was being drafted; he rendered the final version into English; and he edited the text – shortening and sharpening Fagel's original turgid prose.[19] Once the invasion was launched, Burnet took an even more prominent role. As the member of the Orange team with local knowledge, he was a more suitable director of English propaganda than Fagel, and was effectively promoted to this position during the expedition. Burnet accompanied William to England as his chaplain, and used the resulting intimacy with the prince to advise his master on how to present himself to James's subjects.[20] During the expedition Burnet got involved with the physical production of Orange propaganda; he spoke in William's defence at vital moments during the invasion; and he wrote pamphlets to rebut the charges of Jacobite authors. Further, Burnet set up public occasions on which William's message could be propagated. These included religious services to pray for the prince's success, ceremonial entrances into towns, public readings of William's *Declaration*, and formal expressions of support by the prince's English allies.[21]

At first glance, Burnet's activities as a publicist do not suggest that he pursued an alternative to the constitutional arguments of William's manifesto. As must be clear, much of the chaplain's time in 1688 was taken up with

---

[17] See, for example, Gilbert Burnet, *Some letters; containing an account of what seemed most remarkable in Switzerland, Italy etc.* (Amsterdam, 1686); [Gilbert Burnet], *Reasons against the repealing the acts of parliament concerning the test* (1687); [Gilbert Burnet], *A letter containing some reflections on his majesty's declaration for liberty of conscience dated the fourth of April 1687* (1687); [Gilbert Burnet], *Three letters concerning the present state of Italy* (1688); [Gilbert Burnet], *An enquiry into the reasons for abrogation of the test* ([Amsterdam], 1688).

[18] For William's opinion of Burnet as a publicist, see the letter from the prince of Orange to Bentinck, 21 September 1687 (new style), N. Japikse, *Correspondentie van Willem III en van Hans Willem Bentinck* (5 vols., Hague, 1927), I, 33–4.

[19] See Schwoerer, *Declaration of rights*, pp. 110–13; Burnet, *History . . . own times*, III, 300–2.

[20] Some of his advice to the prince during the invasion can be seen in two private memoranda printed in R. W. Blencowe, ed., *Diary of the times of Charles the Second by the honourable Henry Sidney* (2 vols., 1843), II, 281–8, 288–91.

[21] For Burnet's concern over the mechanics of publication see *Notes and Queries*, 2nd series II (1856), 246 – a transcription of BL Harley Ms. 6798, fols. 264–8. For Burnet's concern that public declarations of support for the prince should be broadcast see the letter from Burnet to Admiral Herbert, 29 November 1688, BL Egerton Ms. 2621, fol. 67. Burnet's political tracts included [Gilbert Burnet], *A review of the reflections on the prince of Orange's declaration* (1688); [Gilbert Burnet], *An enquiry into the present state of affairs, and in particular, whether we owe allegiance to the king in these circumstances* (1688); [Gilbert Burnet], *Reflections on a paper entitled his majesty's reasons for withdrawing himself from Rochester* (1689). For speeches, religious services, and ceremonial entrances, see below, pp. 53–8.

the *Declaration*, a document which he part-wrote, advertised and defended in print. Yet the St James's sermon on 23 December was different. Although it was clearly part of the Orange propaganda campaign (it was rapidly published at the prince's 'special command'), it steered clear of the constitutional justifications for the expedition which had dominated the original manifesto. Whilst Burnet endorsed William's actions in his London address, he did so by advancing a case which did not centre on traditional liberties, the rights of parliament, or English law.

The central argument which Burnet used at St James's was the assertion that William's invasion had been favoured by God. Much of the sermon was dedicated to a demonstration that the prince of Orange's success had been brought about by heaven, and that it had proceeded according to some divine plan. The preacher proved this by outlining a series of extraordinary miracles which had marked William's progress to London, and which, he maintained, proved that providence must have guided his advance. In the Channel, Burnet reminded his audience, unusual changes in wind direction had given the Orange fleet the best possible military advantage. In Europe, James's natural supporter, Louis XIV, had unpredictably lost his diplomatic dominance, and united all nations against him. In England, the plots of evil counsellors had been unexpectedly revealed. Remarkably, William had broken through the divisions of the English and 'had turned the hearts of the whole nation as one man to him'.[22] Thus at St James's, William's chaplain had opened up an entirely new strategy for justifying the Orange invasion. Playing down arguments from an earthly and man-made constitution, he made an appeal to divine blessing upon his master's actions.

Of itself, perhaps, Burnet's providentialism was not particularly interesting. Providence has long been recognised as a widely used idea in seventeenth-century political discourse, and it might be thought that it was too imprecise and flexible a concept to form the basis of an alternative Williamite case.[23] Some modern scholars have suggested that God's will was such a fluid notion in the late Stuart era, that it could never have sustained or defined a coherent ideology. For them, the idea that God had willed a particular series of events was an intellectually empty, and very tired, commonplace, which could be used to justify almost any event. J. P. Kenyon, in particular, has called this sort of rhetoric 'a devotional platitude'. For him, it was 'the small change of polemical ... vocabulary' which 'did not change men's minds, [but] only confirmed them in decisions they had reached for other reasons'.[24] Mark Goldie has similarly pointed out that providence could be used to justify

---

[22] Burnet, *Sermon ... St James's ... 23 December 1688*, pp. 10–14, 8.
[23] For an appreciation of its role in justifying the revolution, see Gerald Straka, *Anglican reaction to the Revolution of 1688* (Madison, Wisconsin, 1962).
[24] Kenyon, *Revolution principles*, pp. 24–5.

a wide range of political positions. For him it was an 'agreed' concept, which was generally available to all shades of opinion.[25] Both historians have demonstrated that, even to men in the 1690s, it was clear that providentialism could collapse into an unsatisfactory justification of success by success. William Sherlock's book, *The case of allegiance* (1691), which based its whole defence of Orange rule on providential grounds, was widely ridiculed and condemned by contemporaries.[26]

Yet it would be a mistake to dismiss Burnet's providentialism, either as a crude justification of a fait accompli, or as a conventional gift-wrapping for a case whose substance was other principles. Providence *was* vital to Burnet's argument, but his position was not merely vacuous. His account of God's recent intervention was deepened by placing the events of 1688 within a history of 'reformation'. In the 23 December sermon, William's invasion was given meaning, not just by God's evident support for the prince's forces, but also by explaining it as part of a process of purgation and return to godly purity. Unfortunately, full understanding of this requires a long excursion into early protestant thought. Burnet's arguments at the Revolution emerged from a particular intellectual tradition, which must be explored if his stance and assumptions are to be fully appreciated. The examination has to start in the middle of the sixteenth century. Then protestant Englishmen had been driven by their break with Rome to construct a view of the world which was to be enormously influential in the succeeding decades, and which was to underpin Burnet's rhetoric over a hundred years later.

Early English protestants were faced with a number of intellectual difficulties in the mid-Tudor period. In the thirty years after Henry VIII's first divorce, Englishmen broke away from the catholic communion of Rome, and set up a new church, based upon the doctrines and practices of reformed Christianity. Those who supported this process had to find a justification for what they had done, and had to answer a series of charges laid against them by their catholic opponents. They had to explain the tenets of the protestant faith; they had to rebut accusations of heresy and schism; and they had to establish the authority on which they had acted. The protestants' response to these challenges was worked out in a series of writings produced throughout the mid-Tudor period. In tracts, sermons, biblical commentaries, and even in plays and verse, reformed Christians wrestled with their intellectual difficulties, and gradually developed a legitimising account of their church. Writers such as John Bale, Hugh Latimer, and John Foxe analysed the birth of English protestantism, and explained its conformity to the will of God. In their vision three concepts were crucial, and were to have lasting importance. The first was the notion of

[25] Goldie, 'Tory political thought', p.9.
[26] Kenyon, *Revolution principles*, pp.26–34. Goldie, 'Tory political thought', pp.90–125.

an apocalyptic battle between two mystical churches; the second was the ideal of the godly prince; and the third was a peculiar understanding of the importance of moral reform.

The vision of two battling churches emerged from protestant attempts to justify their separation from Rome. When the English broke away from the continental catholicism, the main charge against them was of schism. Papal polemicists accused the nation of having left a communion which had united western Christendom, and which was the heir of the primitive apostles' church. They therefore suggested that Englishmen had torn the mystical body of Christ – the communion of all believers – and had consequently committed a sin denounced both by the New Testament and by the ancient fathers.[27] For their part, protestants were sensitive to this accusation, and vigorously refuted it. Their main defence was that the Roman faith had become corrupted. They claimed that the spiritual organisation headed by the pope had sunk so far into error and iniquity that its followers could not object if others left to re-establish a pure communion.[28] In this response, the notion of two churches was born. Arguing that the Roman religion had been so corrupted that separation was justified, protestants asserted that it had ceased to be the body of Christ. This demanded that a distinction be made between a wicked church – which could only pretend to embody true religion – and a godly church of real believers – which actually did.

Having formulated their basic riposte to the charge of schism, the English protestants broadened it by borrowing from two early Christian texts. As they worked out their ideology, reformed Christians drew on St Augustine's *City of God* and the biblical book of Revelation to set their vision of competing churches within a complete cosmic history of struggle. The key figure in this process was John Bale.[29] Bale was a bishop of Ossory, and a leading protestant polemicist, who in 1545 finished his most important work, *The image of both churches*.[30] This volume, published initially in Antwerp but widely circulated in England under Edward VI (1547–53), synthesised existing traditions to provide an extraordinarily far-ranging context for the English Reformation.

---

[27] See, for example, Nicholas Sanders, *De origine ac progressu schmatis anqlicani liber* (Rome, 1586). For some discussion of catholic charges of schism over a longer period, see John Spurr, *The Restoration church of England, 1646–1689* (New Haven, 1991), pp. 113–14.

[28] English protestants accused papists of introducing corrupt innovation, unheard of in the primitive church. See F. J. Levy, *Tudor historical thought* (San Marino, c.1967), pp. 78–9.

[29] For Bale see Leslie P. Fairfield, *John Bale: mythmaker for the English Reformation* (West Lafayette, Indiana, 1976); John N. King, *English Reformation literature: the Tudor origins of the protestant tradition* (Princeton, 1982), pp. 61–74; Levy, *Tudor historical thought*, pp. 89–98.

[30] The best modern edition is contained in Henry Christmas, ed., *Select works of John Bale DD, bishop of Ossory* (Cambridge, 1849).

Bale took the idea from Augustine that mankind had always been divided into two distinct bodies. The fifth-century saint had argued that from the earliest times the world's population had been polarised into two great camps. On the one hand, he maintained, there had been a 'heavenly city', symbolically identified with Jerusalem. This consisted of God's true followers, and contained those men and women who tried to live by their Lord's word. On the other hand there was the 'earthly city', the symbolic Babylon. This was a body headed by the devil, which contained those who were deaf to the gospel and who remained in their own fleshly desires. Inevitably, Augustine argued, there would be a rivalry between the two entities. Inspired by Satan, and dedicated to the pursuit of lust and worldly ambition, inhabitants of the earthly city would persecute members of the heavenly, and attempt to deceive them or tempt them away from their spiritual goals. Augustine traced the story of this struggle, starting with the disputes between Cain and Abel, and culminating in the recent attacks upon Christianity by the Roman emperors.[31] In the sixteenth century, Bale found much useful material in Augustine's writings as he prepared his case against the papacy. Relabelling the 'earthly city' of the saint's writings 'the false church', Bale claimed the Roman communion was its modern visible expression, and proved his identification by citing its characteristic perversion and persecution of God's true faith.[32] He therefore added much greater resonance to protestant arguments. Once Bale had adapted Augustine, the contemporary break with Rome would not be seen merely as a local dispute between the English and the papacy, but would be interpreted as the latest instalment in the ceaseless battle between the earthly and heavenly cities. Protestants came to believe that they carried the ancient torch of Christian faith, and that their struggle was the same struggle that the true church had always had to fight against its Satanic opposite.[33]

Bale gave his arguments even greater depth by drawing on the book of Revelation. In this last section of the bible (widely believed to have been written by Jesus' disciple, John) the protestant polemicist saw yet another description of the battle between the two churches. For him, Revelation's narrative of a complex war between God's angels and the forces of an evil Antichrist seemed a symbolic prophecy of the rivalry between false and genuine religion. Accordingly, Bale constructed his *Image of both churches* around apocalyptic scripture, mapping the past advances and persecutions of

---

[31] Augustine, *Concerning the city of God against the pagans* (Penguin classics edn, Harmondsworth, 1984), *passim*, especially book 15.

[32] For Bale's use of Augustine's two cities, see Paul Christianson, *The reformers and Babylon: English apocalyptic visions from the Reformation to the eve of the Civil War* (Toronto, 1978), pp. 15–16.

[33] For Bale's belief in the continuity of struggle, see Fairfield, *John Bale*, pp. 82–5.

true Christianity onto the mystical events described by St John. Yet Bale did not simply use the Apocalypse to confirm his two-church vision. He also employed it to stress God's providential control of history. In Revelation the deity dictated the entire course of the symbolic narrative, and had intervened repeatedly to shape the protagonist's actions. Implementing a pre-ordered plan God had unleashed Antichrist and his supporters upon the world, had granted them opportunities to wreak their particular forms of havoc, and limited their power by throwing up champions against them and ensuring their final destruction. Reading the lesson from this, Bale concluded that God exercised similar control over the actual battle between the two churches. The balance of advantage between the righteous and the corrupt might have shifted over time in a complex fashion; but in Bale's interpretation, every development had followed a divine script, and each event had contributed, in its way, towards a providentially determined victory for Christ.[34] Within this interpretation the English Reformation became still more significant. More than the latest instalment in the endless battle between good and evil, it became a providentially determined stage in the eventual triumph of the true religion. Whilst acted out by men, it had been set in motion by God as part of his plan for the two churches. The Reformation could, therefore, be doubly justified. It was both a blow against Satanic forces, and a fulfilment of God's unfolding project for world history.[35]

Bale's use of Augustine, St John, and the two-church model, met most of the early protestants' intellectual needs. It explained their place in the world, justified their actions, and was widely adopted as a tool of reformed propaganda. Yet for all its usefulness, the two-church model did not, by itself, meet an important difficulty. It did not fully justify the role which secular rulers had played in the English Reformation. The problem was that mid-sixteenth-century protestantism had not triumphed through a spontaneous conversion of the people, but had rather been imposed by monarchs. It had been introduced by kings and queens such as Henry VIII, Edward VI, and Elizabeth, who had used the machinery of the state to enforce the new faith and change patterns of worship. This monarchical leadership posed difficulties for protestants on several counts. It permitted accusations that their religion had been promoted for political rather than spiritual reasons; and it risked embarrassing them by throwing them into alliance with worldly coercion – a force which St Augustine, and so their own account of history, had tended to identify with the earthly city. Perhaps most importantly, however, it required them to rebut catholic charges of sacrilege. Papal polemicists objected to

---

[34] For Bale's use of Revelation, see Fairfield, *John Bale*, ch. 3.
[35] For the eschatological significance of the Reformation in protestant thought see Katherine Firth, *The apocalyptic tradition in Reformation Britain, 1530–1645* (Oxford, 1979); Richard Bauckham, *Tudor apocalypse* (Oxford, 1978).

temporal princes interfering in ecclesiastical affairs since they claimed that spiritual matters must be governed by a spiritual (effectively a clerical) authority. This complaint was given great strength by the traditional separation of lay and church estates, and forced protestants to develop a new account of the relationship between priest and secular magistrate.

The first part of the protestant response to these difficulties was to preach up the spiritual authority of earthly rulers. Following scriptural injunctions that men should obey temporal princes, and cannibalising the arguments of medieval anti-papalists, English reformed Christians insisted that God had given all governors the right to determine forms of worship within their jurisdictions. They thus answered catholic charges of sacrilege by accusing the papacy of usurping divinely bestowed authority through its attempt to carve out an ecclesiastical sphere which would be independent of magisterial control.[36] However, whilst this case provided a technical legitimation of the monarchs' actions, most protestants tried to supplement it with another argument. They had to do this since, unadorned, the theory of divinely granted authority provided only a pinched and uninspiring defence of the role of monarchical power in the Reformation. The protestants' basic case might explain why Englishmen must acquiesce in the recent ecclesiastical policies of their rulers, but it gave them little special reason to celebrate, or to support actively, the royal introduction of protestantism. Although Christians were told to submit to the changes put through by Henry, Edward, and Elizabeth, they were instructed to do so merely on the grounds that they must submit to *any* earthly authority, and were thus given no grounds for enhanced loyalty to reforming monarchs. Something of the weakness of the protestants' case was revealed in 1553. Then Mary Tudor, a committed catholic, had inherited the throne from her brother Edward, and had declared her determination to bring England back to the papal church. In this situation, protestants such as Thomas Cranmer – who had vigorously argued for royal supremacy in spiritual affairs – found it difficult to construct a case which might limit popular support for the queen and her return to Rome.[37] To overcome such shortcomings in their argument, protestant polemicists advanced the ideal of the godly prince. They tried to foster a more active allegiance to reforming monarchs by distinguishing between those rulers – 'godly princes' – whom God had raised to benefit his true faith, and the general run of kings and

[36] For the construction of this case see G. R. Elton, *Policy and police: the enforcement of the Reformation in the age of Cromwell* (Cambridge, 1972), pp. 182–95; Richard Rex, *Henry VIII and the English Reformation* (Basingstoke, 1993), ch. 1.

[37] See Clare Cross, 'Churchmen and the royal supremacy', in Felicity Heal and Rosemary O'Day, eds., *Church and society in England: Henry VIII to James I* (1977), pp. 15–35, especially p. 22.

queens, who might draw their basic authority from God, but who could not claim any special divine commission.

Not surprisingly, the people most active in elucidating this distinction were those polemicists who also acted as royal propagandists.[38] Men such as John Foxe or Hugh Latimer who organised publicity for their monarchs, based their case primarily on historical analysis. Building on their two-church model of the past, protestant royalists suggested that God's providential interventions in history had sometimes elevated champions of the true religion to positions of worldly power, and had encouraged them to rule in the interests of that faith. The writers proved this by citing examples from the bible. They drew attention to Old Testament kings such as David, Solomon, and Josiah, who had been favoured by God for their commitment to his cause; and they interpreted the book of Revelation as a prophecy of good Christian rulers (especially the Emperor Constantine) who would be similarly blessed. From this historical analysis it was a short step to suggest that the reforming Tudors formed part of the same providential pattern. Drawing comparisons between the protestant rulers of the middle of the sixteenth century, and such figures as Solomon and Constantine, royal polemicists argued that contemporary kings and queens bore all the distinguishing marks of godly princes, and implied that they deserved special veneration as peculiar instruments of God's will.[39] To start, protestant writers pointed to the evidence for divine blessing in the personal histories of their rulers. Just as David and Constantine had come to power only through providential protection and promotion, polemicists argued that the reforming Tudor monarchs had received heavenly aid. It was explained, for example, that God had protected Edward and Elizabeth through the political vicissitudes of the mid-Tudor period, and that he had brought them to power to defeat their conservative enemies.[40] In addition to such evidence, royalist writers made much of the military exploits of their heroes. Reminding audiences that David and Constantine had been armed defenders of the true church and had defeated its heathen enemies on the battlefield, the protestant propagandists argued that Tudor defences against catholic powers were continuations of the same struggle.[41] Finally, court

---

[38] For the organisation of protestant/royalist propaganda in the mid-Tudor period, see Elton, *Policy and police*, pp. 171–216; King, *English Reformation literature*, pp. 88–113, 425–36, and ch. 4.

[39] For general comparisons with Old Testament kings and Constantine, see Rex, *Henry VIII*, p. 174; Frances A. Yates, *Astraea: the imperial theme in the sixteenth century* (1975), part 2; William Haller, *Foxe's 'Book of Martyrs' and the elect nation* (1963), pp. 84–9.

[40] For providential imagery surrounding these monarchs' successions see King, *English Reformation literature*, pp. 165, 201–6; Christianson, *Reformers and Babylon*, pp. 29–36.

[41] For anti-catholic war rhetoric, meditations on Christian rulers' use of the sword, and comparisons with earlier godly warriors, see Elton, *Policy and police*, pp. 171–217; King, *English Reformation literature*, pp. 184–206; Yates, *Astraea*, part 2; Bauckham, *Tudor apocalypse*, pp. 173–4.

protestants concentrated upon royal efforts to purge the realm of the false faith. Here the key exemplar was Josiah, the biblical king of Judah, who had led the Jewish people in amending their corrupted doctrine and worship.[42] Given the religious policies of Henry, Edward, and Elizabeth, there were obvious ways in which these monarchs could be placed in a Josiahian context. Tudor attacks upon popish error and superstition could be compared to the Old Testament campaign against paganism and idolatry; and both programmes could be described as national destructions of the devil's false church.[43] With such comparisons made, the early protestant writers had met the difficulties posed by royal involvement in the propagation of their faith. By developing the notion of godly princes they had reversed concern about the political nature of the Reformation; they had met the catholic charge of sacrilege; and they had deepened the loyalty due to their masters beyond bare submission to the secular power.

After the two-church battle and the godly prince, the third significant element of early protestant ideology was a peculiar emphasis on moral reform. Of course, Christians had always stressed the importance of personal virtue within a religious life. Yet for the mid-Tudor reformers the ideal of moral renewal attained a special urgency. Early protestants were urged to repent of their vices with a peculiar vehemence, and personal righteousness gained a unique place in their overall vision. The reasons for this were partly theological (the abolition of the medieval penitential system which had ameliorated anxiety about lapses into vice, and the insistence on sanctification within the philosophies of the early reformers), but the phenomenon can also be explained with reference to the two other crucial aspects of early protestant thought. First, mid-Tudor moralism had sprung from the characteristic depiction of the two-church battle. In protestant rhetoric, the false church was portrayed as a hugely inventive body, which had discovered a baffling variety of ways to attack its faithful enemy. Most obviously, it had persecuted true Christians, and had perverted the Lord's doctrines to try to lead the world astray. More insidiously however, it had relied on moral corruption. Tempting Christ's followers with all manner of luxury and voluptuousness, it had attempted to debauch people from the gospel by offering them greater sensual delights. Its tactics were evident throughout history, from the intemperance of the pagans who had faced the loyal Jews, to the avarice and sexual misconduct which were held to mark the Roman catholic faith. Within such an assessment of the false church's operation, the importance of moral reform was obvious. If people were to be tempted away from true religion, then the only way for anyone to remain within Christ's

---

[42] II Kings 22:3; II Chronicles 34:5.

[43] For comparisons of Henry VIII and Edward VI with Josiah, see King, *English Reformation literature*, pp. 161, 167, 177; Rex, *Henry VIII*, pp. 103, 173–5.

true communion would be to purge themselves of the tendency to sin which could lead to their downfall. Second, emphasis on morality with early protestant thought came from the image of the godly prince. As preachers and propagandists had drawn comparisons between ancient and contemporary rulers to establish that the latter were true instruments of God, they had been at pains to point out zeal for virtue amongst the Tudors' archetypes. Presenting the old godly rulers as wise to the devil's deceptions, protestants had insisted they had understood the subtle threat of immorality, and had stressed their determination to fight against this Satanic weapon. Again the figure of Josiah had been crucial. The Old Testament king was shown to have attacked vice as well as doctrinal error when he campaigned to re-establish true religion, and attempts were made to fit sixteenth-century rulers into this pattern as the essential parallels were drawn. Thus all the reforming Tudors were to be crusaders for moral reform. Henry VIII's break with Rome was accompanied by legislation against vice, especially sodomy; Edward VI was asked to lead England to repentance in the sermons of Hugh Latimer; and much was made of the virgin Elizabeth's moral example to her nation.[44]

Having outlined the essential aspects of early protestant thought, it would be possible to return to 1688 and demonstrate how Gilbert Burnet deepened his account of the events of that year. One could demonstrate that the mid-Tudor development of the two-church model, the godly prince, and moral reform, provided Burnet with all the tools he required to transcend any simplistically providential justification for the prince of Orange's actions. However, whilst such a return to the late seventeenth century might be rhetorically elegant, it would be historiographically impossible. Any premature end to the current diversion would run into an objection from a variety of scholars that the intellectual traditions established in the English Reformation had effectively become unavailable to Burnet. It would run counter to the great secularising hypothesis which has dominated early modern scholarship – namely the belief that the worldview advanced by Bale, Foxe, and Latimer was disrupted in the hundred years following its birth, and that it came to be rejected and reviled in the decades after 1640.

The case for the abandonment of early protestant thought begins from the observation that the two-church model of history became hugely divisive in the run up to the English Civil War. Since the 1970s, scholars such as Paul Christianson, Patrick Collinson, and Peter Lake have traced developments in philosophy in the early seventeenth century, and have noted that ideas originally advanced to unite the nation around its protestant rulers began to have the opposite effect once their consequences were worked out. The main

---

[44] For mid-Tudor attacks on vice, see Rex, *Henry VIII*, p. 173; King, *English Reformation literature*, pp. 173–9; Yates, *Astraea*, part 2.

cause of this change was a shift in the agenda of political and religious debate. As the English protestant regime established itself after the mid-Tudor period, the focus of theological attention moved from the defence of the break with Rome, and began to centre on a series of controversies about the proper nature of the reformed church. Broadly speaking, some English protestants pressed for a thoroughgoing reformation in which Roman corruptions of doctrine, order, and worship would be completely eliminated; whilst others saw value in certain features of the medieval church and mobilised in defence of such catholic survivals as ceremony, episcopacy, and sacramental grace.[45] This basic spiritual issue widened into a set of political disputes as secular factions became identified with different ecclesiastical positions, and tensions rose as religious conflicts were played out at every level from parish to parliament. Most significantly, some Englishmen came to perceive elements at court as sponsors of a more 'catholic' ecclesiology. Especially under Charles I, advocates of further reformation began to oppose royal policy, suspecting that the king had become a prisoner of their spiritual rivals, and worrying the monarchy might no longer be wholehearted in working for moral reform or in its defence of reformed Christianity. This perception appears to have made a major, perhaps crucial, contribution to the outbreak of Civil War in 1642.[46]

In this new situation, the intellectual traditions developed under the Tudors began to play a divisive role. The problem was that although the two-church model had been developed to combat papal arguments, it proved disastrously easy to apply it in debates *between* protestants. The main reason for this was the protean conception of the false church within reformed ideology. In the worldview developed in the mid-Tudor period, Roman catholicism was a living expression of Satan's kingdom, but it did not exhaust the definition of that realm. According to protestant polemicists, the antipathy between good and evil had begun well before the pope's dominion had been established and had taken a variety of forms throughout history as God's faithful had battled with all manner of temptations, lies, and cruelties. Popery was thus but one manifestation of a much wider evil. Believing this, Englishmen in the early Stuart period found they could include even non-catholic enemies within their definition of the false church, and were willing to comprehend fellow pro-testants within Satan's armies if they argued for unacceptable ecclesi-ologies.[47]

---

[45] The growing debates in this area are traced in Diarmaid MacCulloch, *The later Reformation in England, 1547–1603* (Basingstoke, 1990); Peter Lake, *Anglicans and puritans?: presbyterianism and English conformist thought from Whitgift to Hooker* (1988); Nicholas Tyacke, *Anti-Calvinists: the rise of English Arminianism, 1590–1640* (Oxford, 1987).

[46] See the essays in Kenneth Fincham, ed., *The early Stuart church, 1603–1642* (Basingstoke, 1993).

[47] Such labelling is the main theme of Christianson, *Reformers and Babylon*.

Once this identification of opponents with the false church had been made, the established structures of protestant polemic served to widen divisions amongst Englishmen. In the first place, the dichotomous nature of the two-church model ensured that English opinion would become hopelessly polarised. Since the prevailing intellectual tradition tended to categorise people into two great camps, it eliminated any middle ground in debates about the proper nature of the true church, and also cut off possibilities for compromise, as people became convinced that their enemies were irreconcilable partisans of the devil. This tendency to view the world in black and white has been traced through the writings of early Stuart Englishmen, and the scholars who have pursued it have agreed its significance in tensions which led to the Civil War.[48]

Secondly, early protestant ideas encouraged disruptive hopes for the future. The understanding of history as a providentially directed triumph for the true church persuaded many that the final victory for the godly was at hand, and thus encouraged them to adopt even more intransigent attitudes. The vital development here was the emergence of millenarianism in the early seventeenth century. In theological terms the millennium was a thousand-year period described in the book of Revelation, during which God's true followers would rule on earth. Mid-Tudor polemicists had tended to place this era in the past, identifying it with the dominion of the catholic church before its corruption; but later commentators on the Apocalypse – most influentially Joseph Mede (1586–1668) – had begun to interpret it as something to be realised in the future. Many, indeed, suggested that the triumph of the true church was close at hand, and decoded the symbolic dates provided by St John to prove their case.[49] By itself, such millenarianism raised tensions by persuading early Stuart Englishmen that they would soon see the total defeat of their enemies. More damagingly however, millennial expectation came to combine with the rhetorics of godly rule and moral reform to produce an even more dangerous ideological cocktail. In the early Stuart period, the rise of millenarianism – coupled with doubts about the virtue and godliness of the royal court – meant that the traditional notion of earthly rulers as God's instruments could no longer rally Englishmen behind their monarch. Once people were convinced that God's hour was at hand, the expectation that their ruler would aid this triumph increased disappointment

---

[48] Patrick Collinson, *The birthpangs of protestant England: religious and cultural change in the sixteenth and seventeenth centuries* (Basingstoke, 1988), pp. 147–8; Christianson, *Reformers and Babylon*, p. 5; Peter Lake, 'Anti-popery: the structure of a prejudice', in Richard Cust and Anne Hughes, eds., *Conflict in early Stuart England* (Harlow, 1989), pp. 72–106; Richard Cust and Peter Lake, 'Sir Richard Grosvenor and the rhetoric of magistracy', *BIHR*, 54 (1981), 40–53.

[49] Katherine Firth, *Apocalyptic tradition*, ch. 7; Christianson, *Reformers and Babylon*, pp. 127–30.

with an apparently unrighteous and immoral monarchy. Such dissatisfaction pushed many towards radical action in the 1640s. Much of the political nation was driven to rebellion and political experiment as it attempted to replace the corrupt Caroline court with a regime which might do more towards the imminent destruction of Antichrist. As William Lamont has put it, the centripetal apocalypticism of Elizabeth's time, which had consolidated subjects in loyalty around their ruler, degenerated into a divisive, centrifugal force under her successors.[50] The importance of such disruptive millenarianism in the turbulence of the middle of the seventeenth century can be confirmed by a glance through contemporary polemic. Parliamentarians in the Civil War, Oliver Cromwell in his destruction of English monarchy, the novel sects and movements which advanced revolutionary ideas after 1642, all sang similarly apocalyptic tunes.[51]

It is from this history of division that claims for the collapse of the early protestant worldview have been forged. Over the past few decades a number of historians have argued that the practical effects of the old Tudor philosophies were so horrific that they were largely abandoned. In the middle of the seventeenth century, it has been suggested, the two-church model and the notion of godly rule disintegrated as group after group of Englishmen recoiled from their capacity to cause chaos. Christopher Hill, for example, has stressed the shock of Civil War and republicanism for England's elite. He has argued that the traditional leaders of the political nation suffered loss of power and position after 1642; that they hankered for the stability of the old regime; and that this sentiment facilitated the eventual return to monarchy in 1660. Central to this reactionary ideology was the rejection of old thought patterns. After the Restoration, Hill has suggested, members of the political nation distanced themselves from the two-church model and ideals of godly rule which they imagined had caused their afflictions. They were reluctant to identify Antichrists; they were sceptical about the providential significance of events; they doubted that a godly society could be built on earth; and they sublimated millenarian impulses into scientific and commercial endeavour.[52] Similarly J. G. A. Pocock has charted a rapid decline in the use of apocalyptic language in political texts after 1660. He has argued that this reflected a

[50] William M. Lamont, *Godly rule: politics and religion 1603–59* (1969), p. 25.
[51] See Paul Christianson, 'From expectation to militance: reformers and Babylon in the first two years of the Long Parliament', *JEH*, 24 (1973), 225–44; J. S. A. Adamson, 'Oliver Cromwell and the Long Parliament', in John Morrill, ed., *Oliver Cromwell and the English revolution* (1990), pp. 49–92; Christopher Hill, *God's Englishman* (Harmondsworth, 1970); Christopher Hill, *The world turned upside down: radical ideas during the English revolution* (1972); B. S. Capp, *The fifth monarchy men: a study in seventeenth-century English millenarianism* (1972).
[52] Christopher Hill, *The English bible in the seventeenth-century revolution* (1993), ch. 19; Christopher Hill, *Some intellectual consequences of the English Revolution* (1980); Christopher Hill, *Antichrist in seventeenth-century England* (1971).

general nervousness about such discourse, and a tendency to identify it with the dangerous 'enthusiasm' which it was thought had caused the disasters of the Civil War.[53] William Lamont, meanwhile, has demonstrated disillusion-ment with the old worldview amongst even the anti-monarchical elements who had endorsed it most passionately. In a seminal study, he has detected confusion and disappointment amongst middle of the century radicals as they realised that triumph over the royalist Antichrist would not herald a godly utopia. By the 1650s it had become clear that millenarian excitement had merely encouraged contradictory programmes for reshaping church and society, and that politics would still be marked by bitter debate. In this situation, Lamont has suggested, Cromwell and others retreated from their old vision. Disappointed that their allies could neither secure a godly society, nor agree how to pursue it, many dropped the whole project. Whilst still hoping for instruction from divine providence, they were no longer sure they were on the verge of destroying the false church, and even lost confidence that they had correctly identified that evil body.[54] Thus many scholars have argued that after 1660, the influence of mid-Tudor mentality was ebbing rapidly. In their version of events some features of the old worldview might survive, but they were torn from their wider ideological contexts, and no longer had the same apocalyptic resonance. Moral reform, for example, is acknowledged to have remained on the political agenda of Restoration England. However, its purpose was supposed to be merely the creation of hard-working and biddable subjects. It no longer formed part of a cosmic battle between true religion and Antichrist.[55]

Now obviously, the sort of ideological change described above would raise questions about the potential effectiveness of early protestant ideas in 1688. If the English had become so anxious about the two-church model and godly rule, then Gilbert Burnet could not have successfully deployed these notions in support of William of Orange. This being the case, it is vital to assess whether the intellectual metamorphosis proposed by so many scholars had actually occurred. Unless it is possible to challenge the contention that mid-Tudor ideas were discredited in the middle of the seventeenth century, readers would have to conclude that they had lost their persuasive influence after 1660, and that the lengths taken here to elucidate them would have been in vain.

At first glance, the evidence for change appears strong. Political language does appear to have become more sober in the late seventeenth century, with

---

[53] Pocock, *Machiavellian moment*, p. 403.

[54] Lamont, *Godly rule*. For another account of Cromwell's loss of confidence, see Blair Worden, 'Oliver Cromwell and the sin of Achan', in Derek Beales and Geoffrey Best, eds., *History, society and the churches* (Cambridge, 1985), pp. 125–45.

[55] For such an argument, see Lamont, *Godly rule*, ch. 7.

less overtly apocalyptic rhetoric; and new discourses did arise to challenge the early protestant interpretation of history. In particular, it has been claimed that political actors and writers began to analyse their times through classical analogies with Greece and Rome, rather than constantly reaching for the book of Revelation and the examples of Old Testament kings.[56] However, whilst there may have been a change of tone after 1660, there are real grounds for questioning whether the old ideology was eradicated in the late seventeenth century. Even as some scholars have made the case for mental transformation, others have revealed the persistence of traditional thought in the Restoration period. Whilst it is true that some of the survivals which have been unearthed came from a radical underground of republicans and sectaries, and so might say little about 'mainstream' political culture, other examples have come from 'respectable' sources, and have revealed continuing interest in early protestant concepts within the elites and establishments of late Stuart England. After the work of such scholars as Michael McKeon, John Miller, Margaret Jacob, and (ironically) William Lamont and Christopher Hill, it seems probable that traditional protestant ideals were too deeply ingrained in the English political nation to be erased easily. Men as respectable as archbishops, Cambridge professors, and poet laureates have been shown still at home in a 'mid-Tudor' mental universe.[57] In a world where popery still seemed a pressing threat, people continued to use the two-church model, godly rule, and moral reform to try to understand their situation.

Conveniently, evidence for the continued influence of early protestant discourses after 1660 can be garnered from the career of Gilbert Burnet. In the years before 1688, this cleric had achieved popularity and respect through a series of writings which had fitted a distinctly mid-Tudor pattern. In the

---

[56] Stephen Zwicker, 'England, Israel and the triumph of Roman virtue', in Richard M. Popkin, ed., *Millenarianism and messianism in English literature and thought, 1650–1800* (Leiden, 1988), pp. 37–64.

[57] For examples of works stressing the survival of traditional thought patterns, see William M. Lamont, *Richard Baxter and the millennium: protestant imperialism and the English revolution* (1979); William M. Lamont, 'Richard Baxter, the apocalypse and the mad major', *PP*, 55 (1972), 68–90; Michael McKeon, *Politics and poetry in Restoration England: the case of Dryden's 'Annus mirabilis'* (1975); Margaret C. Jacob, *The Newtonians and the English revolution, 1689–1720* (Hassocks, Sussex, 1976); M. C. Jacob and W. A. Lockwood, 'Political millenarianism and Burnet's *Sacred theory*', *Science Studies*, 2 (1972), 265–79; Miller, *Popery and politics*; Christopher Hill, *A turbulent, seditious and factious people: John Bunyan and his church 1628–1688* (Oxford, 1988); Hillel Schwartz, *The French prophets: the history of a millenarian group in eighteenth-century England* (Los Angeles, 1980), especially ch. 2; Tim Hitchcock, '"In true imitation of Christ": the tradition of mystical communitarianism in early eighteenth century England', in Mick Gidley and Kate Bowlen, eds., *Locating the shakers: cultural origins and legacies of an American religious movement* (Exeter, 1990), pp. 12–25; Manuel Schonhorn, *Defoe's politics: parliament, power, kingship and Robinson Crusoe* (Cambridge, 1991).

1670s, for example, Burnet had received recognition for a series of anti-catholic writings which had used apocalyptic analysis and terminology to advance their case.[58] The most important of these works was *The history of the Reformation*.[59] Published in two volumes in 1679 and 1681, the *History* had brought its author financial support from well-placed patrons, the thanks of the royal court, and an official endorsement from Oxford University.[60] Since this work was so important in building Burnet's reputation, it is worth examining it in a little detail to demonstrate the sort of arguments which could still win widespread approval.

At base, the *History* provided a detailed account of the English church's break with Rome. However, the volumes did not only describe the actions of the earliest English protestants: they also borrowed their arguments. They used their nations of two-church struggle, godly rule, and moral reform to justify England's schism. The book thus portrayed the papal establishment as the very image of the false church. According to Burnet, medieval popery had existed solely to serve the lust and avarice of its priests; it had ruthlessly persecuted those who had protested against its perversion; and it had promoted all sorts of debauchery and vice in its quest of worldly power. In contrast, the early protestants were presented as providentially guided adherents of the true faith. Moved by the Holy Spirit, they had battled to restore righteousness, and had suffered the afflictions which any opponent of Babylon must expect.[61] Continuing the parallel with early protestant polemic Burnet presented the reforming English monarchs as godly princes. In his narrative, as in their own propaganda, they had been brought to power by God's providence to serve as divine instruments, and had used their authority to promote the cause of true Christianity.[62] Admittedly, the *History* seems to reveal some awareness of the potential danger of its arguments. This is not surprising, as its author lived in an England deeply scarred by the experience of the Civil War, and faced an audience who knew where over-zealous attention to old ideals might lead. Yet, whatever anxiety surrounded 'mid-Tudor' ideas, Burnet's reaction to this was not to dilute his traditional argument, but merely to employ with care. Far from abandoning the vision of Bale, Foxe, and Latimer, he effectively tried to recreate it, attempting to revive

---

[58] See, for example, [Gilbert Burnet], *The mystery of iniquity unvailed* [1673].

[59] This is most easily consulted as Gilbert Burnet, *The history of the Reformation of the church of England* (6 vols., Oxford, 1865).

[60] For comment on the success of the *History* see Clarke and Foxcroft, *Life of Burnet*, p. 157.

[61] These portraits of catholicism and protestantism are evident throughout Burnet's long work. For a representative sample of them, see his accounts of Cardinal Wolsey, medieval heresy and early protestantism, Burnet, *History of the Reformation*, I, 31–67.

[62] For example, the reign of Elizabeth (when Burnet believed a truly godly prince had established the church on a firm footing) was the great climax to which the *History* moved. See Burnet's comments on the shape of his work, Burnet, *History of the Reformation*, II, 1.

an early version of the philosophy, uncorrupted by the disturbing developments of the early Stuart era. Thus Burnet was careful not to encourage millenarian expectations. The *History* presented the Reformation as a significant blow against the false church, but did not suggest that it was necessarily the penultimate stage in the battle, nor that it would presage the triumph of God's saints on earth. Similarly, Burnet played up the 'centripetal' elements of his discourse, promoting versions of the two-church battle and godly rule which were intended to rally Englishmen behind their monarchs. The *History* not only supported the protestant rulers of the sixteenth century, but was also prefaced with a remarkable panegyric to English monarchy. In a dedication to Charles II, Burnet praised the role the king's predecessors had played in advancing protestantism, and defended the royal prerogative from outside encroachment. Presenting monarchical power and true religion as mutually supportive, Burnet urged Charles to play the godly prince and extend his authority in protection of Christ's faith.[63]

Having said all this, it is possible to return to 1688. Earlier it was mentioned that Burnet used early protestant concepts in his defence of the prince of Orange's invasion. Now it has been established that such ideas were still current in the late seventeenth century, and that Burnet himself had built a considerable reputation using them. With 'mid-Tudor' ideals thus rehearsed, and historiographic objections thus addressed, St James's palace can at last be revisited, and Burnet's position on the 23 December can be more fully explored.

When Gilbert Burnet came to speak to the prince on that early winter day in London, he was fully aware that a political case which rested solely on divine will might easily collapse into a vacuous justification of success by success. The preacher was in fact so conscious of the potential weakness of his position that he recognised it even as he developed his providential defence of William's actions. Almost as soon as his sermon had begun, Burnet warned his audience against invoking divine intervention too frequently when accounting for temporal events. He implied that God was usually content to let the universe take its normal course and stated that everybody should hesitate before ascribing anything to supernatural causes.[64] Later in the address, Burnet explained why such caution was necessary. Considering the case of evil men who had risen to positions of worldly power, the preacher noted how easily providentialism could backfire, and how it could come to legitimate any political position. He predicted that those who pretended that their victories were God's will might come to regret their stance when circumstances turned against them; and he pointed out that they would have little defence if their enemies claimed similar divine sanction for their triumphs.

---

63 *Ibid.* I, 1–2.   64 Burnet, *Sermon ... St James's ... 23 December 1688*, pp. 2–3.

I know how dangerous and deceitful an Argument ... from Providence will ever seem to be ... There are ... such Mysteries in the whole Conduct of the World, that though our Partiality makes us apt to Magnify all that we like [by attributing it to God's will], yet if we carry it too far, we will be in danger to be often out of countenance, when the same Argument turns against us.[65]

Initially, such language would seem to negate the main thrust of Burnet's case at St James's. If providence was such a fickle and unmanageable concept, it was surely pointless to invest as much in it as the chaplain did. Yet examined more closely, Burnet's rehearsal of the danger of his discourse can be seen as part of a subtle rhetorical strategy. The preacher was denouncing the sort of crude argument which ran straight from worldly success to heavenly approval, because he wished to advance a more subtle version of providentialism. In the arguments which Burnet advanced on 23 December 1688, God's will was still paramount, but mere attainment of earthly goals was not the sole grounds for claiming divine agency. Instead, the sermon broadened its defence of William's invasion by drawing upon early protestant concepts. In the address, recent events were justified because God had allowed them to happen; but they were also legitimated because they had furthered the struggle of the true church against the false, because they had led to the rise of a godly prince, and because they had promoted the cause of moral reform.

Burnet adopted a two-church discourse very early in his St James's sermon. Immediately after an initial warning about arguments from providence, he started to list those features of William's invasion which demonstrated its concurrence with God's will. The first of these was simply the magnitude of the political change in 1688, and does seem to have been little more than retrospective justification from the success of William's actions.[66] The second, however, was rather more interesting. Burnet stated that the collapse of James's regime could be proved providential because this event had upheld the deity's 'honour', and he drew upon the two-church model of history to show how it had done this.[67] Presenting the English protestants as a people of God, and blackening the catholic faith as a 'mystical Babylon', the preacher argued that God's will was evident in the Dutch invasion because it had allowed the true church to strike a blow against its Satanic foe. Burnet was, therefore, keen to pin all the standard marks of Antichrist upon the defeated catholic party. Whilst he claimed to eschew 'controversial' attacks upon the Roman faith, he ran through its corruptions and perversion of religion, and, most importantly, he reminded his audience that popery was a cruel and bloodthirsty faith. Citing recent attacks upon protestants in France and Savoy, Burnet cast catholicism in the traditional persecuting role of the false

[65] *Ibid.* p. 10.   [66] *Ibid.* pp. 3–5.   [67] *Ibid.* p. 5.

church, and expressed the hope that William's triumph might lead to some sort of deliverance for those who were suffering. The preacher also presented 1688 in the context of the sixteenth-century Reformation. By alluding to the advent of protestantism in the Tudor period, the preacher argued that William's arrival was the latest stage in England's deliverance from the false faith, and so was able to set recent events within a history of divinely guided struggle. According to Burnet the English had 'reduced Christianity to its primitive purity and simplicity' in the previous century, and had subsequently upheld their truth in contests with wicked opponents. When such a nation's religion was preserved by the Orange expedition, it could be portrayed as 'a re-establishment of that glorious work, which God in a series of many signal providences had set up in the last age', and its deliverance could be 'justly ascribed to that sovereign wisdom that governs the church'.[68]

Burnet's argument from godly rule was developed soon after his two-church case. Continuing the list of features which demonstrated divine approval for William's invasion, Burnet pointed to the remarkable effects it had had upon Englishmen's minds. He showed that the intervention of the prince of Orange had united a nation which had been deeply divided over James's succession, and that old enemies had been reconciled as they had turned to welcome the arrival of the Dutch. The main purpose of this passage was to suggest that only divine power could have produced such a change in something as ungovernable as human opinion, but the imagery used to make the point also suggested that the rise of a godly prince was another reason for believing in the providence of the event. Speaking of the strange transformation of Englishmen's attitudes, Burnet likened this to the sudden concord which had been achieved in Israel when David had succeeded the corrupt and divisive regime of his predecessor, Saul.[69] This was clearly an invitation to the audience to see William as a Davidic figure, and raised the possibility of justifying the invasion as a divine promotion of a godly ruler. Later in the address, this possibility was exploited to the full. The prince of Orange was praised as a true servant of God in a panegyric passage which employed all the conventions of the Tudor propagandists. Like Henry VIII, Edward VI, and Elizabeth, William was portrayed as a man brought to power by God's will, who would act to defend the true church with his worldly power, and who brought godly righteousness to the realms over which he held sway. In the St James's sermon William was 'the instrument, whom God has so highly exalted': a man who seemed 'born to be the greatest blessing of the age'. He was also a man who had brought the benefits of godly rule to Holland, and might be expected to do the same for England.

---

[68] *Ibid.* pp. 5–7.   [69] *Ibid.* pp. 7–9.

His first appearance in the World carried with it a Deliverance to those happy Provinces; for happy they were, from the first time that they came under His protection. We that saw their Peace and Plenty, and the Order and Justice that reigned among them, and the sense they have of that Conduct that procures it saw an earnest of those Blessings that seem to be before us.[70]

If 1688 was important as a promotion of a godly prince, it was also crucial for the opportunity it provided for moral reform. Burnet's case here rested upon his analysis of recent history. In the St James's sermon the last thirty years were presented as a period of advancing vice, which could only be ended now that God had brought William to England. The story began at the Restoration in 1660. According to Burnet, this event had been a divine blessing, which should have encouraged Christian behaviour out of gratitude to God. However, instead of walking in holiness, the English had celebrated Charles II's return with 'criminal excess', and had effectively frustrated God's designs by returning debauchery for his gifts of peace and order.[71] This initial mistake had poisoned the moral atmosphere of the nation and had ensured that the people degenerated yet further in the years that followed. Burnet lamented that in the years after the Restoration

the excesses of Rioting and Drunkeness, and the Disorders of all sorts, grew not only to be practiced, but gloried in, as if those Abominations had been the proper distinctions of a loyal man; a Virtuous man [was] look'd out of Countenance, if he could not go into the madness of the time.[72]

As always, popery lay behind this decline. Burnet insisted that popish agents had plotted to spread immorality, knowing that sin and godlessness had always been bulwarks of their anti-religion. Capitalising upon the popular image of a popishly affected court, the preacher asserted that highly placed catholics had deliberately furthered the infection of vice under Charles II, and had trapped the nation in a literally vicious circle from which it could not escape because of their debauching influence. 'Those', he said, 'who were not concerned any further in religion, than it might advance their ungodly designs, were willing to encourage this spirit of atheism, hoping it would make way for a religion [popery] that in some respects is worse than no religion at all.'[73] The conclusion of this process had been the near-disaster of James's reign. Then English virtue had been so undermined that catholicism had made frightening advances, and English protestantism had almost succumbed to the temptations of its evil opposite.

Given this interpretation of the recent past, it was easy for Burnet to present 1688 as a new opportunity for moral reform. With the political defeat of the

---

[70] *Ibid.* pp. 18–19.   [71] *Ibid.* pp. 22–3.   [72] *Ibid.* p. 23.   [73] *Ibid.*

false church, and the arrival of a protestant magistrate, the preacher could claim God had offered the English a real chance to sweep away the influence of popery and to restore their virtue to its pristine condition. For instance, Burnet showed that William's soldiers understood they were moral as well as military crusaders. Before embarking they had resolved to do their part in reviving godly living, and had entered into solemn engagements of personal amendment and 'serious and universal reformation'.[74] Similarly, Burnet argued that William's arrival in London might allow the entire English population to turn its back on sin. After the debacle of the last decades, the nation could make another attempt to live according to the gospel. Indeed, the preacher went further than this and claimed that the latest divine deliverance *demanded* moral reform. On no account, he warned, was the population to respond to this latest blessing in the way they had greeted the 1660 Restoration. They must exploit the possibilities which God had just opened up and must make every effort to walk in godliness.

As we reflect on [the] Abominations [of Charles' reign], and on the fatal Consequences of them, which have been on us so long; so in order to the preventing the return of the like Evils, we must avoid relapsing into the like Sins ... In a word, if Men think their Fears are over; and that, therefore, they may give themselves up to work wickedness without restraint, then we may justly expect the return of the like, if not greater Miseries.[75]

Thus at St James's Burnet used early protestant concepts to elaborate his argument from God's will. He stressed that the Revolution had promoted the true church, godly magistracy, and moral reform, and so had deepened his basic contention that Englishmen must approve recent events because their Lord had brought them about. In doing this, the preacher had escaped the trap inherent in providential discourse. Reading the December sermon closely, it is clear that Burnet did *not* justify William's invasion merely because it had been successful. The near-miraculous events which had led to the prince's triumph were cited as strong evidence for God's approval; but whilst these signs were necessary to establish the justice of the Orange cause, they were not seen as sufficient to do so. Instead, it was made clear that Englishmen should only support William because his actions had advanced the three long-cherished ideals. Burnet wanted his audience to consider the scale of the prince's triumph, but he only asked them to welcome William as their protector once he had proved that his hero's victory had promoted God's true church, a Christian prince, and purer morality. Furthermore, Burnet's mid-Tudor rhetoric allowed him to make special claims about the significance of William's invasion, which he could not have made if he was

---

[74] *Ibid.* p. 26.   [75] *Ibid.* p. 24.

simply justifying it from its success. Using the three old protestant ideals, the preacher was able to set 1688 in the dichotomous and apocalyptic interpret-ation of history developed by sixteenth-century polemicists and could conse-quently present it as a potential turning-point in world affairs. Once he was operating within the 'mid-Tudor' mind-set, Burnet could argue that an event which did so much to advance God's case was far more than an ordinary political development. The preacher could imply that a change which so advanced the true church, Christian magistracy and morality, was clearly a vital moment in the global battle between good and evil, and might even represent the beginning of the final victory for God's forces. Burnet's deploy-ment of such suggestions is clearest in his use of millenarian imagery. In 1688, the preacher was still wary of applying Revelation too closely or literally to contemporary affairs. Nonetheless he was excited enough by what had just happened to use apocalyptic similes and metaphors. Trying to impress upon his audience the magnitude of the events through which they were living, the preacher suggested that if they were diligent in responding to God's gift of the deliverance, they might create a world comparable to that described in the triumphant last verses of the bible. The English might witness 'the most glorious beginning of a noble change in the whole face of affairs . . . We may, if we are not wanting to our selves, and to the conjuncture before us, hope to see that which may be according to the prophetic style, termed a new heavens and a new earth.'[76] In such language, Burnet had moved far beyond a simple, retrospective justification for William's invasion. He had awarded the prince's expedition a central place in the unfolding drama of human history, and so invested it with a significance denied to other men's advances and achievements.

The St James's sermon, therefore, provided an account of God's dealings with the prince of Orange which escaped the standard criticisms of providen-tialism. The address did not collapse into a tautologous justification for worldly might, and so presented an intellectually meaningful and defensible case. It also, however, did something still more significant. As Burnet care-fully avoided the potential traps in his discourse, he laid the groundwork for a genuine alternative to the arguments of the *Declaration*. The December address contained a comprehensive Williamite ideology, which was quite independent of the case promoted in the Orange manifesto. This ideology, which might be labelled 'Williamite reformation', consisted of a series of interlocking assumptions about the prince and protestantism in England, and was based upon a deeply spiritual analysis of history. Its main tenets have already been implied in discussion of Burnet's sermon. Williamite refor-mation insisted that the decades after 1660 had been a period of godly decline

[76] *Ibid.* pp. 20–1.

in England. Satan's forces, in the form of highly placed popish agents, had worked to undermine the true faith by debauching protestants and had endangered a special relationship which the English had built up with God through their earlier championship of his cause. In this interpretation, 1688 was a moment of divine deliverance. It was justifiable because it had offered an opportunity to reverse the degeneration of recent years, and had opened up an opportunity for the nation to restore its alliance with the deity. Not only had it dealt a blow to the false church, it has set up a godly magistrate in power, and had permitted the English to break out of their cycle of sin. Now that James had fled the people must respond to this divine gift. They must follow the lead of their new Christian prince, and expunge the vices which had nearly led to disaster under the pre-Revolutionary regime. Joining with William, they must effect a wholesale moral and religious reformation to restore the pristine protestantism of England's first break with Rome.

Taken together, these ideas constituted a powerful statement of Orange legitimacy. They were useful, not only in the circumstances of December 1688, but throughout William's reign. Williamite reformation both justified the prince's actions in the Revolution, and provided continuing reasons for supporting the new king once he had come to the throne. It made the new reign comprehensible within a broad historical context; it drew upon deeply engrained English prejudices against popery; and it stood as a standing rebuke to the degeneracy of the displaced Stuart regime. In fact, so convenient was the doctrine that it became the cornerstone of Williamite propaganda. Once the arguments of the prince's original manifesto proved counter-productive, Orange publicists turned to the ideas Burnet adumbrated at St James's, and increasingly utilised them in their appeals for support. Over the winter of 1688–9, Williamite reformation was gradually to replace English constitutionalism as the defence of William's position.

REFORMATION IN ACTION

The Orange camp spent considerable effort in the winter of 1688–9 propagating Burnet's ideal. The 23 December sermon was but one element of an energetic publicity campaign which ran alongside efforts to promote the prince's *Declaration* and spread Williamite reformation through a variety of sermons, speeches, ceremonies, and symbolic actions. The great attraction of the rhetoric was that it avoided the main weakness of the Orange manifesto. Unlike that document, it did not lack a powerful argument for William's *personal* power and prestige. Seeing the prince's own endeavour as integral to the divine deliverance, the rhetoric could present him as a near-sacred instrument of God's providence.[77] He was the longed-for godly magistrate, who might crush the false church and could inspire and lead the purgation which might restore England's holiness. Lionising the prince in this way, the propaganda contained an explicit appeal for William to be given authority. It could thus be used to smooth over those dangerous moments in 1688–9 when the prince's ambition became more stark. Its unchanging glorification of William scored over arguments in the *Declaration*, since it did not suffer embarrassment in the face of the unadvertised accumulations of Orange power.

The language emerged as soon as the prince's intention to invade England became clear. Just before William's fleet sailed (flying pennants vowing to maintain the protestant religion), Burnet preached to the assembled troops.[78] Although the text of this address was not printed, John Whittel, an apocalyptically minded chaplain in the army, later published a report of it. According to Whittel's account, Burnet's sermon was pure Williamite reformation. It asserted that the prince of Orange was engaged in God's work, and stressed that amendment of morals was an essential part of his whole enterprise. Burnet asked that all the fighting men 'be truly reformed' and was 'very pressing unto holy life and conversation'.[79] At about the time this sermon was preached, prayers for the expedition were published.[80] No author was given on the printed sheets, but the *London Gazette*, sneering at these treasonous supplications, claimed they had been written by Burnet.[81] Given their content, and the position of the supposed author within Williamite counsels in this period, such an attribution seems highly likely to be correct. The prayers (which were used constantly by the Orange forces, and supplanted James's prayers in areas which they controlled) continued the themes of Burnet's sermon.[82] They again emphasised that William's invasion of England was a blow for the true faith, and that it must be a moment of moral purgation.

---

[77] William had already been presented in these terms in his Dutch propaganda, especially when at war with the French. See Simon Schama, *The embarrassment of riches: an interpretation of Dutch culture in the golden age* (1987), pp. 51–3, 275–6.

[78] See *The expedition of the prince of Orange for England; giving an account of the most remarkable passages thereof*, printed in *A complete collection of papers, in twelve parts: relating to the great revolution* (1689), part 3, pp. 1–8, especially p. 3.

[79] [John Whittel], *An exact diary of the late expedition of his illustrious highness, the prince of Orange* (1689), pp. 23–4.

[80] *A praier for the present expedition* ([Hague], 1688).

[81] *London Gazette*, No. 2402.

[82] [Whittel], *Exact diary*, p. 32, talked of the prayers being used on ship. Burnet, *Sermon ... St James's ... 23 December 1688*, p. 26, spoke of the vows of reformation (almost certainly in the form of reciting the prayers) made by the whole Orange company on its embarkation. Reaction to the *Gazette*'s report on 19 November that William had forbidden praying for the king, is reported in *Ellis correspondence*, II, 333. See also Ambassador Van Citters to the States General of the United Provinces, 3 December 1688 (new style), BL Additional Ms. 34,510, fols. 184–5.

Grant O Gracious God that all of us, may be turning to thee with our whole hearts; Repenting us truely of all our past sins, and solemnly vowing to thee, as wee now doe, that wee will in all time coming amend our lives, and endeavour to carry our selves as becomes Reformed Christians. And that wee will show our Zeal for our holy Religion by living in all things suteably to it.[83]

Other works which appeared as William sailed reinforced the burden of the Burnetine prayers and sermon. Two prose 'Characters' of the prince presented their subject as the ideal godly magistrate.[84] They praised his diligence, temperance, and piety, and related his efforts to purge corruption from the United Provinces. For these biographers William was not simply a virtuous foreign ruler. They suggested that God had picked him out to save Christians beyond his own realm. One of the pieces stated the prince had acted 'as if he were designed by heaven, not only to be the saviour of his own country and religion, but the champion of the Lord of Hosts, to deliver his true church from the fury, treachery and tyranny of its enemies'.[85] The other asked why righteous men might not 'hope to see this wondrous blessing by providence more diffusive, and not concluded within the narrow boundaries of Belgium'.[86] The pamphlets thus used reformation ideas to hint that, in future, William's authority would extend over new kingdoms. An even more explicit argument for William's sovereignty in Britain was contained in a further 1688 pamphlet, which described a miraculous vision in William's original principality of Orange.[87] On 6 May 1665 when William had acceded to the government of that state, a crown of light had appeared over its chair of state. Now, on the eve of William's expedition to England, it had appeared again.

The production of reformation propaganda continued once William's forces were in England. On 8 November, Burnet was sent by William to Exeter to organise the prince's reception in that town.[88] The local bishop, Thomas Lamplugh, had already interpreted William's actions as rebellion, and fled to avoid association with them. In his preparations, Burnet attempted to get round such doubts over the legality of the invasion by stressing providential protestant deliverance. At the centre of Burnet's Exeter reception were two ceremonies. The first was William's triumphal entry into the city. This was an important piece of propaganda, which was described in a pamphlet printed by the Orange camp for those who had missed the original

---

[83] *Praier ... present expedition.*
[84] *Character [of William, prince of Orange]* (Hague, 1688); *Character of his royal highness, William Henry, prince of Orange* (1689).
[85] *Character ... his royal highness*, p. 6.
[86] *Character [of William ...].*
[87] *A relation from the city of Orange, of a crown of light that was there seen in the air, 6 May 1688*, in *Complete collection of papers*, part 1, p. 22.
[88] Details of his activities can be found in a letter from Burnet (to his wife?) preserved as BL Harley Ms. 6798, fols. 264–8. See also *Expedition of the prince*, p. 6.

event.[89] It is worth analysing the symbolism of the procession, as it reveals what the Orange camp was suggesting about the meaning of the prince's advance. Some of the symbols were obvious enough. In the parade, at least according to the published account, there were 'fifty gentlemen, and as many pages to attend and support the prince's banner, bearing this inscription, "God and the protestant religion"'. Other parts of the procession, however, are harder to analyse. The prince himself appeared 'rid ... on a milk white palfrey. Armed cap a pee. A plume of white feathers on his head. All in bright armour, and forty two footmen running by him.'[90] Although it is clear that William was being presented as a chivalric, Christian warrior in this display, decoding the precise symbolism of the white horse is difficult. It may just have been a striking visual image to draw the viewers' attention to the most important man in the procession. It may have been a simple suggestion of purity.[91] However, it may also have had a millennial resonance. William's appearance echoed passages from Revelation which described God's terrible champions in the last days. 'I saw and behold, a white horse: and he that sat on him had a bow, and a crown was given unto him, and he went forth conquering and to conquer' (Revelation 6:2). 'I saw heaven opened and behold, a white horse, and he that sat upon him was called faithful and true, and in righteousness he doth judge and make war' (Revelation 19:11). William's entry into Exeter may thus have used powerful biblical imagery to suggest that the prince was the ultimate godly magistrate. He had come to vanquish evil, to conquer and, most importantly, to gain kingship. This millennial element may have been reinforced by the symbolic suggestion that William was a world ruler, whose God-given writ ran everywhere. The celebration included 'two hundred blacks brought from the plantations of the Netherlands in America' who, also dressed in white, took their place in the procession.[92]

The second Exeter ceremony was a service of thanksgiving in the cathedral. A later story, accusing Burnet of using muskets to threaten the local clergy into changing the form of prayer, may suggest his zeal in organising the event.[93] At this service, constitutional propaganda was used, but the occasion did not rely on it. The reading of William's *Declaration* was preceded by the singing of the *Te Deum* (with its appeal for God to save, lift up, and govern his

---

[89] *A true and exact relation of the prince of Orange his public entrance into Exeter* ([Exeter], 1688).
[90] *Ibid.*
[91] White is a common symbol of purity in scripture, II Chronicles 5:12; Daniel 12:10; Matthew 17:2, 28:3; Mark 16:5.
[92] *True and exact account ... entrance into Exeter.*
[93] [Nathaniel Salmon], *The lives of the English bishops from the Restauration to the Revolution* (1731), p. 229. [Edward Bohun], *History ... desertion*, p. 41 confirms, from a Williamite source, the need to use threats in Exeter to get prayers changed.

people) and was succeeded by the prayer for the expedition.[94] Burnet also preached in the cathedral on William's first Sunday in Exeter. Although this address – like that at the Hague – has not survived, contemporary accounts of it report that it had a strongly providential theme, and its text, from the last verse of psalm 107, might indicate it was an exposition of Williamite reformation.[95] Psalm 107 called for repentance from the Jews as a response to God's deliverance. Such a message suggests that Burnet was using this biblical passage to encourage the English to see themselves as a people divinely protected by William's arrival, who must amend their lives in gratitude.

The language of reformation was again prominent as William moved on from Exeter. On the march east, Burnet accompanied William, and was noted both for his vehement promotion of the prince's claims and his hostility to Jacobite prayers.[96] Williamite publications, which reported their hero's advance, presented his army as living up to the highest ideals of reformed Christian behaviour. One spoke of the soldiers' 'civil deportment, and their honesty of paying for what they have'.[97] Meanwhile, William himself assiduously cultivated his image as a godly champion. He was careful to ensure the good behaviour of his troops, and told a crowd as he rode through Salisbury, 'I am come to secure the protestant religion, and to free you from popery'.[98] An extraordinary account of the prince's meeting with deserting commanders from James's army even cast him as the biblical David. At Sherborne, he was described greeting men including Lord Churchill, and Prince George of Denmark, with David's salutations at the moment he was acclaimed king. In one of the most unlikely reports on the whole expedition, William is supposed to have asked that his heart be knit with those of the commanders. They promptly replied, 'thine are we, David, and on thy side, thou son of Jesse'.[99]

Once William had arrived in London in mid-December, reformation propaganda became even more important. Arguably, the prince's entry to the English capital was the moment of most acute ideological danger for the Orange forces, since it was at this point that the Stadholder most obviously went beyond his initial constitutional claims. His arrival at the national centre

---

[94] *Expedition of the prince*, p. 7.

[95] [Whittel], *Exact diary*, p. 48; *Expedition of the prince*, p. 6; *Notes and Queries*, 2nd series II, 245.

[96] S. W. Singer, ed., *The correspondence of Henry Hyde, Earl of Clarendon* (2 vols., 1828), II, 214, 217, 227, 242.

[97] *A further account of the prince's army, in a letter from Exon. Novemb. 24*, printed in *Complete collection of papers*, part 3, pp. 8–9.

[98] Singer, *Correspondence ... Clarendon*, II, 215. For more on William's time in Salisbury, see *Great news from Salisbury* (1688). William's own efforts for an ordered army are recorded in Burnet, *History ... own times*, III, 331; and [Whittel], *Exact diary*, p. 46.

[99] *Expedition of the prince*, pp. 7–8. The original scene is I Chronicles 12:17–18.

of power with a large army monopolised authority in his hands, and led to difficult questions about his ultimate aims. After he had come to London, William had clearly taken more power than he had first laid claim to, and his opponents started to use the moderation of his original manifesto against his latest actions. Burnet coped with these dangers by stepping up his reformation propaganda. He sent the prince a memorandum reminding him of the symbolic importance of his actions during his early days in London, and suggesting that he put himself at the head of a campaign for moral purgation. In this way, the preacher hoped to balance his master's actual dominance with an ideological justification for William's power which was drawn from reformation ideals, and so was not compromised by his earlier constitutional position. Part of the memorandum read 'I humbly propose that, when the Lord Mayor and the aldermen of London come to wait on the prince, he may recommend to them the suppressing of vice and the excesses of drinking', and Burnet went on to advise that William attack vice in the army, remove scandalous ministers from the church, and be careful to promote an image of personal piety.[100]

Not all of this advice was followed. In particular there was no immediate proclamation against debauchery. However, Burnet's memorandum set the general tone of William's self-presentation during his first days in London, and did something to raise the moral expectations of those who first met the prince in his new capital. The prince certainly expounded Burnet's message in his physical entry into the metropolis. On 18 December, when he arrived at St James's, he indulged in a blaze of symbolic ceremonial which echoed his Exeter triumph.[101] William again wore white, a cloak of this colour being thrown over his shoulders as he drove through the park. His military commanders rode in coaches pulled by six white horses, and crowds cheered, as they had done from Exeter, that they would live and die protestants. The effect was only spoiled by heavy rain, and the fact that most Londoners had gathered in the city streets, not realising that the prince would go through the park to the palace.[102] William was also careful to publicise his piety during his early days in London. He attended several religious services, including the one at St James's on 23 December and one on 30 December during which he listened to a sermon and heard prayers read by Burnet. On this second occasion he also took communion in a public enough manner that the

---

[100] Blencowe, *Diary ... times of Charles the Second*, II, 287. Burnet's advice was quite explicit about its propagandist objectives. The chaplain cited with approval the effect of earlier campaigns for moral reformation on public opinion.

[101] *A true account of the prince of Orange's coming to St James, on Tuesday 18 December 1688, about three of the clock in the afternoon* (1688).

[102] Burnet, *History ... own times*, III, 358. Burnet seems to have been upset at this slip-up in public relations.

city gentleman Richard Lapthorne could report that 'his highness received the sacrament from the bishop of London with an exemplary devotion'.[103]

Reformation was again used in January. The second half of this month, when the convention began to gather in Westminster, was another moment of great ideological difficulty for William, in which he again found his initial constitutional propaganda troublesome. By this stage, the prince wanted to be offered the throne quickly, so that he could settle the political uncertainty which had been racking England for months, and lead his new nation swiftly into war with France. Unfortunately, however, his manifesto prevented him simply requesting or demanding the crown. The *Declaration* suggested that all constitutional questions should be decided by an uncoerced legislature, and would have offered even more ammunition for his opponents if the prince had infringed the parliamentary freedom which his document had promised. As a result William had to adopt a stance of public neutrality on England's settlement and had to watch in some discomfort as members of the convention openly debated his claims and canvassed solutions which would have excluded him from the throne. Yet even though Orange constitutional propaganda had stalled, reformation rhetoric could still be deployed and developed. On 31 January a public day of thanksgiving was held. Officially, this event was intended to show the nation's gratitude 'to almighty God for having made his highness the prince of Orange, the glorious instrument of the great deliverance of this kingdom from popery and arbitrary power'.[104] Unofficially, it was designed to bring Burnet's ideals to the widest possible audience, and to advance William's claims as a godly magistrate at the height of the convention's debates about his future.

The historical record provides few clues as to who exactly promoted the thanksgiving in January 1689. However, there is strong circumstantial evidence that Burnet, or men close to him, encouraged it in order to boost William's image at a time when the prince was unable to join directly in political discussions. From what happened, it is clear that there must have been an organised effort to promote the thanksgiving, and to ensure its message was controlled by William's chaplain. When the idea was moved in the upper house of the convention – that body's first official action – the assembled peers accepted it and chose William Lloyd, bishop of St Asaph's, to preach to them on the coming occasion.[105] Lloyd was an old friend of Burnet who had become very close to him over the winter of 1688, and was actively

---

103 Russell J. Kerr and Ida Coffin Duncan, eds., *The Routledge papers: being extracts from the letters of Richard Lapthorne, gent., of Hatton Garden, London to Richard Coffin, esq., of Routledge, Bideford, Devon* (1928), p. 57.
104 *An order of the Lords spiritual and temporal and Commons assembled at Westminster in this present convention for a publick thanksgiving* (1688), dated 22 January 1689.
105 *LJ*, 14, 102.

drumming up support for the prince of Orange.[106] After the lords' decision had been relayed to the lower house, the commoners assembled there swiftly agreed to the thanksgiving, and chose as their preacher none other than Burnet himself.[107] When he went to the pulpit, the prince's chaplain took the opportunity to repeat the message of the St James's address. He reminded his audience of William's importance in a divine scheme of reformation, and again argued that the invasion had been divinely promoted to end the debauchery and corruptions of the last two reigns. It had shown that God was willing to renew his protection of England's godly nation; and that the people must now respond to the gift of the prince by following his reforming lead.[108]

This thanksgiving was important because it allowed Burnet to engage in a mass publicity exercise. The event was designed to bring the Williamite message to the *whole* English population. Up to the end of January, Orange propaganda had relied on published descriptions of the prince's words and actions. It had, therefore, been limited to those with access to printed literature. The thanksgiving, by contrast, attempted to ensure that *all* Englishmen heard a legitimation of recent events. The order from the lords which established the event urged every Londoner into his local church on the 31st, where they were to hear a special religious service.[109] This act of worship was to include a sermon from the local minister on the theme of deliverance, and a form of prayer specially composed for the occasion.[110] These supplications put William's actions in a Burnetine context, replacing the collect for the day with one thanking God for protecting the protestant religion through the ages. The special collect blamed the ravages of James's reign on national sin, and viewed William's invasion as a divine event, heralding a new age. God had 'raised up for us a mighty deliverer' and caused 'light to spring out of darkness'. Other parts of the prayers suggested that the work of reformation was to continue, and that William would need to be in England to see it through. 'Go on to perfect', they asked, 'O gracious God, the work that thou hast begun among us. Bless and prosper the hands, by which thou hast

---

[106] See Clarke and Foxcroft, *Life of Burnet*, p. 254; Arthur T. Hart, *William Lloyd, 1627–1717* (1952); Singer, *Correspondence ... Clarendon*, II, 226–7. Burnet once wrote that Lloyd had criticised his *History of the Reformation* so closely before publication that it was almost his own work. See Gilbert Burnet, *A letter writ by the lord bishop of Salisbury, to the lord bishop of Coventry and Litchfield* (1693), pp. 2–3.

[107] *CJ*, 10, 11–12.

[108] Gilbert Burnet, *A sermon preached before the House of Commons on 31 January 1688, being the thanksgiving-day for the deliverance of this kingdom from popery and arbitrary power* (1689), especially pp. 29, 32–3. William Lloyd did not deliver his sermon as he was ill.

[109] *Order of the Lords.*

[110] *A form of prayer and thanksgiving to almighty God for having made his highness the prince of Orange the glorious instrument of the great deliverance of the kingdom from popery and arbitrary power* (1688). This had been ordered by the Lords and sent to a committee of bishops for composition, *LJ*, 14, 102.

conveyed this mercy to us. Direct our governors with the spirit of wisdom and righteousness, rule thou in the midst of our public councils.' Men and women in the provinces were to go to church for the thanksgiving on 14 February, two weeks after London. The fortnight's delay gave areas outside the capital time to plan the day, and for news of what had been preached in London to spread.[111] Where the provincial sermons have survived by being published, they seem to have echoed the themes of Burnet's address. They promoted reformation as a necessary response to deliverance, and portrayed the prince as the only possible leader of this purgation. John Ollyffe, preaching in Almer, Dorset, talked of the desperate need, after a deliverance, to join the renewal promoted by William.

> Our chief Work is yet to come. And that is, that we labour for a thorow and National Reformation, which though we that are in private Capacities cannot do much, yet we should labour to do what we can; ... And what we cannot of our selves, let us help by devout and earnest Prayers at the Throne of Grace, that Holiness beginning at the Throne, may flow down through all the Channels of Office and Magistracy to the meanest Persons of the Land.[112]

Similarly, John Flavell, a Devonshire divine, told his audience that 'a national reformation is now expected by the Lord', and that William was 'a second Hezekiah', 'a great example of virtue, to correct thy lewdness'.[113]

The effort put into promoting the thanksgiving of 31 January indicates the progress Williamite reformation was making in Orange circles. By the early weeks of 1689, it had filled the gap created by the failures of the *Declaration*, and had effectively taken over from constitutional language in the presentation of the prince's case. Avoiding the caution of the original manifesto, reformation ideology had allowed William to argue for kingship even at those dangerous moments when his actions had exceeded the intentions declared in his first tract, and when he had been forced into silence by that document. The final triumph for Burnet's rhetoric came after the prince had become king. Once this had happened, his second set of arguments became still more attractive because they proved as well adapted to defending a court as to attacking one. Whereas the original constitutional case had been critical of monarchical authority and had stressed its tendency to abuse, reformation argument allowed a more open celebration of kingship, and was therefore more useful to the incoming regime. Based in the ideals of godly rule and

111 The Harley family correspondence shows that at least as far away as rural Herefordshire (over 125 miles from London, on the Welsh border), services were organised and attended; see letter from Robert Harley to Sir Edward Harley 14 February 1689, *HMC Portland*, III, 428.

112 John Ollyffe, *England's call to thankfulness for her great deliverance ... in a sermon preach'd in the church of Almer in Dorsetshire on Feb 14 1689* (1689), p. 30.

113 [John Flavell], *Mount Pisgah: a sermon preached at the publick thanksgiving, Febr. 14 1689* (1689), pp. 23, 46, 24.

Christian magistracy, it contained a potential justification and celebration of royal power, and so could more easily survive the shift from opposition to government ideology. To see this one need look no further than the coronation of William and Mary on 11 April. Then, reformation was employed to bolster both the dignity and the authority of the nation's new masters.

The 1689 coronation has been the subject of recent historical study. Both Carolyn Edie and Lois Schwoerer have described the ceremony, and have outlined its role in establishing an image of the new monarchy. Schwoerer concentrated on the new coronation oath taken by William in Westminster Abbey. This, she argued, performed the delicate task of appearing to preserve the old forms of royal authority, whilst actually making concessions to the men who had pushed for a declaration of subjects' rights.[114] Edie studied the coronation medals and the sermon preached during the ceremony. Both these, she believed, served as expositions of the legal principles the Revolution was held to represent.[115]

This work is valuable, but it stresses constitutional rhetoric at the expense of a reformation message which had become much more useful to William and his allies. Schwoerer's work on the oath, for instance, ultimately confirmed Orange weakness in controlling constitutional propaganda since she demonstrated that the duty of preparing this vital public statement passed to a committee of independently minded MPs, who were suspicious of the new king, and wished to make the limitations on his power explicit.[116] By contrast, the historian underplayed those parts of the ceremonial which propagated a reformation message, and used it to underline William's authority. Whilst, for instance, Schwoerer noted that the bible played a novel role in the coronation, she did not provide a full analysis of its possible significance. In her work on the new rite (in which an impressive volume of scripture was presented to the king and queen with the request that they make it their rule of life and government), Schwoerer interpreted the ceremony simply as a confirmation of the protestantism of the new regime.[117] This was an important observation, but it did not bring out the extent to which the presentation was part of an ongoing attempt to portray William as a powerful reforming magistrate. The offer of the bible, linked to the suggestion that the king accept it as his guide, was almost certainly intended to boost royal authority by reminding its audience of Hebrew rulers. The ideal model of kingship

[114] Lois G. Schwoerer, 'The coronation of William and Mary, April 11 1689', in Schwoerer, *Revolution of 1688/9*, pp. 107–30.
[115] Carolyn A. Edie, 'The public face of royal ritual: sermons, medals and civic ceremony in later Stuart coronations', *Huntingdon Library Quarterly*, 53 (1990), 311–36, especially 322.
[116] Schwoerer, 'Coronation', p. 118.
[117] Schwoerer, 'Coronation', p. 115; for other accounts of the ceremony see *An account of the ceremonial at the coronation of their excellent majesties King William and Queen Mary* (1689); and Hester W. Chapman, *Mary II, queen of England* (Bath, 1972), p. 171.

contained in scripture was the familiar image of godly magistrates such as David, Solomon, and Josiah. These were potent figures, who had used their divinely bestowed majesty to lead their people to righteousness. The ceremony in the abbey was therefore intended to cast William's monarchy in an Old Testament mould, and so stress his God-given mastery over polity and society.

A similar message was carried by Burnet's coronation sermon. Some of this address dealt, as Carolyn Edie noted, with the constitution. Burnet took just government as his theme and reminded men how it could be subverted. Justice, he said, could only be maintained when monarchs were 'not breaking through the limits of their power, nor invading the rights of their people; neither inventing new pretensions of prerogative, nor stretching those that do belong to them, to the ruin of their subjects'.[118] However, this argument was not to be the meat of the sermon. Despite the echoes of William's *Declaration* in the early passages of the address, Burnet was not concerned to develop a legal case. He did not apply his definition of just rule to explain exactly how James had forfeited the throne, nor did he provide any concrete descriptions of the bounds of English prerogative. Instead, Burnet quickly developed a much wider definition of justice. *Really* just government, the preacher stated, involved more than constitutional correctness. It meant taking the fear of God as the rule for the exercise of authority.[119] This echoed the message of the bible ceremony, and explained that real righteousness went far beyond mere obedience to national law. True justice meant the encouragement of godly religion and morality implied by the ideal of reformation.

When the encouraging and promoting of a vigorous Piety, and sublime Vertue, and the maintaining and propagating of True Religion ... is the chief design of their Rule: When Impiety and Vice are punished, and Error is repressed ... : When the decency of the Worship of God is kept up, without adulterating it with Superstition: When Order is carried on in the Church of God, without Tyranny: And above all, when Princes are in their own deportment, Examples of the *Fear of God*, but without Affectation; and when it is visible that they *honour those that fear the Lord*, and that *vile men are despised by them*, then do they truly Rule in the *Fear of God*.[120]

The explanation for Burnet's change of tack lay in the growing nervousness about constitutionalism in the Orange camp. Defining English fundamental law too closely at the coronation would risk reopening the campaign to limit the prerogative which had been noticeable in the convention's debates, and might encourage all sorts of unwelcome investigations into the monarch's legal position. To avoid this danger, Burnet chose a reformation idiom which

---

[118] Gilbert Burnet, *A sermon preached at the coronation of William III and Mary II, king and queen ... in the abby-church of Westminster, April 11, 1689* (1689), p. 11.
[119] *Ibid.* p. 17.   [120] *Ibid.* pp. 19–20.

enabled him to preach up the new court's power. The position the cleric adopted allowed him to suggest that, since justice was secured more by righteousness than by limitation of the prerogative, a monarch willing to rule in the fear of God should be allowed to retain his influence. Following this line, Burnet turned his coronation address into a hymn to godly magistracy – a song of praise for what monarchical power could achieve. National reformation, he argued, would begin at court, and would be effected by William's sway over his subjects. 'Kings' examples', he pointed out, 'have an efficacy which few can resist.'[121] William, he suggested, would play the same role as the Emperor Hadrian after the debauchery of Nero and Caligula. He would change the whole tone of society and restore ancient virtues.[122] At his most impassioned, the preacher engaged in what might be called centripetal millenarianism. He presented royal power as a vital element in God's providential plan for the world. In a glorification of the court, the king's authority was portrayed as the necessary stimulus to Christ's reign on earth. 'When we see kings become ... truly Christian philosophers, then we may expect to see the city of God, the *New Jerusalem*, quickly come down from heaven to settle among us.'[123]

In such passages Orange reformation demonstrated its impressiveness as a *executive* rhetoric. In fact, the coronation could be seen as the point at which 'Williamite' reformation was transformed into an ideology of 'courtly' reformation. Instead of undermining a court (that of James), Burnet's arguments were now used to support a court (that of William). The rhetoric had thus become the legitimating message of a regime. It was ready to take its place, not just as the prime defence of William's actions, but also as the official language of the English government.

---

[121] *Ibid.* p. 20.   [122] *Ibid.* p. 24.   [123] *Ibid.* p. 20.

2

The resources for royal propaganda

REFORMATION PERSONNEL

On 31 December 1701, William III went to Westminster to deliver his last speech to parliament. Two months later, a rodent would succeed where Jacobite plotters had failed, and the king would die after his horse had stumbled over a molehill in Hyde Park. William's last speech was given nearly twelve years after he had first addressed the English as their monarch, but in that time the royal message had changed little. For one last time he rehearsed his claims for courtly reformation. Towards the end of his speech he hoped 'what time can be spared, will be employed about those other very desirable things, which I have so often recommended from the throne; I mean, the forming of some good bills, for employing the poor, for encouraging trade, and the further suppressing of vice.'[1] As William's words suggested, this last appeal for moral renewal was merely the most recent instance of a continuing performance. Throughout his reign, the king had constantly advanced the tenets of reformation, and had tirelessly repeated his invitation to godly renewal. By 1701, William's subjects had experienced one of the heaviest polemical bombardments ever suffered by loyal Englishmen. The next two chapters will attempt to do justice to this royal effort. The first will describe the human and material tools which were available to William. The second will go on to demonstrate how these were used within a series of ideological strategies, and will show how a variety of campaigns were launched to legitimate the king as a righteous reformer.

Any account of courtly reformation in the 1690s must start with the men who promoted the rhetoric. Gilbert Burnet may have done most to develop and advertise Williamite ideals during the invasion of 1689, but he did not work alone, and much of the credit for the king's publicity must go to those with whom Burnet co-operated. Even during the early days of William's

---

[1] *LJ*, 17, 6.

invasion the prince's chaplain was dependent upon the Dutch printers, polemicists, and politicians who constituted Fagel's communications machine.
More significantly for the future, Burnet spent his first weeks back in England
contacting a number of old friends whom he rapidly marshalled into a tightly
knit team of Orange publicists. By the summer of 1689 he had persuaded a
number of clerics to oversee his master's propaganda and had opened up lines
of communication between these men and their monarch. Throughout the
rest of the reign, it would be this group of people, acting collectively, who
would direct the presentation of the king's moral crusade.

The first sign that Burnet was attempting to recruit helpers was contained
in the paper the chaplain wrote to William in December 1688.[2] As well as
suggesting that the prince initiate an amendment of the capital's manners, this
memorandum recommended a batch of the city's clergy, whom William
might consider for preferment. John Tillotson, the dean of Canterbury and a
preacher at Lincoln's Inn, was mentioned; along with Simon Patrick, the dean
of St Paul's. Also on the list were Edward Fowler, the rector of St Giles,
Cripplegate; Thomas Tenison, the minister at St Martin's-in-the-Fields; John
Sharp of St Giles-in-the-Fields; Edward Stillingfleet; William Wake; and
Anthony Horneck, the charismatic preacher at the Savoy.

There are good reasons for believing that Burnet was trying to bolster
William's propaganda machine as he made these recommendations. First,
the chaplain made much of the clergy's polemical abilities as he promoted
them. The December paper dwelt upon the communication skills of its
subjects, and stressed their success in attracting the population's support.
It described Patrick as a 'great' preacher; it informed William that Horneck
was a pious preacher, with a huge personal following; and it puffed Wake
as 'the most popular divine now in England', the force of whose writing was
'amazing'. Second, the men listed in December were Burnet's ideological
allies. Not only were they old personal friends, who had helped him compile
the *History of the Reformation*, they had also had careers in the press, parish
and pulpit which suggested they might concur with the notion of Williamite
reform.[3]

Amongst the works published by Burnet's clergy before 1688, two genres
of literature had stood out. The first was anti-catholic polemic. The men
recommended to William had been some of the foremost protestant writers of
the 1670s and 1680s, whose activities had reached a fever pitch under James.[4]
The other speciality of Burnet's clergy had been English jeremiads. Particu-

---

[2] See above, p. 57.
[3] For Burnet's earlier contacts with these clergy, see Burnet, *History of the Reformation*, I, 7–8;
II, 3–4; Clarke and Foxcroft, *Life of Burnet*, pp. 143–4.
[4] Burnet, *History ... own times*, III, pp. 105–6, talks of a concerted effort amongst anglican

larly in their sermons in the late 1670s, the men listed in 1688 had analysed England as a nation falling deeper and deeper into sin.[5] These two forms of literature were linked because their authors blamed catholics for the moral temptations to which England had succumbed. They saw popish conspiracy behind depravity, and feared a plot to weaken England's attachment to the godly cause. Edward Stillingfleet, addressing the House of Commons in 1678, spoke for all Burnet's clergy when worrying that popery would come in 'at the back door' of profanity.[6] Echoing the other London ministers, he called for a concerted amendment of morals as the only means of averting the Roman danger. Obviously, such a philosophy brought the men Burnet listed in 1688 close to the position of their sponsor. Their hatred of popery amounted to the same 'two-church' vision which Burnet espoused during William's invasion, and their calls for national repentance anticipated the rhetoric of the Orange camp.

The parallel between Williamite ideology and the personal beliefs of the men mentioned in December was strengthened by the London clergy's pastoral work. Whilst ministering to the capital in the 1670s and 1680s, these men had participated in a spiritual and ecclesiastical revival, which the modern historian, Gordon Rupp, has labelled the 'small awakening'.[7] Possibly inspired by frequent meetings in one another's houses, the London clergy had initiated a drive to improve the quality of religious life in the city and had developed a pastoral style of intense personal care. Concentrated upon catechising, frequent public worship, and the establishment of parochial schools, libraries, and religious societies, the ministers had tried to reach out to their flocks, and involve them far more deeply in church life. Above all else, this religious awakening had emphasised the defeat of corrupt catholicism through the reformation of manners. Preaching, prayers, education, preparation for communion, and the spiritual exercises of the societies, had all been intended to foster an awareness of popish sin, and promote

---

clergy to publish against popery, organised by Tillotson, Stillingfleet, Tenision, and Patrick. For William Wake's efforts against catholic theology throughout the Restoration period see Norman Sykes, *William Wake, archbishop of Canterbury, 1657–1737* (2 vols., Cambridge, 1957), I, 17–43.

5 See, for example, John Sharp, *A sermon preached on the day of the publick fast, April 11 1679 at St Margaret's Westminster, before the honourable House of Commons* (1679); Simon Patrick, *A sermon preach'd at St Paul's Covent Garden, on the day of fasting and prayer, Novemb. 13 1678* (1678); Simon Patrick, *Angliae speculum: a glass that flatters not: presented to a country congregation at the late solemn fast, April 24 1678* (1678).

6 Edward Stillingfleet, *A sermon preached on the fast day, November 13 1678, at St Margaret's, Westminster before the honourable House of Commons* (2nd ed, 1678), p. 47.

7 Gordon Rupp, *Religion in England 1688–1791* (Oxford, 1985), pp. 40–51.

general repentance.[8] Thus in their actions, as well as in their words, the men of Burnet's list had suggested themselves as exponents of Williamite reformation. Whilst their publications had shown they agreed with the moral pathology of England offered by Orange spokesmen, their work as ministers indicated that they might contribute to the proposed cure.

If Burnet was indeed trying to recruit his London clerics as reformation publicists in December 1688, he succeeded. Contrary to the account of their careers given by G. V. Bennett (who dated their association with the new court no sooner than the late spring of 1689), the men on Burnet's list entered into a close alliance with William from his very first days in England.[9] Although some of the group had initial doubts about the Revolution, most quickly lent their services to the Orange party.[10] From the start, they visited the prince, and used their good offices to try to win over key political figures to his cause. Tillotson helped to convince William's sister-in-law, Princess Anne, not to make damaging claims over the succession; whilst Tenison worked on the archbishop of Canterbury, William Sancroft, to stop distancing himself from England's deliverer.[11] The clerics also lent their rhetorical skills to the prince. They preached to his entourage at St James's, and promoted him to a wider public. Tillotson, for instance, addressed William as early as 6 January, whilst Simon Patrick first preached at the palace two weeks later.[12] These two men went on to join in the thanksgiving propaganda of 31 January. From their prestigious pulpits in St Paul's, Covent Garden, and Lincoln's Inn, they

---

[8] For post-Revolution comment on some of this activity in London, see Josiah Woodward, *An account of the rise and progress of the religious societies* (1701); Richard Kidder, 'The life of Anthony Horneck', preface to Anthony Horneck, *Several sermons on the fifth of St Matthew* (2nd edn, 1706); Gilbert Burnet, *A sermon preached at the funeral of the most reverend father in God, John ... lord archbishop of Canterbury* (1694); John Sharp, *A sermon preached on 28 June at St Giles in the Fields ... at his leaving the parish* (1691). For more recent accounts, see Rupp, *Religion in England*, pp. 40–51; Edward Carpenter, *The protestant bishop; the life of Henry Compton, bishop of London* (1956), pp. 208–32; Edward Carpenter, *Thomas Tenison, archbishop of Canterbury, his life and times* (1948), pp. 16–30; Arthur Tindal Hart, *The life and times of John Sharp, archbishop of York* (1956), pp. 62–81.

[9] G. V. Bennett, 'King William III and the episcopate', in G. V. Bennett and J. D. Walsh, eds., *Essays in modern English church history* (1966), pp. 104–32.

[10] John Sharp's early doubts are discussed in Thomas Sharp, *A life of John Sharp, DD, lord archbishop of York* (2 vols., 1825), I, 99–102.

[11] Edward Gregg, *Queen Anne* (1980), p. 70; Sarah Churchill, *An account of the conduct of the dowager duchess of Marlborough* (1742), pp. 23–4; Simon Patrick, *The autobiography of Symon Patrick, bishop of Ely* (Oxford, 1839), p. 140.

[12] Thomas Birch, *The life of the most reverend Dr John Tillotson, lord archbishop of Canterbury, copied chiefly from his original papers and letters* (1752), p. 143; Patrick, *Autobiography*, p. 142.

delivered sermons (soon published) which rejoiced that William's invasion had made possible the reformation for which they had long called.[13]

In return for these services, William showed Burnet's men considerable favour. He promoted them, brought them into his circle, and gave them ample opportunity to propagate their message. On 22 January 1688/9, when Patrick went to speak at St James's, William revealed he was aware of the men Burnet had recommended and announced his intention to work with them. He told Patrick he had heard of him before and that he 'was glad to hear' him preach. He went on to state that he had 'always had a great esteem for the clergy of London, and a value for the service they have done religion; and will take care they shall live at ease'.[14] Promotions from these men began the same day when Wake and Horneck joined Burnet as the prince's chaplains.[15] Over the next couple of years, William accelerated the careers of most of those who had been recommended in 1688, building up a corps of clerics closely tied to the new regime. On his accession to the throne, the prince appointed Burnet his clerk of the closet. This was a high court office which brought the chaplain influence over patronage, and in which he would be succeeded by Tillotson in April 1689.[16] In the summer of William's first year, the king granted still more prestigious plums, moving the Burnetine clergy into the bishoprics he had found vacant on his elevation. He installed Burnet as bishop of Salisbury, made Edward Stillingfleet bishop of Worcester, and sent Simon Patrick to the diocese of Chichester. In the same period, John Tillotson was advanced to the deanery of St Paul's, and John Sharp was sent to replace him as dean of Canterbury. When, early in 1690, Archbishop Sancroft and some of his episcopal colleagues refused to take the oaths to the new monarchs, William got a further opportunity to show his favour. He proposed to deprive these non-jurors, and fill their sees with the men of Burnet's list. Despite some reluctance on the part of the clergy concerned to displace erstwhile colleagues, the king eventually persuaded Tillotson to go to Canterbury to replace Sancroft; he ordered Patrick to be translated to Ely, where the old bishop Turner had been deprived; and he sent Edward Fowler to Gloucester, where Robert Frampton had been ejected.[17] John Sharp's implacable refusal to step into the shoes of a deprived colleague was overcome by offering him

[13] John Tillotson, *A sermon preach'd at Lincoln's Inn chappel on 31 January 1688, being the day appointed for a public thanksgiving* (1689); Simon Patrick, *A sermon preached at St Paul's Covent Garden on 31 January 1688, being the thanksgiving day for the deliverance of the kingdom* (1689).

[14] Patrick, *Autobiography*, pp. 142–3.

[15] Luttrell, *Relation*, I, 497.

[16] John Bickersteth, *The Clerks of the Closet in the royal household: five hundred years of service to the crown* (Stroud, 1991), pp. 35–41.

[17] Tillotson's reluctance to take the archbishopric, first mooted to him by the king in 1689, is illustrated in a series of letters to Lady Rachel Russell. See BL Additional Ms. 4236, fols. 32, 293–4.

the archdiocese of York, whose metropolitan, Lamplugh, had died. By the time Thomas Tenison was promoted to Lincoln in 1691/2, the men of Burnet's list were dominating the episcopal bench. They had secured the most illustrious appointments in the English church, and were trusted to run ecclesiastical affairs in areas where the monarchs did not take a direct interest. In 1690, for instance, Burnet, Patrick, Stillingfleet, Sharp, Tillotson, and Tenison were appointed to supervise the reconstruction of the Irish establishment after the Jacobite revolt. Similarly in 1694, Tenison, Sharp, Patrick, Stillingfleet, and Burnet were put onto a commission to handle ecclesiastical patronage after Queen Mary's death.[18] These clerics – reform-minded, indebted to William, and elevated to prestigious platforms – would constitute the core of the court's propaganda machine.

Other clergymen, whilst not on Burnet's list, were drawn into his polemical activity, and must be considered key courtly reformers. One such man was Bishop William Lloyd of St Asaph's (promoted to Coventry and Lichfield in 1692). He was left off the December paper because he was already on the episcopal bench by 1688, and so would not have appeared amongst recommendations for preferment. Nevertheless he was to continue the close association with Burnet which has been noted in 1688/9, and would maintain his ideological alliance with him. Richard Kidder, the preacher at the Rolls, was also omitted from Burnet's original memorandum; but like Lloyd he must be considered an integral member of Burnet's team. He had been a popular London clergyman, was sponsored for ecclesiastical preferment by Tillotson and Burnet, and was a close friend of Horneck.[19] After the Revolution, his career mirrored those of the other courtly reformers. He was appointed to the Chapel Royal early in 1689, replaced the non-juring Thomas Ken at Bath and Wells in 1691, and did much to preach the virtues of Williamite reformation. Also important for royal propaganda were the bishops' clerical clients. Ministers such as Ralph Barker, George Royce, and John Hartcliffe – all patronised by Tillotson – weighed in to back the message of their masters.[20] Royce, for instance, would preach on William's Irish campaign in 1690, and Hartcliffe was to publish *A treatise of the moral and intellectual virtues* (1691) whose explicit purpose was to outline the righteousness made possible by 'our late wonderful Revolution'.[21] Mention should also be made of Henry Compton, bishop of London. Although this man was to drift out of the core group of courtly reformers in 1691 (he

---

18 *CSPD, 1690–1*, pp. 158–9; Luttrell, *Relation*, III, 446.
19 Kidder's popularity as a preacher at the Rolls and at Blackfriars is chronicled in *DNB*, XI, 96. For his recommendation by Burnet and Tillotson to replace Patrick at Covent Garden, see *CSPD, 1689–90*, p. 246. Kidder wrote an affectionate 'Life' of Horneck.
20 For patronage of these clerics, see Birch, *Life ... Tillotson*, pp. 260–3, 392.
21 John Hartcliffe, *A treatise of the moral and intellectual virtues* (1691). For Royce's sermons and his recommendation by Tillotson, see below, p. 141.

withdrew in disgust when Tillotson was translated to Canterbury over his head), his links with the others went back before the Revolution, and he worked amongst the Burnetine allies in the early months of Orange rule. As the capital's diocesan since 1674 Compton had promoted the 'small awakening' through a series of clerical conferences; and he had played an active part in the anti-popery campaign during James's reign.[22] In 1688/9, he was an enthusiastic Williamite, and lent his weight to Burnet's propaganda. He joined Patrick in a communion service for the prince of Orange in early January; he consecrated the new bishop of Salisbury in March; and he crowned the new king on 11 April.[23]

Although the bishops were to be at the heart of reformation publicity, they were aided by secular writers and politicians. Obviously, some of the king's ministers played vital roles within the propaganda campaign, especially advising on the wording of royal speeches, and organising public ceremonies. The earl of Nottingham, Secretary of State from 1689 to 1693, was particularly active. He had been an old patron of Sharp, Tenison, Stillingfleet, and Tillotson; and he had aided the production of Burnet's *History of the Reformation*. When in office under William, he continued to consult closely with his clerical friends, and contributed to their promotion of the new regime.[24] Later in the decade, the episcopal propagandists worked closely with Lord Somers.[25] In addition, Burnet's circle recruited some of the growing band of professional pamphleteers who were becoming a feature of public debate at the end of the seventeenth century.[26] One especially interesting example was Daniel Defoe. As Manuel Schonhorn's study of this writer has made clear, Defoe was a fervent Williamite in the 1690s, and his works of the period shared many of the assumptions about providential kingship and godly magistracy which animated courtly reformation thought.[27]

Most importantly, the bishops had the support of Queen Mary. This was vital because communications between the king and his chief propagandists were not always easy. Not only was William frequently out of the country, fighting in Ireland or Flanders, his personal relationship with his advisers, especially Burnet, was sometimes tense. There seems, for instance, to have been a particularly cool period over the summer of 1689, during which William refused to entertain his bishop of Salisbury, and privately expressed his irritation with the man. The two men were back on intimate terms by the

[22] Carpenter, *Protestant bishop*, parts 1–2.
[23] Kerr and Duncan, *Routledge papers*, p. 57; Luttrell, *Relation*, I, 516.
[24] Henry Horwitz, *Revolution politicks; the career of Daniel Finch, second earl of Nottingham, 1647–1730* (Cambridge, 1968), pp. 262–3; Sharp, *Life of ... Sharp*, I, 104–5; Burnet, *History of the Reformation*, II, 4.
[25] See Bennett, 'William III and the episcopate', p. 124.
[26] For such sponsorship of pamphleteers, see Goldie, 'Revolution of 1689'.
[27] Schonhorn, *Defoe's politics*.

spring of 1690, but William never quite got used to his chief propagandist's self-importance, and hectoring approach to his royal majesty.[28] By contrast, Mary was much easier for Burnet and his allies to approach. Her intimacy with the Scotsman in Holland had extended to his colleagues once she was back in England, and she showed the whole group great support and encouragement during her reign.[29] As the person to whom William delegated ecclesiastical policy, Mary saw much of the bishops on business. She also took a close interest in the clerics' careers and publications, and constantly sought their spiritual and political counsels.[30] Burnet in particular remained in close attendance, spending most of his summers at Windsor. This was a convenient location which was just inside his diocese, but was near enough to Whitehall to allow weekly audiences with the queen.[31] Such intimate relations meant that Mary could act as a channel of communication between the king and his ideologues. She was keenly aware of the importance of public appearances, and played a pivotal role in the development of royal propaganda.[32] It was she who adopted, organised, and promoted many of the courtly reformation initiatives described below.

REFORMATION MEDIA

With the queen, the roll-call of leading courtly reformers is complete. However, whilst a description of the people involved in Williamite publicity is important, it is not a complete account of the resources available for the promotion of the Orange worldview. It was obviously an advantage for the king to be able to call on the services of dedicated and experienced publicists, but this would have been of little value if his servants had lacked the means to transmit their message to their intended audience. The problem of broadcasting ideology was particularly acute in the late Stuart period, since for reasons discussed below, traditional mechanisms for conveying royal propaganda were becoming increasingly ineffective for their purpose. Given this, it is vital to pay at least as close attention to the *media* of courtly reformation, as has been devoted to its message and its personnel.

[28] Clarke and Foxcroft, *Life ... Burnet*, pp. 266, 286. For the expressions of irritation, see H. C. Foxcroft, ed., *The life and letters of Sir George Savile* (2 vols., 1898), II, 216.

[29] Mark Goldie, 'John Locke, Jonas Proast, and the politics of toleration', in John Walsh, Colin Haydon and Stephen Taylor, eds., *The church of England c.1689–c.1833: from toleration to tractarianism* (Cambridge, 1993), pp. 143–71; Craig Rose, 'Providence, protestant union and godly reformation in the 1690s', *TRHS*, 6th series 3 (1993), 151–70.

[30] Tillotson and Burnet both spoke warmly of the queen's interest in their work and careers. See, for instance, *The letters of Lady Russell* (7th edn, 1809), p. 282; BL Additional Ms. 4239, fols. 316–17; Gilbert Burnet, *An exposition of the thirty nine articles of the church of England* (1699), preface.

[31] Clarke and Foxcroft, *Life ... Burnet*, p. 286.

[32] Chapman, *Mary II*, pp. 173–4.

The first set of media to be considered were the most traditional, and have been those subject to the most intense historical study by early modern scholars. These were a series of tactics, centring upon life at court, which had been used to convey royal ideology for over two hundred years. Since at least the early Tudor period, English monarchs had communicated with their nation by gathering political elites within their households, and then manipulating their social, cultural, and visual environment to convince them of the ruler's power. The most obvious example of such techniques was the building and adorning of royal palaces. Monarchs from Henry VII onwards had spent fortunes constructing and decorating houses, which were intended to convince visitors of the glory of their owners. Buildings such as Hampton Court, Whitehall, and Nonsuch – whose grandeur had spoken of the magnificence of English kings – had been complemented by paintings, tapestries, and sculptures whose iconography had proclaimed the legitimacy of these rulers. Display had been similarly important in the activities which these palaces accommodated. Ceremonies, rituals, and etiquette had been developed to structure the courtiers' existence, and had involved political elites in visual performances confirming the monarch's majesty. Even non-ceremonial life at court was organised to make ideological points. Court manners had confirmed hierarchies of prestige centring upon the king or queen, and strict rules of access to monarchs had created an aura of mystery and sanctity about their persons. Political elites had thus lived saturated with royal propaganda. Clustering around their monarch they had daily breathed the messages his household was organised to convey.[33]

All these ideological tactics were available in the 1690s and were used in the service of royal reformation. The dual monarchs were careful to establish their godly image within their household, and presented their moral zeal through the usual courtly means. For example, William and Mary were energetic builders. Investing in new wings at their palace at Hampton Court, converting Kensington House into a royal residence, and initiating the Royal Naval Hospital at Greenwich, they proclaimed reformation to their courtiers in paint, brick, and stone.[34] At Hampton Court, for instance, a coherent iconographic programme, based upon the presentation of William as

---

[33] For introductions to these themes, see David Starkey, 'Representation through intimacy: a study in the symbolism of monarchy and court office in early modern England', in Ioan Lewis, ed., *Symbols and sentiments: cross cultural studies in symbolism* (1977), pp. 187–224; Roy Strong, *Splendour at court: renaissance spectacle and illusion* (1973); Neville Williams, 'The Tudors', in A. G. Dickens, ed., *The courts of Europe: politics, patronage and royalty, 1400–1800* (1977), pp. 147–68; Penry Williams, *The Tudor regime* (Oxford, 1979), pp. 359–74; Sydney Anglo, *Images of Tudor kingship* (1992); Kevin Sharpe, *The personal rule of Charles I* (New Haven, 1992), pp. 207–31.

[34] For royal building, see John Harris, 'The architecture of the Williamite court', in Robert P. Maccubin and Martha Hamilton-Phillips, eds., *The age of William III and Mary II: power, politics and patronage, 1688–1702* (Williamsburg, 1989), pp. 225–33.

Hercules, was devised to adorn the walls of the rising wings. Hercules (a symbol of virtue and fortitude and so an appropriate representation of the godly king) was depicted in roundels above the new Fountain Courtyard, and was again portrayed on the pediment of the facade facing London. Within the palace, Verrio's murals on the King's Staircase took up the Herculean theme, and sculptures and fountains echoed it from outside the building.[35] Other forms of cultural patronage similarly promoted Orange reformation at court. Portrait painters depicted the monarchs as champions of virtue, and their works were hung in the public galleries at Hampton Court and Kensington.[36] Religious music was performed in royal chapels; and on special court occasions – such as the monarchs' birthdays – composers as eminent as Henry Purcell were commissioned to write odes to celebrate their rulers' zeal.[37] Still following their predecessors' example, William and Mary used court ritual to confirm royal ideology. We have already seen how careful William had been to demonstrate his piety in the winter of 1689 by processing publicly to the chapel at Whitehall.[38] Later we shall see Mary using exactly the same technique once she had arrived in the country.[39] Again, court social life was used as reformation propaganda. The monarchs cracked down upon frivolous manners in their household, and vowed to exclude immoral persons from the inner recesses of their palaces. William's court, therefore, was not entirely the stiff and lifeless place which has traditionally been imagined. It was still used to display royal ideology to sections of the political elite, and was capable of producing cultural and artistic works of considerable interest and merit.[40]

Nevertheless, the potential reach of court-based propaganda was contracting under William and Mary. As was mentioned in the introduction to this book, the number and importance of those who came to court was declining in the later seventeenth century, with the result that display and ritual within the royal household were losing their ability to persuade. Tudor and early Stuart monarchs had invested heavily in household display because they knew they could reach all their most important subjects that way. The elimination of regional magnates in the Wars of the Roses at the end of the fifteenth century, and the monarchy's increased ability to suppress rival

---

[35] Stephen B. Baxter, 'William III as Hercules: the political implications of court culture', in Schwoerer, *Revolution of 1688/9*, pp. 95–106.

[36] See for example the twin portraits of William and Mary as respectively a Christian warrior, and a virtuous and rational princess by William Wissing hung at Kensington.

[37] Franklin B. Zimmerman, 'The court music of Henry Purcell', in Maccubin and Hamilton-Phillips, *Age of William III*, pp. 311–18.

[38] See above, pp. 57–8.

[39] See below, pp. 94–5.

[40] Andrew Barclay, 'The impact of King James II on the departments of the royal household' (unpublished PhD dissertation, University of Cambridge, 1994), p. 225.

centres of power, had ushered in an age of household government in which most significant Englishmen were packed into the royal palaces. For nearly two centuries the court had been the main point of contact between ruler and nation, and politics had been played out between factions immediately surrounding the sovereign. In the middle of the seventeenth century, however, the household system began to unravel. It became progressively less certain that all significant people were at court, and the royal household ceased to be the forum for political activity.[41] Consequently, old forms of propaganda became increasingly irrelevant, and government publicists were forced to rethink the monarch's self-presentation.

Serious problems with the household system of government first surfaced in Charles I's reign. The precise processes by which this king's court lost its dominance between 1625 and 1642 are the subject of intense historical debate, but it seems clear that this period saw the emergence of an effective political movement which did not owe its power to contacts near the king. Whilst it is true that the leaders of the emerging 'parliamentary' opposition enjoyed support from aristocrats who still expected to engage in household politics, it is impossible to deny that men such as John Pym, who challenged Charles's government, came to owe their position to sources outside court circles. In 1640–2, for instance, Pym's attacks upon royal policy exploited both suspicions of the king amongst the provincial elites represented in parliament, and the Scottish military occupation of Northumberland. The focus of political life thus moved away from Whitehall towards Westminster and the Scottish camp, and the state of opinion in localities all over the country assumed an unprecedented importance.[42] Obviously, conditions in the run up to the Civil War were extraordinary, and should not be used to claim a permanent breakdown of household government. Nevertheless the situation in the early 1640s did point towards the future. Although the Cromwellian regime which replaced Charles I developed an effective court around the Lord Protector, and although the Restoration re-established a glittering and powerful royal household, the changes inherent in Pym's challenge were to continue, and were steadily to sap the court's leadership of the political nation.[43]

[41] See David Starkey, ed., *The English court from the Wars of the Roses to the Civil War* (1987), introduction.

[42] A detailed account of politics between 1640 and 1642, which stresses pressure from localities in the course of events is Anthony Fletcher, *The outbreak of the English Civil War* (1981). For arguments that an independent political culture was developing away from court from the 1620s onwards, see Richard Cust, 'Politics and the electorate in the 1620s and Anne Hughes, 'Local history and the origins of civil war', both in Cust and Hughes, *Conflict in early Stuart England*, pp. 134–67, 224–53 respectively.

[43] For Cromwell's 'court' see Roy Sherwood, *The court of Oliver Cromwell* (Cambridge, 1977); for a short account of the Restoration court, see R. O. Bucholz, *The Augustan court: Queen Anne and the decline of court culture* (Stanford, 1993), pp. 12–22.

In the first place, parliament gained influence and permanence after the Civil War. The 1660–3 settlement might have restored many of the monarchy's formal powers, but it did not grant Charles II sufficient revenue to live without parliamentary grants, with the result that the legislature became a regular part of English government. Whilst James I and Charles I had survived long periods without meeting the legislature, their successor never ruled alone for more than three years at a stretch, and found himself devoting much of his time to managing an often-unruly Lords and Commons. Consequently, parliament developed into a new crucible of debate and power to rival Charles II's household, and the English elite's interest and ambition came to centre increasingly on the two chambers at Westminster. At the same time, and partly as an effect of parliament's new position, political life in the wider country continued to assume importance. Pym's efforts in the early 1640s to mobilise a public opinion were to have sequels after the Restoration as politicians realised they might influence government actions by exerting popular and electoral pressure on legislators. In the exclusion crisis of 1679–83, for instance, a vigorous political sphere opened up, well away from the previously recognised centre of power. The whig and tory groups who competed for dominance in these years stooped to street level in their attempts to sweep opponents from the field, and thus moved the focus of political life further from the royal palaces. They contributed to a vigorous political press which produced a vast outpouring of controversial literature; they stimulated debate amongst ordinary English people in the rapidly expanding number of clubs and coffee-houses; they organised popular demonstrations against their enemies; and they mobilised local supporters in election campaigns of increasing sophistication and bitterness.[44]

Perhaps even more damagingly for the prestige and position of the court, the relative loss of political importance coincided with a decline in the social and cultural leadership of the royal household. In the 1660s, Charles II had managed to restore something of the brilliance of his father's court. Lavishly hospitable, and keen to secure the services of the best artists and musicians, the king had made himself a trend-setter in fashion, and had attracted the upper echelons of English society into regular visits to his palaces. He had consequently benefited by becoming the centre of elite life, and had gained considerable personal prestige. Unfortunately, however, this early success had been gradually eroded as the king had been forced to cut back on his magnificence by financial shortages, and worries about the unfavourable impression that his sumptuous court was creating out in the country. Consequently, the court lost much of its social and cultural cachet, and the king

---

[44] For good introductions to the new politics outside court, see Tim Harris, *London crowds*; Mark Knights, *Politics and opinion in crisis, 1678–81* (Cambridge, 1994).

forfeited the influence this had bestowed.[45] Under his brother, James II, the situation worsened still further. A parsimonious and pious king had baulked at the cost of even his brother's later, more restrained, style, and had drastically curtailed spending on his household.[46] Whilst the court's social position declined, rival sites of cultural life, especially in London, burgeoned. By the later seventeenth century, the capital had developed to a point where it could offer a range of attractions, and had began to divert those who had previously looked to the royal household for entertainment and artistic innovation. Slowly, there came into existence a new realm of theatres, promenades, coffee-houses, concerts, clubs, and taverns, which provided many opportunities for gossip, recreation, and fashionable display which had previously only been available under royal roofs. Thus in cultural, as in political, affairs, the royal court was losing its hold on national life after the Restoration. No longer was Whitehall the fulcrum of English society, and the king found it steadily more difficult to persuade his subjects even to visit his household.[47]

All the processes outlined above persisted, and even accelerated, under William III. As has already been noted, parliament in the 1690s became a still more permanent and regular element of the English polity. As a result, elites concentrated upon it ever more closely, and made alliances and conducted campaigns in its chambers rather than in palace rooms. Similarly, a wider public opinion increased in importance. This was especially true after the passage of a triennial act in 1694 which ensured general elections at least every three years. With new legislatures being selected so frequently, political parties and factions were forced into virtually continuous cultivation of their popular constituencies, and had to divert energies away from court politics.[48] At the same time, new centres of political influence and debate continued to develop. The press, in particular, gained added momentum after 1695, when licensing legislation, which had imposed an albeit ramshackle government censorship, lapsed and was not renewed. In response, newspapers and political pamphlets flourished, and attentions were drawn further from the royal entourage.[49] Nor could William's court regain the cultural initiative. The challenge from rival attractions in London continued to strengthen; and despite the new regime's efforts at Hampton Court and Kensington, the

---

[45] Bucholz, *Augustan court*, pp. 12–22.

[46] *Ibid.* pp. 22–6; Barclay, 'Impact of King James II'.

[47] For the classic reflection upon this emergence of a wider 'public sphere', see Jurgen Habermas, *The structural transformation of the public sphere*, translated by Thomas Burger (Boston, 1989), especially ch. 3.

[48] Harris, *Politics under the later Stuarts*, p. 176; Geoffrey Holmes and W. A. Speck, eds., *The divided society: parties and politics in England, 1694–1716* (1967); and the essays in Clyve Jones, ed., *Britain in the first age of party, 1680–1750* (1987).

[49] J. A. Downie, 'The development of the political press', in Jones, *Britain in the first age of party*, pp. 111–28; G. C. Gibbs, 'Press and public opinion: prospective', in Jones, *Liberty secured?*, pp. 231–65, especially pp. 256–64.

financial needs of the war prevented any return to the artistic and social largesse of the Tudors and early Stuarts. In sum, the court was rapidly becoming peripheral to the English priorities at the end of the seventeenth century. The situation was such that the leading modern historian of the royal household in this period, Robert Bucholz, has portrayed a largely bankrupt institution. Abandoned by much of the elite, it could not compete with the new social and political worlds opening up in Westminster, London, and beyond.[50]

All this, of course, had profound implications for the conduct of royal publicity. In the 1690s, William's courtly reformers faced the difficulty that traditional forms of court-based propaganda would not be very effective. First, with so many of the king's leading subjects living lives largely beyond the household, it was very doubtful how far intimate royal display could reach them. Second, the increased importance of parliament, and of a broader public opinion, ensured that even if the aristocrats who had originally attended court could be won back, there would still be a need to persuade the wider political nation. In the changing circumstances of the later Stuart era, members of the House of Commons, and the electorate and populace behind them, had gained considerable influence, but could not realistically be integrated into the ideological theatre of the royal household. Therefore Burnet and his allies could not rest satisfied with court iconography and ritual as means of persuasion. They had to find ways to reach audiences beyond the monarch's immediate circle. At the risk of terminological anachronism, they had to contrive strategies for *mass* propaganda.

Some of the answer to the courtly reformers' difficulties was found in parts of the traditional royal round which had not been bound up with the monarch's household. Although Tudor and early Stuart rulers had concentrated upon their courts, they had not been entirely cloistered within them, and had always tried to extend their display beyond the walls of their palaces. Monarchical rites of passage, for instance, had always been semi-public affairs. Much of the actual business of royal coronations, marriages, and funerals had taken place in private spaces in front of courtier audiences, but these events had included processions through the streets of London and had thus brought the monarch's visual propaganda to a wider populace. Similarly certain rulers, most famously Elizabeth I, had gone on progresses through their realms; and many had participated in civic ceremonial, particularly joining the public festivities of the City of London. Most importantly, perhaps, Tudor and early Stuart monarchs had left their households to visit their parliaments. On the occasions on which their legislature had met, they had

---

[50] Bucholz, *Augustan court, passim*, especially conclusion.

processed from their palaces down to Westminster, and had attended opening and closing sessions. This not only gave them another ceremonial opportunity to present themselves to a broader public, but set them at the symbolic heart of the entire nation. When they sat on the throne amongst the Lords and Commons, they were surrounded by people who were believed to represent all Englishmen. As they addressed the two houses, they could claim to be speaking to the whole realm.[51]

In the 1690s, these traditional tactics could still be used to widen royal publicity, and were exploited by the courtly reformers to that end. For example, the joint monarchs used royal rites of passage to considerable effect. As has already been shown, William's coronation was used to inculcate the ideal of reformation.[52] Mary's funeral was similarly staged to spread the word. In fact, the solemnities surrounding the queen's death in 1694–5 were to be some of the most carefully organised and impressive pieces of reformation propaganda. The whole event was conceived to remind the nation of Mary's virtue, and to stress what a loss the godly cause had suffered with her demise. Thus a full state funeral was planned. Reversing the trend towards more private royal interments which had been noticeable since James I's reign, William revived much of the Tudor ceremonial, and buried his wife with the most pompous ritual and trappings. Mary's body lay in state at Whitehall for two weeks, and orders were given that all should be admitted to her coffin displayed in the purple-draped Privy Chamber. On 5 March, the largest royal funeral procession ever mounted made its way from the palace to Westminster Abbey. This accompanied an elaborate chariot which bore the queen to her final resting place, and allowed onlookers to see her coffin adorned with crown and sceptre. Once inside the church, the queen was placed inside a huge mausoleum temporarily erected at the crossing, and a full funeral service commenced which included a sermon by the archbishop of Canterbury and specially composed anthems by Purcell. Perhaps most impressively, the abbey, and all buildings along the funeral route, were draped in black crepe. Over £50,000 was spent to transform the appearance of the capital's streets, and the effect was enhanced by moving the timing of the service from midnight (a traditional, but dark, hour) to the full light of the morning. Taken together, the elements of this ceremony must have made a remarkable spectacle. Combined with the sale of medals and picture prints to act   as   souvenirs

---

[51] For the public presentation of early modern English monarchy, see Williams, *Tudor regime*, pp. 364–6; Anglo, *Images of Tudor kingship*, pp. 106–12; D. Bergeron, *English civic pageantry, 1558–1642* (Columbia, South Carolina, 1971); Jennifer Loach, 'The function of ceremonial in the reign of Henry VIII', *PP*, 142 (1994), 43–68; Roy Strong, *The cult of Elizabeth: Elizabethan portraiture and pageantry* (1977).

[52] See above, pp. 61–3.

of the occasion, they seem to have inspired an outpouring of genuine national grief not often equalled on the death of English monarchs.[53]

Mary's funeral was extraordinary, but it was not the only public display designed to persuade the English of reformation ideals. William and Mary, like their predecessors, participated in civic rituals, and occasionally progressed through their realm to show themselves to their people. In 1689, for instance, the monarchs joined in a London Lord Mayor's Show which took their triumph over popish vice as its theme.[54] Similarly, William's 1690 journey to Ireland via Chester was used to present him to his people as a diligent Christian warrior.[55] Heavy use was also made of the king's excursions to parliament. Since the legislature met more often under William than any previous monarch, this ruler had more frequent opportunities to come among his Lords and Commons, and visits to Westminster consequently became one of the regime's main channels of communication. Especially towards the end of the reign, the king urged action against vice on parliament, and asked its members to take the message of reformation back to the localities which had first sent them.[56]

Yet despite the regime's use of more public occasions to widen the appeal of its campaign, there were still strict limitations on what this kind of display could achieve. The potential reach of funerals and visits to parliament was wider than private court ritual, yet such propaganda did not escape the need to witness it directly. Londoners, and those on the routes of royal tours, might see and be impressed by a royal procession, but most provincials could not be won over by events in distant places. Similarly, Lords and MPs might hear the king's speech to parliament, but they remained a tiny elite in a rapidly broadening political nation. To overcome these constraints, the new regime needed to employ still more penetrative media. Here the king benefited both from his control of the machinery of the English state, and from the choice of people who had been recruited to direct his public relations. Whilst the local and national agencies of government provided one vehicle of comprehensive communication, the men of Burnet's circle enjoyed the position and experience to master the other two mass media available in late Stuart England. As

[53] *The form of the proceeding to the funeral of her late majesty Queen Mary II* (1695); Francis Sandford and Samuel Stebbino, *A genealogical history of the kings and queens of England and monarchs of Great Britain* (1707), pp. 719–21; Paul S. Fritz, 'From "public" to "private": the royal funerals in England, 1500–1830', in Joachim Whaley, ed., *Mirrors of mortality: studies in the social history of death* (1981), pp. 61–99; Paul S. Fritz, 'The trade in death: the royal funerals in England', *Eighteenth Century Studies*, 15 (1985), 291–316.

[54] See [Matthew Traubman], *London's great jubilee, restor'd and perform'd on Tuesday October 29 1689* (1689).

[55] For comment on the progress to Chester see letters from the earl of Portland to the earl of Nottingham, 7 June 1690, and from Sir Robert Southwell to the earl of Nottingham, 9 June 1690, *HMC Finch*, II, 290–1.

[56] See below, p. 117.

leading clerics, and as successful writers, the bishops commanded both the church and the press.

The institutions of the English state had been evolving for many centuries before William III arrived. Even in the middle ages England had developed an impressive administration, which came into far more direct contact with its subjects than most of its rivals in Europe. An extensive system of royal courts, financial institutions such as the Exchequer, and local government officials such as the sheriffs, had ensured that the English realm was remarkably closely governed by the standards of the day. In more recent centuries, Tudor and earlier Stuart monarchs had elaborated upon this medieval core, and had developed additional institutions to cope with emerging problems. New bodies, such as the Treasury and the Excise, had been established to collect new forms of tax; military administration had been expanded through the organisation of the Admiralty, the Army Office, and the militia; and foreign trade had come to be regulated by a network of customs officials. Most importantly, perhaps, the court had answered the needs of local government by boosting the powers of town corporations and of county commissions of the peace. These bodies had been given responsibility for maintaining order in their areas; they had been charged with the implementation of court policy at ground level; and they had been granted judicial powers to enforce the increasing number of statutes which the crown secured through parliament. By the late seventeenth century, therefore, English monarchs stood at the centre of a network of administrative establishments which had penetrated their society to a considerable degree.[57]

Obviously, the early modern state just described had some clear advantages as a propaganda machine. Its variety of institutions provided it with agents in every locality who might publicise the king's ideology through their official statements and actions. For example, and as we shall see, county commissions supported William's campaign for reformation in the 1690s by local drives to enforce statutes against vice.[58] However, despite such possibilities, the late Stuart system of administration had weaknesses which might lead to doubts about its efficiency as an instrument of royal publicity. It was, by modern standards, rather loosely constructed and it often lacked rational bureaucratic organisation. Although individual government agencies had extensive contacts with the general population, centralised control over them was often relatively weak, and many of them lacked efficient administrative or financial structures. Most particularly, local government escaped tight

---

[57] For the development of the English state down to, and in, the late seventeenth century, see Williams, *Tudor regime*; J. P. Kenyon, *The Stuart constitution: documents and commentary* (Cambridge, 1966), especially pp. 492–7; J. R. Western, *Monarchy and revolution: the English state in the 1680s* (1972).

[58] See below, p. 117.

royal management. In the administration of the English regions, the king could not rely on paid officials whose duty lay unequivocally to his administration and to whom he could issue detailed and direct orders. Rather, the monarch was dependent on the justices of the peace who made up the county commissions, and on members of town corporations who controlled urban areas. These were men who did their jobs voluntarily, who were drawn from influential local elites, and who expected (and had proved powerful enough to secure) a degree of independent control over their jurisdictions.[59] At first sight, this was not the best arrangement for the use of local administration in propaganda. There was, it might appear, too much scope for JPs or corporation members to set their own priorities in the administration of their areas, and therefore too much danger that propagation of the court's message might be ignored or distorted in the complexity of neighbourhood politics and concerns.

Yet, although the relative autonomy of English local government did cause some inconvenience for courtly reformers, there was a paradoxical sense in which this apparent weakness could be a strength. It is true that William lacked tight control over his local agents, and that his publicists had to devote much time to cajoling justices to propagate the doctrines of reformation. But the very fact that they had to do this illustrates an advantage of the early modern state in the field of publicity. Precisely because English monarchs had lacked integrated structures which might have given them close administrative contact with their agents, they had come to rely on less direct, *but more public*, means of signalling royal wishes to their local agents. Since English government often meant co-ordinating voluntary groups of independent gentlemen, and not issuing orders through an enclosed bureaucracy, the state had had to act more as a persuader than an executive, and had developed *open* mechanisms for communicating with its servants. Rather than being able to send internal memoranda to departmental officials, the state had operated through widely broadcast statements of its position, which, it was hoped, would encourage the vigorous implementation of its policies by the independently minded local justices. As a result, English monarchs had increased the means by which they could publicise their thinking, so that the courtly reformers in the 1690s inherited a system which generated propaganda as an integral part of its operation.

Some examples will clarify this point. Over the 1690s, there were several instances of courtly reformers spreading Williamite publicity through the instruments which had been developed to communicate between central and

---

[59] For the complex relations between centre and locality in this period see Anthony Fletcher, *Reform in the provinces: the government of Stuart England* (New Haven, 1986); Kenyon, *Stuart constitution*, pp. 492–7; C. G. F. Forster, 'Government in provincial England under the later Stuarts', *TRHS*, 5th series 33 (1983), 29–48.

local government. One of these was the propagandists' use of assize judges. For many generations these judges had been one of the most important bridges between the court and neighbourhood justices. Roving on circuit around the English provinces, they had sat in on special annual sessions of each county commission, and had relayed messages from the executive as they had done so. Through their 'charge' – a speech delivered to justices and other substantial citizens at the beginning of the special assize sessions – they had instructed local officials about the latest details of government thinking; they had encouraged them to enforce certain statutes with particular vigour; and, most importantly, they had offered justifications for the existing regime and its actions.[60] The assize charge was thus a prime example of the English state's 'open' style of communication with its local servants. Whilst technically a means of conveying administrative instructions, it also provided an opportunity for public relations, legitimating the regime as it implemented its policies. In the 1690s, courtly reformers exploited this medium, instructing assize judges to stress the importance of William's moral reformation in their charges, and ordering them to encourage local campaigns against vice on their circuits.[61] More impressively, perhaps, the courtly reformers used proclamations against popery and debauchery to advance their cause. Proclamations consisted of an order to subjects from the king to pursue a particular policy, and they had emerged over the preceding centuries as the most direct means of conveying royal instructions to local agents. At the same time, however, they had been developed as instruments of royal publicity. By the 1690s, proclamations had become central to the court's self-presentation and provided English monarchs with a comprehensive, and multi-faceted, medium for the spread of its ideas. Once a proclamation was issued in the late Stuart period, it was not only published in the *London Gazette* (the authoritative and widely circulated government newspaper), but was also reproduced in large numbers by the royal printers, and sent out to the country in bundles. Special messengers conveyed the documents to sheriffs and mayors in every locality, and also delivered an accompanying writ, which ordered the receiving officials to broadcast the text of the proclamation in their jurisdictions. In towns this was often done by crying out the royal message in the streets, and in the counties proclamations were frequently read out at quarter sessions, when local elites, at least down to the level of grand jurymen, would be assembled. Sheriffs and mayors were also expected to distribute extra copies of the document to magistrates and clergymen, who intoned them in

---

[60] For the importance of assize judges as co-ordinating instruments see Fletcher, *Reform*, pp. 47–55; Clive Holmes, 'The county community in Stuart historiography', *JBS*, 12 (1980), 54–73, especially 63–5.
[61] See below, p. 116.

pulpits and petty sessions and posted them in public places.[62] Thus, whilst the administrative machinery of the late Stuart state was sometimes ill co-ordinated, it could still be used to soak the English in royal ideology. The example of proclamations demonstrates that courtly reformers could benefit from a system which not only employed agents in every locality, but had to persuade Englishmen of the rightness of its policies in order to work at all.

After the state, the second great medium of mass propaganda available in late Stuart England was the church. The church had been used as the major organ of government publicity since the sixteenth-century Reformation. Once the monarchy had been placed at its head, the established ecclesiastical machinery had offered many advantages as a carrier of state ideology, and the Tudors and Stuarts had been quick to take these up. Exploiting the fact that the church's network of parish ministers and its regular religious services gave it close contact with the great mass of the population, rulers had ordered the clergy to announce public policy from the pulpits; they had issued directions on what should be preached; and they had shaped the ceremonial forms of public worship to inculcate royal ideas in the people. Burnet's men followed these examples closely. As bishops they were in a position to direct the messages broadcast by the church, and in the 1690s they used their influence to advertise courtly reformation. At the most direct, Williamite ideals were contained in the sermons which the bishops themselves delivered. Since these addresses were often given on prominent occasions before prestigious audiences, they were intended to become a model for what should be preached by other clergymen, and were frequently printed so that they could be widely available. Of course, local ministers might ignore these hints about what they should be telling their congregations. However, if they did, they found themselves up against another manifestation of the bishops' power. Throughout William's reign, a torrent of circular letters and visitation charges rained down upon dioceses from episcopal palaces, and firmly instructed ministers to preach on reformation themes.[63] These documents strongly implied that any who neglected to inform their flock of William's moral renewal were failing in their pastoral duties, and might be subject to ecclesiastical discipline. The clergy also received firm instructions to publicise royal initiatives against vice. On several occasions in the 1690s ministers were ordered to read out monarchical condemnations of sin and irreligion as part of Sunday services, and were sometimes commanded to back up these sentiments with some pulpit words of their own.[64] Even liturgy was used to convey the royal gospel. Working closely with William and Mary, the bishops of Burnet's circle organised a series of extraordinary religious occasions on which

---

[62] Robert Steele, ed., *Tudor and Stuart proclamations 1485–1714* (2 vols., Oxford, 1910), I, ix, xvi–xvii.

[63] See below, pp. 173–5. [64] See below, pp. 116–17.

England's population was expected to suspend its normal work, and attend church for public services. Each of these events inspired a specially composed form of prayers which were to be read in every parish, and which emphasised the reforming zeal of the current regime.[65]

Naturally, the effectiveness of such church-based propaganda would depend on levels of church attendance in the late Stuart period. The bishops might have hoped for mass communication through the ecclesiastical machinery, but the actual effectiveness of their efforts could be limited if most of the population stayed away from public worship. Unfortunately the evidence on this vital question is thin and circumstantial. Traditionally, ecclesiastical historians have been pessimistic about church-going after the Revolution. They have blamed the 1689 toleration act (which permitted religious services outside anglican buildings) for breaking the clerics' hold over the population, and have suggested that the legislation created so much confusion about the obligation to attend public worship, that many people evaded it altogether.[66] If this is correct, then none of the propaganda strategies described above would be a powerful means of persuasion. On the other hand, this picture of declining religiosity may be too gloomy. Recently, some historians have suggested that, whilst not every late Stuart service was well attended, much of the population did go to church regularly, and that public worship retained a central place in people's cultural and social lives.[67] Moreover, it has been argued that services with sermons were the most popular kind of worship, and that ecclesiastical discipline in the 1690s continued to come down hard on those who stayed at home on Sundays (unless they were specifically protected by attendance at a dissenting meeting house).[68] If *this* view is correct, then it would clearly be a mistake to see the church as a spent ideological force. The courtly reformers would have enjoyed audiences for the sorts of worship which could convey their ideas most effectively, and most of the English would still be contactable through the ecclesiastical machine.

Whatever the truth about church-going, there can be much less doubt

---

[65] See below, pp. 107–8.

[66] The classic statement of this view has been G. V. Bennett, *Tory crisis in church and state: the career of Francis Atterbury* (Oxford, 1975); and G. V. Bennett, 'Conflict in the church', in Holmes, *Britain ... Glorious Revolution*, pp. 155–75. See also A. D. Gilbert, *Religion and society in industrial England* (1976), pp. 6–7; J. H. Pruett, *The parish clergy under the later Stuarts* (Urbana, Illinois, 1978), pp. 177–8.

[67] Donald A. Spaeth, 'Common prayer? popular observance of the anglican liturgy in Restoration Wiltshire', in S. J. Wright, ed., *Parish, church and people: local studies in religion, 1350–1750* (1988), pp. 125–51; W. J. Gregory, 'Archbishop, cathedral and parish: the diocese of Canterbury, 1660–1805' (unpublished DPhil dissertation, University of Oxford, 1993); Jonathan Barry, 'Cultural patronage and the anglican crisis in Bristol, c.1689–1775', in Walsh et al., *The church of England*, pp. 191–208.

[68] W. J. Gregory, 'Archbishop, cathedral and parish', ch. 6; C. E. Davies, 'The enforcement of religious uniformity in England, 1668–1700, with special reference to the dioceses of Chichester and Worcester' (Unpublished DPhil dissertation, University of Oxford, 1982).

about the effectiveness of the third mass media at the courtly reformers' command. Burnet and his circle were enthusiastic and successful participants in an English publishing industry which, by the 1690s, had become the most comprehensive and efficient vehicle for the transmission of ideas. From its importation into the country in the early sixteenth century, print had rapidly penetrated English society. It is difficult to assess the level of reading skills at any one time, and so it is hard to tell how many people had direct access to the new medium. However, records of the ability to sign names imply that about 30 per cent of English males were literate by the end of the seventeenth century.[69] Moreover, it is clear that literacy rates were very high in London by William's reign, and anecdotal evidence suggests that reading was a far more widespread accomplishment than writing.[70] It is thus probable that a substantial proportion of the English population could follow a text by the time of the Revolution, and so formed a large potential audience for the regime's printed polemic.

In this advance of print, the decades before William's arrival had been particularly important. The Interregnum, and the Restoration period, had seen a rapid expansion in English publishing, as the book trade burst through old restrictions, produced more material, and restructured to improve the distribution of its wares. During the mid-century wars, government control of the press had broken down, and the prevailing ideological turmoil had encouraged many writers into print.[71] Consequently, when the Stuarts returned, they found it hard to control the publishing industry. Although some attempt was made to reimpose restrictions through the 1662 print act, this was only partly successful. The law left loopholes; the licensing system it instituted was never watertight; and its limitations on the number of printers were never properly implemented.[72] As a result the book trade continued to develop, so that by William's reign its scale and vigour were remarkable. For the period between 1688 and 1725, the historian Henry Plomer listed over a thousand publishers and booksellers active in London, and recorded bookshops in a large number of provincial and local centres.[73] In one three-month

---

[69] David Cressy, *Literacy and the social order: reading and writing in Tudor and Stuart England* (Cambridge, 1980); Lawrence Stone, 'Literacy and education in England 1640–1900', *PP*, 42 (1969), 69–139.

[70] Margaret Spufford, *Small books and pleasant histories: popular fiction and its readership in seventeenth-century England* (1982); Margaret Spufford, 'First steps in literacy: the reading and writing experiences of the humblest seventeenth-century spiritual autobiographers', *Social History*, 4 (1979), 407–35; Thomas Laquer, 'The cultural origins of popular literacy in England', *Oxford Review of Education*, II (1976), 255–75.

[71] John Feather, *A history of British publishing* (1988), pp. 50–63.

[72] F. S. Siebert, *The freedom of the press in England, 1476–1776* (Urbana, Illinois, 1952), pp. 239–57.

[73] Henry R. Plomer, *A dictionary of the printers and booksellers who were working in England, Scotland and Ireland, 1686–1725* (Oxford, 1922).

period alone, the Hilary term of 1690, the catalogues of the Stationers' Company revealed an industry producing 117 new titles, brought out by fifty-three different publishers.[74] As it attained this scale, the book trade took important new initiatives in marketing, distribution, and promotion. In the late Stuart era, book wholesaling grew rapidly, and publishers showed greater sophistication and imagination in the advertisement of their wares.[75] Having said all this, books were expensive. Even an octavo volume cost at least five shillings, and most titles did not sell enough to exhaust their first edition. (The first edition usually had a print run around 1,000 – any subsequent editions were generally larger.) However, the seventeenth century saw the rapid development of smaller and cheaper products, such as ballads, broadsides, pictorial prints, and chapbooks, which sold for as little as a penny and would have enjoyed a rather wider circulation.[76]

William's polemicists (successful authors in their earlier careers) were quick to take advantage of the opportunities offered by this developing market. Not only did they produce a steady stream of works for publication in the 1690s, they demonstrated a good understanding of the book trade, using those parts of the industry which were likely to be most efficient in broadcasting their ideas. For a start, they fostered close working relationships with a small group of leading London publishers, whose reputations and extensive business contacts would guarantee effective distribution for their works. For example, Gilbert Burnet, Simon Patrick, and Thomas Tenison published almost exclusively with Richard Chiswell. John Dunton, the some- what maverick printer, whose autobiography provided thumbnail sketches of the men in his business, described Chiswell as the most successful and influential bookseller in London. He headed Dunton's list of the most 'emi- nent' men of his trade, and was said 'to [deserve] the title of metropolitan bookseller of England, if not of all the world. His name at the bottom of a title page, does sufficiently recommend the book.'[77] Stillingfleet, Wake, Kidder, and Tillotson also cashed in on this success by occasionally using Chiswell to bring out their works. John Sharp, meanwhile, sent his writings to Walter Kettilby, 'an eminent episcopal bookseller', whilst Kidder and Tillotson, along with Edward Fowler, had most of their works handled by Brabizon

---

[74] Edward Arber, *The term catalogues, 1688–1709* (3 vols., 1905), II, 297–309.

[75] Feather, *History ... publishing*, p. 61; Graham Pollard, 'The English market for printed books', *Publishing History*, 4 (1978), 9–48, especially 9–17; Marjorie Plant, *The English book trade: an economic history of the making and sale of books* (2nd edn, 1965), pp. 248–52.

[76] Feather, *History ... publishing*, p. 60; Spufford, *Small books*; Carolyn Nelson, 'English newspapers and periodicals', in Maccubin and Hamilton-Phillips, *Age of William III*, pp. 366–72, especially pp. 367–8.

[77] John Dunton, *The life and errors of John Dunton esq., late citizen of London* (1705), p. 280.

Aylmer, another aristocrat of the book world, whom Dunton, a co-publisher and friend, described as 'well acquainted with the mysteries of the trade'.[78]

The bishops' skill in selecting publishers was augmented by their choices of literary genre. Whilst they produced some thick intellectual tomes in the 1690s, the courtly reformers also tapped into the more popular end of the print market, producing a number of short, cheap pamphlets which might convey their message to a wide audience. Some of this lighter material was designed to broaden the reach of other, more limited media. For example, royal ceremonial which could only be observed at court was described for the country at large, often with pictorial representations of processions included.[79] Similarly, the already-open media of communication between the central executive and the local organs of the king's administration were publicised even more broadly through the book trade. Assize charges were printed, as were proclamations; and the king's speech to parliament was produced in pamphlet or broadside form. Most significantly, perhaps, the courtly reformers produced a very large number of sermons. In fact, the single, paper-bound sermon was to become the most important unit of courtly reformation propaganda in the 1690s. It was used *ad nauseam* by Burnet and his allies to outline the basic elements of their doctrine to the literate public, and to repeat their message at regular intervals throughout the reign. This was important, because, by broadcasting their views in this form, the courtly reformers were participating in one of the most vigorous markets developed by the emerging print industry. By the later seventeenth century sermons dominated book production, and, selling for as little as two pence, formed one of the most reliable parts of the publishers' market. In 1690 alone, fifty-four new sermons were advertised in the Stationers' catalogues, and printed versions of pulpit-preaching would have headed lists of best-sellers throughout the period.[80] Thus, by couching their political arguments in sermon form, William's divines were cashing in on an extremely popular genre. They were incorporating their Orange message within the usual expositions of morality and providence which they knew the public would buy, and as a result they gained a considerable audience. Many sermons produced as part of the campaign for courtly reformation ran into multiple editions in the 1690s, and a few were phenomenally successful, becoming some of the most widely purchased works of the entire late Stuart period.[81]

Obviously not all the pro-Orange material produced in Britain during

---

78 *Ibid.* pp. 226, 282.
79 See, for example, *Form ... funeral ... Mary II.*
80 C. J. Somerville, *Popular religion in Restoration England* (Gainesville, Florida, 1977), tried to ascertain late Stuart best-sellers by counting the number of editions in which books appeared. Many individual sermons made his list of the period's most popular works.
81 For examples, see below, pp. 97, 110.

William's reign was produced directly by Gilbert Burnet and his associates. There were independent writers, songwriters, engravers, and craftsmen who supported the king (or saw cash to be made from promoting his image) and produced their own forms of propaganda. Their products – from pamphlets and newspapers to broadside ballads and decorated pottery – often popularised the case made by the court's publicists and may have played a considerable role in attaching the people to their ruler. For example, a number of pictorial prints (many of them originally produced in Holland) portrayed William's providential advance to the English throne through a variety of allegorical designs, or by illustrating his miraculous expedition from the Hague.[82] Similarly, much of the popular Delftware pottery produced in the 1690s depicted the king in heroic poses on plates, tiles, and bowls.[83] Again, a plethora of cheap periodicals, pamphlets, verse, and ballads lauded the monarch's God-given martial triumphs, or his honest and Christian rule.[84] Yet despite the undoubted importance of this independent and commercial material, the palm for royal publicity must still rest with the bishop of Salisbury and his associates. Within a few months of William's arrival in England, Burnet had managed to construct an impressively efficient official propaganda machine. Very rapidly – especially considering the disruptions of the Revolution – he had recruited a close-knit band of ideological allies; he had appropriated the established publicity instruments of the English church and state; and he had began a vigorous and sophisticated use of the press. Most importantly, perhaps, he had made great efforts to overcome the problems caused by the declining position of the royal court. His campaign of courtly reformation was pursued through a great variety of media, some of them relatively new, and many of them with power to reach

---

[82] See Christiaan Schuckman, 'Dutch printing and printmaking', in Maccubin and Hamilton-Phillips, *Age of William III*, pp. 281–92; Mary Ede, *Arts and society in England under William and Mary* (1979), pp. 112–19; and the items listed in Mary Dorothy George, ed., *Catalogue of prints and drawings in the British Museum. Division 1: personal and political satires* (11 vols., 1870), I, 730–52; II, 1–161.

[83] Anthony Ray, 'Delftware in England', in Maccubin and Hamilton-Philips, *Age of William III*, pp. 301–7, especially pp. 305–6.

[84] One of the most solidly Williamite of early periodicals was John Dunton's *The Athenian Gazette, or Casuistical Mercury* (first published 17 March 1691). For its comments on the providence of William's arrival, see I no. 2; I no. 5; III no. 3. For a small, but representative, selection of Williamite ballads and verse, see *England's great deliverance* (1689); *An heroic poem upon his majesties most gracious releasing the chimney-money* (1689); Matthew Morgan, *A poem to the queen, upon the king's victory in Ireland, and his voyage to Holland* (Oxford, 1691); *The protestant commander; or a dialogue betwixt him and his loving lady* [1690]. Some of the numerous popular songs and poems were collected by entrepreneurial publishers into more substantial volumes. See, for example, *The muses farewell to popery and slavery, or a collection of miscellaneous poems, satyrs, songs &c* (1689). For the early work of Daniel Defoe, a Williamite pamphleteer who viewed 1688 in distinctly millenarian terms, see Schonhorn, *Defoe's politics*. For pamphleteering more widely, see Downie, *Robert Harley*; Goldie, '1689 and the structure of political argument'.

far beyond the confines of the royal palaces. Burnet's publicity was, therefore, doubly significant. It not only demonstrated the energy and imagination of William's regime in its self-promotion, it also served as a reminder of the ideological resources which monarchs could call upon in the late Stuart period, even after the rise of parliament, parties, and a wider political public. At the end of the seventeenth century, the royal household might no longer dominate the sites and substance of debate. Yet, despite this, the king could still make a substantial contribution to public discussions, and could still hope for real influence over the political perceptions of his subjects.

3

The propagation of courtly reformation

COURTLY REFORMATION STRATEGIES

Having identified the human and material resources available to William, it is time to investigate how these resources were actually used. Broadly, the government's propagandists attempted to legitimate the regime by proving that it was reforming many different areas of national life. They justified William's claim to be an instrument of God through a number of publicity campaigns designed to show his reformation acting in a variety of spheres. These campaigns were to some extent interdependent, and it is thus somewhat crude to separate them out. For the sake of clarity, however, six main strategies can be identified. First, William's publicists attempted to prove that the new monarchs had cleared the court of sin, and that they had made the royal household an appropriately virtuous engine of reform. Second, the king's men promoted a series of fasts and thanksgivings. These, they hoped, would cast their master in an Old Testament role and portray him turning his people back towards God. Third, a mantle of royal patronage was thrown over a number of initiatives to reform the nation's manners through the use of statute law. Fourth, William's pro-Dutch foreign policy was presented as a promotion of true godliness. Fifth, the king was shown improving the moral guidance and pastoral resources of the English church. Finally, William was depicted as an honest and frugal executive, purging waste and corruption from the machinery of his government. Within the ideology of courtly reformation, all of these programmes argued for the legitimacy of William's rule. However, only the first three will be described in detail in this chapter. Whilst the publicists' work in the later areas complemented their other efforts to justify the basic fact of Orange government, they also had additional functions, and are best analysed in later sections when the problems of English xenophobia and parliamentary management are considered.

THE VIRTUOUS COURT

The Williamite regime faced a number of obstacles to its first aim – proving that the new monarchs had reformed their court. The most serious was the reputation for immorality from which royal households had traditionally suffered, and which circumstances in the 1690s did little to cure. By the late Stuart period the English were so convinced that palaces were natural sinks of vice, that it would take propaganda of considerable flair to do anything to counter that impression.

Early modern suspicion of courts had two main philosophical roots. The first was the denunciation of imperial luxury found in much classical writing, whilst the second was the standard Christian distrust of worldly grandeur. In seventeenth-century England, these two traditions had combined into an established critique of royal circles, which suggested that the power and wealth of courts corrupted those who entered them and led to all manner of dishonesty, lust, and avarice. In the early Stuart period, for example, the evils of the court had become a common, perhaps the dominant, idiom of discourse across a surprisingly wide political spectrum. On the one hand, puritan critics of Charles I had accused his courtiers of debauching the nation, and destroying the godliness which was its only true defence. On the other hand, the monarch himself had claimed to be the antidote to household vice, and had argued that his virtue was purging the corruption which usually gathered in Whitehall.[1] Both sides had thus wrestled with the problem of ensuring the probity of the king's intimates, and had assumed those around him had a tendency towards moral degeneration. Similarly the image of a corrupted court had dominated the later Stuart period. Charles II had had to tackle it immediately he was restored in 1660 (his first proclamation asked his followers to desist from drunkenness and debauchery), and was faced with accusations of royal profligacy throughout his reign.[2] Even William III's rhetoric of courtly reformation reinforced the tradition. Arguing that papists at the Caroline and Jacobite courts had promoted debauchery, Orange publicists underlined the sensual and luxurious image of royal circles, and so increased the difficulty of their own task. Proving that William had turned his household into a bastion of virtue would be doubly difficult once his spokesmen had emphasised the potency and danger of court vice.

---

[1] Perez Zagorin, *The court and the country: the beginning of the English revolution* (New York, 1969); Kevin Sharpe, *Criticism and compliment: the politics of literature in the England of Charles I* (Cambridge, 1987); Kevin Sharpe and Peter Lake, eds., *Culture and politics in early Stuart England* (Basingstoke, 1994).

[2] For the rapid emergence of such criticisms see Paul Seaward, *The Cavalier Parliament and the reconstruction of the old regime, 1661–7* (Cambridge, 1989), pp. 244–5, 256–7.

It might be thought that 1688 offered an easy opportunity to break the spell of anti-court rhetoric. The Revolution had seen an extensive turnover of household personnel, and it seems logical that William would argue that court corruptions had been swept away with the displaced men. Obviously this line was adopted; but the installation of a new monarch, and a new team of household servants, was no panacea. Members of the incoming court were not so spotless that their reputation for godliness would convince a sceptical nation, and William's circle was soon subject to as much adverse comment as either of his uncles' had been.

Some of the difficulty here lay with the new holders of household offices. Those who were brought into the king's service under Lord High Steward Devonshire and Lord Chamberlain Dorset, were largely whigs who had been excluded from court posts in the previous reigns. They were thus people who had resented the profits their opponents had gained in office before the Revolution, and who now tended to view their recently acquired positions as an opportunity to secure their own share of reward. A rigid system of household economy which had been introduced under James II was abandoned; and experienced royal servants, who had ensured the basic competence and honesty of court management before 1688, were removed. As a result, new fortunes were made rapidly in William's service, and complaints began about the waste, corruption, and extravagance of household finances.[3] However, whilst the new courtiers besmirched the image of the royal circle, an even bigger problem was caused by the king himself. His personal morality was suspect, and his peculiar manner towards his subjects hampered efforts to dispel the impression of vice hidden behind palace walls.

Rumours about William's sexual misconduct began to circulate as soon as he had arrived in England. He was known to have a mistress (Elizabeth Villiers, countess of Orkney); and many suspected him of homosexual relationships with two of his Dutch friends (Willem Bentinck, made duke of Portland in 1689; and Arnald Joost van Keppel, created earl of Albemarle in 1696). The evidence for the latter two liaisons was, and is, highly circumstantial, but the king's behaviour provided enough material for speculation.[4] James's supporters in particular fanned rumours. Jacobite pamphleteers, Jacobite poets, and even Jacobite playwrights, seized upon the king's supposed intimacy with the Dutchmen, and wove it into a wider moral pathology of Orange rule. Arguing that no virtue could survive in a court based upon the sin of usurpation, they portrayed a court where all restraints of conscience

---

[3] Paul A. Hopkins, 'Aspects of Jacobite conspiracy in England in the age of William III' (unpublished PhD dissertation, University of Cambridge, 1981), p. 108; Barclay, 'Impact of James II', pp. 219–23.

[4] Sensible discussion of William's sexuality can be found in Baxter, *William III*, pp. 348–52.

had been abandoned, and where men were enmeshed in the most unnatural practices.[5]

The regime's difficulty in constructing a virtous court were compounded by William's monarchical style. Despite his continued use of his court as an instrument of cultural propaganda, William was one of the most reserved and reclusive kings ever to sit upon the English throne. He not only recoiled from close contact with Englishmen, but, still more unfortunately, betrayed this aversion to his new subjects. Uncomfortable amongst people whose jokes and habits he never fully understood (and suffering from a respiratory complaint which made life in smoky London unbearable) the king withdrew his court from the accessible palace of Whitehall and spent much of his time amongst foreign advisers in his more remote houses at Hampton Court and Kensington. Worse still, William disliked and disapproved of public entertainments. Reducing royal hospitality to a bare minimum, he gave every impression of having to force himself into what few social events he did offer to the English elite. These traits in the king's character were extremely damaging. They hid him from public scrutiny and fed doubts about what went on within his tightly knit circle. Both Gilbert Burnet and Mary recognised the trouble William was storing for himself. During the king's early months in England, Burnet made desperate attempts to persuade his master to show himself to his new subjects, and incurred considerable royal anger for his graphic warnings about the consequences of monarchical seclusion.[6] Mary, meanwhile, tried to compensate for her husband's reserve with a more open and hospitable royal style. Yet her gaiety, party-throwing, and theatre-going could not entirely compensate for the social absence of her husband, and also created an embarrassing tension between the public presentations of the king and queen.[7]

Overall, therefore, William's publicists had a difficult task in persuading the country of the new court's virtue. The basic problem that courts had never been seen as bastions of godliness, was compounded by suspicions about the new ruler and his servants, and by William's unhelpful approach to his role. Yet despite their daunting nature, these obstacles did not block attempts to portray a reformed court. Rather, they shaped the propagandists' strategy, dissuading them from a direct assault on the adverse image of the king.

---

[5] Monod, *Jacobitism, passim.* Much Jacobite innuendo took the form of scurrilous verse. See W. J. Cameron, ed., *Poems on affairs of state: Augustan satirical verse, 1660–1714* (9 vols., New Haven, Connecticut, 1971), V, xxxvii, 37–8.
[6] Burnet mentions his worries about William's coldness throughout his *History ... own times,* and in other writings. For the incident in 1689, see an extract from his original memoirs, Bodl. Additional Ms. D 24, fol. 211, reprinted in H. C. Foxcroft, ed., *A supplement to the 'History of my own times'* (Oxford, 1902), p. 496.
[7] For comment on the strains, see Hester W. Chapman, *Mary II*, pp. 181–5.

Instead of emphasising William's personal morality in the face of rumours to the contrary, Burnet and his circle turned to establish the rectitude of his wife. In the early 1690s Mary became the linchpin of the regime's publicity. She was presented as a woman of immense personal piety, whose example and censure were clearing the court of vice.

As a symbol of the Orange court's virtue, the queen had several advantages. In the first place, she had a long-standing reputation for household godliness. Mary had been admired whilst growing up at Charles II's court for her ability to resist the temptations which it had offered, and she had been respected in Holland for the modesty she had brought to the Stadholder's palaces.[8] Next, the queen was relatively untouched by the stories which surrounded her partner. There were few suggestions that she herself had been unfaithful, and there may even have been a perverse sense in which the supposed misdeeds of William enhanced her innocence by casting her as a patiently suffering victim. Finally, the attempt to portray the queen as a reformer of the court chimed with Mary's own character and priorities. The private journals which she wrote up at the end of each year reveal an intensely spiritual person, who was deeply anxious about her own morality, and was genuinely concerned to promote religion and good manners amongst her intimates.[9] She thus led and inspired government publicity as well as featuring in it, and so became a doubly valuable asset in the presentation of a godly court.

The campaign to portray Mary as a court reformer began inside the royal palaces. From her first months back in England, the queen laboured to promote a more godly and sober atmosphere within her husband's household. At the end of 1689, her journal recorded her dismay at arriving in a 'noisy world full of vanity', and revealed her determination to instill greater spirituality in her court.[10] Whilst the queen enjoyed courtly entertainments and spent much on the adornment of her houses, she balanced these more extravagant activities with an exemplary personal morality. She tried to set an upright tone at court by her own modest behaviour, and announced her intention to promote only people of good character within the royal household. Most importantly, Mary increased the quantity and quality of the court's divine service. Hoping to ensure that public worship was 'looked on as it ought' amongst members of her circle, she urged her entourage to attend prayers frequently, and to take them seriously when they did so.[11] At Whitehall, she established a new round of religious services in the afternoons, which included sung prayers, and a novel series of Wednesday sermons.[12] At

---

[8] *Ibid.* pp. 75–83; Mary's avoidance of the luxurious temptations of courts was to be the main theme of Gilbert Burnet, *An essay on the memory of the late queen* (1695).

[9] R. Doebner, ed., *Memoirs of Mary, queen of England 1689–1693* (1886).

[10] *Ibid.* p. 11.   [11] *Ibid.* p. 12.   [12] *Ibid.* p. 16.

Hampton Court, frequent worship was also provided, and the chapel was remodelled so that the queen could be seen joining in worship in an enlarged and more open royal gallery. At both palaces, the queen set an example by her own diligent and public attendance at services. She also demanded unusually close attendance by the chaplains seconded to the royal household, and encouraged wider participation in worship by abolishing private communions for the monarchs and replacing them with sacraments more accessible to her officers and servants.[13] Even Mary's gardening can be read as an attempt to enhance the experience of worship in the royal household. The 'wilderness' which she created at Hampton Court was planned as a place of spiritual contemplation. Courtiers, it was hoped, would reflect upon what they had heard in the chapel as they wandered amongst its trees and hedges and lost themselves in its famous maze.[14]

The queen's personal efforts for a court reformation formed a solid base for Williamite propaganda. However, by themselves they would have been of limited use in persuading the nation of the legitimacy of the new regime. For reasons already rehearsed, only a small proportion of the political nation would have entered the royal household and so few would have experienced Mary's initiatives for themselves. Strategies therefore had to be devised to publicise the godly queen more widely.

The first step in this direction was taken as early as December 1688. As with so much else, the origins of a royal publicity campaign lay in the paper that Burnet had written to the prince of Orange when he first arrived in London. Amongst the many recommendations contained in this document was the following suggestion.

The whole number of the king's Chaplains, which consist of good men for the most part, ought also surely to be dissolved, and a new set to be formed with more choice, for the rule was formerly to take all Bishops out of that Body. It may be fit for his Highness to have Chaplains, that every one may wait his week.[15]

Burnet was here arguing that William should remodel the clerical personnel of the royal household. Traditionally, the English court had included forty-eight chaplains whose job was to attend the king and cater for his spiritual needs. Burnet now suggested that James's ministers be dismissed, and that William surround himself with clerics of his own choosing. The incoming king took up this suggestion, and, on his accession, issued a new list of chaplains, who, unsurprisingly, included Sharp, Wake, Patrick, Fowler,

---

[13] *Ibid.* p. 19. For the close attendance expected of chaplains, see letter from Tillotson to Ralph Barker (his chaplain), 25 April 1689, BL Additional Ms. 4292, fol. 150.
[14] Roy Strong, *Royal gardens* (1992), p. 30.
[15] Blencowe, ed., *Diary . . . times of Charles the Second*, p. 286.

Tillotson, Tenison, Stillingfleet, Horneck, and Kidder.[16] At one level, of course, these promotions were merely rewards for Burnet's proteges. Yet at another they served as propaganda. The preferments were widely advertised through the *London Gazette*, and involved some of the most famous and respected clerics of the day. The men advanced to the Chapel Royal were not only heroes of the church's battle against popery, and recognised leaders of the spiritual awakening in London, but successful religious authors, whose books had been popular under Charles and James, and would remain so under William.[17] In making these appointments, therefore, William was supporting, and giving publicity to, his wife's initiatives at court. He was tacitly announcing that Mary would be surrounded by the nation's most famous and popular pastors, and that these clerics would work closely with her in efforts to Christianise her household.

If any failed to read the message of the chaplains' appointments, they would be less likely to miss the next stage in the advertisement of Mary's court reform. This was the mass publication of court sermons. Monarchs before the Revolution had ordered that some of the preaching they heard in their regular round of religious services be printed to make it available to a wider audience. Mary, however, extended this practice massively. Before 1688 only a small trickle of court sermons had been recorded as newly published in the Stationers' Company catalogues. After that date however, this trickle turned into a great flood, and came to dominate a substantial section of the book trade. Whereas under Charles only an average of three new sermons had appeared a year (and none had come out under his brother after 1686); under the new monarchs vast numbers were advertised. Nine appeared in 1689, twenty came out in 1690, there were twenty again in 1691, fourteen in 1692, sixteen in 1693, and a record twenty-two in 1694. Even without any publications which evaded the Stationers' catalogues, this was a production rate of nearly one a fortnight.[18] The clergy of Burnet's list played a large part in this bibliographic phenomenon. In the 1690s Burnet published at least fifteen of his court addresses; Tillotson printed at least nine before his death in 1694; Stillingfleet produced six between 1689 and 1693; and Sharp, Wake, Patrick, and Tenison were all repeated performers.

At first reading, it may not be obvious how all these sermons enhanced the image of a reforming queen. Most of the output was superficially 'apolitical',

---

[16] *An historical account of the memorable actions of the most glorious monarch, William III* (1689), appendix.

[17] Many editions of the courtly reformers' earlier works were produced in the 1690s; see their entries in Donald Wing, ed., *Short title catalogue of books printed in England ... 1641–1700* (2nd edn revised, 3 vols., New York, 1972). John Dunton praised the business acumen of those who had secured the right to print the bishops' work. See Dunton, *Life and errors*, p. 286.

[18] Arber, *Term catalogues*.

making surprisingly little reference to the monarch before whom they were preached, and dealing mainly with prosaic pastoral and spiritual themes. They simply guided the Christian through life, and urged him to godly faith and behaviour.[19] Yet despite their lack of explicit Williamite ideology, these works could still be important carriers of royal propaganda. The constant printing of even 'apolitical' sermons confirmed that the court under Mary was a centre of Christian instruction and edification, and advertised the fact that the queen listened regularly to the prestigious clerics who worked alongside her. The effect was to bestow an almost evangelical air upon the royal household. Here, these works implied, was a truly pious, serious, and godly monarchy. This message was driven home by the form in which the sermons appeared. The works had the words 'PREACHED BEFORE THE QUEEN' or 'PRINTED BY HER MAJESTY'S SPECIAL COMMAND' emblazoned in large or bold Gothic type across their title pages. This would have stressed the monarch's personal interest in the original palace preaching to anyone who so much as browsed the volumes in bookshops, and would even have advertised this concern to people who merely walked city streets. Title pages were posted as flysheets by publishers to advertise their wares, so the court's devout Christianity would have been announced to those who merely glanced at walls or notice-boards, or rested in taverns and coffee-houses where publishers promoted their material.

There is some evidence that this strategy of using sermons to promote a godly image of the court had an impact. Some of the religious addresses to the monarchs were very popular in the 1690s, and became minor classics of their time. Tenison's sermons *Concerning the folly of atheism*, and *Concerning the coelestial body*, given at Whitehall in 1691 and 1694, both had second editions in 1695; and Sharp's *Sermon about the government of the thoughts* went through three editions in 1694 (the year it was preached in the palace), and got a fourth imprint in 1698. Towering over even these efforts was William Beveridge's *Of the happiness of the saints in heaven*, an address preached before the queen in 1690. This went through multiple editions and became one of the best-selling works of the whole late Stuart period.[20] Moreover, the series of court sermons were sufficiently prominent for both William's allies and his enemies to comment upon them. Thomas Manningham, a royal chaplain, believed that the quality of religious literature emanating from the court proved that a transformation had come over royal circles since the Revolution. In an oration to mark Mary's death he stated

---

[19] Tillotson, Horneck, and Stillingfleet's court sermons were in this mould, as were those produced by most of the lesser clerics and chaplains who preached before the monarchs. See the works of Thomas Staynoe, Charles Hickman, Richard Meggot, Edward Pelling, and Edward Young.

[20] Somerville, *Popular religion*, p. 55.

'Tis to the *Queen* that we owe many of those *Pious Treatises* which have been lately Publish'd amongst us; And that multitude of *plain, useful* and *Practical Sermons,* which She approv'd of, and cause'd to be *Printed,* are Her Gift to the Publick. ... It is judiciously concluded by many, that there was not such *Preaching* in the whole World besides, as at *Whitehall* and never such in England before.[21]

On the other side, Charles Leslie, a non-juror who hated both William and his clerical allies, complained about such sanctimoniousness, and the sermons which promoted it. He scowled that the monarchs had hired 'foulmouthed' preachers of 'prostitute consciences', had put their 'own stamp' upon their words, and then published them 'to the kingdom by special command'.[22] Such comment suggests that large numbers of Englishmen were aware of these publications, and it seems probable that they would have understood them as a signal that the court was reforming and edifying itself. A royal household with such preachers, and, more importantly, with such pious and attentive monarchs, might well have convinced its audience that it was fit to power a religious and moral revival.

The final, and most direct, technique for advertising the queen's reformation was the production of panegyric. Throughout her reign, Mary was praised in a great mass of prose and poetry which lauded her godliness and the effect she had on her immediate contacts. Again, Burnet and his circle led the regime's activities in this area. They complimented the queen in their sermons and pamphlets, and contrasted the household which she led with the debauched courts of her predecessors.[23] The most intense burst of such polemic occurred at the time of Mary's funeral. The queen's death from smallpox in the winter of 1694 was a personal tragedy for William, and a moment of acute political danger for a regime which had benefited from Mary's claims to hereditary legitimacy. Nevertheless, the royal demise did provide an excellent opportunity for retrospective propaganda, allowing royal polemicists to review the queen's virtuous life and to stress her beneficial influence at court. The tone here was set by Thomas Tenison. Preaching Mary's funeral sermon at Westminster Abbey, he gave a fulsome eulogy, concentrating upon the power of her moral example. For Tenison, the queen was a woman of immense charity, moderation, and Christian devotion, whose godly example set the pattern for those around her. Her life, he stated, was not a scene 'of vain pleasure, and soft and unprofitable ease, but of true usefulness'. 'If all

---

21 Thomas Manningham, *A sermon preach'd at the parish church of St Andrew's, Holborn, 30 December 1694. On the most lamented death of our most gracious soveraign Queen Mary* (3rd edn, 1695), p. 10.

22 [Charles Leslie], *Remarks on some late sermons: and in particular, on Dr Sherlock's sermon at the Temple, Dec 30 1694* (1695), p. 10.

23 See, for example, John Tillotson, *A sermon preach'd at Whitehall before the queen on the monthly fast day, Sept. 16, 1691* (1690), pp. 36–7; Gilbert Burnet, *A sermon preached at Whitehall on 26 Novemb. 1691, being the thanksgiving day* (1691), pp. 27–8, 32.

were as diligent in examining and noting the condition of their souls, and comparing the former and the present estate of them, heaven would in some measure be upon earth.'[24] Similar sentiments were expressed by other leading Williamite polemicists, who also published pulpit or pamphlet elegies. Gilbert Burnet, for example, wrote an *Essay on the memory of the late queen* which spoke of her personal piety and temperance, and compared her to Josiah – another monarch whom he claimed had begun a national reformation in his own household. Like her Old Testament archetype, Mary had risen above her upbringing in a luxurious and flattering court, and had determined to amend its ways as a first step to renewing her country as a whole.[25] Similarly, Edward Fowler praised the queen's attempts to end frivolous fashions amongst the English elite; and William Wake praised her efforts to improve religion within her household.[26] The latter cleric expanded upon his theme at some length, yet still regretted that he had too little time to do it full justice. His *Sermon on the death of our late royal sovereign* apologised that his description of the court under Mary was

to pass by Her constant Attendance upon the Publick Service of God, and those Opportunities for Instruction which she provided for, as all the more solemn Returns of it. To say nothing of Her frequent and useful Conversations with those who Ministered unto Her in Holy Offices.[27]

The queen thus remained central to Williamite efforts to prove the virtue of the new court even after she had died. Indeed, paradoxically, she may have made her greatest contribution to royal polemic in this area once she had relinquished her mortal efforts for it. The lead taken by Tenison, Burnet, and the others, was followed by a huge number of poets and preachers, who produced a vast outpouring of lament for such an exemplary paragon as Mary. Numerous sermons, tributes, and pieces of verse – often bound together by booksellers into extensive memorial volumes – reinforced the impression of a devout royal household, presided over by a truly righteous ruler.[28]

Of course William was not left entirely out of the portrayal of household reformation. It would in fact have been dangerous to ignore the king's image in this area. Any such neglect might have suggested an embarrassing contrast

---

[24] Thomas Tenison, *A sermon preached at the funeral of her late majesty queen Mary of ever blessed memory in the abbey church in Westminster upon March 5 1694/5* (1695), pp. 16, 8.

[25] Gilbert Burnet, *Essay ... late queen* (1695), pp. 38–40.

[26] Edward Fowler, *A discourse of the great disingenuity and unreasonableness of repining at afflicting providences* (1695), preface; William Wake, *Of our obligation to put our trust in God rather than in men ... a sermon preached before ... Gray's-Inn, upon the occasion of the death of our late royal sovereign, Queen Mary* (1695).

[27] Wake, *Of our obligation*, p. 32.

[28] For more on Mary's contribution to royal virtue, see Speck, 'William – and Mary?', pp. 140–6; Schwoerer, 'Images ... Mary II'.

between the two sovereigns whilst Mary was alive, and would have left the regime's publicists with no strategy for asserting the virtue of the court once she had died. William was therefore associated with many of his wife's activities before 1694 and was shown to have continued her domestic moral duties once he was left on his own. He was portrayed listening to sermons, surrounding himself with godly courtiers and chaplains, and following Mary's example of devout prayer.[29] Nevertheless, the portrayal of court reformation lost much momentum without the queen. After Mary's death there was noticeably less emphasis on the devotion and decorum of the royal household, and the publication of court sermons declined rapidly. Following the peak of twenty-two sermons produced in Mary's last year, the number fell to four in 1696, and never approached the old levels again. This contrast between the two halves of the reign underlines Mary's importance within William's rhetoric. She had become crucial to the presentation of the court once the reputation of the king and the new household servants had been tarnished by expense and rumour. After she had gone, royal publicists would have to rely more heavily on other strategies to establish the reforming legitimacy of the regime.

FASTS AND THANKSGIVINGS

Of the alternative strategies for proving William's righteousness, one of the most important, and hitherto one of the least studied, was the court's programme of public fasts and thanksgivings. Between 1689 and 1702, the Orange regime staged a remarkable series of national days of humiliation and prayer, which have received extraordinarily little attention from the historical profession. Perhaps because fasting has been associated with the sort of biblically based mentalities which were supposed to have been in rapid decline in the seventeenth century, many scholars have ignored what is perhaps the single most important ideological initiative taken by the post-Revolutionary government. Whilst students of the 1690s have barely mentioned the public solemnities which punctuated their decade with great regularity, those examining the history of fasting in England have assumed that late Stuart activities in this area were pale shadows of their Tudor, early Stuart, and Civil War precursors. This section will attempt to redress this

---

[29] Court sermons continued to be published after 1694, though in reduced numbers, and royal proclamations banished vicious persons from court. See *By the king, a proclamation for preventing and punishing immorality and prophaness ... given 24 February 1697* (1697). Three years after William's death, the personal prayers he had used, composed by Tillotson, were published. These demanded a rigorous programme of self-examination and repentance which would have served as an example to his circle. See [John Tillotson], *A form of prayers used by his late majesty K. William III when he received the holy sacrament* (1704).

imbalance and bring into the light one of the prime elements of William III's self-legitimation.

National fasts and thanksgivings had been held in England since Tudor times.[30] Based on biblical models, these events aimed to win God's favour for the nation by demonstrating the population's adherence to his cause. Fasts were intended to avert divine judgements by staging a day of mortification and prayer. On fast days, the population was urged to reform itself through abstinence; and specially organised religious services insisted on 'an unfeigned and universal repentance' and 'a visible amendment' of lives to atone for the nation's sins.[31] Thanksgivings were more joyful in mood, being intended to celebrate divine blessings upon England. However, their ultimate message was similar to that of fasts, because true gratitude to God was held to include resolution to walk in righteousness. Both fasts and thanksgivings were, therefore, designed as instruments of godly renewal, and were consequently easy to integrate into the campaign of courtly reformation.

The court's strategy in the 1690s was built around an annual calendar of fasts and thanksgivings established at the Restoration in 1660. Since the return of the Stuarts after the civil wars, the English people had been required to gather in their churches three times a year on the anniversary of significant occasions in the country's history. On 30 January, they fasted to atone for the execution of Charles I in 1649.[32] On 29 May, they gave thanks for the return of Charles II in 1660.[33] On 5 November, they celebrated the frustration of the 1605 Gunpowder Plot. These occasions could generate a good deal of popular enthusiasm, and were used by Restoration governments to promote the image of their regimes. The proclamations, sermons, and liturgy of the days were used to reassert Stuart claims by arguing that the events of 1605, 1649, and 1660 had established the sanctity of the monarchy, and God's ultimate protection of it.[34]

---

[30] Roland Bartel, 'The story of public fast days in England', *Anglican Theological Review*, 37 (1955), 190–220; W. S. Hudson, 'Fast days and civil religion', in W. S. Hudson and L. J. Trinterud, eds., *Theology in sixteenth- and seventeenth-century England* (Los Angeles, 1971), pp. 1–24.

[31] The quotes are from William Talbot, *A sermon preached at the cathedral church of Worcester upon the monthly fast day, September 16 1691* (1691), p. 9; James Gardiner, *A sermon preach'd before the House of Lords at the abbey church of St Peter's Westminster on Wednesday 11 December, 1695, being the day appointed for a solemn fast and humiliation* (1695), p. 25.

[32] *By the king, a proclamation for the observation of the thirtieth day of January as a day of fast, ... given 25 January 1660* (1661). This document ordered that it be read out and the fast kept every year.

[33] *By the king, a proclamation for the observation of the nine and twentieth day of May instant, as a day of publick thanksgiving ... given 20 May 1661* (1661). Compulsory observation of this thanksgiving was enacted by 20 Charles II c. 14.

[34] See John Spurr, 'Virtue, religion and government: the anglican uses of providence', in Goldie *et al.*, *Politics of religion*, pp. 29–47, especially pp. 29–30.

In 1689, the new Williamite regime inherited this calendar. Although the fasts and thanksgivings had been associated with the ideology of the displaced government, they were retained. They did, after all, remain a good opportunity for mass propaganda, and it proved possible to adapt them to carry a Williamite message. The 5 November solemnity was easiest to convert. It had always sat least easily with Charles and James's claims, since the defeat of the 1605 plotters was usually interpreted as a providential salvation of a *protestant* monarchy. After the Restoration, when the court was widely suspected of popish sympathies, the 5 November celebration had become a focus of opposition, spawning popular demonstrations against the supposedly catholic policy of the government.[35] An occasion which sometimes embarrassed Charles and James could be useful to William. His reformation propaganda presented him as the saviour of the same cause which had been rescued in 1605, and the coincidence of the prince's landing at Torbay on 5 November 1688 added to the anniversary's Orange resonance. The ceremonies of the day could thus be used to establish the providential link between England's two salvations from popery, and to legitimate the later event with reference to the earlier.

The Williamite regime exploited this possibility and turned 5 November into a key occasion for the propagation of courtly reformation. Before the new government's first Gunpowder Day, the official reason given for its observance was altered to make it a day of gratitude for William's deliverance, as well as for 1605.[36] Throughout the 1690s, 5 November sermons celebrated William's arrival as a providential protection of the true religion, and developed the reformation theme by asserting that the prince had come to renew English virtue and piety. Gilbert Burnet, as so often, set the tone. In a published address to the House of Lords on Gunpowder Day, 1689, he compared 1605 and 1688, and outlined the new monarchs' role as God's instruments. 'We have now a king and queen, whose examples we hope shall have as great an influence over us for making us truly good, as their government has for making us really happy.'[37] Two years later, John Sharp told the same audience they must obey William and Mary, and purge themselves of lustful sin to show their gratitude to the delivering deity.[38]

The 30 January and 29 May services could be almost as useful to the

---

[35] Harris, *London crowds*, pp. 93, 108–13; David Cressy, *Bonfires and bells: national memory and the protestant calendar in Elizabethan and Stuart England* (1989), pp. 178–84.

[36] Cressy, *Bonfires and bells*, p. 185.

[37] Gilbert Burnet, *A sermon preached before the house of peers in the abby of Westminster on 5 November, being the gunpowder treason day, as likewise the day of his majesties landing in England* (1689), p. 31.

[38] John Sharp, *A sermon preached before the lords spiritual and temporal in parliament assembled in the abbey-church at Westminster, on the fifth of November, 1691* (1691), pp. 25–6.

Williamites. J. P. Kenyon has seen these fasts and thanksgivings as points around which forces hostile to William could organise.[39] With their inherent condemnation of usurpation, they did provide an opportunity to cast veiled aspersions on the Revolution. A few of William's supporters, disgusted with the near-Jacobite atmosphere the days sometimes encouraged, called for their abolition.[40] However, the fasts and thanksgivings were not uncontested ground. The ideology of courtly reformation was flexible enough to absorb their power, and turn these occasions against the Restoration regimes. The rhetoric's providential interpretation of English history allowed 1649 and 1660 to be remembered, without derogating the achievement of 1688.

The sermons of William Lloyd in the 1690s show how the trick was performed. In two addresses preached on 30 January in 1691 and 1697, Lloyd rooted Williamite propaganda in the conventions of the occasion. He began his case by utilising the cult of the royal martyr which had been fostered since 1660. Following the line laid down by Restoration clerics, he asserted that Charles I had been a saintly monarch, and argued that the effects of his sinful and treacherous execution (the Cromwellian tyranny) had been a divine punishment for it.[41] From this point, however, Lloyd skilfully altered the message of the old king's cult. As the preacher developed his argument, it became clear that he was not simply concerned to deplore the rebellion of the 1640s. He also wanted to condemn the sins which had led the English to butcher their godly king. He reviewed the lust, greed, and intemperance which had prevailed in the early Stuart period, and argued that these were the true sources of disaster in 1649. Once this was done, Lloyd could suggest that the real lesson of 30 January was the danger of irreligion and immorality. Personal debauchery was the reason the English had lost their royal paragon, so the proper purpose of the commemorative fasts must be moral renewal as well as denunciation of regicide.[42] In 1691 the bishop stated that each man's duty on the anniversary of Charles's death was 'within the sphere of his calling, to bring others to a sight and sense of their sins; and to persuade them to join with us, every one, by his particular, to help on the public reformation.'[43]

In following this line, Lloyd was not being completely innovatory. The 30 January preachers had traditionally distinguished between the 'instrumental' causes of the king's murder – rebellion and treason – and the 'meretricious'

[39] Kenyon, *Revolution principles*, pp. 69–75.
[40] See, for example, *Some observations upon keeping the thirtieth of January* (1694).
[41] William Lloyd, *A sermon preached before the queen at Whitehall, January 30, being the day of the martyrdom of King Charles the first* (1691), pp. 1–20.
[42] William Lloyd, *A sermon preach'd before the House of Lords, at the abbey-church of St Peter's Westminster on Saturday 30 January 1696/7* (1697), pp. 5–21.
[43] Lloyd, *Sermon ... Whitehall ... January 30*, p. 22.

ones – the general sins of the nation.[44] However, unlike earlier preachers, Lloyd used this analysis to attack the Restoration regime. Charles II, Lloyd implied, may have established a fast to mark 1649, but his moral laxity had defeated the proper point of his initiative. Charles had not read the true lesson of his father's murder because he had not resolved to lead his nation to godliness. Rather, his return had been marked by a 'corruption of morals' which had 'spread from the court downwards into all parts of the nation'.[45] 'Instead of glorifying God, [Charles' supporters] fell to drinking of healths. Instead of being stricter in religion, they grew looser in their lives. Instead of frequenting God's worship, they filled the playhouses and worse places.'[46] From here, Lloyd could convert 30 January into a thoroughgoing Orange occasion. Following the courtly reformation case, he could claim that 1688 was essential to the national renewal demanded by 1649. It was only after the Revolution, he argued, that a godly court was attempting to purge the nation's sins, and so honouring properly Charles I's sacrifice. Thus, even in a 30 January sermon which lauded the executed Stuart as a new Josiah, Lloyd was able to celebrate William.

It is plainly the design of God by this turn, to establish the Protestant Religion in these Kingdoms ... And especially to unite us in that common design, of driving out all immorality and prophaness ... It is the purifying and Reforming of [men's lives] that is the chief business of Religion. And this is the chief design of God's Providence, in this Revolution.[47]

Lloyd's treatment of 29 May in the 1690s fitted this pattern. Again, the event commemorated by this thanksgiving could be interpreted as a divine call for reformation, frustrated by the Restoration governments. In Lloyd's rhetoric, 1660 became a providential opportunity to restore national righteousness, which could only be properly utilised once the corrupt court had been cleared away at the Revolution. As with the 5 November thanksgiving, 1688 was legitimated by comparing it to an event already accepted as a divine deliverance.[48] As with the 30 January fast, courtly reformation turned an old Stuart propaganda weapon back against its creators.

The 5 November, 30 January, and 29 May solemnities were extremely useful occasions for the spread of Williamite propaganda. However, Burnet and his circle did not rest satisfied with them. Very early in the new reign, it was realised that the courtly reformation message could be broadcast even more effectively, if the programme of national repentance was expanded beyond the inherited Restoration calendar. Burnet and the queen seem to

[44] Spurr, *Restoration church*, p. 242.
[45] Lloyd, *Sermon ... House of Lords ... 30 January 1696/7*, p. 25.
[46] Lloyd, *Sermon ... Whitehall ... January 30*, p. 28.
[47] *Ibid.* p. 29.
[48] See William Lloyd, *A sermon preached before her majesty on May 29, being the anniversary of the restoration of the king and royal family* (1692).

have reasoned that the new monarchs might present themselves more effectively as godly and reforming magistrates if they promulgated *extra* fasts and thanksgivings to supplement the established occasions. In the first place, additional events might provide more opportunities for sermons, prayers, and proclamations to urge reformation, and to link this call with 1688. Secondly, the very act of instigating fasts and thanksgivings might give the king and queen a righteous air, revealing them as rulers determined to use every means to remind their subjects of their duties to God.

The campaign to expand the number of solemnities began as early as the spring of 1689. Soon after the start of the war with France, Burnet approached Queen Mary with the suggestion that a public fast be held to secure God's blessing on England's armies.[49] The queen agreed. A solemn day of fasting and humiliation was observed in London on 5 June, with Burnet's circle playing a major role in the solemnities.[50] Early next year a royal proclamation ordered that a fast be held on the third Wednesday in every month for the duration of William's war in Ireland.[51] This was discontinued by an order of 1 October 1690, because the king's success at the battle of the Boyne called for gratitude rather than humiliation, but the idea of monthly fasting was revived the next year to cover the summer campaigning against France. Fasts were held on the third Wednesday of each month from April to October 1691. Monthly fasts were repeated the following year between April and October, and in 1693 the only changes were that the fasting season did not begin until May, and that the day was moved to the second Wednesday in each month. 1694 did not see monthly fasts, but two special days of public humiliation for the war were called on 23 May and 29 August (in London – fourteen days later in the provinces). After Mary's death the frequency of humiliations declined, but further individual fasts for the war were held in 1695, 1696, and 1697.

This endless round of national humiliation was not as concentrated as the activity William induced in Ireland, where *weekly* fasts were ordered for a short period in 1690.[52] However, it was still the most intense period of fasting England had seen since the 1640s, since neither Charles, nor James, had used public days of humiliation to anything like the same extent. Apart from the summer of 1665, when God was to be propitiated to stop the plague, neither

[49] Doebner, *Memoirs of Mary*, p. 14.
[50] *By the king and queen, a proclamation for a general fast, ... given 23 May 1689* (1689). Both Tenison and Wake preached before the House of Commons on the day. Thomas Tenison, *A sermon against self-love &c preached before the honourable House of Commons on 5 June 1689, being the fast day* (1689); William Wake, *A sermon preach'd before the honourable House of Commons at St Margaret's Westminster, June 5 1689, being the fast day* (1689).
[51] *By the king and queen, a proclamation for a general fast, ... given 20 February 1689* (1689).
[52] *By the king and queen's most excellent majesties, a proclamation for a fast, ... given 1 August 1690* (Dublin, 1690).

monarch had used monthly fasts, and there were long periods in their reigns (between 1660 and 1665, 1666 and 1672, the middle of the 1670s, and after 1680) when there had been no extraordinary fasts at all. It is true that Charles and James were not so often at war as William, and that war, along with natural disaster, was the usual stimulant for national humiliation in the seventeenth century. Yet even when Charles had been at war – with the Dutch (1665–7 and 1672–4) – he had not used monthly fasting, but had contented himself with one day of humiliation at the beginning of the campaigning season. In 1674 even this had been omitted; so the intensity, consistency, and regularity of William's fasting were new and remarkable features of royal policy.

The new king's thanksgivings for blessings were not quite as punishing as his humiliations. In the hardships of war, the regime had rather less occasion to show gratitude than to fast. Nevertheless, the regime did hold a significant number of thanksgivings in the 1690s, being particularly careful to ensure that each of its major military victories, and the safe end of difficult military seasons, were followed by a national expression of gratitude.[53] Extra occasions were also staged to mark the conclusion of peace in 1697, and the discovery of a plot against William's life in 1696. When added to the fasts, this meant that none of William's first nine years in power passed without at least five national solemnities designed to illustrate the monarch's reforming mission.

Fast and thanksgiving were not only frequent, however. They were also meticulously planned to convey courtly reformation ideology with the greatest possible efficiency. William's propagandists spent much time and care preparing the events, and attempting to maximise their impact amongst the public. To show how detailed the organisation was, it is convenient to describe the efforts made for the programme of fasts and thanksgivings in 1692. The evidence for this particular programme is untypical because it is unusually rich. However, there is no reason to doubt that it reveals the care which was taken year after year to organise public solemnities, and it does provide extraordinarily good insights into the internal workings of William's propaganda machine.

In 1692, the first problem facing the Williamite bishops was to decide when to hold the year's events. A letter from Tillotson to Burnet revealed the detailed consideration given in the Privy Council to the question of when to start the series of summer humiliations. The archbishop reported that Mary

[53] See, for example, *By the king and queen, a proclamation . . . given 1 October 1690* (1690), to give thanks for the battle of the Boyne; *By the king and queen, a proclamation for a publick thanksgiving, . . . given 22 October 1691* (1691), to give thanks for the preservation of the king in Flanders and successes in Ireland; *By the king and queen, a proclamation for a publick thanksgiving, . . . given 2 November 1693* (1693), for success in Flanders.

had initially fixed upon 13 April as the first fast, but that when the proclamation was brought to the Council, it was objected that that date was the first day of the Easter legal term. The 20th of the same month was proposed 'but that was thought not so convenient, because some action abroad might happen sooner' and the first fast was eventually fixed for 8 April.[54] This early date was confirmed in a proclamation of 24 March, but in May a military victory caused further agonising about when to stage a national solemnity. Admiral Russell inflicted a heavy defeat on the French fleet at La Hogue, and the question arose as to whether to greet it with a public thanksgiving. The queen again consulted with her clerical allies, and spent many days deliberating over the precise organisation of the celebration. She recorded that she waited to hear what success was had in Flanders 'before I would have a public thanksgiving. I thought, and so did several bishops, we must stay for that, and so did for, I believe, a fortnight together at least, every hour expecting to hear of a battle.'[55] Mary's concern with the staging of such events was further underlined when no such military success materialised, and the La Hogue thanksgiving was put back to the end of campaigning in October. The queen blamed herself for missing the opportunity for a national sign of gratitude, and believed that political rancour over the summer was a direct and divine punishment for her indecision.[56]

Once the basic date for the fasts and thanksgivings of 1692 had been decided, the chief tasks were to advertise them, to choose the speakers for the prestigious pulpits at court and parliament, and to compose a form of prayers for the occasions. Officially, the bishops were given the last of these jobs by the Privy Council.[57] In 1692, however, Tillotson was so certain that there would be a series of fasts in the summer, that he had the office composed and printed over a month before the Council requested it.[58] Once the supplications had been written, they were published and sent out to the clergy of every parish. In 1692, as was usual, they followed closely the daily liturgy in the *Book of common prayer* with certain passages added or replaced to emphasise the tenets of courtly reformation. The form of prayer for the first Williamite fast in 1689 had replaced the collect for the day with one outlining England's national history, and asking God to stimulate repentance now that the English had been rescued from popery.[59] The 1692 form of prayer was

[54] Tillotson to Burnet, 12 April 1692, Birch, *Life ... Tillotson*, p. 291.
[55] Doebner, *Memoirs of Mary*, p. 51.
[56] *Ibid.*
[57] The fast and thanksgiving proclamations called on the bishops to write a form of prayers for the occasion. For a typical example of their involvement in this stage of the preparations, see the register of the Privy Council for 9 April 1691, PRO PC2 74/149.
[58] Birch, *Life ... Tillotson*, p. 291.
[59] *A form of prayer to be used on 5 June coming, being the fast day* (1689).

similar in tone, and included a new supplication to be said on the coming fast day, and 'constantly' whilst the king was abroad. It read

Almighty and most gracious God, who hast been our Deliverer in the day of our Distress, and hast called up thy Servant King WILLIAM to be the happy Instrument of our Deliverance: ... We humbly beseech thee still to continue him under the merciful Ease and Protection of thy good Providence, ... And likewise to give us Grace to be worthy of these Mercies in all thankful Obedience to thee, and in dutiful Subjection to their Majesties, whom thou hast set over us.[60]

Whilst these prayers were composed, the Attorney-General was told to draft the proclamation which would officially announce the fast. This document explained the occasion for the coming solemnities, and expressed the monarchs' personal concern that their nation take the opportunity offered to amend their lives. The 1692 proclamation explained how the fast could help the war and requested that William's subjects do their part to secure divine favour on his enterprise.[61] Once finished, the proclamation was distributed through the usual channels, giving the monarch's hopes and motives a wide audience. Meanwhile, Burnet's circle was arranging who would preach before the court and parliament, and so set the tone for the day. On 31 May, whilst Mary was deciding about a thanksgiving for La Hogue, the earl of Nottingham wrote to Burnet. He expressed the hope that the bishop would recover from a recent illness, because the queen wanted him to give the sermon at Whitehall when Russell's naval victory was celebrated.[62] Burnet had given the court sermon on the previous two thanksgivings, and was becoming the automatic choice for the job. He prepared an address, but also showed a canny concern for public opinion, telling Mary that if he performed again 'it would look as if nobody else was willing to perform that office'.[63] The queen saw the strength of this point, and when the thanksgiving day was finally held, it was Tillotson who went to the Whitehall pulpit.[64]

When, at last, the fast days arrived, an extensive machinery for ensuring their observance sprang into action. On the secular side, the pains of English law were threatened against those who did not take the public solemnities seriously. The proclamation which established the series of fasts decreed punishment for those who should 'contemn or neglect so religious a work' and urged local officials to enforce the day's privations with vigour.[65] This order was taken to heart by at least some local magistrates, so that several Londoners who were caught playing bowls on the 13 July fast were fined or

[60] *A form of prayer to be used on Friday the eighth day of April next ... being the fast day* (1692).
[61] *By the king and queen, a proclamation for a general fast, ... given 24 March 1692* (1692).
[62] Nottingham to Burnet, 31 May 1692, Bodl. Additional Ms. A 191, fol. 107.
[63] Gilbert Burnet, *Some sermons preached on several occasions* (1713), preface, p. xxii.
[64] John Tillotson, *A sermon preached before the king and queen at Whitehall, October 27, being the day appointed for the publick thanksgiving* (1692).
[65] *By the king, ... proclamation ... 24 March 1692*.

sent to prison.[66] Meanwhile on the ecclesiastical side, the bishops ensured that all their subordinate clergy provided the prayers and, services which had been prescribed. Simon Patrick, writing to ministers in the diocese of Ely, warned against negligence in the preparing and keeping of fasts, and then had his letter printed so that it could influence clerics in other areas of the country as well.[67] At the same time the bishops wrote and delivered their own sermons, and made arrangements to publish them so that they could serve as encouragements and models for local ministers. The first of the 1692 crop of publications, Patrick's *Sermon preached before the queen at Whitehall, 8 April*, repeated the gospel that 1688 had given the English a royally inspired opportunity to repent.[68]

Of course, it is hard to assess what effect such efforts had in 1692, or in any other year. No historian can be sure how seriously ordinary Englishmen took William and Mary's fasts, or whether they absorbed the ideology which lay behind them. It is always possible that the solemnities were extensively evaded, or that people who participated were merely happy to have a day off work. Certainly, many clerics preaching on fast days complained that these national humiliations were not being properly observed. However, since the point of pulpit oratory on these occasions was to berate a sinful nation to repentance, clerics were hardly likely to praise the population for its piety and diligence. When the structure of their rhetoric required, the men of Burnet's circle were quite capable of suggesting that fasting was going splendidly. In the autumn of 1690, for instance, Burnet himself wished to prove that the humiliations of the summer had resulted in the king's success in Ireland. He accordingly opined

We have been this last Summer frequently brought together to fast and pray for Success and Victory ... We have never seen a more solemn Observation, as to all outward appearance, of such Days as was on those monthly Returns; and tho many were very bare-faced in their neglect of them, and others that should have animated the Publick Zeal, were extream cold in the observance of them, yet much earnestness and fervour showed itself in many places.[69]

Contemporary records of public observance of William's humiliations backs Burnet in this mood. According to some eyewitness reports, the early fasts were kept 'very strictly' in London.[70] A leading chronicler of the period, Narcissus Luttrell, noted how the town regularly shut up shop on the

---

[66]   Luttrell, *Relation*, II, 513.

[67]   Simon Patrick, *The bishop of Ely's letter to the clergy of his diocese* (1692), p. 7.

[68]   Simon Patrick, *A sermon preach'd before the queen at Whitehall, 8 April 1692, being the fast day appointed to implore God's blessing on their majesties persons* (1692).

[69]   Gilbert Burnet, *A sermon preached before the king and queen at Whitehall on 19 October 1690, being the day of thanksgiving for his majesties preservation and success in Ireland* (1690), pp. 33–4

[70]   Singer, *Correspondence ... Clarendon*, II, 313.

humiliations and thanksgivings, whilst the famous diarist, John Evelyn, always noted the occasions in his journal.[71] Meanwhile Lady Russell found she could withdraw from society on fast days without being missed by her acquaintances; and an incident in London early in William's reign suggests that the fasts generated genuine popular enthusiasm.[72] In the autumn of 1690 there was some confusion about when the fasts would be suspended for the winter. In September, some of the London clergy assumed the series of humiliations had finished, but the capital's population was less sure and many of them left their work and turned up at closed churches expecting to participate in appropriate religious services.[73] The fact that some of the published sermons became best-sellers also indicates a degree of real popularity; as does the fact that Jacobites seem to have felt a need to try to disrupt the fasts and thanksgivings.[74] Some publicly mocked, or wrote against these public occasions, whilst others, such as the earl of Clarendon, staged surly retreat into the depths of their households.[75]

Given this evidence, it appears that the court's promotion of fasts and thanksgivings was a successful ideological strategy. Not only were these events frequent, regular, and compulsory occasions, backed by the coercive resources of the regime, they also seem to have attracted considerable public support and participation. It thus seems possible that the fasts and thanksgivings were the element of William's propaganda which made most impact amongst ordinary Englishmen. The fact that they were designed to disrupt people's ordinary lives, and were promoted through a wide variety of media, makes it likely that more people noticed these events, and reflected upon their meaning, than other forms of propaganda. Despite their historiographic neglect, therefore, fasts and thanksgivings were crucial to the wide dissemination of a Williamite view of the world. They deserve to be better studied, and better known.

REFORMATION THROUGH THE LAW

If the Orange regime's programme of fasts has received too little attention from historians, the next initiative for the promotion of courtly reformation has almost received too much. Whilst many aspects of the 1690s have

---

[71] Luttrell, *Relation*, I, 542; II, 20, 45, 217, 301–2, 603.
[72] Lady Russell to Dr Fitzwilliam, 21 July 1692, *Letters ... Lady Russell*, p. 299.
[73] Kerr and Duncan, *Routledge papers*, p. 85.
[74] Both John Sharp, *A sermon preached before the honourable House of Commons at St Margaret's Westminster, Wednesday 21 May 1690, being the day of the monthly-fast* (1690), and Edward Fowler, *A sermon preached at Bow-church, April 16 1690; before the Lord Maior and court of aldermen, and citizens of London being the fast day* (1690), sold more than one edition.
[75] Monod, *Jacobitism*, p. 122; Singer, *Correspondence ... Clarendon*, II, 318.

remained underresearched, the past few decades have seen an explosion of interest in the numerous contemporary campaigns to use English law to promote moral reform. Relative to other topics, the number of studies of this phenomenon published since the middle of the 1950s has been remarkable. Repeatedly, works on the late Stuart period have outlined efforts to secure new statutes to curb immorality; they have covered campaigns by local magistrates to enforce existing laws against debauchery; and they have described the societies for the reformation of manners – bodies of volunteers who reported vicious offenders to local constables and JPs.[76] As a result, there has been a curious distortion in the modern understanding of William III's England. Specialists in this period seem to know far more about the statutory campaign for a reformation of manners in the 1690s than they do about almost any other part of their field.

At first sight it may seem strange that a historian of courtly reformation should complain about the attention devoted to the reformation societies and to reforming JPs and MPs. It might appear that legal campaigns against vice would fit into William's ideological agenda, and that their study should provide much information about popular participation in the king's crusade for virtue. Yet despite the excellence and usefulness of most of the writing on these initiatives for reform, there is an unfortunate sense in which the historiographic popularity of the theme has made the task of describing courtly reformation more difficult. With the notable exception of Dudley Bahlmann (who opened up the field with his 1957 book *The moral revolution of 1688*), most scholars of statutory reformation in the late Stuart period have denied the court's close involvement in, and its leadership of, the movement.[77] They have presented reformation initiatives as largely independent of William's regime, and have suggested that they became a source of embarrassment, or even a centre of opposition, to the government. For example, some of those who have studied the local operation of the reformation campaign have shown that it caused considerable anxiety for central government officials. They have shown that William's ministers and higher judges, worried that reformation initiatives had sprung up outside government control, sought to

---

[76] Apart from the works cited in the next few notes, see Shelley Burtt, *Virtue transformed: political argument in England, 1688–1740* (Cambridge, 1992); Tina Isaacs, 'The anglican hierarchy and the reformation of manners', *JEH*, 33 (1982), 391–411; Tina Isaacs, 'Moral crime, moral reform and the state: a study in piety and politics in early eighteenth-century England' (Unpublished PhD dissertation, University of Rochester, New York, 1979); Rose, 'Providence, protestant union'; Eamon Duffy, 'Primitive Christianity revived: religious renewal in Augustan England', in Derek Baker, ed., *Renaissance and renewal in Christian history* (Oxford, 1977), pp. 287–300; Robert B. Shoemaker, 'Reforming the city: the reformation of manners campaign in London, 1690–1738', in Lee Davison, Tim Hitchcock, Tim Kearns, and Robert Shoemaker, eds., *Stilling the grumbling hive: the response to social and economic problems in England* (1992), pp. 99–120.

[77] Dudley W. R. Bahlmann, *The moral revolution of 1688* (New Haven, Connecticut, 1957).

investigate these movements, and suspected them of various kinds of sedition and disruption.[78] Even more damagingly, many of the studies of reformation in the 1690s have tried to demonstrate a direct link with opposition politics. Scholars including William Speck, Tim Curtis, and A. G. Craig have presented the reform movement as a sort of social manifestation of 'country' attitudes. For these historians, the reforming initiatives sprang from the old fear that the court was corrupting the nation's virtue, and were driven by the belief that only vigorous moral action could distance citizens from the vice of their governors.[79] David Hayton has gone further still. Looking closely at the voting and other records of late Stuart MPs, he has claimed a statistical correlation between those who criticised William's administration in the House of Commons, and those who are known to have supported reformation societies, or to have been reforming justices in their localities.[80] Thus an area of study which might have expanded understanding of William's ideology has actually posed serious problems for it. In order to integrate legal campaigns for moral renewal into the court's programme of reformation (as this section will attempt to do), it has become necessary to dispel an impression that reformers were critical of William's administration.

The history of the attempts in the 1690s to improve morals through the law can be briefly summarised. Most of the campaigns did result from the enthusiasm of independent gentlemen. As early as December 1688, the self-publicising clergyman, Edward Stephens, drafted a proclamation against vice which called for the enforcement of the existing statutes against such offences as drunkenness, prostitution, and profane swearing. Stephens claimed to have presented his work to the prince of Orange as his highness advanced on London, but had been disappointed that the Dutch camp had shown little interest in its contents.[81] By May 1689, Sir Richard Bulkeley, an Irish baronet, had joined Stephens in lobbying the new government. Bulkeley also drafted orders against vice, and hoped that William would endorse them with his authority.[82] In 1691, these two projectors, enthused by a local drive against bawdy houses in Tower Hamlets, set up the first society for

---

[78] A. G. Craig, 'The movement for the reformation of manners 1690–1715' (Unpublished PhD dissertation, University of Edinburgh, 1980), pp. 41–63; Robert B. Shoemaker, *Prosecution and punishment: petty crime in London and rural Middlesex c. 1660–1725* (Cambridge, 1991), pp. 261–2.

[79] T. C. Curtis and W. A. Speck, 'The societies for reformation of manners: a case study in the theory and practice of moral reform', *Literature and History*, 3 (1976), 45–64; Craig, 'Reformation of manners', p. 299; David Hayton, 'Sir Richard Cocks: the anatomy of a country whig', *Albion*, 20 (1988), 221–46.

[80] David Hayton, 'Moral reform and country politics in the late seventeenth-century House of Commons', *PP*, 128 (1990), 48–91.

[81] [Edward Stephens], *A specimin of a declaration against debauchery, tendered to the consideration of his highness, the prince of Orange* (1688).

[82] Craig, 'Movement for reformation', pp. 10–11.

reformation of manners. Based in Westminster, this body urged its members to inform magistrates of drunks, profane swearers, and prostitutes; it printed blank warrants for the arrest of miscreants; and it financed prosecutions of debauched offenders. By the end of the decade, the society's model had been copied all over the country. In 1699, Josiah Woodward – the moral activist and first historian of the movement – was able to boast that societies for reformation existed in a host of towns, including such dispersed and varied places as Carlisle, Westminster, Bristol, York, and Nottingham.[83] Whilst the fashion for reforming associations took hold, local magistrates launched their own campaigns against vice. Active JPs such as Sir Ralph Hartley in Middlesex, or Sir Richard Cocks in Gloucestershire, imposed the full rigours of the English law against debauchees under their jurisdiction, and the mayor and aldermen of London also began to crack down on offenders in their city.[84] In addition, certain MPs began calling for more and tougher statutes against immorality. Moves in this direction early in the decade came to little, but in the parliamentary session of 1697/8, many back-benchers rallied behind attempts by Sir John Phillips to enact a comprehensive programme of measures against sacrilege, profanity, and debauchery.[85] Whilst the House of Commons eventually thought better of Draconian provisions against sin, a blasphemy act was passed, and agitation for extra moral legislation persisted throughout the rest of the reign.

In these campaigns, the historian of Williamite propaganda does face ideological and political confusion. Although there is a temptation simply to integrate legal movements for moral renewal into the regime's reformation programme, it must be admitted that those scholars who have claimed these movements were hostile to the court have evidence for their case. The attempts at moral renewal through the law were very diverse; they were often led by gentlemen with little direct connection with the king; and amongst the babble of initiatives it can be difficult to trace the court's influence. This is particularly true since not all the men involved in reforming activities acknowledged the regime as their inspiration. Whilst most of those trying to purge England through its law were Williamite in the sense that they saw 1688 as a providentially provided opportunity to make their attempt, the

---

[83] [Josiah Woodward], *An account of the societies for the reformation of manners, in London and Westminster, and other parts of the kingdom* (1699).

[84] For Hartley, see Craig, 'Movement for reformation', pp. 26, 43. For Cocks, see Hayton, 'Sir Richard Cocks', pp. 236–7. For London, see CLRO PD 10.91 – an order by the Lord Mayor for the suppression of vice, 19 November 1689; CLRO Rep. 95, fols. 310, 318, 321–4 – orders to put the laws against vice in execution, July/August 1691; CLRO Rep. 98, fols. 304–5 – similar orders in May 1694; CLRO Rep. 97, fols. 153–61 – an order of 24 February 1692 for sabbath observation and suppression of vice.

[85] For Phillips' bills, see PRO SP 32 9, fols. 333–4; PRO SP 32 10, fols. 3, 23–4, 65, 202. For support by backbenchers, see BL Loan Ms. 29/186, fol. 225; BL Loan Ms. 29/189, fols. 21, 67.

reformers were not always impeccably loyal to William's administration and policy. Some of them had a higher loyalty to their moral ideal than to the Orange regime. They were prepared to judge the court according to its record of helping the cause of moral virtue, and could criticise the government when they found it wanting. There was thus a real risk that William's subjects might prove more zealous for reform than his administration, and that the king's publicists might be hoisted by their own petard.

The capacity for trouble was shown early. Edward Stephens, perhaps smarting from the neglect of his specimen declaration, complained that little was done in the first years of William's reign to institute a legal campaign for public virtue. He had a point. Before 1691, the court's only move in this area had been to issue a letter from William to the bishop of London, ordering all clergy to read out the statutes against vice.[86] In a series of works published between 1689 and 1691 Stephens complained about this lack of action, and warned that debauched and powerful factions at court were blocking legislation to curb sin.[87] Even the bishops fell under suspicion as Stephens issued dark warnings that the king and queen themselves might fall victim to the prevailing corruption.[88] The late 1690s saw more rumblings from the independent reformers. By the end of the decade the societies for reformation of manners in London and Westminster were publishing quarterly sermons to act as publicity for their movement. Many of these worried that little progress was being made in rolling back vice, and expressed suspicion of the men in whom William had placed trust. Sermon after reformation sermon spoke of wholesale neglect amongst magistrates, and the poor moral example set by those in positions of authority. One address, by John Woodhouse in 1697, openly criticised the court by talking of a 'false step' taken in the early months of the regime. In 1689, Woodhouse claimed, debauched politicians had persuaded William to settle the government before tackling national manners, so that 'little was at first done to reform the court, city, country, army, navy, magistracy, and ministry'. Only the bench of assize judges had been effectively purged and the task of reformation had been entrusted to those who wished to see it thwarted.[89]

Such evidence suggests that William's propagandists had lost control of the

---

[86] William III, *His majesties letter to the lord bishop of London, to be communicated to the two provinces of Canterbury and York* (1689).

[87] [Edward Stephens], *A plain relation of the late action at sea, between the English and the Dutch, and the French fleets from June 22 to July 5 last* (1689); [Edward Stephens], *An admonition concerning a publick fast* (1691); [Edward Stephens], *An appeal to earth and heaven against the Christian Epicureans, who have betrayed their king and countrey* (1691).

[88] [Stephens], *Plain relation*, pp. 30–2; *Admonition concerning a fast*, p. 3.

[89] John Woodhouse, *A sermon preach'd at Salters Hall to the societies for reformation of manners, May 31 1697* (1697), pp. 37–8.

legal campaign for reformation. It appears to confirm claims that reform of morals through the law was basically an opposition phenomenon in the 1690s. Yet whilst there were clear signs of discontent with William amongst reformers, the instances which have been cited so far do not provide a complete picture of the movement. They must be balanced by the efforts made by Burnet and his allies to cope with the threat to their position. Through vigorous action, William's publicists were able to limit the damage to their master's cause by erecting an umbrella of royal patronage over the campaigns for legal reformation. As efforts to strengthen and enforce the laws gathered pace, the court propagandists joined the movement, appropriated its rhetoric, and cut off potential criticism by proving the king's enthusiasm for statutory moral reform. It was a virtuoso piece of tiger-riding, which at least partially reintegrated independent reformers with the court's programme of moral renewal.

The manoeuvring began in the second half of 1691. Soon after the formation of the first reformation society, Edward Stillingfleet came to patronise the body. He consulted with the association's leaders, and put pressure on Queen Mary to become their sponsor. The result of the bishop's initiative was a letter written by the queen to the Middlesex justices. This encouraged the reformation society's work by requiring the JPs to apply the statutes against vice, and asking ordinary men and women to bring offences to the magistrates' notice.[90] Later in the year, the court's propagandists again elicited royal action when the 'pious address of our archbishops and bishops' produced a proclamation by William and Mary against vicious and debauched persons.[91] This asked all judges, justices, and constables to be diligent in enforcing the law, and again succoured the reformation societies by stressing the need for action by all their majesties' subjects. The vigorous expansion of the reformation movement in the late 1690s, and its efficient publicity, elicited more court response towards the end of the decade. William issued two further proclamations against vice in 1698 and 1699, and called for more laws to suppress debauchery in six separate speeches to parliament between 1697 and 1701.[92] As the monarch made his contribution, other propagandists

---

[90] Craig, 'Movement for reformation', p.27. Mary II, *Her majesties gracious letter to the justices of the peace in the county of Middlesex, July 9 1691, for the suppressing of prophaness and debauchery* (1691).

[91] *By the king and queen, a proclamation against vitious, debauched and profane persons, ... given 21 January 1691/2* (1692). BL Additional Ms. 70, 015, fol. 276 is a petition for the proclamation from thirteen bishops including Tillotson, Burnet, Patrick, Sharp, and Stillingfleet.

[92] *By the king, ... proclamation ... 24 February 1697; By the king, a proclamation for preventing and punishing immorality and prophaness, ... given 9 December 1699* (1699); *LJ*, 16, 175, 344, 352, 366, 476; *LJ*, 17, 6.

worked to propagate and magnify his efforts. Edward Fowler, who maintained close links with the reformation societies, attempted to have them
officially endorsed, and collected signatures of fellow bishops on a paper
commending their work.[93] Thomas Tenison responded to the king's
1699 speech to parliament by sending out a letter to the clergy of his province
giving advice on how best to achieve a 'universal reformation'. He advised
ministers to form associations to combat debauchery, and to encourage
their flock to inform JPs of vicious offenders.[94] Gilbert Burnet approved
Tenison's epistle, and added his endorsement of it in an appendix to the
copies sent out in his Salisbury diocese. Secular politicians and officials were
also involved. A paper read in 1699 by Secretary of State James Vernon to the
Privy Council referred to Tenison's letter and told circuit judges to remind JPs
of its content at assizes. Vernon also told these men to punish 'vice and
prophaness' on their rounds, and to encourage local magistrates to do the
same.[95]

It is true that some in court circles, and even some of Burnet's bishops, had
doubts about aspects of the legal reform movement. In some cases Williamite
involvement was not always rapid or enthusiastic, and certain supporters of
the king were careful to investigate the initiatives before they backed them.
For instance, Vernon asked for reports on the societies for reformation of
manners since he feared they might become subversive cells; whilst Archbishop Sharp temporarily forbade the clergy in his diocese to join these bodies
because he believed they might constitute illegal conventicles. However, in
both cases, these initial reservations were overcome, and both men became
readier supporters of reform through the law. Vernon dropped his opposition
to the societies on learning nothing disturbing about them, and Sharp eventually permitted clerical participation once he had drawn up strict rules about
the sort of groups which clergymen might aid.[96]

The regime's leadership of legal reformation was further emphasised by
efficient broadcasting of its initiatives. Both Mary's letter to the Middlesex
bench, and William's to Compton, were published. The latter epistle was sent
to every parish priest in the country, along with copies of the statutes which

---

[93] Craig, 'Movement for reformation', p.225. The endorsement of the societies, including
Patrick's signature, appeared as a preface to the 1699 edition of Woodward, *Account ...
societies.*
[94] Thomas Tenison, *His grace the lord archbishop of Canterbury's letter to the right reverend
the lords bishops of his province* (1699).
[95] PRO SP 32 11, fols. 308–11.
[96] For Secretary of State Vernon's suspicions of the reform movement in the late 1690s, see
G. P. R. James, ed., *Letters illustrative of the reign of William III from 1696 to 1708
addressed to the duke of Shrewsbury by James Vernon esq.* (3 vols., 1814), II, 128–9. For
Sharp's policies see Sharp, *Life of ... Sharp*, I, 172–88.

the clergy were to read out. William's proclamations were sent out through the usual publicity machine, and, in addition, contained the specific provision that they be read by all ministers from the pulpit four times a year.[97] Assize judges were ordered to check that this was being done.[98] William's speeches to parliament, especially those at the end of sessions, were similarly designed to transmit the court's enthusiasm for legal reform to the whole nation. They were published, and contained a request that peers and MPs act as carriers of royal ideology as they returned to their estates and constituencies. The legislators were asked to go back to their localities and be active 'in all your several stations ... in a due and regular execution of the laws, especially those against profaness and irreligion'.[99]

This saturation coverage of the court's legal reformation headed off the worst dangers of the independent reformers' campaign. Effectively, it established a rhetorical universe in which potential criticism of the regime could be neutralised. Appropriating the independent reformers' polemic, the bishops associated the monarchs so closely with their cause, that it became difficult for the campaigners to call for godly rule without endorsing the court's position. The process could be observed amongst reforming magistrates. When the Middlesex justices took action against vice in 1691, they thanked Queen Mary for her letter to them, and so presented their local action as an aspect of court policy.[100] The case was similar with the reformation societies. The royal letters, speeches, and proclamations against vice were a powerful endorsement of these bodies' campaigns, which naturally found their way into their literature. As the societies drew attention to the royal action in their promotional publications, they automatically portrayed themselves as embodiments of the monarch's personal wishes. For example, the men involved in one of the first initiatives for the reformation of manners, the 1690 push against bawdy houses in Tower Hamlets, printed a broadside to advertise their campaign. The Hellenicly titled *Antimoixeia* cited two stimulants to reforming action which had originated at court.[101] The first was a proclamation for the apprehension of highwaymen (just issued by the king and queen), whilst the second was William's letter to Bishop Compton. When the societies were founded, they too cited royal literature in support of their actions. Their sermons and pamphlets constantly referred to a canon of court documents: most especially the queen's Middlesex letter, the proclamations,

---

[97] *By the king, ... proclamation ... given 24 February 1697.*
[98] PRO SP 32 11, fol. 310.
[99] *LJ*, 16, 344.
[100] For a citation of the queen's letter by local magistrates, see Middlesex Quarter Sessions, *Mid. ss. Ad. general. Quateral session [public order respecting vice and immorality]* (1691).
[101] *Antimoixeia: or the honest and joynt-design of the Tower-Hamlets for the general suppression of bawdy houses, as incouraged thereto by the publick magistrates* (1691).

and the king's speeches to parliament.[102] So keen were the societies to quote this material, that they effectively became part of the Williamite propaganda machine. In 1691 it was the first society which was responsible for the wide distribution of the queen's letter.[103] They paid for its printing and sent it out to the provinces. Later in the decade, the societies provided a platform for leading court spokesmen. Gilbert Burnet and Edward Fowler were invited to preach before the bodies, and the addresses they delivered, full of the royal concern for reformation, were published at the members' request.[104]

The propagandists' attempts to place the monarchs at the head of legal reformation were particularly impressive when they neutralised suggestions that royal efforts had been inadequate. As has been seen, criticism of the court was a disturbing undercurrent in reform movements of the 1690s. The royal propagandists recognised this, and fashioned a rhetorical response to cope with the problem. Their approach is evident in the altered wording of the reforming proclamations. The texts of William's orders against vice were largely formulaic, since they borrowed much of their phraseology from documents previously produced by Charles and James.[105] However, whilst the proclamations issued after 1688 were very traditional, they also contained two significant innovations. First, they expressed pessimism about the progress of official reformation. Whilst Charles's third proclamation against vice had spoken of his pleasure that his first was having such a good effect, William's edicts were far more gloomy, expressing 'resentment' that 'impiety, profaness and immorality do still abound in this our kingdom'.[106] Second, William was prepared to blame negligent magistrates for the continuance of

---

102 [Woodward], *Account ... societies for reformation of manners*, opened with Mary's 1691 letter and William's 1697 proclamation against vice; [Josiah Woodward], *An account of the progress of the reformation of manners in England, Scotland and Ireland* (1701), p. 9, mentioned a lost booklet, *A help to reformation*, which also led with William's proclamation. [Edward Fowler], *A vindication of an undertaking of certain gentlemen, in order to the suppressing of debauchery and profaness* (1692), defended the societies by quoting Mary's Middlesex letter.

103 Woodward, *Account ... of the religious societies*, pp. 70–1.

104 Gilbert Burnet, *Charitable reproof: a sermon preached at St Mary-le-Bow to the societies for reformation of manners, 25 March 1700* (1700); Edward Fowler, *A sermon preached at St Mary le Bow to the societies for reformation of manners, June 26 1699* (1699). The societies sent their sermons out to the provinces and distributed them widely. See William Hayley, *A sermon preach'd at the church of St Mary le Bow before the societies for reformation of manners upon Monday October 3 1698* (1699), preface.

105 Both Charles and James had issued proclamations against vice, though only at moments of political expediency. Charles's edicts dated from the very beginning of his reign, and were aimed chiefly at securing order in the streets of London, and countering the suggestion that his party was morally lax. James issued *By the king, a proclamation, ... given 29 June 1688* (1688) as his contribution to moral reform. This dated from the period when the king wanted to ally with dissenters against anglican opposition, and may have been intended to win their support.

106 *By the King, a proclamation for the suppressing of disorderly and unseasonable meetings, ... given 20 September 1660* (1660); *By the king ... proclamation ... given 24 February 1697*.

sin. Both he and James noted 'frequent and repeated instances of dissolute living', but only William went on to state that these had 'in great measure been occasioned by the neglect of the magistrates not putting into execution those good laws which have been made for suppressing and punishing thereof, and by the ill example of many in authority'.[107] These innovations were designed to deal with the regime's detractors. They formed part of a wider strategy, in which the monarchs admitted shortcomings in their legal reformation, so that the court could place itself at the head of its own critics. If the regime could acknowledge that its crusade had met with limited success, and that certain royal servants seemed to be blocking its progress, it might moderate complaint by seeming to concur with it. The king and queen's image as zealous reformers might be preserved, as the monarchs were shown to share the prevailing concern about their failure. It was in accordance with this strategy that Mary's letter to the Middlesex bench warned of JPs who 'refused or neglected to discharge the duty of [their] place', and that William's closing speech to parliament in 1699 had expressed disappointment at how little progress had been made towards new laws to promote virtue.[108]

In certain cases this rhetorical gambit was very effective. Some society activists, who had been worried by the government's reluctance to join in reformation, were able to express their anxiety in words borrowed from court propaganda. For instance, the author of the *Account of the progress of the reformation of manners* (1701) talked of recalcitrance amongst those responsible for suppressing sin, but was able to illustrate his point by citing the proclamation of 1697 which had talked of 'the negligence of magistrates in the execution of their office, and their ill example'.[109] What might have been an attack on William's choice of servants was therefore transformed into an endorsement of the king's sentiments. Even Edward Stephens and John Woodhouse were convinced by royal suggestions that vicious officials were obstructing William and Mary's designs, and accepted that the monarchs themselves were sound on reform. Stephens greeted Mary's Middlesex letter as evidence that the corrupt remnant at court had been defeated and that true royal reformation would begin.[110] Woodhouse attacked the state's general apathy in meeting the challenge of immorality, but he cleared William and Mary personally of blame. After the initial mistake of relegating reformation amongst official priorities, Woodhouse argued 'there were vigorous overtures made, by our excellent king, and nonsuch queen, to retrieve this false step: I

---

107 *By the king, … proclamation … given 29 June 1688; By the king, … proclamation … given 24 February 1697.*
108 Mary II, *Her majesties gracious letter; LJ,* 16, 466.
109 *An account of the progress of the reformation of manners in England and Ireland* (1701), p. 37.
110 [Edward Stephens], *The beginnings and progress of a needful and hopeful reformation in England* (1691), p. 7.

need not recite their vigorous application, to officers sacred, and civil'.[111] In the light of such examples, it is necessary to refine any suggestion that the reformation movements of the 1690s were hostile to the court. There was some criticism of the regime in reformation circles, but William's bishops found ways to cope with this, and even managed to absorb some of its energies into the royal propaganda campaign.

None of this, of course, is to claim that Burnet and his circle achieved a greater propaganda success and managed to convince a wider public that the king should be supported for his interest in a moral English law. There is, in fact, considerable evidence from the 1690s that the general run of William's subjects were highly ambivalent about having their manners reformed by statutes, and that many viewed the movement as an excuse for hypocritical interference in private lives. More Englishmen, perhaps, encountered legal reformation as its persecuted victims than as active participants, and poets and pamphleteers certainly attacked the movement for either reviving the puritan terror of Cromwell's day, or unjustly torturing the poor.[112] Perhaps the best example of this critical genre is a satirical pamphlet play of 1698, *The puritanical justice*. It mocked the reforming magistrates of London for using religious zeal to hide their own sin, and for becoming so crazed with enthusiasm that they subverted the social order. At the height of the crusade, the work portrayed the wives of respectable citizens locked up with common prostitutes as over-enthusiastic constables swept the streets for all signs of luxury.[113]

Nevertheless, and despite this vital caveat, the bishops' actions in taming legal reformation must be viewed as an important part of William's campaign for legitimation. By posing as the patron of the reformation movements, the king had again presented himself as a true godly magistrate. Moreover, he had involved a considerable portion of the political nation in his moral campaign, and had perhaps cemented them more securely to his regime as a result. Taken together with the attempts to present the virtues of the royal household, and the programme of fasts and thanksgivings, the king's patronage of legal reformation formed an impressive claim for royal authority based on the tenets of Burnet's ideology. Through this initiative the court had given

---

[111] Woodhouse, *Sermon ... reformation of manners*, p. 37.
[112] Bodl. Rawlinson Ms. D 1396, is a register book of warrants issued by magistrates on information supplied by the societies for the prosecution of vicious individuals. It lists numbers of ordinary subjects proceeded against for Sunday trading, drinking, and swearing. For critical publications, see *The modern fanatical reformer, or the religious state tinker* (1693); *The mystery of phanaticism, or the artifices of the dissenters to support their schism* (1698); *The poor man's plea, in relation to all the proclamations, declarations, acts of parliament &c, which have been ... for a reformation of manners* (1698); *Reformation of manners: a satyr* (1702).
[113] *The puritanical justice: or the beggars turn'd thieves. A farce as it was late acted about the city of London* (1698).

concrete expression to its moral promises of 1688, and had gone a considerable way to prove its credentials as a purging instrument of God.

The rest of this book will continue to explore how the Williamites tried to live up to their Revolution rhetoric through further claims to righteous zeal. At the same time, however, it will turn to consider questions wider than the basic justification of Orange rule. The other strategies implemented by Burnet and his allies to sell their master to the English people were also designed to overcome war-weariness and anti-Dutch prejudice, and to allow the king to deal with the problems of parliamentary politics. They thus tackled the difficulties which William had stored up for himself when involving England in his personal crusade against Louis XIV.

⋘ 4 ⋙

Courtly reformation, the war, and the English nation

ENGLISH XENOPHOBIA AND ANTI-WAR SENTIMENT

William III was always extremely vulnerable to anti-Dutch xenophobia in England. Throughout the 1690s, his national origins, his policies, and his personal behaviour, all laid him open to accusations that he was a foreign monarch, with foreign interests at heart. The very Revolution which had brought William to power had been an affront to English sensibilities. Recent studies by Jonathan Israel have shown that the expedition of 1688 was, at base, a Dutch invasion. The adventure was launched in the interests of the United Provinces; Hollanders had provided most of William's navy and army; and those few English soldiers who had defected to the Orange camp were held at arm's length.[1] As the new king took power, his continental priorities, and especially his overriding desire to protect the Netherlands from French aggression, became steadily more apparent. During his first weeks in London, William ordered the English navy to attack Louis XIV's fleet and urged the constitutional convention to come to the Low Countries' military aid.[2] Even before he was crowned, he sent regiments of English soldiers to Flanders to defend the Provinces' borders.[3] Once he was king, William's ambition to secure his original territories involved his new realm in the sort of European entanglement which she had avoided for nearly a century. All this suggested a distance from the English and their concerns. The monarch appeared determined to uphold Dutch interests, whatever the cost to his new subjects.

Critics of William's regime were not slow to take advantage of the opportunities brought by the king's apparent bias towards foreigners. The Jacobites, in particular, exploited English xenophobia and made it the central

---

[1] Jonathan Israel and Geoffrey Parker, 'Of providence and protestant winds: the Spanish armada of 1588 and the Dutch armada of 1688', in Israel, *Anglo-Dutch moment*, pp. 335–64; Israel, 'Dutch role'.

[2] J. R. Jones, *The revolution of 1688 in England* (1972), p. 310; *LJ*, 14, 101–2.

[3] John Childs, *The British army of William III, 1689–1702* (Manchester, 1987), pp. 19–20.

122

element of their rhetoric. From the first, James's supporters played upon fears of Holland's domination, and raised the old spectres of Dutch universal monarchy. One of the very earliest Jacobite pamphlets, a work produced in the autumn of 1688 and entitled *The Dutch design anatomised*, warned the English of a foreign take-over of their country. It told its audience that if William succeeded in his ambitions, Hollanders would soon be stalking the court, the streets of English cities, and the Royal Exchange.[4] Other Jacobite pamphlets appearing over the winter of 1688–9 outlined a Dutch plan to undermine all the key features of English national life. They charged the Hollanders with attempting to snuff out English commerce; with trying to impose excises and other foreign taxes on the people; with hoping to export their tyrannical version of republicanism; and with aspiring to spread their ungodly presbyterian religion.[5]

These first Jacobite publications were hurtful enough, but as time wore on, James's supporters put still further effort into encouraging English xenophobia. The increasingly apparent cost of the king's continental war played into his opponents' hands as the seemingly boundless royal enthusiasm for French defeat allowed them to claim that England was being exploited in a battle not her own. The Dutch, the Jacobites could argue, were using William to bleed his new country dry and were appropriating English troops and coin to obtain security at little cost to themselves. Estimates of the damage done by William's war appeared even before any bills came in. One author, writing very soon after the prince of Orange's seizure of power, listed the results of the Revolution as 'reproach, violence, taxes, blood and poverty'. Under 'taxes' he estimated the cost of war at £3 million per annum. This included the expense of seventy ships to patrol the Channel, 15,000 troops for Flanders, and as many more to defend the English shore. Under 'blood' and 'poverty' he outlined the loss of life and economic disruption of the coming conflict, and concluded that 'these are like to be the sad consequences of this celebrated change'.[6] After England had officially opened hostilities against France, the unfair, draining, and disruptive cost of the conflict became even more central to Jacobite literature. The theme was addressed by numerous clandestine pamphlets, in James's messages to his old subjects, and even by a Dryden

---

[4] *The Dutch design anatomised, or a discovery of the wickedness and unjustice of the intended invasion* (1688), p. 20.

[5] *Some reflections upon his highness the prince of Orange's declaration* (Edinburgh, 1688), pp. 4, 13; *The prince of Orange his declaration, shewing the reasons why he invades England, with a short preface, and some modest remarks on it* (1688), p. 17; *Min Heer T. Van C.'s answer to Min Heer H. Van L.'s letter of the 15th March 1689; representing the true interests of Holland and what they have already gained by our losses* [1689]; *England's crisis: or the world well mended* (1689); *The ballance adjusted: or the interest of church and state weighed and considered upon this revolution* [1689?].

[6] *A remonstrance and protestation of all the good protestants of this kingdom, against deposing their lawful sovereign, king James II* (1689).

prologue spoken (once – before it was banned) from the stage.[7] The very titles of Jacobite works betray their content: *The dear bargain*; *The sad estate of the kingdom*; *The price of the abdication* (that is, James's supposed abdication); *Great Britain's just complaint for her late measures, present sufferings*.[8] All accused the Dutch of seizing control of English affairs and raiding English resources for their own ends.

This polemic was extremely worrying for William's regime. At a basic level, anti-Dutch and anti-war rhetoric risked conversions to James's cause. The government was so nervous about one pamphlet, the *Remarks on the present confederacy* (1693), that it executed its Jacobite printer, William Anderton.[9] Worse still, xenophobia began to cross over to men supposedly loyal to William. As the strains of war grew, anxiety about Dutch power was expressed in parliament, and the Commons came to ring to angry warnings of foreign influence. In the 1690s anger was expressed at Westminster over the number of Dutchmen amongst the king's advisers; over the drain of cash out of the country; over the pensions and land grants given to foreigners; and over the fact that Englishmen were commanded by Hollanders in the armies in Flanders.[10] A flavour of this rhetoric is provided by Sir Thomas Clarges. In the winter of 1692–3 (a Commons session marked by particular sourness towards the Dutch) this parliamentarian spoke repeatedly to warn that England was suffering a vast drain of cash to the Low Countries.[11] In a famous interjection on 9 December, he openly accused Portland of fostering the conditions which allowed this haemorrhage to occur, and accused the duke of favouring his country of origin over his new English home.

I cannot but take notice that though we were drawn into this war by the Dutch – they being the principals – yet we must bear a greater share of the burden. These things, I am afraid, are occasioned by having one of the Dutch [E]states in your council.[12]

Such bitterness continued throughout the war, and shaped politics even after the conflict had finished. In the last year of his reign William found that he had

---

[7] Dryden's prologue for *The prophetess*, which likened the expense of opera to the expense of war, and complained of the current economic recession caused by the conflict, was banned after its first performance in May 1690, H. T. Swedenberg, ed., *The works of John Dryden* (20 vols., Los Angeles, 1969), III, 255–6, 507n.

[8] See also, in the same vein, *The people of England's grievances inquired into* [1693?]; *A letter to a member of the committee of grievances, containing some seasonable reflections on the present administration of affairs, since managed by Dutch councils* [1690].

[9] The Jacobites were able to make political capital out of this, accusing the whole Williamite judiciary of corruption and tyranny. See *A true copy of the paper delivered to the sheriffs of London and Middlesex by William Anderton, at the place of execution* [1693].

[10] See, for example, Luttrell, *Diary*, pp. 243, 267; Cobbett, V, 777, 794; Knight, *Speech ... against the bill*.

[11] For expressions of anti-Dutch feeling in this session, see Luttrell, *Diary*, pp. 250, 288.

[12] *Ibid.* p. 304.

to make concessions to the House of Commons when trying to determine who would gain the English throne after he and his sister-in-law, Anne, had died. In order to secure the succession of the House of Hanover, which he favoured, the king had to reassure the English that they would never again be victims of policies advancing alien interests. As a result, clauses of the 1701 act of settlement, which fixed the succession through the House of Hanover, stated that any future foreigner who came to the throne could only appoint Englishmen as Privy Councillors, and could neither leave the country, nor use English troops to defend foreign possessions, without parliamentary approval.[13] This legislation stood as an implied rebuke to William's lack of English patriotism over the previous ten years.

However, despite the vigour of the Jacobite press, and the signs of real disaffection with William's bias towards Holland, English xenophobia ultimately had only a limited impact on politics in the 1690s. Most importantly, the anti-war sentiment sometimes apparent in parliament proved a relatively minor irritant to the court. As Robert McJimsey has shown, few MPs or peers advanced any real alternative to the European policy William was pursuing; and most parliamentarians restricted their criticism of continental warfare to efficiency or tactics.[14] The Commons readily made money available for William's adventures, and there were many instances of parliamentary enthusiasm for continental escapades.[15] Moreover, attacks upon Hollanders often ran alongside considerable sympathy for their plight. In many quarters, the English and Dutch were recognised as sharing a genuine community of interest. For example on 5 December 1693, Sir Charles Sedley rose in the Commons to berate those who repined at William's request for a large army. Sedley was an MP who frequently spoke and voted with Sir Thomas Clarges against the Treasury bench, yet he could not condone any move which might place the Dutch in danger. The army, he claimed, 'is not so dangerous as is said. It is to defend us from France and popery. If Holland be destroyed, it is our turn next.'[16]

There were several good reasons why the anti-Dutch xenophobia stirred by the Jacobites did not become triumphant. Most obviously, the United Provinces were the nation's chief ally against the French. In the later seventeenth century, France was increasingly seen as England's main strategic and trading rival. A belief that one's enemy's enemy was one's friend may, therefore, have served to limit hatred of the old antagonist. In addition, Louis XIV's support for the discredited James drove many Englishmen into Dutch arms, especially

[13] 12 and 13 William 3 c. 2.
[14] Robert D. McJimsey, 'A country divided? English politics and the Nine Years War', *Albion*, 23 (1991), 61–74.
[15] For instances, see Horwitz, *Parliament, policy and politics*, pp. 53–4, 72, 106; Luttrell, *Diary*, pp. 46–9.
[16] Cobbett, V, 795.

in 1701 when French declarations of Jacobitism encouraged parliamentary support for renewed warfare.[17] However, any explanation of English acceptance of a foreign ruler, and of the need to defend the Netherlands, must include some space for courtly reformation. As its fourth strategy to promote reformation, Burnet's rhetoric provided a neat response to anti-Dutch prejudice. Presenting the king as the champion of an *international* cause, Williamite polemic answered the xenophobic case by advancing a conception of Englishness very different from that held by the king's critics. It eased the royal position by providing an open account of who the English were and a flexible definition of what exactly 'England' was.

VERSIONS OF NATIONALITY

In order to follow the Williamites' strategy, it is necessary to understand the sense of English nationality which the king's propagandists had to combat. The Jacobites, and other critics of William's continental bias, took a largely economic (what might almost be called a 'mercantilist') view of England. As they questioned royal policy, they presented their country as a set of material resources which had to be husbanded for her born citizens. In tracts and speeches which attacked the Dutch, 'England' was portrayed as a stock of men, money, and land, which was in danger of depletion by the activities of strangers. Underpinning this xenophobic vision, was an image of the realm as a glorified gentry household. Colin Brooks has pointed out that many MPs who complained about the costs of William's government in the 1690s conceptualised England by employing an analogy with their own country estates.[18] They saw their nation as a sort of ancient family, with its own fortune, and worried that current extravagance would prevent this inheritance being passed on to the next generation. Such familial imagery was particularly strong amongst Jacobites. They saw James as the father of his people, and presented William and Mary as ungrateful and rebellious children who were ruining the clan's wealth by their ambitious selfishness.[19] This vision of nationality was dangerous to the new regime because it was so exclusive. It first defined the nation as a body of kinsmen – and so denied that a foreign-born monarch could be part of it – and then concentrated on the preservation of national resources – thus casting William, with his tax demands, as a plunderer of England's estate.

The courtly reformers countered this dangerous conception of the nation by advancing a different account of Englishness. Whilst their alternative view was not a direct contradiction of the 'household' vision, it did have a sharply

[17] Luttrell, *Relation*, V, 94; Horwitz, *Parliament, policy and politics*, pp. 296–301.
[18] Brooks, 'Country persuasion', p. 140.
[19] For this rhetoric, see Monod, *Jacobitism*, pp. 55–6.

different focus, which centred around the moral and spiritual condition of the people. For William's propagandists the essence of 'England' – the thing which defined who Englishmen were and which held them together – was not simply a national stock, or a set of inherited resources. Rather, it was a national covenant with the deity. To answer the broadly economic fears of their xenophobic countrymen, Burnet and his circle advanced a 'Hebraic' view of their nation which described it as a body united by its peculiar relationship with God.

The courtly reformers' sense of nationality sprang from their attempts to bring out the full significance of 1688. Endeavouring to present the Revolution as a providential salvation of the true church in England, court spokesmen were drawn to discuss previous occasions on which the deity had apparently intervened to restore pure faith in their nation. Because the reformers found that their account of William's arrival was strengthened if they pointed to other times when the deity had secured English protestantism, they tended to emphasise such earlier events, and consequently presented English history as a series of heavenly deliverances. For example, William Wake drew on a standard catalogue of divine mercies when preaching his eulogy to Mary in 1695. Countering Jacobite suggestions that the queen's death had demonstrated God's anger with the Revolution, he reminded his audience that the deity had repeatedly led protestant Englishmen into danger in order that he might demonstrate his support for them by rescuing them from their plight. As examples the preacher cited the death of Mary Tudor, the miscarriages of conspiracies against Elizabeth, and the discovery of the Gunpowder Plot; and he then drew the advent of William into this series of preservations by adding 1688 to his list.[20]

This use of history fed into a peculiar view of nationality because the reformers offered an explanation for the pattern of divine concern they outlined. They accounted for repeated mercies by suggesting that God had entered into a covenant with the English. They argued that the deity had offered the nation a binding contract, under which he would protect the people, in return for their espousal of his cause. This notion of a national covenant owed much to an old habit of drawing an analogy between England and Old Testament Israel. Since Tudor times, English protestants had sensed that they were specially favoured by God, and had understood their position by analysing the covenants Jehovah had offered to the Jews at Beer-sheba and Sinai.[21] The courtly reformers continued this tradition, and made it a characteristic feature of their Williamite propaganda. Trying to account for the mercy of 1688, they maintained that the English had been taken into the

[20] Wake, *Of our obligation*, p.25.
[21] The best summary of this tendency in Tudor and early Stuart thought is Collinson, *Birthpangs*, ch. 1.

'protection and favour' once enjoyed by the Hebrews and presented their nation as the successors to that first-chosen people.[22] Consequently, the propagandists constantly compared the state of England and Judah, and referred to their nation as 'our Sion', or 'our Israel'. In the bishops' rhetoric London was Jerusalem, whilst William retained his role as David.[23] Burnet made explicit the connection between old and new chosen people when preaching to the House of Lords in 1689. Discussing the Revolution, he claimed, 'we have had as many of the distinguishing characters of the Jewish nation upon us ... as any nation under heaven'.[24]

[God] has given us a plain and simple Religion; he has delivered us from all Bondage, both in Spiritual and Temporal Concerns; and he has sent us mighty Deliverers; *Aarons* in the Church, and *Moses* and *Miriams* in the State, an *Elizabeth* and a MARY, as well as an *Edward*, a *Charles* and a WILLIAM.[25]

John Sharp was as adamant two years later when he argued before his monarchs for a mystical translation of election from Israel to England; and an anonymous pamphleteer of 1694 spoke for the whole courtly reforming camp when apotheosising his country as 'A nation of [God's] peculiar love and protection; the vineyard which his own right hand hath planted, and watered, and fenced, and preserved both night and day, ... the signet on his right hand, and the labour of his endearing love'.[26]

At first sight this 'Hebraic' view of England might appear no less exclusive than the alternative 'household' vision. There may seem nothing in it which could solve the problem of William's foreignness since Hebraism contained a strong sense of national identity, a feeling of specialness, and a belief in English separation from the rest of mankind. Indeed, Linda Colley, in her stimulating work on Britishness in the eighteenth century, has used the identification with Israel to portray a confident pride in country, which gave her subjects a sense of who they were by contrasting them with a foreign 'other'.[27] Yet, studied again, the courtly reformers' sense of nationality can be

---

22 The quote is from Gilbert Burnet, *A sermon preached at Bow church before the court of aldermen on March 12 1689/90, being the fast day* (1690), p. 10.

23 William Wake was especially fond of presenting William as David. See Wake, *Sermon ... House of Commons ... 5 June 1689*, p. 27; William Wake, *A sermon preach'd before the Lord-Mayor ... on Thursday 26 November, being the day of the publick thanksgiving* (1691); William Wake, *A sermon preached in the parish church of St James Westminster, April 26 1696, being the day of thanksgiving* (1696). See also Thomas Tension, *A sermon concerning holy resolution preached before the king at Kensington, December 30 1694* (1695).

24 Burnet, *Sermon ... House of Peers ... 5 November 1689*, pp. 3–4.

25 *Ibid.* p. 7.

26 John Sharp, *A sermon preach'd before the king and queen at Whitehall, 12 Nov. 1693, being the day appointed for a publick thanksgiving* (1693), pp. 22–3; *Proposals for a national reformation of manners, humbly offered to the consideration of our magistrates and clergy* (1694), p. 3.

27 Linda Colley, *Britons: forging the nation, 1707–1837* (1992), ch. 1

seen to have been more open than this rather exclusive model. English Hebraism contained two ambiguities which allowed its adherents to shift and redefine the boundaries of Englishness. In the hands of Burnet and his allies these ambiguities could be exploited to anglicise a foreign king, and even to suggest that William's wars, damaging as they appeared to the nation's narrowly material interests, were in fact England's highest national duty.

THE NATIONALISATION OF THE KING

The first ambiguity in the Williamites' Hebraism was its curious lack of confidence. Although royal rhetoric presented the English as a chosen nation, it also reminded the people that their salvation, either temporal or eternal, was not secure. The analogy between England and Israel could provide comfort in times of adversity, but it also made it clear that the national covenant with God did not guarantee continuing protection. The Old Testament was not an idyllic story of unbroken divine favour. Rather, it was a chronicle of judgements upon a backsliding people. The Jews had suffered plagues, defeats, and famines as punishment for their incorrigible sins, and had eventually been scattered when Jehovah lost patience with his children. Jewish history thus proved that God's grace towards a people would always be conditional, and that chosen nations had continually to earn their blessings by obedience to divine law.

This sense of insecure election fed an uneasy uncertainty into Williamite propaganda. Burnet and his circle argued that, whilst England's position as a new Israel was a privilege, this very status meant that she was subject to the same judgement which had hung over the Jews. The English were on trial, the bishops warned, and, like their predecessors, would be destroyed if they did not improve their moral and spiritual condition. In the very Lords' sermon in which Burnet had drawn out the similarities between the English and the Hebrews, he compared the two nations in their sins as well as their blessings. For him, the 'distinguishing characters' that marked England as a new Israel included ingratitude to God. The bishop chillingly observed that the 'parallel' between the two cases agreed 'too exactly', and reminded his audience that God's favour to the Jews had lasted no longer than their observation of his covenant.[28] John Tillotson similarly warned his countrymen of the consequences of their chosen status. He told them that just as the English resembled the Jews 'in their many and wonderful deliverances', they also mirrored them 'too much in their faults and follies'.[29] For Edward Fowler also, the analogy

---

[28] Burnet, *Sermon ... House of Peers ... 5 November 1689*, pp. 3, 6, 12.
[29] John Tillotson, *A sermon preach'd at St Mary le Bow before the Lord Mayor ... of London on Wed. 18 June, a day appointed by their majesties for a solemn monthly fast* (1690), p. 25.

between England and Israel was a cause for consternation rather than rejoicing. Addressing the London Corporation on a fast day he exclaimed

O let us not of *this City*, and *this Kingdom*, be acting the *Israelites* still over and over, those fearfully hardened People who had even made a Covenant with death. .... [If the English did this] we are more desperate than *they* were, because we are fore-warned of the dismal consequence of such doings, by their fearful Example.[30]

The element of Hebraism in courtly reformation rhetoric thus transformed Williamite propaganda into a haunted language of apprehension. The sermons which promoted the king's cause were frequently jeremiads, which echoed the lamentations of Old Testament prophets. The bishops even took surprisingly little comfort from 1688. At the Revolution, they asserted, God had proved that he still cared about the English nation. Yet the people's behaviour since that deliverance threatened to reverse their special blessing. In particular, fast sermons and the propaganda of the societies for reformation of manners used Hebrew scriptures to express horror at the state of England. To take just two examples, Edward Fowler and Simon Patrick berated their fellow subjects in fast sermons in 1690 and 1692. The former preacher wanted to know 'what reformation hath our late deliverance wrought amongst us', whilst the latter asked 'are we not lovers of pleasure, more than lovers of God?'[31]

This ambiguity within English Hebraism was important because it allowed the courtly reformers to nationalise their king. Since the analogy between England and Old Testament Israel contained a brooding fear of failure as well as a sense of election, it undermined any celebratory nationalism, and posed questions about whether the English were so different from the rest of mankind. A language which insisted that a chosen people might lose their status cast doubt upon that people's separation from other nations, and opened the way for a more inclusive account of nationality which might even include space for William III. In the 1690s the courtly reformers exploited these possibilities within their rhetoric. Using the strange lack of confidence within English Hebraism they developed three strategies by which they might admit the foreign-born William to a version of English nationality, and counter the damaging impression that he still had Dutch interests to heart.

First, William's spokesmen used Hebraism to discourage any direct connection between the hardships England was suffering and the king's policy of protecting Holland with English arms. Within the Hebraic worldview, national misfortunes were to be analysed, not simply in temporal terms, but as trials or judgements, episodes in the divine drama of God's dealings with his people. The bishops' favourite explanation for the costs of war was,

---

30 Fowler, *Sermon ... Bow-Church April 16 1690*, p. 21.
31 *Ibid.* p. 27; Patrick, *Sermon ... Whitehall, 8 April 1692*, p. 12.

therefore, that they were just deserts for the people's failings. This distracted attention from the king's part in bringing hardship on England, and neatly transferred blame to the English themselves. Thus in a speech delivered to the clergy of his Salisbury diocese, Burnet urged that when flocks complained of England's fortunes, they should be told to reflect on their own part in bringing disasters about.

If some years are less prosperous than others have been, we ought to reflect on former Successes, and the ill use that we have made of them, which may have provoked God to change his methods ... Can one reflect on the Blasphemy and Infidelity, the dissolution of all good Morals, and the Impieties and Vices of all sorts that are among us, and not wonder rather, that we have not been made a scene of Earthquakes and Ruins, as *Sicily, Malta* and *Jamaica* have of late been. It is to these sins that we ought to turn the minds of our people, when they are at any time dejected with ill success.[32]

Royal proclamations reinforced this message, stressing that an end to national sufferings, particularly through victory in the war, depended on individual Englishmen propitiating God, as much as on royal policy.

Second, the bishops deployed Hebraism to advance a new account of national loyalty which could turn William into an English patriot. This account began from the simple assumption that sin could be equated with treason. The unrepentant were disloyal to their nation because they risked the withdrawal of God's protection, and all the dangers which would follow from that. Burnet spelled this out towards the end of William's reign, telling sinners they were no less treacherous than the Jacobite conspirators who invited in French force. Now that many of the English walked in luxury, and now that atheism and impiety stalked the land, 'storms may shatter our fleets, and if God should for our sins deliver us so far to the enemy that they should but once land upon us, how naked and defenceless are we?'[33] The obvious reverse of this view of treason was an account of patriotism, which defined it as zeal for reformation. Since those who followed God's law secured blessings on England, they were truly loyal. Preaching to the prince of Orange on 20 February 1688/9, Simon Patrick stated that anyone who 'loves his country' would have to 'do his part' in bringing the nation back to its primitive purity.[34] All 'estates and conditions of men', Patrick assured the prince's retinue, 'are obliged to discharge their several duties conscientiously; that they may contribute to the peace and quietness, prosperity and happiness of the society whereof they are members'.[35] Tillotson echoed this a year later. He told the House of Commons that the only way for men 'to engage the

---

[32] Gilbert Burnet, *Four discourses delivered to the clergy of the diocese of Sarum* (1694), preface, pp. 18–19.

[33] Burnet, *Charitable reproof*, p. 26.

[34] Simon Patrick, *A sermon preached in the chappel of St James' before his highness, the prince of Orange, 20 January 1688* (1689), p. 34.

[35] *Ibid.* p. 35.

providence of God for us' was to do all they could, in their 'several places from the highest to the lowest ... to retrieve the ancient piety and virtue of the nation'.[36] The clear implication of this rhetoric was that William could be an English patriot. Since the king's campaign of reformation would bring down God's blessings, it proved his concern for his new realm. The presentation of the monarch as a purging ruler therefore became a simultaneous assertion of his love of England.

Third, Burnet and his circle exploited Hebraism to present William as the very embodiment of his new nation. The case here was built on two principles (discoverable from close reading of the Old Testament) by which God decided when a nation was ripe for punishment. First, the bishops pointed out that the righteous often brought disproportionate relief for a sinful nation. Though usually a minority, they could act as intercessors for their people to God, convincing him that an otherwise debauched and incorrigible nation was still worth protecting. Effectively, they became national attorneys, men whose virtue could represent that of the general population. The bishops proved this from the Hebraic analogy, making much use of passages such as Genesis 18:32, where the Lord promised not to destroy Sodom if he could find ten righteous men there. In 1690, Edward Fowler applied the principle to contemporary England, warning of impending judgements on English sinfulness, but speculating that God's punishment might be delayed. Fowler could not tell 'how merciful he may be to us, for the sake of his great name; or what respect he may yet farther have to the intercessions of those many good people in the land, who sigh and mourn for the abominations of it'.[37] He went on to suggest that if a way could be found for those good men to discipline the 'blacker crimes' of their neighbours, 'we know not what blessings such a partial reformation may prove for us'.[38] Preaching in the same year, William Lloyd agreed. Having stated that those who would not reform could not be good subjects, he urged his audience at court to strive for purity of life.[39] 'Oh! if we could all attain to this! if any number of us could do it! I will not say the whole nation, but if a considerable part of it! What favours might we not hope, the whole nation would have for their sakes?'[40]

To this principle of minority intercession, the bishops added the second observation that God paid particular attention to political authorities when reviewing the moral state of the nation. They pointed out that the magistrate's

---

[36] John Tillotson, *A sermon preached before the honourable House of Commons on Wednesday 16 April. A day appointed by their majesties for a solemn monthly fast* (1690), pp. 32–3. See, in a similar vein, Sharp, *Sermon ... House of Commons ... Wed 21 May 1690*, pp. 36–7.

[37] Fowler, *Sermon ... Bow Church ... April 16 1690*, p. 32.

[38] *Ibid.* p. 32.

[39] William Lloyd, *A sermon preached before the king and queen at Whitehall, March the twelfth 1689/90, being the fast day* (1690), pp. 30–1.

[40] *Ibid.* p. 31.

obligation to suppress godlessness was more onerous than that of the private man, since rulers owed their very position to the need to control sin. The biblical text, Romans 13:3–4, which explained temporal power as a divine grant made with the intention that governors suppress evil, became a reformation favourite. Holding this view of authority, Williamites saw any magisterial failure to impose reform as a particularly heinous example of treachery. The Williamites insisted God saw a nation as worthy of punishment, less when sin became widespread, than at the moment when the magistrates ceased to check it. It was, Simon Patrick claimed, 'this bold commission of sin *without correction*' (my emphasis), which God would 'account the sin of the kingdom'. 'It will lie especially at the door of the magistrates and officers of justice, if they can, and yet will not redress such impieties.'[41] Edward Stillingfleet underlined this with the essential biblical analogy.[42] He told the story of the punishment of Israel in Eli's time when the ark of the covenant was lost to the Philistines (1 Samuel chs. 2–4). Stillingfleet showed the greatest fault for this tragedy lay with the magistrate Eli, because he did not restrain his two sons who had set the people a sinful example. 'It was not for Eli's personal miscarriages, that God thought himself so dishonoured by him, but for want of taking due care for the suppressing profaness and corruptions of manners in others.'[43] Since Stillingfleet pointed out that the loss of the tabernacle was a *national* punishment (the ark was the symbol of Israel's deliverance from bondage and idolatry), it is clear that the bishop saw the magistrate as standing for the nation in God's eyes. Eli was punished in his private capacity by the loss of his sons in battle with the Philistines. The nation as a whole, however, had to bear a punishment occasioned by Eli's failings as a ruler. It was magisterial negligence which effectively nationalised sin, and provoked God to vengeance on the whole people.

Bringing their two principles together, the courtly reformers used them to suggest that William, in a sense, could become England. Since God was prepared to accept the righteousness of the few as the justification of the many, and since he paid particular attention to magistrates, William could become the supreme intercessor for, and representative of, his people. By pursuing his campaign of reformation, William could thus become more than a patriot for his new nation. He could become the very embodiment of it. His actions could stand for its actions, and it could receive blessings for his sole sake. Edward Fowler brought out the implications of this in a sermon preached in 1690. Asking why God had not yet punished such an incorrigibly

---

41 Patrick, *Sermon ... Whitehall ... 8 April 1692*, p. 19.
42 Edward Stillingfleet, *Reformation of manners, the true way of honouring God. With the necessity of putting the laws in execution against vice and profaness. In a sermon preach'd at Whitehall* [1709?]. This sermon was probably first delivered on 29 Nov. 1691.
43 *Ibid.* p. 12.

sinful nation as his own, he found part of the solution in William's person and the programme of courtly reformation which he had instituted. Fowler reflected upon the continued blessings enjoyed by the English and told his audience they could not tell if the divine hand had been stayed by

these *Monthly Days* of Humiliation [the public fast days] (which Their Majesties, like Religious and Pious Princes, have obliged us to the Observance of) as they are a *Publick Owning of Him*, and Solemn Acknowledgements of his absolute Soveraignty over us, and of our ill-deserving at his hands, in the Face of the World: ... Or whether God may still be merciful to us and prosper our Forces by Land and Sea, for the sake of that Glorious Work, he is *now* in all likelihood a doing in the World, (wherein we trust he will make our Soveraign a Blessed Instrument) we know not.[44]

In such rhetoric the bishop's Hebraic view of nationality had produced an almost complete identification between king and realm. William's drive to reform morals, considered in the light of England's covenant with God, had nationalised the foreign-born monarch.

THE NATIONALISATION OF THE WAR

Aside from its inherent anxiety about punishment and failure, the Williamites' Hebraism contained a second ambiguity, which could anglicise the king's war with France, as well as his person. Despite providing the English with a strong sense of their special status, the language of reformation denied that they had been set aside from the rest of mankind. The chosen people were presented as the particular recipients of God's favour, but, paradoxically, were also shown to be only one small part of a godly international.

The tension between the national and the universal had always been present in English Hebraism. The ambiguity had initially emerged as writers tried to identify the new Israel within the framework of Calvinist thought which dominated Tudor protestantism. 'Israel' was, by definition, the collective name for God's people. Calvinism, however, made it impossible to identify this people with any earthly nation since the creed's theory of predestination by inscrutable divine will made it most unlikely that any national body of men and women would coincide with God's true church. Even if a nation appeared outwardly righteous, Calvinists insisted it was likely to contain many reprobate hypocrites, who were damned because they had not received the gift of grace.[45] They thus had difficulty conceiving of an unproblematic godly nation, and showed an increasing tendency to limit their

---

[44] Fowler, *Sermon ... Bow Church ... April 16 1690*, pp. 31–2.

[45] For discussion of the problems Calvinism caused the idea of an elect nation, see Jane Facey, 'John Foxe and the defence of the English church', and Catherine Davies, ' "Poor persecuted little flock" or "commonwealth of Christians": Edwardian protestant concepts of the true church', both in Peter Lake and Maria Dowling, eds., *Protestantism and the national church in sixteenth-century England* (1987), pp. 162–92 and 78–102; Michael McGifford, 'God's controversy with Jacobean England', *AHR*, 88 (1983), 1151–74.

definition of Israel. By the early Stuart period, the term was widely used to refer, not to England as a whole, but to the hidden remnant within it.[46] Moreover, Calvinist soteriology made it unlikely that the Holy Spirit would confine its attentions to a single nation. Tudor protestants saw the true church as a universal body, which was scattered throughout Europe in many kingdoms, and existed wherever isolated individuals received God's grace. Thus despite claims by the historian William Haller that John Foxe's *Acts and monuments* established England as the true elect nation, the Calvinist author of the book of martyrs was not himself convinced that God's people were contained within England's political boundaries.[47] He viewed the survival of the godly as a European drama and made the Frenchman Waldo, the Czech Hus, and the German Luther, heroes of his story. Patrick Collinson has summarised this universalism by writing of the Tudor sense 'that the church achieved its truest identity above nationality'. He charted the resulting confusions in English Hebraism, which could use 'Israel' to mean the universal and international community of the godly; or the temporal English nation, or the righteous remnant in England, or an ambiguous combination of these.[48]

Burnet and his circle cleared up some of this difficulty for themselves by abandoning rigid Calvinism. Like most of their contemporaries (though not the king), they had moved towards a 'holy living' soteriology before 1688, which insisted that the divine gift of grace was, to some degree, conditional upon repentance and efforts to a righteous life.[49] This shifted responsibility for salvation from God's irresistible gift, towards the efforts of the sinner, and incidentaly allowed a less troublesome identification of England with Israel. Under the new theology, it was always possible that the whole English population might be persuaded to repent, and so become a true people of God by all gaining election. However, despite clarifying the conception of a godly nation, Burnet and his circle were no less ambiguous than their Tudor predecessors about England's peculiar status within Christendom, since their new doctrine forbade any exalted claims for English uniqueness as effectively as Calvinism had done. Precisely because the bishops had less room for God's inscrutable gifts of grace, and because they argued that simple repentance was the qualification for election, they were unable to claim any special favour

---

[46] See Collinson, *Birthpangs*, pp. 20–7.

[47] Haller, *Foxe's 'Book of martyrs'*.

[48] Collinson, *Birthpangs*, ch. 1. See also Firth, *Apocalyptic tradition*, pp. 106–9; Bauckham, *Tudor apocalypse*, p. 86; David Loades, 'The origins of English protestant nationalism', and A. J. Fletcher, 'The first century of English protestantism and the growth of national identity', both in Stuart Mews, ed., *Religion and national identity* (Oxford, 1982), pp. 297–308 and 309–19 respectively.

[49] The standard work on this theological shift is C. F. Allison, *The rise of moralism* (1966). For the future courtly reformers' role in promoting holy living theology, see John Spurr, ' "Latitudinarianism" and the Restoration church', *HJ*, 31 (1988), 61–82; Hill, *Turbulent, seditious and factious people*, pp. 130–5.

bestowed upon Englishmen. In the propagandists' theology, their country-
men might become Israel by living in righteousness – but this was an option
available to all other peoples. There was nothing peculiar or mysterious about
the way the English might gain God's favour: it was laid out in the bible for all
mankind. The bishops did admit that, in the sixteenth century, God had given
the English special providential help to further their Reformation, but they
were also heirs to the Tudor tradition of studying European history as a
whole, and accordingly admitted that the Lord had been active elsewhere at
the birth of godly protestantism. Thus, although some of the beliefs and
structures of the English ecclesia were unique, the Williamites never used
these features to deny that foreign protestants were part of God's true church.
Burnet demonstrated this clearly when prefacing one of his most impassioned
comparisons between England and Israel with a warning that his audience
must listen 'without any arrogant preferring our own nation to others, or any
partiality for our selves, in imagining that we are God's favourite people'.[50]

All this left Williamite rhetoric in some confusion. Consideration of
England's past deliverances suggested she was special. Yet, since the covenant
which explained these deliverances was identical to covenants God might
reach with other nations, full analysis of it undermined England's uniqueness.
This ambiguity ran through the whole courtly reformation campaign. Burnet,
for instance, celebrated England's avoidance of the disasters which had
recently afflicted European protestants. Yet he denied that God had given his
kingdom any special security against them. Short of repentance, there was no
way to be sure what had happened abroad would not happen in his own
country. In an unpublished sermon on William's first fast day he told
members of the court that the persecution faced by protestants in France,
Hungary, Piedmont, and Transylvania, and the military danger faced by
those in Holland and Ireland, contained a message of direct relevance to their
own country.[51] In his *Discourse of the pastoral care* (1692), he told his
readers to 'look at the instruments of the calamities that have fallen so heavily
on so many protestant churches'.[52] Similarly, Simon Patrick, writing to the
clergy in Ely in the year Burnet's book was published, told them

you ought to warn your People of the heavy Judgements of God, which the sins of the
Land give us just cause to apprehend; and that the rather, since God has spared us so
long, whilst he has visited so many Nations round about us in so terrible a manner.[53]

On their own, these warnings about possible punishments might simply be
taken as more reminders of God's conditional favour upon his favourite

---

[50] Burnet, *Sermon ... House of Peers ... 5 November 1689*, p. 3.
[51] Burnet, *Some sermons*, p. 39.
[52] Gilbert Burnet, *A discourse of the pastoral care* (1692), preface, p. x.
[53] Simon Patrick, *A letter of the bishop of Chichester to his clergy* (1690), p. 2.

people. Yet other examples of courtly reformation rhetoric make it clear that a genuinely international vision lay behind such pronouncements. The reformers' Hebraic language (which seemed at first to set the English apart) also had the effect of reabsorbing them into some sort of universal church. For example, on 26 November 1689, Gilbert Burnet preached a sermon at St Lawrence Jewry which implied that English protestants were unique, but which also suggested that they were but one part of a larger godly entity. Essentially this address was an appeal to national unity based on the text Acts 7:26. It included the phrase 'Ye are brethren' and gave two accounts of what these words implied for his audience.[54] The first was straightforward enough, and contained a strong sense of English nationality. The congregation were brethren because they were Englishmen: they were bonded together because they were united by the same laws, lived under the same ruler, and inhabited the same island.[55] The second account was, however, much less clear. After commenting upon a unifying Englishness, Burnet used the Jewish analogy, and the idea of a covenant, to unite his auditors in brotherhood. At precisely this moment in his oratory, Hebraic language began to disrupt the preacher's national sense. 'In this "Ye are Brethren"', Burnet stated,

there is a closer relation implied; That as the *Jews* were all *Brethren* with regard to that Covenant to which they had a Right, as they were *Abraham*'s Seed; so we *Christians* are *Brethren*, as we profess the same common Christianity, and look for the same common Salvation. As we are *Christians*, or as we are *Protestants* we are *Brethren*, believing the same Gospel, owning the same God.[56]

In this passage the Jewish covenant became the type, not of a peculiar English relationship with God (there was no such thing), but of a covenant offered to all protestants. This implied a brotherhood of all those of the reformed faith, and so allowed a vision of the church universal to break through the English-ness outlined in the early minutes of Burnet's speech. From this point on it was not clear whether the preacher was taking a national, or a supranational, view of his situation. He slid unconsciously between his two visions, speaking of English national history, but also of events in the Savoy, Germany, and France as if they were part of the same story. In a passage towards the end, the preacher told his audience they stood at the beginning of a deliverance from bondage, and could be 'made one of the most glorious nations that ever was'. Yet it was not clear whether the nation referred to was England, or whether it was a sort of spiritual nation, uniting all European protestants. The evidence for deliverance consisted of the close union of the British 'kingdoms' (my emphasis) with the United Provinces, and the fact that the 'great persecutor of

[54] Gilbert Burnet, *An exhortation to peace and union in a sermon preached at St Lawrence-Jury on Tuesday 26 November 1689* (1689).
[55] *Ibid.* pp. 6–10.   [56] *Ibid.* p. 10.

protestants' (Louis XIV) had raised a strong alliance of princes against himself. Burnet also stated that the deliverance could not be complete until the Irish had been rescued from popery. All this implied that William's work for England was just one small part of the process.[57] The blessings that God was promising were intended for the English, but not solely for the English.

Eight months later, Burnet's shadowy universalism emerged even more clearly from his Hebraism. Giving a fast sermon to court in July 1690 the preacher performed his usual trick of relating Jewish history to draw contemporary lessons. Yet the lessons this time were not for England, but were rather for the whole of reformed Christianity. The Israelite backslidings and punishments were types of a series of international crises which European protestantism had had to face as one body. These had included such periods as the 1550s (when catholic rulers in both England and France had started to roll back the Reformation in their realms); the 1580s (when both the Dutch and the English had faced the power of Spain); and the 1620s (when protestantism everywhere was put at risk by the disastrous early years of the Thirty Years War). Burnet was careful to present the latest crisis, the one resolved by William's intervention in England, as similarly European. It had started in 1685, the date not only of James's popish accession in England, but of the revocation of the edict of Nantes which had opened the way to persecution of the protestant Huguenot population of France, and of Louis XIV's pressure on the protestants on the Rhine.[58] Burnet's reading of God's new Israel transcended national divisions to unite all reformed religions in common peril, suffering, and resistance.

In so far as the confusion between the English and the universal was resolved in Burnetine rhetoric, it was so through the subordination of local patriotism to supranationalism. The bishops found in the bible a way to reconcile national and universal impulses which their own scriptural studies had produced. Using the Isaiahan formula that God had never intended to confine his grace to Israel, but had wanted that country to be 'a light to the gentiles' (Isaiah 49:6), the bishops could assure England that she could be a special nation, but only by zeal in the *international* protestant cause. England's true destiny, like Israel's, came not through setting herself aside from other nations, but by being the blessed core of God's world community. Burnet asked England to be a beacon 'with a benign influence on all the foreign churches'.[59] She was to be the 'pattern and glory' of the Reformation, and had a chance to become 'more and more, that which she truly is, the

---

[57] *Ibid.* pp. 18–19.
[58] Gilbert Burnet, *A sermon preached before the queen at Whitehall on 16 July 1690, being the monthly fast* (1690), pp. 24–8.
[59] Burnet, *Essay . . . late queen*, p. 147.

praise of all the churches, and the joy of the whole earth'.[60] William Lloyd shared these hopes. He talked of the Lord's 'meaning to set us up like a light on a hill, that we should be a pattern to all other nations'.[61]

So far, the ambiguity between the national and the universal in Williamite rhetoric has been discussed as if it were an illogical flaw in their argument. In fact, however, it was one of the language's great strengths as propaganda. By confusing the grounds for England's separateness, and incorporating the country within a protestant international, the bishops could address criticism of William's continental wars. They could try to sell the king's battles to protect protestants abroad as vital to England's true national interests. If the country's destiny could be presented bound up with the whole European Reformation, William's military exploits could be interpreted as a defence of an international church of which England was the heart and core.

Williamite use of a universal cause to justify their leader's military action was first evident during the invasion of England. Jonathan Israel has suggested that in 1688 the Orange camp tried to avoid discussion of the European situation. He has pointed out that William's *Declaration* did not analyse events outside England, and has claimed that this omission was part of a deliberate strategy to minimise Dutch involvement in the expedition.[62] This may have been true of the manifesto itself, but it did not hold for the rest of Orange propaganda. Other productions were willing to risk resentment at Dutch interference, and boldly placed William's adventure in a European context. The invasion was described as part of an international protestant crusade, in which Holland and England must be partners. For example, the biographies of the prince which appeared in 1688 sold him as an appropriate ruler of England by advertising his record as a protestant commander abroad.[63] His resistance to the French in the Netherlands was presented as his best qualification for the crown. Another pamphlet lengthened the focus to show that the Orange family had engaged in a generations-long, and Europe-wide, struggle against the false church.[64] In a similar vein, the speech William gave to his troops as they embarked emphasised that he was the commander of God's *international* forces. He boasted that his army was composed of men of many countries, and warned that England and the United Provinces, the

---

[60] Burnet, *Sermon ... Whitehall ... 19 October 1690*, p. 35; Burnet, *Exhortation to peace and union*, p. 24.

[61] Lloyd, *Sermon ... May 29 ... king and royal family*, p. 24. See also Sharp's presentation of the church of England as a pillar of the international protestant cause in John Sharp, *To the reverend clergy of the diocese of York* (1699), p. 1.

[62] Israel, 'Dutch role', pp. 122–4.

[63] *Character [of William ...]*; *Character of his royal highness*.

[64] *The history of the most illustrious William, prince of Orange: deduced from the first founders of the ancient house of Nassau, together with the most considerable actions of this present prince* (1688).

protestant pillars of Europe, must stand together if they were to defeat 'the cankered hearts of our irreconcilable enemies'.[65] Later, Gilbert Burnet, in his St James's sermon, treated William's enterprise as a salvation for protestants everywhere. The man who had once saved Holland now offered 'a check to the spirit of persecution, which [had] of late raged so furiously against our brethren in so many different places of Europe'.[66]

Once William was crowned, and had taken the English into alliance with the Dutch, this supranational rhetoric of crusade was maintained. In fact, it was remarkable how loyal the king's propagandists were to it. It dominated the regime's justification of conflict, even in theatres where less 'universal' languages were available. In the case of the Irish war, for instance, the ideal of a pan-European church was upheld, despite the close links between London and Dublin, which might have suggested a more parochially 'British' approach to the problem of selling this particular struggle.

The situation in Ireland before 1691 was very threatening to the English regime. As soon as William had come to power in Westminster, forces loyal to James had risen against Orange rule, and had been joined by French troops and the old king himself. Although the protestant population was loyal to the London government, and held on to enclaves in Ulster, the Jacobites rapidly overcame resistance and controlled most of the country by the autumn of 1689. Expeditions were sent to help the Williamite Irish, but progress was disappointing, and Orange armies were tied up fighting the revolt for two years.[67] To support this military effort, it might have been possible for government propagandists to develop a feeling of 'Britishness'. They could have encouraged a sense of community between the peoples of the British Isles, and then appealed to the English to help fellow Britons as they faced a foreign invasion. To some extent, the king's spokesmen attempted this. They claimed that Ireland was legally part of England, and argued that whoever was crowned in Westminster Abbey, was automatically ruler in Dublin.[68] Yet this was about the limit of a 'British' dimension in Williamite propaganda. Rather than develop a patriotism which would include the inhabitants of both islands, Burnet and his allies handled the Irish war by gearing straight up from an English, to a universalist, rhetoric. Their language never spoke of 'Britain', but instead recognised only a chosen nation (England) on the one hand, and the pan-European cause on the other.

---

[65] William III, *The prince of Orange his speech in defence of the protestant religion* (1688).
[66] Burnet, *Sermon ... St James'* ... *23 December 1688*, p. 4.
[67] See David Hayton, 'The Williamite revolution in Ireland, 1689–91', in Israel, *Anglo-Dutch moment*, pp. 185–214; J. C. Simms, 'Schomberg at Dundalk', in his *War and Politics in Ireland 1649–1730* (1986), pp. 91–104.
[68] The 1689 declaration of rights had assumed this constitutional connection, offering William and Mary the crown of 'England, France, Ireland and the dominions thereunto belonging', Cobbett, V, 110–11.

The language surrounding William's personal expedition to Ireland in 1690 proves the point. On 14 June, the king landed at Belfast to lead his forces against the rebellion. Soon after disembarking he went to divine service and heard a 'most eloquent sermon' by George Royse, a chaplain travelling in the royal party who had been recommended for his post by John Tillotson.[69] Royse's task was to provide pious encouragement for the military campaign ahead. He did so by reminding the army of the eternal battle between the two Europe-wide churches.

How much the general interest of the Reformed Church and Religion does depend upon the present Juncture and success of things, I need not tell you; and since God has interposed his word for the Maintenance of his True Religion in the World, we may reasonably build our confidence on this, and face our Enemies with a true heart and courage.[70]

Royse demonstrated that William was not a national, or a British, ruler only, but a universal instrument of God's providence, who acted in many different realms to secure the true religion. He had come from saving Holland's reformation, to save England's, and had now come to promote God's cause in Ireland. William was 'a prince, who as he was miraculously brought amongst us to begin our deliverance, so he seems to be acted now by a new commission from heaven to complete it'.[71] William's own speech on his landing in Belfast echoed these universal themes. He presented his life as one of service to his deity which had taken him right across Europe in defence of protestantism.[72] William's thanking the duke of Schomberg for his command in Ireland may also have served to remind his audience of the international protestantism of his forces. Schomberg was a half-English, half-German protestant, who had been in Dutch service since fleeing France with the Huguenots on the revocation of the edict of Nantes.[73]

Williamite propaganda for the rest of the 1690 campaign stuck to these themes. For example, the newsletters, which kept Londoners informed of events over the water, did not develop a sense of 'British' community. In them, William's allies abroad were described as 'protestants', whilst his enemies were labelled 'the Irish'. An Englishman's friends in the west were thus linked to him by a universal term, whilst the national name of another 'British'

---

[69] Sir Robert Southwell to the earl of Nottingham, 15 June 1690, *HMC Finch*, II, 298.
[70] George Royse, *A sermon preached before the king at Belfast on 14 June 1690* (1691), p. 20.
[71] *Ibid*. p. 21.
[72] *A full account of King William's royal voyage and safe arrival at the castle of Belfast in Ireland* (1690).
[73] Schomberg himself could be presented as a supranational leader of the protestant cause. See *His grace the duke of Schomberg's character ... together with some old prophecies, fore-telling the conquest of that kingdom by the protestant army under his grace's command* [1689].

people was used to tag foes.[74] This message was rammed home in sermons by Irish clerics, printed ballads, and plays published in London as the Irish battles unfolded. All of these stressed religious, rather than 'British', links between William's army and its local supporters.[75] Gilbert Burnet capped the campaign with a thanksgiving sermon for the king's success. William, he said, had been born with very few advantages, but now had the hopes of all the continent fixed upon him. It was from this monarch that 'Europe expects liberty and peace, and the Reformation a recovery and a new lustre'.[76]

The international language of godly crusade also dominated discussion of the Flemish war. At first sight, it appears obvious why this should be so. An appeal to protestant solidarity should have been appropriate to sell the defence of the reformed Dutch against papist French invaders. Unfortunately, however, the propagandists' task with regard to the Low Countries was not as simple as this, since William's conflict in Flanders was not an unambiguous clash of faiths. In the Low Countries, the king *was* fighting to protect a reformed nation, but this religious end was not his prime objective. His chief desire was to restrain French ambitions, and in order to achieve this, he had made pacts with catholic states. In the period before 1689, William had persuaded Spain and the Austrian Empire into his camp, and had even exploited the pope's francophobia.[77]

In this inconvenient situation, it might have been possible for Williamites to abandon reformation rhetoric, and stress the importance of restraining Louis on secular grounds. They might have talked about the strategic and commercial dangers of allowing France to dominate Europe, and explicitly endorsed a 'balance of power' doctrine. Yet, like the 'British' language for Ireland, this option was rejected. William's camp did sometimes mention the 'geo-political' or economic threat posed by Louis XIV, and occasionally drew attention to the wide spectrum of powers (including catholic powers) opposed to him.[78] Nevertheless, the emotional heart of their appeal remained the doctrine of reformation. In his 1692 speech to parliament, William admitted he

---

[74] See, for example, *A true and perfect journal of the affairs in Ireland since his majesties arrival in the kingdom* (1690); *A true and faithful account of the present condition of the kingdom of Ireland* (1690); *A full account of the two great victories lately obtained before Limerick by K. William's forces over the French and Irish rebels* (1690); *Great news from Limerick giving an account of the successful victory over the Irish rebels* (1690).

[75] See, for example, Edward Weterhall, *A sermon preached at Whitehall, before the queen, on the fourth Sunday in Lent, March 22 1690, reflecting on the late sufferings and deliverances of the protestants in the city and county of Cork* (Cork, 1691); *The soldiers return, or his promise to his country-men perform'd* [1690]; *The valiant souldiers misfortune: or his grace the duke of Schomberg's last farewell* [1690]; *The couragious souldiers of the west* [1690]; *The royal flight, or the conquest of Ireland* (1690); *The royal voyage, or the Irish expedition* (1690).

[76] Burnet, *Sermon ... Whitehall ... 19 October 1690*, pp. 16, 17, 26.

[77] Carswell, *Descent on England*, p. 126.   [78] *LJ*, 17, 6.

was in league 'with most of the princes and states of Europe' but went on to stress his defence of God's cause, and requested support from all who had 'any zeal for our religion'.[79]

The courtly reformers preserved their rhetoric in the face of William's catholic alliances by subtly reorientating their attack upon popery. In the war propaganda of the 1690s, censure of popish behaviour fell, not upon the catholic church in general, but upon a much narrower entity – the French court. Arguing that the main threat to God's cause in contemporary Europe was Louis XIV's government, rather than the entire Roman system, the propagandists concentrated upon the clash between their godly ruler and the French prince of darkness, and so passed over the catholicism of Spanish and Austrian allies. This redirection was signalled as early as Burnet's St James's sermon in 1688. In this address, the preacher had been careful to point out that many catholics were deluded rather than evil, and asked that such men be left in peace.[80] This rhetoric tried to calm the waves of anti-catholic violence which marked William's invasion, and may have been part of a coherent attempt to reassure William's continental allies that he was no protestant zealot.[81] It also, however, refined the equation between the Roman faith, and the evil forces which had opposed God's cause through history. In Burnet's sermon, 'popery' was no longer the Roman religion *per se*, but was confined to those parts of it, currently embodied in Louis's regime, which posed the most pressing threat to righteousness.

The shift was continued by dressing the French king as Antichrist. If Versailles, rather than Rome, could be identified as Babylon, then the iniquities of non-French catholics would fade in comparison, and alliance with such men would appear less strange. In accordance with this strategy, the courtly reformers put much stress on Louis's persecution of reformed Christians. After Foxe's *Acts and monuments* Englishmen would always view such cruelty as the classic mark of the Beast. Consequently, the declaration of war against the French in April 1689 cited the harassment of protestants as one of the *causae belli*, and Burnet's circle homed in on horrors of Louis's rule in the rest of their war propaganda.[82] Simon Patrick, for example, preaching at a fast in 1690, thanked God that the Revolution in England had stopped 'the whips, and gibbets, and racks, and fires, and other instruments of cruelty, wherewith we have seen it [popery], torturing the bodies and souls of

[79] *Ibid.* 15, 102–3.

[80] Burnet, *Sermon ... St James' ... 23 December 1688*, pp. 28–30.

[81] For the anti-catholic violence see Robert Beddard, *A kingdom without a king: the journal of the provisional government in the revolution of 1688* (Oxford, 1988), pp. 41–5. For William's need to please a catholic audience on the continent, see Jonathan Israel, 'William III and toleration', in Ole Peter Grell, Jonathan I. Israel and Nicholas Tyacke, eds., *From persecution to toleration: the Glorious Revolution in England* (Oxford, 1991), pp. 129–70.

[82] William III and Mary II, *Their majesties declaration against the French king* (1689).

innumerable good men and women in France, and in other places'.[83] In the same year Burnet warned the English that they should not be deluded into thinking their French enemies were 'not quite so bad as our fears may have pictured them to us'. Their record in treating those they conquered suggested they were even worse.[84] Similarly, an anonymous defence of Tenison's funeral sermon for Mary in 1695 accused the archbishop's Jacobite detractors of supporting French power. The French, the author reminded his audience, were those who had persecuted protestant subjects, and had hung the citizens of Heidelberg by the hair and then burnt them in their private parts.[85] According to William Lloyd, the issue in contemporary Europe was the very survival of the reformed religion. The French king had hunted the Huguenots out of his country like wild beasts, and lent his guards to the duke of Savoy to extirpate his reformed subjects. 'This he doth for his glory, as being the most Christian king; and if other princes will follow him, no protestant shall live in this world.'[86]

With such brutality described, William's propagandists could go on presenting William's foreign wars as a protestant crusade, notwithstanding co-operation with pope, Spain, and Austria. They had painted the struggle between their king and Louis in such black-and-white terms, that William's catholic alliances could be virtually ignored. Thomas Tenison certainly made no mention of his master's pro-papal diplomacy when opening the war propaganda with his fast sermon to the Commons on 5 June 1689. In this, he assured MPs, they were 'engaged in the evangelical cause against popish superstition', and stated that English armies would go abroad 'in the name of that God who is truly the Lord of Hosts'.[87] Subsequently, the Williamites kept up a barrage of pan-European rhetoric which stressed the common cause of all protestants. The English were endlessly updated on the situation on the continent, and reminded that their status as a chosen nation entailed sacrifice to protect their co-religionists across Europe. Burnet's sermon to the corporation of London early in 1690, and the supplications published for fast days, were particularly good examples. Burnet's address combined the most vivid Hebraic imagery, with an appeal for William's war to be properly manned and funded. The preacher told the mayor and aldermen that their city faced the same destruction as Jerusalem when Jesus had wept over it, and warned

[83] Simon Patrick, *A sermon preached before the king and queen at Whitehall, April 16 1690, being the fast day* (1690), p. 28.

[84] Burnet, *Sermon … Bow church … March 12 1689/90*, p. 15.

[85] *A defence of the archbishop's sermon on the death of her late majesty of blessed memory* (1695), pp. 8, 13–14.

[86] William Lloyd, *A sermon preached before their majesties at Whitehall, on the fifth day of November, 1689* (1689), p. 28.

[87] Tenison, *Sermon against self-love*, pp. 23, 27.

them that their duties in avoiding this catastrophe must include both moral reform and full support for William's war effort.

> If we have any Regard either to our Selves, our Families or Posterities, to our Religion or our Country, to the present or the succeeding Generations, we must now unite our whole Strength, and turn our whole Forces against those Enemies of Humane Nature...
> If while things are in this State, every one will look on, and fancy, That this lies on the Government, and not on himself; if Men will neither with their Persons, nor their Purses contribute what is in them to our preservation ... this gives us yet a more terrible Prospect than the Jews had.[88]

The forms of prayers for the war's fast days included a new collect 'for all the reformed churches', which was designed to remind Englishmen of the fate of their continental brethren. It lamented the sad state of the continental reformation and went on to appeal to God, 'who hast united us into the mystical body of Christ (that is his church)', to have mercy upon the Englishman's fellows abroad.[89]

It is difficult to state exactly why so much investment was put into courtly reformation's vision of a universal church, and why other rhetorics which might have helped to sell the war were downgraded. In this particular area there is no explicit evidence of choices between languages being made in Williamite circles. However, it is possible to offer some suggestions. There were, for instance, good reasons why a 'British' rhetoric might have been rejected when discussing campaigns in Ireland. Work by John Morrill on the 1640s and 1650s has suggested that Englishmen were unwilling to see the islands on which they lived as a political or spiritual entity in that period.[90] If this attitude persisted after the Revolution, then propaganda based upon a 'British' patriotism would have been ineffective, since its audience would have been unused to thinking in these terms. Certainly, the bishops themselves did not often think of a single 'British' entity. The catalogue of divine interventions they used to establish their people as a chosen nation was limited to events in *English* history, and in their account of the past Scotland and Ireland were treated as sources of potential popish threat, rather than as protestant allies. Henry VIII, Cranmer, and Elizabeth were the heroes of their story, not Scottish or Irish reformers. Moreover, it is possible that the use of internationalist rhetoric in the Irish arena might have had a strategic purpose. It was obvious from the first that Flanders, not the British Isles, would be the main site of William's military effort against France. In this situation it might

---

[88] Burnet, *Sermon ... Bow Church ... March 12 1689/90*, pp. 20–1.
[89] *Form of prayer ... Friday the eighth day of April next.*
[90] John Morrill, 'The Britannic revolution, 1640–60' (Unpublished seminar paper read at the Cambridge seventeenth-century seminar, autumn term, 1992).

have been dangerous to use a 'British' rhetoric to cover the battle in Ireland, since such a language risked placing the Irish and continental conflicts in different categories, and might render the Flemish war less vital to Englishmen. The danger of such a decoupling was evident as early as June 1689 when parliamentary debates revealed a growing mood of alarm at the lack of progress in Ireland, associated with angry swipes at the Dutch as the cause of England's troubles.[91] A rhetoric which excluded any concept of 'Britain' might help to stem this tide by giving all William's conflicts abroad equal importance.

The relative neglect of 'balance of power' and commercial rhetorics to sell the continental war is harder to explain. These alternative languages neatly side-stepped the ideological difficulties of a protestant crusade, and were perfectly familiar to late Stuart audiences. Perhaps the propagandists were reluctant to ditch arguments based on courtly reformation, because they tied in so neatly with the rest of their message. Having staked so much on William's godliness to promote his domestic government and his Irish campaigns, Burnet and his circle might have feared that it would have been damaging to retreat from their image of the king when he was directly facing the shock troops of popery. Perhaps, too, the propagandists genuinely believed the providential purpose of William's war, and wished to convince their countrymen. It is also possible that Burnet's allies thought the English would be most easily roused by a vigorously anti-catholic rhetoric. As Linda Colley has rightly pointed out, Englishmen's willingness to fight abroad was often based upon the threat of an encircling popery, not only in the late Stuart period, but on into the eighteenth century.[92] For all the problems associated with William's popish alliances, his spokesmen clearly felt they could gain most capital by continuing to present their master as the reforming champion of God's cause.

Whatever the reasons for their choice of rhetoric, the courtly reformers' attempts to calm xenophobia and anti-war sentiment had been coherent and cogent. The men of Burnet's circle had in fact used Hebraic language to take their fight deep into their opponents' territory. They had exploited the ambiguities inherent in the analogy between England and Israel to reverse completely the logic of their critics' position. In the household vision of Englishness used by Jacobites, and by those who complained about the cost of William's conflict, the drain of resources abroad to fight other people's battles was a sin against the nation. Once, however, the English were presented as a people in covenant with God, sending aid to protestants abroad could be presented as England's highest national duty. If the English were a chosen

[91] Horwitz, *Parliament, policy and politics*, pp. 32–3.
[92] See Linda Colley, 'Britishness and otherness. An argument', *JBS*, 31 (1992), 309–29; Colley, *Britons*, ch. 1

people, this did not mean that they could retreat into a proud insularity. Their very status as an elect nation demanded that they embrace a godly champion, even if he was foreign-born; and it demanded that they act as leader of all protestants by supporting struggles for godliness beyond their shores.

5

Courtly reformation and the politics of party

One of the most remarkable features of William's invasion of England in 1688 was the degree of support it received from both whigs and tories. For a few brief weeks over the winter, old enemies united in defence of the protestant religion, and in agreement that James could no longer be trusted with the exercise of uncontrolled monarchical power. Whigs such as Wharton and Montagu, who pressed William's case amongst the political elites in London, were joined by tories such as Sir Edward Seymour, flocking to the prince's banner in the West Country. On coming to power, William tried to capitalise upon this broad alliance, and attempted to unite his new realm behind his new regime. The ministry he first constructed combined men of both parties in an attempt to force them to work together, and to bury factional jealousies for good. William balanced a whig Secretary of State, the earl of Shrewsbury, with a tory one, the earl of Nottingham, and constructed a Treasury Commission from men of differing political backgrounds. Whilst the royal household, judiciary, and admiralty were mainly whig preserves, the marquis of Halifax, who was no species of whig, was made Lord Privy Seal, and a leading tory, the earl of Danby, was promoted to the marquisate of Carmarthen, and to the Lord Presidency.

William's first ministry was a bold attempt to break with the recent pattern of English history, and to dispel the problems which factionalism would cause as the king tried to work with the English parliament. Unfortunately, however, inherited bitterness proved too strong for the royal plan for reconciliation. Very rapidly, partisan disputes re-emerged to break the brief consensus against James, and began to plague William's relations with the legislature. In order to secure support for his war in parliament the king found that he had to pay close attention to English politics, and had to devote virtually all his winters to constant meetings with English political leaders. He had to respond to rapid shifts of mood in the Lords and Commons; he had to try to manage the more extreme manifestations of party activity at West-minster; and he had to attempt to calm the disruptive factional hatreds which dominated public life. In this daunting set of tasks, the propaganda of courtly reformation was to prove invaluable. As the court's spokesmen advanced their case for moral renewal, and especially as they deployed their fifth strategy to promote their campaign (the presentation of the monarch as a reforming supporter of the established church), they developed a rhetoric which could help the king deal with his divided realm.

At the risk of vastly oversimplifying a complex parliamentary situation, in which political groupings were fluid, and in which there was rivalry and diversity of opinion within the two camps, three main sources of division between whigs and tories can be identified under William. The first, naturally, was argument over the personnel of government. The battles of the 1680s had bred such mutual mistrust that few Englishmen could bear the sight of their old enemies in power, with the result that politics came to be dominated by factional struggles for office. Accordingly, William's first ministry broke down as the two groups of ministers worked to exclude one another from their posts, and the rest of the reign was to be marked by bitter battles between the parties for the king's favour. The other two issues to divide England into whig and tory camps were extensions of the disputes which had split the country before William arrived. Politics was still centred upon the civil problem of the constitution, and the religious question of dissent, even though the Revolution had transformed the content and context of these arguments.

On the civil side, the dispute after William had arrived was obviously no longer whether James should have been allowed to inherit royal power. Everyone who welcomed William's intervention in 1688 had accepted that a papist ruler could not be trusted with the actual exercise of authority. However, even though this much had been agreed, debate about the nation's fundamental law continued. Throughout William's reign, the parties squabbled over the constitutional significance of 1688, and clashed repeat-edly over which legal principles underpinned the new regime. The first point of division was the nature of the Revolution. The issues here were complex, but if the wide differences within the whig and tory camps can be ignored, the fundamental dispute turned on whether 1688 had witnessed legitimate resistance by the English to a tyrant. By and large, whigs insisted that it had. Although they disagreed about the precise circumstances in which resistance might occur, about the theoretical basis of the right, and even about who precisely might resist, whigs generally concurred that James had been tyrannous, and had been properly removed by his subjects.[1]

---

[1] Kenyon, *Revolution principles*, ch. 4.

Tories, by contrast, rejected this logic. Although many whigs were keen to stress that 1688 had been an extraordinary situation, which would not be a precedent for regular cashiering of monarchs, their opponents feared that their principles dissolved royal authority, and would rapidly lead to anarchy. In response to this anxiety, tories championed interpretations of James's removal which preserved their old ideal of non-resistance. For instance, in the convention of 1689 they worked for settlements which denied the people's right to disobedience. Some argued that James himself had taken the decision to abdicate, and that Mary, as his next heir, should inherit the throne. Others pressed for a regency, arguing that whilst monarchs could not be deposed by their people, they could prove themselves incapable of actually exercising authority. Even after these arguments had been defeated and William had been placed on the throne, tories clung to their non-resistance theories. They either passed into Jacobitism, or, more usually, insisted that whilst James's days were over, they had not been ended by legitimate, popular deposition. He had lost the throne through his own decision to withdraw, because he had been defeated in a just war, or because his land had been conquered by a sovereign prince, who had had no duties as a subject towards him.[2]

The second point of constitutional contention was William's title. Whilst whigs held that William was a lawfully chosen monarch, with a full legal right to his position, tories were worried that his ascent to the throne had broken the hereditary principle. Many of those who accepted the Revolution salved their unease by maintaining that although William was an authoritative monarch, he was so *de facto*, not *de jure*. They argued that the prince of Orange should be obeyed because he was actually in power, and was protecting his subjects from disorder and foreign invasion; but they maintained that he did not have a complete legal title to the throne, since that rested, following heredity, with James. This controversy over the basis of allegiance was complemented by a third constitutional debate about the succession. Tories, hoping to avoid any suggestion of election to monarchy, were keen to settle exactly who would accede to the English throne, and in which order. Whigs, less disturbed by the threat to the hereditary principle, were more relaxed about delineating the succession. Arguments in 1689 soon defined these differences. In the first year, the debates over the throne in the convention were echoed by divisions on the oath of allegiance, and on succession clauses in the 1690 bill of rights. Whilst whigs pressed for an early and widespread tendering of oaths to William, tories tried to protect those unsure about the Revolution by delaying and limiting the requirement to swear loyalty to the

---

[2] Goldie, 'Tory political thought', pp. 61–129.

new monarch. As tories attempted to tie up the English succession in a strict hereditary settlement, whigs resisted and prevaricated.[3]

On religious issues, the context of party debate was also transformed by the collapse of the old tory ideal. If tories before the Revolution had worked to impose anglican uniformity, that policy ceased to be an option in 1688. The first blow against it had been struck by James. The favour he had shown to catholics and dissenters had ended royal support for the national church, and so terminated the alliance between crown and bishops on which the tories had traditionally relied for the realisation of their ideal. James had been removed at the Revolution, but his replacement did little to brighten tory hopes. The prince of Orange was a known supporter of toleration, whose political position demanded he establish religious indulgence in England. Jonathan Israel has shown that William was not only personally committed to freedom of worship, but that his alliance with a wide range of protestant and catholic princes also forbade persecution for fear of alienating his foreign friends.[4] In addition, the prince was relying on whig support in 1688–9, and was in close contact with English dissenters who had fled into exile after the exclusion crisis.[5] Tories were thus denied a monarch who would co-operate with their ecclesiastical plans, and had to resign themselves to losing an exclusive national church.

However, if the possibility of securing uniformity receded, this did not end partisan strife on religious issues. Both parties were galvanised into action by the changed atmosphere of ecclesiastical politics after William's arrival. The tories were motivated by the fear that the new regime was fundamentally hostile to their church. They were worried by the new king's preference for toleration, by his close association with nonconformists, and by disturbing events in both Scotland and England. In Scotland, the victory of Williamite forces in 1689 led rapidly to the disestablishment of the episcopal church, and fuelled anxiety amongst English clerics that a similar loss of status might occur in their country.[6] Meanwhile, in England, danger loomed as it became clear that the new regime would deprive those clergy (including the primate and several bishops) who refused to swear the oath of allegiance. It thus appeared that the king was about to remove several of the church's most experienced leaders at a time when she faced a serious challenge from her enemies.[7] In response to these perceived dangers, tories organised to preserve anglican dominance. From the moment of William's arrival they worked to

---

[3] Horwitz, *Parliament, policy and politics*, pp. 21–6, 28, 30; *CJ*, 10, 126; Grey, X, 237–42.
[4] Israel, 'William III and toleration'.
[5] Robert Beddard, 'The unexpected whig revolution of 1688', in Robert Beddard, ed., *The revolutions of 1688* (Oxford, 1991), pp. 11–101.
[6] Bennett, 'King William III and the episcopate', p. 119.
[7] For the deprivations, see George Every, *The high church party, 1688–1715* (1956), ch. 4.

uphold the church's privileges (particularly the tests which reserved public office for her communicants), and sought to limit the freedom granted to dissenters. Whigs, meanwhile, saw William's advent as an opportunity to ease the plight of their nonconformist supporters. Whilst not all of the party was hostile to the anglican church, nor wished the establishment to lose all legal advantage, whigs were generally less concerned to uphold the predominant authority of the clerical establishment, and wanted a generous treatment of dissenters. They were sceptical of tory claims that widespread evasion of anglican control would threaten social and moral chaos, and acted to secure a wide degree of religious liberty. The battle lines were drawn immediately. In March 1689, certain of the more radical whigs tried to repeal the sacramental tests. In a series of motions and draft bills they attempted to open up national and local government posts to nonconformists, and so break one of the central guarantors of the church's leading position.[8] Horror at this threat stimulated tories to organise. On the 16th, over one hundred and fifty MPs met in the Devil's Tavern in Westminster and vowed to defend the religious establishment in the subsequent debates. Over the next weeks this Devil's Tavern group acted together to preserve the test, attack the influence of dissenters at Whitehall, and protect the old forms of anglican liturgy and government.[9] Religion thus joined personal and constitutional disputes in destroying political harmony in the first months of the new regime.

This failure to calm party politics haunted the reign. Factional struggle divided a nation the king wanted united against France, and delayed decision-making as parliament engaged in endless partisan argument. Party also hindered the construction of ministerial teams. If William pursued his initial policy of appointing officers from both parties, he found his servants disunited, and had to watch them plotting to overthrow their colleagues. For instance, whigs in the government in the autumn of 1689 did not defend their tory colleagues when they were attacked by their enemies in parliament, and the mixed Treasury bench of 1692–3 was so paralysed by internal dissension that it could not provide a lead in the Commons.[10] On the other hand, if the king tried to rely on only one group, his problems were as severe. Quite apart from his reluctance to become a prisoner of faction, William found that constructing a party administration merely encouraged opposition by providing a target on which it could focus. When the government consisted of ministers from one side only, their partisan enemies united in attacking the administration, and discovered that they only had to attract a few floating or loosely committed parliamentarians to secure an anti-government majority.

---

[8] *CJ*, 10, 43 – an attempt on 7 March to repeal the corporation acts; *LJ*, 14, 148 – an attempt on 15 March to abolish the tests.
[9] Horwitz, *Parliament, policy and politics*, p. 22.
[10] *Ibid.* pp. 37–44, 104–14.

William's first attempt to rule through party came to grief in this way. The largely tory administration which took power in 1690 collapsed in 1693 when whigs persuaded independent MPs and peers that the king's servants could not be trusted to organise the war. As a result of such problems, William's ministries were impermanent and shifting. The king had to update his team constantly, moving men in and out of office as he searched for an elusive formula which would guarantee stable support in parliament. Thus the mixed administration of 1689 became a tory one between 1690 and 1692, before swinging back to the whigs in the years of the mid-decade, and then switching violently between the two parties in the last years of the reign.[11] Factional division had thus turned royal political management into a difficult and time-consuming job, which required considerable skill, patience, and tact on the part of the monarch.

Given the intricacies of parliamentary politics in the 1690s, any propaganda which could address William's problems with partisan factions needed to satisfy a complex web of demands. Obviously, the central requirement was that a royal case contain an appeal for national unity. It had to condemn party and throw the court's weight against partisan attacks on fellow Englishmen. However, this denunciation of faction had to be made with care. William could not afford to alienate too many party politicians, as he had to work with them to secure majorities in parliament. He was unable, therefore, to express anger at politicians too openly. Closely linked to this need for diplomacy, was the demand that any royal propaganda take a middle ground on the issues which divided whigs and tories. Since a single party could rarely control parliament for long, the regime had to ensure it was always free to court the opposition. This meant it had to adopt a position on the royal title, the succession, and the status of the church of England, which might appeal to both sides, and would retain its freedom to manoeuvre between them. Courtly reformation could satisfy this difficult list of demands. It could make a powerful appeal for unity, do this with a certain amount of tact, and help to construct a royal position which compromised between whigs and tories.

THE COURTLY REFORMATION RESPONSE: TACTFUL DENUNCIATION

A vigorous denunciation of party battle could be easily integrated into the arguments of Burnet and his circle. All the courtly reformers had to do was to equate political division with debauchery, and then insist that William's deliverance demanded unity as part of the general post-Revolution repentance. The initial step was to establish a convincing connection between party

---

[11] The clearest short account of William's ministries is E. L. Ellis, 'William III and the politicians', in Holmes, *Britain ... Glorious Revolution*, pp. 113–34.

and other forms of vice. Broadly, two rhetorical techniques were used to achieve this end. First, the preachers argued that debauchery and division stemmed from the same root. They held that the two evils were manifestations of a single underlying sin, which when eliminated, would cure both ills. Thomas Tenison, in his 1689 fast sermon to the House of Commons, expressed this view most clearly. Tracing all the wrongs of his day back to a self-love, which blinded men to God's injunctions, he blamed this moral flaw for civil conflict as well as depravity.

From a false and unnatural Self-love it is that Discord arises and separates Brother from Brother, whilst each covets the greatest Share of the Inheritance: that Friends divide, and after Professions of the sincerest Love, exercise the bitterest Hatred.[12]

The second way to link division and sensuality was to stress their similar roles within history. Faction and luxury could be presented as the great weapons of Antichrist, the tools with which popery attempted to sabotage God's unfolding reformation. Burnet in particular stressed that papal agents had both debauched the righteous from their cause, *and* attempted to break the united front of the godly. In his thanksgiving sermon for William's invasion, he outlined the twin plan, explaining that the adversaries of reformation had advanced their projects by setting divisions between protestants.[13] Preaching on the same day, Tillotson endorsed this analysis as he outlined his vision of English history.

Almost from the beginning of our happy Reformation the Enemy had sown these Tares, and by the unwearied Malice and Arts of the *Church of Rome* the seeds of Dissention were scattered very early amongst us; and a sowre humour had been fermenting in the Body of the Nation, both upon account of Religion and Civil Interests.[14]

Using these techniques, the courtly reformers could integrate party into the general run of vice. When Sharp wondered in a thanksgiving sermon why God had not yet brought the English to their promised land, he blamed the following factors for the delay.

Our Ingratitude for God's former Mercies; our Lewdness and Debauchery; the Spirit of Atheism, and Prophaness, and Irreligion that still reigns among us as much as ever; and above all, our unaccountable dividing ourselves into Parties, and pursuing particular *Picques* and *Quarrels*.[15]

Similarly Burnet, preaching to the corporation of London in 1690, praised the capital city, but noted it had 'contracted so much guilt, is covered with so

---

12 Tenison, *Sermon against self-love*, p. 10.
13 Burnet, *Sermon ... House of Commons ... 31 January 1688*, p. 14.
14 Tillotson, *Sermon ... Lincoln's Inn ... 31 January 1688*, p. 23.
15 John Sharp, *Sermon ... Whitehall ... 12 Nov. 1693*, p. 26.

much defilement, luxury and excess; is agitated with such factions, and these acted with so much animosity, that we should share in Christ's weeping'.[16]

Once 'sins and divisions' had been so closely associated, it was easy to move on to the second stage of the argument, and set partisan politics in the context of William's providential salvation.[17] The bishops maintained that since 1688 was a blow struck for God's reformation, and since it demanded the English repent of all vice, then it followed that the people must renounce their sins of disunity as well as debauchery. As Tillotson put it when asking for moral reformation at the beginning of 1689: 'Let us endeavour, for once, to be so wise, as not to forfeit the fruits of this deliverance, and to hinder our selves of the benefit and advantage of it, by breaches and divisions among our selves.'[18] Burnet reinforced this message a year later, when warning Londoners that the opportunity to repent was not being taken. According to the bishop, England was facing a 'melancholy prospect' because the great work of improving upon God's deliverance was sticking in birth.[19] The reason for delay was not only reluctance to abandon vice, but division. Faction had made the population 'sharp-sighted to find out one another's faults', but had ensured that no use was made of this perception 'but to reproach others for them'. Burnet concluded that although William recommended a forgiving temper, men were 'so soured by the leaven of a party' that they would not avoid the heavy judgement of God by following his example.[20] In this way, courtly reformation became the regime's standard idiom for the condemnation of party struggle.

Paradoxically, although Burnet's language against faction was vehement, it satisfied the royal need for tact as well as vigour. It conveyed the king's case in a way which reduced the risk of alienating politicians. In the first place, the form of the propaganda – the use of clerics preaching ethical and religious reformation – may have rendered attacks on recent actions more acceptable. Churchmen, as spiritual authorities, had a recognised duty to reflect on the morality of contemporary events; and the jeremiad (the usual form of reformation rhetoric) was a familiar genre of polemic, in which it was possible to say extremely harsh things about public behaviour.[21] Moreover, putting appeals for unity in the mouths of men such as Burnet distanced the king from attacks upon his subjects. Sermons could hint at the monarch's exasperation, but since they did not come directly from William himself, they were less likely to be seen as royal insults of English statesmen.

[16] Burnet, *Sermon ... Bow church ... March 12 1689/90*, p.3.
[17] The quote is from Burnet, *Sermon ... White-hall ... 26 Nov. 1691*, p.34.
[18] Tillotson, *Sermon ... Lincoln's Inn ... 31 January 1688/9*, p.33.
[19] Burnet, *Sermon ... Bow church ... March 12 1689/90*, pp.28, 17.
[20] *Ibid.* pp.17–18, 30–1.
[21] Jeremiads had been a favourite device of the Restoration church as it called the nation to account. See Spurr, *Restoration church*, pp.236–49.

The best example of this strategy in operation came in the autumn of 1689. By this stage in his reign, William had become fearful that party division might nullify his gains in attaining the throne, and made urgent calls for past heats to be forgotten.[22] Yet, despite the pressure on the king, he did not himself express wrath at party actions. Indeed, William's personal response to his political difficulties was to launch a campaign of hospitality to try to woo his leading subjects into co-operation. In the second half of 1689 the monarch went to Newmarket to participate in the elite's horse-racing and gambling; he moved from Hampton Court to Kensington to be nearer London; he dined publicly at Whitehall for the first time since his coronation; and he threw a magnificent ball for his birthday.[23] In contrast to this friendliness, anger in court circles was revealed in reformation language by the king's clerical allies. In November, Burnet preached two sermons which lambasted party politics and accused political leaders of endangering the deliverance of 1688. The first address, the 5 November sermon to the House of Lords, was a relatively mild affair which called for repentance and stressed that division could threaten the blessing provided a year before.[24] The second, preached at St Lawrence Jewry on the 26th, was an extraordinary performance, which all but named guilty parties. In an impassioned address, the bishop utilised the standard Hebraic analogy in an explicit denunciation of contemporary politicians. The sermon used Jewish history to show the sin of civil discord, and then described two groups of men who were transgressing in 1689. Its account of their behaviour left little doubt as to whom the preacher had in mind. The sermon talked of one faction of Englishmen who were driven by a crazed desire to destroy those who had wrestled with them in the past. Burnet denounced those who 'acted with [an] extreme of fury, and under pretence of punishing past errors, seek only to gratify their own revenges'.[25] This was certainly an attack upon the whigs, who, at the time, were trying to limit any indemnity for past actions, in order to dislodge tories who had served Charles and James.[26] On the other hand, the sermon denounced a second group of people who were raising up religious disputes, and wished to persecute their brethren.[27] This was addressed to tories, who had just launched a full-scale pamphlet offensive vilifying dissent.[28] As a finale to his fiery address, Burnet presented William crucified between the two parties.

If Men will forget their present Danger, and only think of former Provocations, if both sides are studying to aggravate Matters one against another, and seeking and

---

[22] *CJ*, 10, 64, 215.
[23] See Luttrell, *Relation*, I, 586, 590, 592, 595, 600.
[24] Burnet, *Sermon ... House of peers ... 5 November*.
[25] Burnet, *Exhortation to peace and union*, p. 22.
[26] Grey, IX, 244–51; Horwitz, *Parliament, policy and politics*, pp. 37–8.
[27] Burnet, *Exhortation to peace and union*, p. 22.
[28] See below, pp. 181–3.

improving all the Advantages they can find; if the repeated Interpositions of Him, to whom, under God, we owe our present Quiet, and our late Deliverance, cannot inspire us with softer Thoughts ... What must the conclusion of all this be?[29]

Courtly reformation thus allowed the court to use both carrot and stick in urging an end to party politics. As the king cooed and encouraged reconciliation through cordial approaches to both sides, churchmen barked, warning the English of the brooding displeasure which lay beneath their ruler's sunny disposition.

THE COURTLY REFORMATION RESPONSE: FINDING THE MIDDLE GROUND

Despite Burnet's angry growls at St Lawrence, courtly reformation was not used simply to denounce party. It was also employed to help William occupy the middle ground. On both the great issues of principle which divided whigs and tories, the rhetoric aided the development of a court position which might appeal to both sides. It prevented William becoming too bound up with either whig or tory ideology, and thus retained his freedom of political manoeuvre.

On the constitutional issues, the role of courtly reformation can be considered briefly. In this area, the chief concern of the court's propagandists was not to alienate tories by becoming entangled in the whig position. Obviously, whig theories on resistance, title, and succession were superficially more attractive to the regime than those of their opponents. They did not (as tory arguments might) deny the new king full legal rights to his throne, or flirt with a future restoration of the legitimate Stuarts. Yet, despite these apparent advantages of whig theory, William's propagandists were careful to avoid espousing it as official philosophy. Whilst not openly criticising whig ideals, the courtly reformers feared that embracing them would alienate tories, and acted to prevent them becoming prescriptive.

The earl of Nottingham took the first step in this direction in February 1689. Advising the House of Lords in that month, he suggested a change in the wording of the oaths of allegiance which might allow tories as well as whigs to take them.[30] He pointed out that the form of oaths used by William's predecessors would endorse whig principles if they were applied to the new monarch, and so would risk narrowing the incoming regime's base of support. To remove this danger, the earl urged the abandonment of the traditional references to the king's 'rightful and lawful' title, and of the promises of obedience to his heirs and successors, so that those Englishmen who were sceptical about the Stuarts' deposition could submit to the new

[29] Burnet, *Exhortation to peace and union*, p. 24.
[30] Singer, *Correspondence ... Clarendon*, II, 261.

government in good conscience.[31] The Lords followed the earl's advice, and new oaths were produced accordingly.[32] In the months that followed, courtly reformers tried to cool the issue further by limiting the number of men who would have to swear. For instance, Gilbert Burnet was active, trying to persuade parliament not to insist that the oaths of allegiance be proffered to clergymen.[33] Burnet lost this battle, but he and his colleagues continued their conciliation of tories, particularly stressing that the principles of non-resistance and *de facto* power were acceptable to the new regime, so long as they did not lead to disloyalty. For example, Burnet and Nottingham helped to co-ordinate a vigorous press campaign through the 1690s which espoused *de facto* theories of obedience. As Mark Goldie has shown, the bishops wrote their own political pamphlets to support this interpretation of the regime's legitimacy, and sponsored other writers who were prepared to do the same.[34] Similarly, the court discouraged whig attempts at statutory recognition of William's legal position. It did so particularly when these efforts aimed to make the explicit endorsement of the royal title a qualification for office. There was a series of such whig initiatives throughout William's reign, but none received the backing of the monarch they claimed to protect.

The rhetoric of courtly reformation played an important role in this constitutional balancing act. It provided the new monarchs with a powerful argument for their legitimacy, which did not rely on interpreting England's fundamental law, and so did not offend either whig or tory positions on the constitution. On the question of resistance, for example, the courtly reformers' central notion – that providence was the chief force behind William's accession – was compatible with both sides of the argument. The idea that God could change a nation's rulers did not directly contradict the claim that the people had the same right, and so did not offend the doctrine held by whigs.[35] It was also acceptable to many tories. This was because the chief intellectual prop of tory theory was the surprisingly equivocal argument that monarchs were God's vicegerents on earth. This notion, propagated vigorously by the Restoration clergy, forbade resistance to rulers because it was the same as resistance to divine will, but paradoxically gave princes little security of tenure. As both John Spurr and J. C. Findon have noted, the insistence that men must not rise against those set over them never implied that God would

---

[31] Nottingham urged all Englishmen to swear to the new monarch as a king *de facto*, Andrew Browning, ed., *The memoirs of Sir John Reresby* (2nd edn, 1991), pp. 558–9.

[32] *LJ*, 14, 119–20.

[33] Clarke and Foxcroft, *Life ... Burnet*, pp. 272–3.

[34] Mark Goldie, 'Revolution ... structure of political argument', pp. 510–17.

[35] For example, John Locke's political writings (radical statements of the whigs' case for resistance) conceded the role of providence by maintaining that rebellion by subjects constituted an appeal to heaven. Richard Cox, ed., *John Locke's 'Second treatise of government'* (Arlington Heights, Illinois, 1982), p. 147, para. 241.

not remove his deputies himself.[36] The deity elevated magistrates for his own purposes; there was no guarantee that his unfolding plan would not overturn regimes and replace them by new rulers. Tories thus paralleled their awe for monarchy with a sense of an all-embracing providence, very similar to that found in Burnetine propaganda.[37]

Courtly reformation also avoided entering the dispute on William's title. Overwhelmingly it concentrated on godly magistracy and protestantism as the justifications for William's rule. It was the fact that the king beat down popery and was prepared to lead the nation to righteousness which argued for loyalty to him, not his precise position in law. Courtly reformers even stayed remarkably clear of the issue of succession. Although they welcomed the removal of an heir in 1688 who would certainly be raised a catholic (James II's son), the propagandists did not generally espouse any strict position on the inheritance of the English crown. In fact, their rhetoric was so centred on William that it tended not to reflect on the future. In reformation propaganda, the death of the king was treated less as a potential political problem, which would pose the question of succession, than as a possible apocalypse – God's ultimate punishment on the English for not living up to his reformation.[38] Describing the horror of William's demise thus prevented the need to look beyond it, and again avoided taking a recognisably whig or tory line.

The role of courtly reformation in religious disputes must be considered at much greater length. This is partly because matters of faith remained the main cause of division between whig and tory in the 1690s. Not only did the legacy of bitterness between anglicans and dissenters carry over from Charles II's reign, but political circumstances also served to concentrate debate on ecclesiastical issues. The Revolution's religious arrangements were slow to emerge in 1689; and they were completed, not by a definitive settlement, but by the failure of a royal policy which left many matters ambiguous and contested.[39] Religious issues will also have to be studied in depth because the thesis to be offered here will be controversial. Below, it is suggested that the bishops used a rhetoric of reformation to pursue an ecclesiological compromise between whig and tory. This goes against the grain of much historiography, which has presented the movement for reformation in the 1690s as essentially hostile to tory ideals. Portraying moral reform as part of a 'whiggish' programme to conciliate dissent, many scholars have not recognised that the programme (at

---

36 Findon, 'The non-jurors', p. 131; Spurr, 'Virtue, religion and government'.
37 William Lloyd was careful to stress that the line taken by the courtly reformers was perfectly consistent with established anglican doctrine. See William Lloyd, *A discourse of God's ways in dispensing of kingdoms* (1691), especially the epistle to the reader.
38 See Wake, *Of our obligations*, p. 22; Burnet, *Essay . . . late queen*, pp. 192–3; Edward Fowler, *A sermon preached before the House of Lords in the abbey-church at Westminster, upon Thursday 16 April 1696* (1696), especially p. 23.
39 See below, pp. 171.

least as promoted by Burnet and his allies) could find a theological middle
ground between the parties.

Two broad strands of historiography have contributed to this 'anti-tory'
interpretation of reformation. First, there has been an attempt to identify a
distinct 'latitudinarian' churchmanship within the Restoration establishment. This has presented the key courtly reformers as a minority group who
were unusually sympathetic to dissent, and has seen interest in moral reform
as a badge of their position. The background here was a standard account of
the church before 1688 which portrayed uniformity as the overwhelming
objective of most of its clergy. In the works of numerous scholars, pre-
Revolutionary anglicans were assumed to have been so shocked by the
religious chaos of the mid-century civil wars that they devoted all their efforts
to preventing its recurrence. They were thought to have sought security in
universal acceptance of their prayer book and episcopal government, and
were shown to have advocated a vigorous persecution of nonconformists as a
way to achieve this.[40] Within this interpretation, William's future propagandists were seen as mavericks. Labelled 'latitudinarians', they were thought to
have been strangely uninterested in uniformity, and were believed to have
shared a distinctive philosophy which did not fit with their colleagues' desire
to attack non-anglicans. As elucidated by a generation of scholars, this
latitudinarian creed consisted of a simple definition of true religion which
could transcend differences between Christians, and of a faith in the power of
reason to resolve misunderstandings between protestants. Most importantly,
moral reform was seen as a cornerstone of the minority's position. Tillotson
and his circle were reputed to have advanced virtue – rather than strict
uniformity – as the most important end of religion; and they were held to have
stressed morality as the heart of the simple gospel through which they hoped
to unite all believers.[41] The result of this historical framework was to suggest
that reformation was hostile to tory ideals. By presenting spiritual and ethical
renewal as the programme of an unusually tolerant party in the church, study
of latitudinarianism implied that there was some opposition between support
for anglican uniformity, and enthusiasm for moral reform.

This impression was strengthened by a second strand of historical writing.

---

[40] See Robert Beddard, 'The Restoration church' in J. R. Jones, ed., *The restored monarchy,
1660–1688* (1979), pp. 155–76; Paul Seaward, 'Gilbert Sheldon and the London vestries', in
Goldie *et al.*, *Politics of religion*, pp. 49–75; Norman Sykes, *From Sheldon to Secker: aspects
of English church history 1660–1768* (Cambridge, 1959), ch. 1; Seaward, *Cavalier Parliament*, pp. 162–96.

[41] See B. J. Shapiro, *Probability and certainty in seventeenth century England* (Princeton, 1983);
Jacob, *Newtonians*; Isabel Rivers, *Reason, grace and sentiment: a study of the language of
religion and ethics in England, 1660–1780* (Cambridge, 1991), I, 25–88, especially pp. 30–4;
J. Gascoigne, 'Politics, patronage and Newtonianism: the Cambridge example', *HJ*, 27
(1984), 1–24; G. R. Cragg, *From puritanism to the age of reason* (Cambridge, 1966).

The study of attempts to amend manners through the law in the 1690s has also tended to present reform in connection with appeals to nonconformity. Particularly, the glut of works on the societies for reformation has stressed how they involved dissenters as active participants in their campaigns. Although reluctant to label these bodies 'whig' (their membership was far too heterogeneous for that), their students have emphasised the broad religious base of the societies, and the hostility they engendered from clerics who worried about the influence of nonconformists.[42] In particular Tina Isaacs has suggested that tory-leaning clerics were deeply worried about the presence of dissenters within the reforming groups, and that they were concerned that these bodies threatened the church's ethical leadership of society.[43] On a different tack, Craig Rose has read the whole movement for moral reform in the 1690s as an attempt to dissolve anglican exclusivity. Pointing out that ethical and religious renewal were goals around which all protestants could unite, he has argued that they were promoted to foster a 'godly union' of all denominations which could come together in the struggle for righteousness.[44]

The historiography just reviewed was not misdirected. The ideal of reformation did contain an ecumenism, and William's propagandists did use this to appeal to dissenters. Building on a broad view of the true church (a view which has already been shown to have embraced different groups of protestants across Europe) the courtly reformers deployed their rhetoric to assure nonconformists that they would not be vilified under the new regime. They comforted dissenters, promising that they could be members of the new godly nation, and reserving for them a key role in bringing it into being. For example, as early as the winter of 1688–9, Burnet and his circle were preaching general protestant reconciliation as an integral part of William's providential deliverance. In their first sermons under the new regime, they suggested that the recent decline of godliness could not be blamed solely on the moral failings of rulers; but that it also stemmed from the needless division of Englishmen into sects. They argued that disunity had weakened spiritual supervision of the population and had allowed papists to spread debauchery; and consequently they insisted that William's moral renewal must include protestant co-operation if it were to succeed.[45] Throughout the decade this early message was repeated, and calls for moral reform were often

---

[42] Craig, 'Movement for reformation', pp. 96–7; Isaacs, 'Moral crime', p. 169.
[43] For such tory suspicions of the societies, see Isaacs, 'Anglican hierarchy'.
[44] Rose, 'Providence, protestant union'; see also Goldie, 'John Locke, Jonas Proast'.
[45] Burnet, *Sermon ... St James' ... 23 December 1688*, p. 28; Burnet, *Sermon ... House of Commons ... 31 January 1688*, p. 33; Tillotson, *Sermon ... Lincoln's Inn ... 31 January 1688*, p. 23; Patrick, *Sermon ... St James' ... 20 January 1688*; Simon Patrick, *A sermon against murmuring preached at St Paul's Covent-Garden, on the first Sunday in Lent; being a second part of the sermon preached before the prince of Orange* (1689); Simon Patrick, *A sermon preached before the queen at Whitehall, March 1 1688/9* (1689).

accompanied by arguments for protestant unity. This was especially true within the societies for reformation of manners. Not only did these bodies recruit members from both the established church and dissent, they organised their promotional activities to stress the importance of such joint participation. Their regular London sermons were preached by both anglican and nonconformist ministers; they were delivered to mixed congregations; they alternated between a dissenting venue, Salters Hall, and the anglican church of St Mary-le-Bow; and they contained repeated and extended praise for the societies' spirit of co-operation.

Yet such ecumenism was only half the picture. If established historiographies have correctly pointed out the Williamite appeal to dissent, they have done a disservice by preventing a balanced assessment of royal propaganda as a whole. Most existing interpretations of the Restoration church, and most histories of the reformation movements of the 1690s, have drawn too stark a distinction between the courtly reformers and tories and have distracted attention from parts of the royal case which might appeal to the more rigid breeds of churchmen. The ideology of reformation was not, in fact, hopelessly entangled with the conciliation of dissent. The rhetoric could criticise, as well as comfort, nonconformists, and could be used in an attempt to reassure established clerics of their status under the new regime.

Before demonstrating the 'tory' aspects of reformation in the 1690s, it is worth noting two strands of historical revisionism which have paved the way for their recognition. One of these strands has been a re-evaluation of the Restoration church. Recent work on the anglican establishment before 1688 has begun to dissolve the picture of courtly reformers as a maverick group, whose espousal of moral reform was a sign of their heterodoxy. In particular, the work of John Spurr has allowed an appreciation of the common ground between the supposed latitudinarians and the bulk of their colleagues. In the first place, Spurr's investigation of the general tenure of Restoration churchmanship has demonstrated that the concerns of the courtly reformers were very similar to those of the clergy in general. Whilst Spurr has acknowledged obsession with uniformity amongst Caroline clergy, he has complemented this with a description of their sense of providence and religious mission very close to that felt by Burnet and his circle.[46] In Spurr's view, the characteristic features of the church after 1660 were not only the defence of the prayer book and episcopal authority, but also a feeling of challenge – a profound fear that God was about to judge and condemn England, and a consequent awareness that the English must be persuaded to righteousness in order to avoid divine smiting.[47] Spurr has also helped to re-evaluate the supposed latitudinarians.

---

[46] Spurr, *Restoration church*, chs. 5–6; Spurr, 'Virtue, religion and government'.
[47] Spurr, *Restoration church*, pp. 236–49.

Along with other scholars, he has questioned the extent to which their views on dissent differed from those of their colleagues. Spurr himself has argued that (apart from a brief period in the early 1660s) the latitudinarians were not identified by contemporaries as a separate group in the church, and did not exhibit the peculiar attitudes ascribed to them by many historians.[48] Other historians have provided evidence that men like Tillotson and Patrick joined a united anglican defence of a monopolistic national church, and were not unduly sympathetic to dissent. Amongst others, Richard Ashcraft and John Marshall have shown that supposed latitudinarians helped to develop a view of nonconformists as undisciplined schismatics.[49] Echoing their colleagues, the future courtly reformers condemned separatists as heinous sinners who had not only disobeyed Christian injunctions to peace and union, but had placed their own wilful opinions above the guidance of spiritual authority.

This revision of the Restoration church has obviously reduced the impression that the courtly reformers' initiatives were the programme of an unusually tolerant group of clerics. Instead, Spurr's work reveals that reform in the 1690s was promoted by men who had been loyal apologists for the old establishment. The Williamite platform of moral and religious renewal was not an alternative to entrenched anglican ideals, but was rather the continuation of a crusade begun by the very institution tories wished to defend. The reformers' language of transgression, providence, and repentance was familiar from the rhetoric of the Restoration clergy; and many reforming initiatives under William can be traced back to the activities of the Caroline church.[50]

The second historiographic revision which might suggest a 'tory' face to reformation, was that attempted in the third chapter of this current work. In that chapter it was noted that study of late Stuart moral reform has been dominated by work on a narrow part of the field. It was argued that historians had become remarkably fixed upon one specific aspect of moral reform, centring upon the societies for the reformation of manners, and that this limitation had given them a distorted view of the phenomenon which should be remedied by closer concentration on the activities of the court. Here this point can be taken further by suggesting that the restricted historiography has also blinded scholars to *tory* aspects of reformation. As has been noted, scholars who have looked closely at the societies have stressed their strong

---

[48] Spurr, '"Latitudinarianism"'; John Spurr, 'The church of England, comprehension and the toleration act of 1689', *EHR*, 104 (1989), 927–46.

[49] Richard Ashcraft, 'Latitudinarianism and toleration: historical myth versus political history', in Richard Kroll, Richard Ashcraft, and Perez Zagorin, eds., *Philosophy, science and religion in England, 1640–1700* (Cambridge, 1991), pp. 151–77; John Marshall, 'John Locke and latitudinarianism', in the same volume, pp. 253–82.

[50] See John Spurr, 'The Restoration church of England and the moral revolution of 1688', in Walsh *et al.*, *Church of England*, pp. 127–42; Duffy, 'Primitive Christianity revived'.

call for 'whiggish' co-operation between protestants, and have emphasised suspicions of these bodies amongst more rigid anglicans. Once, however, the obsession with the societies is abandoned, and the campaigns of William's propagandists are examined, it becomes clear that reformation could have a tory as well as a whig face. There was much sympathy for tory ecclesiology amongst Burnet and his circle, and these clerics used Williamite rhetoric to reassure tories about the position of their beloved church. As a result, signs of ecclesiastical anxiety amongst tory Englishmen in the 1690s were met by bursts of propaganda, which intertwined an insistence that the establishment was safe with calls for national renewal. Despite a series of set-backs, Burnet's circle retained a belief that they could appeal to committed churchmen, and put faith in courtly reformation as their chief instrument of persuasion.

The propagandists began their struggle to reassure tories on 14 January 1689. Then Sharp, Tillotson, Tenison, Patrick, and Fowler met in Stilling-fleet's house in London.[51] At an initial glance, this conference might appear to have endangered tory ideals, since the clerics discussed possible concessions which might be made to dissent. Yet, although the courtly reformers were intending to make overtures to nonconformists, their talks were also designed to preserve the church's dominant position in society. The origins of their initiative lay less in some radical latitudinarianism, than in an approach made the previous summer by William Sancroft, the archbishop of Canterbury, to the leaders of London's dissenting community. Sancroft, who had always been an unbending supporter of a monopolistic church, had suggested that anglicans might consider concession as the price of strengthening themselves in the battle with James's popery. He was thinking of bringing dissenters back into the church to restore its universal government of English protestants, and so add to its authority.[52] This basic intention was retained by the courtly reformers the following winter. When, in February, their discussions were translated by Nottingham into two parliamentary bills, the design was still to secure the church's predominant position. Nottingham put forward a toler-ation bill to meet William's demand for freedom of conscience – but this proposed only a limited indulgence for nonconformists, who would still be excluded from public office by the tests. The Secretary's main hopes were fixed on his second measure, a bill of comprehension, which was intended to reincorporate all but an irreconcilable rump of dissenters into the national church.[53]

Sadly for Nottingham and his allies, these plans for protestant reunion ran into two difficulties. The first was the failure of William to give them his full

---

[51] Patrick, *Autobiography*, p. 141.
[52] Sykes, *From Sheldon to Secker*, pp. 85–91; Every, *High church party*, pp. 20–4.
[53] Horwitz, *Revolution politicks*, pp. 86–90.

backing. Although the king had benefited from his alliance with Nottingham's clerical affinity, the ecclesiastical settlement was one area in which he disagreed with his propagandists. Here William's preference for a generous toleration contradicted the clerics' desire to preserve the church's dominance. In mid-March, this difference became public when the king gave a speech to parliament which appeared to question the religious tests.[54] The Secretary's second problem was tory reluctance to accept the reassurances in his religious package. Such was the anxiety amongst the more rigid anglicans in 1689, that they backed away from the scheme for protestant reunion even though it was designed to strengthen the establishment, and was based upon Sancroft's earlier initiative. Consequently when the reformers' measures reached parliament, tory peers cut down the scope of the proposed concessions in the comprehension bill, and the Commons added clauses to the coronation oath which would bind the king to uphold the church in its current form.[55]

This tory rage was a considerable setback for Nottingham and his clerical allies. However, it did have one good result. The vehemence of the churchmen's reaction appears to have altered the king's position, and brought him into line behind his propagandists' strategy. The details of court politics in this period are patchy, but in early April William does seem to have turned his back on the whig advisers who had accompanied him from Holland, and to have come under greater influence from his Secretary and Burnet. Contemporary rumour held that the king had begun to follow Nottingham in ecclesiastical affairs, and the monarch's change of tack after his March speech appeared to bear this out.[56] On 9 April, when the Commons came to debate the comprehension bill, Sir William Harboard, a Privy Councillor, rose to suggest that instead of discussing the measure, the House should address the king on the ecclesiastical settlement. Harboard proposed that MPs first thank the monarch for his concern for the church of England, and then request that convocation, the church's own legislative body, be called to consider the issue of comprehension.[57] Both these proposals were intended to help William conciliate the tories. The first (the inclusion of an expression of gratitude in the parliamentary address) gave the king an opportunity to make a formal statement of his support for the establishment. Replying to the Commons' document once he had received it, the monarch wrote

As My Design in coming hither [to England] was to rescue you from the Miseries you laboured under; so it is a great Satisfaction to Me; that, by the Success GOD has given

---

[54] *CJ*, 10, 51.
[55] Horwitz, *Revolution politicks*, pp. 90–1; Grey, X, 190–8, 200–4.
[56] Bodl. Ballard Ms. 45, fol. 35.
[57] Doctor Williams' Library Morrice Ms. Q, fol. 530–1.

Me, I am in a Station of defending this Church, which has effectually shewn her Zeal against Popery, and shall always be My peculiar Care.[58]

Harboard's second proposal (the suggestion that a convocation be called) was designed to calm tory fears by reconciling them to compromise with dissent. The tactic here followed arguments by Burnet and Stillingfleet, who had suggested that anglican clerics might be happier to accept plans for protestant reunion if they could influence them through their own legislative body.[59] The call for convocation thus opened up another conciliatory strategy, which William adopted, both by promising in his reply to the address that he would convene the clerics' parliament 'as soon as conveniently may be', and by establishing an ecclesiastical commission which would prepare measures for consideration by that body.[60]

The language of courtly reformation played a central role in developing this attempted reassurance of tories. It was first used to comfort churchmen in the sermons preached by Burnet and his circle early in 1689. Above, it was stressed that these early reformation sermons denounced persecution, and advocated mutual protestant understanding as an integral part of the deliverance of England.[61] Here, it should be noted that they did not simply comfort dissent. They were preached as Nottingham's scheme of union was being planned, and can be seen as an attempt to prepare public opinion for it. The sermons did condemn persecution, but, in accordance with the policy of reuniting protestants in the anglican communion, they also made it clear that dissenters must end their separation at this providential moment. They emphasised that, after God's deliverance, there had to be *mutual* accommodation. The divine purpose in recent events had been to re-establish a united English ecclesia – not to uphold the nonconformists' right to schism. These reflections on dissent were carried furthest by William Wake in May. Preaching at Hampton Court, he delivered a millennial hymn to unity on the text 'grant you be like-minded one towards the another'.[62] In his address, he looked forward to a 'general reformation' to be marked by universal harmony; but he hinted at two possible hindrances to this blessing, which demonstrated that he saw dissent as well as rigid anglicanism as a threat to his cause.[63] First, Wake's appeal for tolerant attitudes suggested he still feared the old persecuting spirit of the establishment. Second, however, he echoed

---

[58] *LJ*, 14, 183. The exchange of messages was published as *The address of the Lords and Commons, to the king's most excellent majesty, for maintaining the church of England as by law established, with his majesty's most gracious answer thereunto* (1689).
[59] Stillingfleet to Nottingham, 8 March 1689, *HMC Finch*, II, 194.
[60] *CSPD, 1689–90*, pp. 242–3.
[61] See pp. 161.
[62] William Wake, *An exhortation to mutual charity and union among protestants in a sermon preach'd before the king and queen at Hampton Court, May 21 1689* (1689).
[63] *Ibid.* p. 33.

Restoration arguments about the stubbornness of nonconformists.[64] Speaking of those who had objected to the details of anglican liturgy, he said

[Those] who at this day *separate* from us, for the sake of those few *Constitutions* that have been made for the *Order* and *Decency* of our *Publick Worship*, must for the same reason have *separated* from all the *Churches* of the *Christian World*, for above 1500 Years.[65]

Wake had thus adapted the idiom of reformation to criticise dissent. Even more significantly, he had associated the new monarchs with this balanced point of view. His May sermon was originally delivered at court and was ordered to be printed by their majesties' special command.

As 1689 wore on, and the full depth of tory fear was revealed, the courtly reformers were ever more careful to stress elements in their rhetoric which soothed churchmen's worries. Particularly, the burden of their message shifted from the need for reconciliation with dissent, to the crucial role which the establishment would play in William's reformation. Although they continued to insist that protestant harmony would help the king's godly crusade, the propagandists also began to emphasise that the personnel and institutions of the church would be the main engine of renewal. William was shown to be counting on the anglican clergy as his elite troops in the battle for righteousness. This move allowed the reformers to address the tories' central anxiety – the suspicion that the new king was hostile to the establishment. If the church could be portrayed as the chief instrument of William's purgation, it naturally followed that he would want to defend its position in society, and strengthen its spiritual provision and authority. In fact, with the help of reformation rhetoric, William could be slotted into the traditional anglican ideal of monarchy. Apologists for the English establishment had always stressed the benefits of having the king as the supreme governor of their church. They had pointed out that the English owed their Reformation to royal action in the 1530s, and that subsequent monarchs, whilst not enjoying sacerdotal power, had been invaluable protectors and guarantors of the church's ministry.[66] Courtly reformation allowed William to turn this anglican belief in royal supremacy to his advantage. By stressing the importance of the church within his reform, William could try to reassure clerics by presenting himself as their ideal of a godly governor. He was, he could claim, a man who would defend and strengthen the establishment as he used it to fulfil his providential mission.

The key element in this strategy was the warrant issued in September 1689

---

[64] *Ibid.* pp. 26–8.   [65] *Ibid.* pp. 27–8.

[66] For the Tudor and early Stuart development of these doctrines, see Clare Cross, *The royal supremacy in the Elizabethan church* (1969); and Patrick Collinson, *The religion of the protestants* (Oxford, 1982), ch. 1.

to institute the ecclesiastical commission to prepare reforms for the coming convocation. The wording of this document was almost certainly determined by Nottingham and his clerical allies. It embraced proposals which had been circulating amongst the earl's affinity through the summer, and nominated all the leading members of Nottingham's circle to the body it instituted.[67] In its first paragraph, the warrant put the case for comprehension. It opened the way for concessions to dissent by stating that the precise form of worship in the church was 'indifferent and alterable'.[68] The second paragraph, however, turned to the theme of moral renewal. This passage was crucial for the development of courtly reformation, because it represented the first occasion on which William himself went beyond mere rhetorical acceptance of his godly magistracy, and suggested a concrete, practical initiative to amend England's manners. Listing a series of reasons for summoning the clerics, the warrant stated that

the book of canons is fit to be reviewed, and made more suitable to the state of the Church; ... there are divers defects and abuses in the ecclesiastical courts of juris-diction, and particularly there is not sufficient provision made for the removing of scandalous ministers and for the reformation of manners, either in ministers or people; and ... it is most fit that there should be a strict method prescribed for the examination of such persons as desire to be admitted into Holy Orders, both as to their learning and manners.[69]

What is remarkable about this first concrete project for reformation was that it was to be church-led. It assigned the task of moral purgation to the personnel and institutions of the anglican establishment. For example, the warrant's consideration of the quality of ordinands, and its concern to remove scandalous ministers, stressed the centrality of an exemplary anglican clergy in the coming campaign for virtue. Similarly, the proposals about ecclesiastical courts suggested an improvement of clerical discipline, in which the clergy's legal authority over the population could be strengthened to enforce popular righteousness. The September warrant, therefore, implicitly countered the tories' perception of William as hostile to their church. By suggesting that the new king intended anglican ministers to retain consider-able spiritual influence, and by presenting William as the author of schemes to remedy the church's shortcomings, the document portrayed the monarch as a faithful ecclesiastical governor. Consequently, the third and final paragraph of the warrant could open with a reassuring statement of the king's love for

---

[67] Tillotson, Stillingfleet, Patrick, Burnet, Sharp, Kidder, and Tenison served. For suggestions within Nottingham's circle that the church be reviewed along the lines mentioned in the warrant see Stillingfleet and Tillotson's proposals for church reform in 1689, Lambeth Palace Library Ms. 1743, fols. 111–18, 151–3. See also letter from Nottingham to Burnet, 19 September 1689, Bodl. Additional Ms. A 191, fol. 103.

[68] *CSPD, 1689–90*, p. 242.   [69] *Ibid.*

the anglican communion. Their majesties, it claimed, were motivated, not only by the desire to reconcile differences amongst their subjects, but also by 'their pious and princely care for the ... order, edification, and unity of the church of England'.[70]

These tactics were continued into the autumn when Nottingham's scheme of comprehension came under renewed fire. Almost as soon as the September warrant had been issued, a pamphlet attacked it. William Jane, the Regius Professor of Divinity at Oxford, refused to be comforted by the document's pro-ecclesiastical passages, and in his anonymous *Letter to a friend*, lambasted it for its conciliation of dissent.[71] He strongly objected to altering ecclesiastical constitutions at a time of turmoil, and attacked the clerics chosen to prepare concessions as ambitious traitors. In the ensuing exchange, several pieces were written to defend the king's initiative. Most were anonymous, and it is unclear how large a hand the royal propagandists had in their production. One of them, however, is known to have been written by Tenison. His *Discourse of the ecclesiastical commission* answered Jane's charges by using reformation arguments to stress the advantages to the church of William's rule. His key tactic was to use the September warrant, with its vision of reform through the establishment, to prove that the royal initiative 'tended to the well-being of the church'.[72] After defending the men William had named on the commission as loyal anglicans, he quoted the whole document to demonstrate that in the king's order, 'there is no unreasonable thing designed, neither is it at all probable that the commissioners should pervert the good ends of it. ... The support, and improvement, and well-being of the church is directly aimed at'.[73] Tenison also used the warrant to develop the image of William as a faithful protector of the establishment. He drew parallels between the new reforming king and other virtuous governors of the church by comparing the 1689 commission with the similar entities which had been instituted by Edward VI and Elizabeth and which had produced the anglican prayer book and articles of religion.[74] Most powerfully, Tenison used the king's September warrant to suggest that William had actually revived godly church government after a damaging lapse. He stated that the ecclesiastical duties of English monarchy had been ignored in the late reigns, and that it was only with the advent of William's reforming rule that they had again been taken up. Pointing a finger at the Restoration Stuarts, he observed that 'no warrant could be procured for the support and improvement of the

---

[70] *Ibid.* p. 243.
[71] [William Jane], *A letter to a friend, containing some quearies about the new commission for making alterations in the liturgy, canons &c of the church of England* [1689].
[72] [Thomas Tenison], *A discourse concerning the ecclesiastical commission open'd in the Jerusalem-Chamber, October 10 1689* (1689), p. 1.
[73] *Ibid.* p. 13.   [74] *Ibid.* pp. 2–3.

church, during the reign of King Charles the Second; much less were we to expect it from King James'.[75] This argument was calculated to appeal to tory churchmen who, as John Spurr and Mark Goldie have shown, had become increasingly disenchanted with recent kings, and had been pushed to the brink of resistance by their ecclesiastical indifference.[76]

William himself joined in stressing the ecclesiastical benefits of his rule. As Nottingham's scheme moved forward, he repeatedly expressed his love and concern for the church, and hinted that his moral renewal of the country would strengthen its position. His first move was a series of statements in the late summer and early autumn in which he praised the English establishment, and emphasised his loyalty to it. So public and sustained was such comment that the diarist Narcissus Luttrell could write

His majestie hath been lately pleased to express himself in favour of the church of England as the best constituted church in the world, and nearest to the primitive; and that he was resolved to die in its communion, and to venture his life in defence thereof.[77]

These themes were taken up again on 19 October, when William opened parliament. Addressing Lords and Commons with another pean to the church, he called the English establishment 'one of the greatest supports' of the protestant religion and asserted his readiness to 'venture his life' in its defence.[78] When convocation finally met in November, William continued his strategy by asking the body's members to seize the providential opportunity which he had provided to secure and strengthen their church. Issuing a letter to the clerics assembled, William commended the work of his ecclesiastical commission, and then reassured his audience

His Majesty has summoned this convocation not only because it is usual upon holding of a Parliament, but out of a pious zeal to do everything that may tend to the best establishment of the Church of England, which is so eminent a part of the reformation . . . and therefore does most signally deserve and shall always have both his favour and protection; and he doubts not but that you will assist him in promoting the welfare of it, so that no prejudices, with which some men have laboured to possess you, shall disappoint his good intensions or deprive the church of any benefit from your consultations.[79]

Subsequent communications reinforced the message that the king wished to protect the church as he pursued reformation through it. On 26 November,

---

[75] *Ibid.* pp. 24–5.
[76] Spurr, *Restoration church*, p. 248; Mark Goldie, 'The political thought of the anglican revolution', in Beddard, *Revolutions of 1688*, pp. 102–36.
[77] Luttrell, *Relation*, I, 606.
[78] *LJ*, 14, 320. The speech was published as William III, *His majesties most gracious speech to both houses of parliament, 19 October 1689* (1689).
[79] Message from the king to convocation, 4 November 1689, *CSPD, 1689–90*, p. 314. This was published as William III, *His majesties gracious message to the convocation sent by the earl of Nottingham* (1689).

he wrote to the bishop of London, who was acting as president of convocation, granting the body authority to discuss the package of measures mentioned in the September warrant.[80] Two weeks later the king 'authorised and required' the bishop to raise the problem of shortcomings in the church's moral jurisdiction and ordered convocation to consider proposals for 'taking away the abuses relating to excommunication in the ecclesiastical courts'.[81]

Unfortunately for the courtly reformers, the immediate impact of their propaganda was disappointing. The sense of unease in tory circles persisted through the second half of 1689, and fuelled a continuing mistrust of Nottingham's plans. Sancroft came out against comprehension, and several clerics who had been nominated to the commission, but came from outside courtly reforming circles, either refused to attend, or walked out after its first meetings.[82] Worst of all, a tory political machine began to work for the election of a convocation which would oppose any changes to the church. G. V. Bennett has shown that a group of men centred on Henry Aldrich's deanery in Oxford co-ordinated efforts to return intransigent clerics.[83] As a result, the courtly reformers' programme was doomed. When convocation met, Tillotson's bid to become prolocutor (speaker of the lower house, composed of non-episcopal clergy) was defeated by William Jane, and the body was almost immediately addled by disputes between its two chambers.[84] Once convocation had demonstrated its log-jammed uselessness, the king was forced to prorogue it, and it was dissolved in January when new elections for parliament were called. The courtly reformers had thus failed to conciliate tory churchmen and had consequently lost their preferred ecclesiastical settlement. Although their measure of toleration passed parliament in the late spring of 1689, its terms now applied to a substantial number of English protestants, not to a marginalised rump as had been hoped.

However, this setback did not end the use of courtly reformation as an appeal to tory anglicans. The propaganda campaign of 1689 had not convinced its audience, but curiously, its failure opened up new possibilities for the rhetoric. Whilst comprehension was still an option, Nottingham and his supporters had been bound to support it, and so had undermined their attempted reassurance of tories by adherence to that unacceptable measure.

---

[80] Royal warrant granting authority to Henry Compton, bishop of London, 26 November 1689, *CSPD, 1689–90*, p. 332. This was published as William III and Mary II, *A copy of the king and queen's commission sent to the convocation now assembled at Westminster* [1689].

[81] The king to the bishop of London, 12 December 1689, *CSPD, 1689–90*, p. 354.

[82] Every, *High church party*, pp. 37–59; Sykes, *From Sheldon to Secker*, p. 87.

[83] L. S. Sutherland and L. G. Mitchell, eds., *The history of the University of Oxford* (Oxford, 1986), V, 24–9.

[84] A contemporary account was given in 'An historical account of the present convocation', printed as an appendix to [Thomas Long], *Vox cleri: or the sense of the clergy concerning making alterations in the established liturgy* (1690).

Once, however, it was clear that union was impossible, the royal spokesmen could play down those parts of their propaganda which had been found offensive. After 1689, the new bishops did not generally use reformation rhetoric to advocate anglican concessions to nonconformity.[85] Instead, they highlighted the benefits to the church of William's purgation, and stressed the image of the faithful ecclesiastical governor which they had welded onto the king's godly persona.

The court's first ecclesiastical initiative after the loss of comprehension was a letter William wrote to Compton in February 1690. There is no evidence of who had the idea for this epistle, but its tone suggests the men who had worked to reassure tories in 1689 were behind it. Essentially, the letter repeated the rhetorical strategies which had been used the preceding autumn. Once again, it confirmed the church's importance to the new regime by ordering the pursuit of a royal reformation through the establishment. For instance, the letter indicated that the church was to be at the core of the king's action against vice by requiring anglican ministers to read out and preach upon the laws against debauchery. The royal epistle also contained proposals to strengthen the clergy's influence, and again linked schemes to remedy known ecclesiastical deficiencies with the drive for national righteousness. The 1689 programme of church renewal thus reappeared – this time to be implemented by direct royal order. The February letter, echoing William's warrant of six months earlier, insisted on measures to improve the quality of the clergy. It instructed bishops to 'examine into the lives and learning of those desiring to be admitted into holy orders, to see that the clergy are resident in their livings, and to admonish them to religiously observe the canon as to sober conversation'.[86] The epistle also repeated the attempt to breathe new life into the church's system of moral jurisdiction, ordering 'all churchwardens to impartially present [before the ecclesiastical courts] all those guilty of adultery and fornication'. As during the first year of William's reign, such suggestions allowed the courtly reformers to stress the ecclesiastical benefits of a royal campaign of moral renewal. Burnet, for instance, asserted in a letter to the clergy of his diocese in 1690, that William's letter demonstrated the king's 'zeal for this our church'.[87]

The bishops too continued the tactics of 1689. Throughout the rest of William's reign they looked for opportunities to associate the king with ecclesiastical initiatives along the lines of the original royal warrant, and tried to present their master as a faithful ecclesiastical governor as they did so. Letters written by the bishops occasionally catch them in the very act of

---

[85] The one exception came in the summer of 1697, when it was rumoured that Tenison was considering reviving comprehension plans. Horwitz, *Parliament, policy and politics*, p. 223.
[86] *CSPD, 1689–90*, p. 460.
[87] Bodl. Additional Ms. D 23, fol. 85.

planning such publicity. In the last months of 1694, for example, Tillotson began to consult with Burnet and Stillingfleet about issuing yet further orders to tighten control of ordination.[88] Early in the deliberations, the archbishop raised the suggestion that these measures should be introduced by royal injunction, and gave reasons for this method which showed he had an eye to their use as propaganda. The archbishop stated that getting the court to issue his orders would give them a more secure legal basis, but then went on to admit that he had 'another reason which moved me herein'. He was, he told Burnet, hopeful that by associating the monarchs with his reforming scheme, 'Their ma[jesties] concernm[ent] for religion and the church might appear to the nation'.[89] This careful nursing of public relations was refined further in September when Tillotson mentioned the project to the queen. She proved an even craftier master of political advertisement with her suggestion that the injunctions wait until William returned from Flanders. She worried that producing the orders solely in her name might create the suspicion that she was the only one of the royal couple to care about the church.[90] Similarly, Burnet can be seen using ecclesiastical reform to improve the king's image after Mary's death. In a memorandum to William in January 1696, he recommended that the king give up his income from first fruits and tenths and apply them to augment poor livings.[91] This was a scheme, eventually realised as Queen Anne's Bounty, which would have increased the money the church could offer to its ministers, and so would have improved pastoral provision in many poorly served parishes. However, whilst stressing the spiritual advantages of his idea, Burnet also emphasised its value as publicity. In the memorial, and in a follow-up note of the next year, the bishop commended his scheme to his master saying it would 'give such an impression of him [the king], as would have a good effect on all his affairs'.[92]

The bishops also continued the tactics of 1689 at diocesan level. After the failure of comprehension they worked for the sort of ecclesiastical renaissance promised by William's September warrant, and presented their efforts as proof of the reforming regime's care for the establishment. At the core of their strategy was the attempt to improve the workings of the church through their own episcopal influence and authority. G. V. Bennett, writing of the style and energy of William's bishops, claimed that they set new standards of diligence. He suggested that Tillotson and his colleagues paid more attention to their dioceses than had been usual, and struggled harder to improve

---

[88] Tillotson to Burnet, 10 September 1694, BL Additional Ms. 4236, fols. 257–8.
[89] *Ibid*. fol. 258.
[90] Letter from Tillotson to Burnet, 10 September 1694, *Ibid*. fol. 261.
[91] Bodl. Additional Ms. D 23, fol. 112.
[92] *Ibid*. 112, 115.

spiritual provision within them.[93] If this claim implied negligence on the part of the courtly reformers' predecessors, it may have been misleading, since there are good examples of energetic and conscientious bishops under Charles and James.[94] Yet, there can be no doubt of the enthusiasm which William's men took to their episcopal duties. Perhaps spurred by the stirring sermons delivered at their consecrations, they arrived at their cathedrals determined to encourage a spiritual awakening amongst the clergy in their charge.[95] The bishops were most concerned to ensure a high standard of parish ministry in their sees. They were, therefore, quick to address abuses such as non-residence, the admission of unsuitable men to the ministry, and scandalous living. They were also careful to get to know their clergy through extensive tours into the localities, and used pastoral letters and their powers of visitation to sift out inadequate pastors.[96] As primate, Tillotson's scope for action was even wider. During his time at Canterbury, the archbishop discussed remedies for the church's shortcomings with his colleagues, and used his metropolitan power to impose them. In 1692 for instance, a meeting of bishops called by Tillotson at Lambeth Palace led to a circular letter to all the dioceses of the province. This demanded action to ensure strict control over ordinations, residence at cures, removal of scandalous clergy, and rigorous moral discipline over flocks.[97] All this activity was explicitly linked to William's reformation. The episcopal messages which demanded higher clerical

[93] Bennett, *Tory crisis*, pp. 22–3; G. V. Bennett, 'Archbishop Tenison and the reshaping of the church of England', *Friends of Lambeth Palace Library, Annual Report* (1981), pp. 10–17, especially p. 14. Neither of these assertions is footnoted.

[94] See, for example, E. A. O. Whiteman, 'The episcopate of Dr Seth Ward, bishop of Exeter (1662–1667) and Salisbury (1667–1688/9), with special reference to the ecclesiastical problems of his time' (Unpublished DPhil dissertation, University of Oxford, 1951); also William M. Marshall, 'Episcopal activity in the Hereford and Oxford dioceses, 1660–1760', *Midland History*, 8 (1983), 106–22.

[95] For the consecration sermons, see Anthony Horneck, *A sermon preached at Fulham, in the chappel of the palace, upon Easter-day, 1689, at the consecration of the right reverend father in God, Gilbert, lord bishop of Sarum* (1689); John Scott, *A sermon preached at Fulham on Sunday Oct. 13 1689 at the consecration of ... Edward, lord bishop of Worcester, Simon, Lord bishop of Chichester* (1689); Ralph Barker, *A sermon preached at St Mary le Bow on Whitsunday, May 31 1691, at the consecration of ... John, lord archbishop of Canterbury* (1691); Joshua Clarke, *A sermon preached at St Mary le Bow on Sunday 5 July 1691, at the consecration of ... John, lord archbishop of York, and ... Edward, lord bishop of Gloucester* (1691).

[96] Richard Kidder, *The charge of Richard, lord bishop of Bath and Wells to the clergy of his diocese at his primary visitation begun at Axebridge, June 2 1692* (1693); Amy Edith Robinson, ed., *The life of Richard Kidder, D. D. bishop of Bath and Wells, written by himself* (Frome, 1924), pp. 64–5; Patrick, *Bishop of Ely's letter*; Patrick, *Letter of the bishop of Chichester*; Patrick, *Autobiography*, pp. 155–8; Gilbert Burnet, *Injunctions to the archdeacons of the diocese of Sarum* (1690); Burnet, *Four discourses*; Edward Stillingfleet, *The bishop of Worcester's charge to the clergy of his diocese in his primary visitation, begun at Worcester, Sept 11 1690* (1691); Sharp, *Life of ... Sharp*, I, pp. 265–6.

[97] Letter from Tillotson to Burnet, 12 April 1692, BL Additional Ms. 4236, fol. 253; heads of a circular letter by Tillotson to be sent to his suffragans, Bodl. Tanner Ms. 25, fols. 15–16.

standards also ordered ministers to implement the government's moral reform by organising fasts and obeying royal proclamations.[98] This implied that the bishops' attempts to build a strong and effective church were central to the wider project sponsored by the king, and advertised the monarch's continuing concern for the religious establishment.

The bishops' appeal to tory churchmen can even be traced through two of the most substantial works of theology published in the 1690s. The volumes in question, the *Discourse of the pastoral care* (1692), and the *Exposition of the thirty nine articles* (1699), were written by Burnet, but were both products of the whole courtly reforming circle. They had been inspired and supervised by Tillotson, and had been read by the queen and Burnet's episcopal colleagues prior to publication.[99] At first sight, the claim that these works contained an appeal to tories may seem surprising. Recent studies of the *Discourse* and the *Exposition* have suggested that they were polemical pieces, deeply hostile to tory ecclesiology. Mark Goldie, working on the *Discourse*, has linked it to John Locke's advocacy of toleration; and has interpreted it as an attempt to replace the tories' persecuting church with a non-coercive ministry.[100] Similarly, Martin Greig, reviewing the *Exposition*, has presented it as an appeal for a flexible approach to the articles, which might allow concessions to dissent.[101] There is much in these arguments. The *Discourse* certainly deplored religious intransigence, and the theological methodology of the *Exposition* was clearly loathed by some breeds of tory churchmen.[102] However, it is doubtful that the bishops' sole aim in producing the volumes was to condemn rigid churchmanship. The works were, in many ways, a stout apology for anglican principles, which might have been intended to garner tory support. Burnet claimed that his *Exposition* provided the first comprehensive defence of the church's beliefs against her sophistical enemies; and it is questionable how far his argument for religious indulgence in the other work went. Far from consistently conciliating dissenters, the *Discourse* could criticise their stubbornness – reminding them that the legal tolerance they had gained did not absolve them from the duty to seek Christian unity.[103] Moreover, the *Discourse* was not dominated by an appeal for concessions to nonconformists, but by a pastoral vision of the clergy's work, centring upon

---

[98] Sharp, *Life of ... Sharp*, p. 265; Burnet, *Four discourses*, preface, p. 4; Patrick, *Bishop of Ely's letter*, pp. 8–9; Kidder, *Charge of Richard, lord bishop*, pp. 18–19, 29–30.

[99] Burnet, *Discourse ... pastoral care*, p. 124; Burnet, *Exposition of the thirty nine articles*, preface; Tillotson to Burnet, 23 September 1694, Bodl. Additional Ms. D 23, fol. 61; Tillotson to Burnet, 12 April 1692, BL Additional Ms. 4236, fol. 253.

[100] Goldie, 'John Locke, Jonas Proast'.

[101] Martin Greig, 'The thought and polemic of Gilbert Burnet, c. 1673–1705' (Unpublished PhD dissertation, University of Cambridge, 1991), ch. 5.

[102] *Ibid.* pp. 223–44.

[103] Burnet, *Discourse ... pastoral care*, p. 101.

exemplary piety, charity, and discipline. This vision was not a party platform, but was shared by all breeds of anglican, including those most hostile to dissent.[104]

Given this, it is possible to read the *Discourse* and the *Exposition* as further episcopal efforts to win over tories. Studied in the light of the courtly reformation campaign, the two volumes can be seen to have employed all the standard devices to reassure those worried about the establishment. The *Discourse* opened with an impassioned appeal for moral and spiritual renewal in the wake of the Revolution. Its preface spoke of a nation plucked from the fire, which must amend its ways if it were not to be thrown back into the conflagration. It then presented the church as the prime instrument of this necessary purgation, and told its clerical audience that they had the greatest responsibility at this time.

We who are the *Priests and Ministers of the Lord*, are under more particular Obligations, first to look into our own ways, and to reform whatsoever is amiss among us, and then to be Intercessors for the People, committed to our Charge.[105]

Finally, the book used the royal programme of reformation, in conjunction with its reliance on the establishment, to demonstrate that the church would be protected and strengthened by the new monarchs. In the dedication to Queen Mary, Burnet spoke of the 'great designs for which God hath raised you up', and repeated Tenison's assertion that William and his wife stood in the great tradition of faithful ecclesiastical governors.

Tho Your MAJESTY's Royal Ancestors have done so much for us, there remains yet a great deal to be done for the compleating of our Reformation, especially as to the Lives and Manners of men. This will most effectually be done by obliging the Clergy to be more exemplary in their Lives, and more diligent and faithful in the discharge of their Pastoral Duty. And this Work seems to be reserved for Your MAJESTIES, and designed to be the Felicity and Glory of Your Reign.[106]

Despite its rather different subject matter, the *Exposition of the thirty nine articles* complemented the *Discourse*'s line. In the second work, Burnet placed his theological defence of anglicanism in the context of moral and ecclesiastical reform, and insisted that William was the inspiration for this renewal. In a fulsome dedication to the king, the author thanked him for his encouragement of the church, and again set his monarch in the context of his illustrious predecessors.

---

104 For discussion of this point, see Rupp, *Religion in England*, p. 74; W. Jeremy Gregory, 'The eighteenth century reformation: the pastoral task of the clergy after 1689', in Walsh *et al.*, *Church of England*, pp. 67–85, and the introduction to that volume.
105 Burnet, *Discourse ... pastoral care*, p. x. Much of the book – especially chapters 8 and 9 – can be read as a handbook for clerics pursuing moral reformation in their parishes.
106 *Ibid.* epistle dedicatory.

The Title of *Defender of the Faith*, the Noblest of all those which belong to this Imperial *Crown*, that has received a New Lustre by Your MAJESTY'S carrying it, is that which You have so Gloriously acquired, that if Your MAJESTY had not found it among them, what You have done must have secured it to Your self by the Best of all Claims. ... May God Preserve Your MAJESTY, till You have gloriously finished what You have so wonderfully carried on.[107]

Of course, Burnet's theological works were advocating a change in the direction of anglican policy. They did attempt to shift the clerical agenda away from rigid uniformity, to a less formal and more spiritual understanding of godliness. Yet none of this means they were hostile to the established church, nor that they wished to diminish its substantial dominance over the English population. In fact, the two works saw 1688 as the opportunity for an anglican renaissance. They informed the clergy that the monarchs brought to power at the Revolution might preside over a golden age of their church, if they all took the rulers' desire for moral reform seriously. As the conclusion of the *Discourse* put it:

While we have such an invaluable and unexampled blessing, in the *Persons* of those *Princes* whom God has set over us; if all the considerations which arise out of the Deliverances that God has given us by *their* Means, of the Protection we enjoy under *them*, and of the great hopes we have of them: If, I say, all this does not oblige us, to set about reforming of every Thing that may be amiss or defective among us, to study much and to labour hard; to lead strict and exemplary Lives, and so to stop the Mouths, and overcome the Prejudices of all that divide from us; this will make us look ... cast off and *forsaken of God*.[108]

Such words were certainly sung to a reformation tune. That is not to say, however, that they could not harmonise with tory aims.

WHIG AND TORY RESPONSES TO COURTLY REFORMATION

Having outlined the ways in which courtly reformation was used to ameliorate party strife in the 1690s, it is appropriate to ask how effectively it did its work. Obviously, the language's basic denunciation of division was a failure. Burnet's censures on partisan behaviour in 1689 fell on deaf ears, and party remained a source of division throughout William's reign. Indeed, it is arguable that disputes between whigs and tories became more divisive as new issues began to join the old trinity of personnel, constitution, and religion. In the next chapter, we shall see how court–country issues came to coincide with and deepen party hatreds after 1697. On the other hand, it seems possible that reformation had more effect in preventing the alienation of politicians from the king. For most of the 1690s the court avoided becoming so associated with either party that it could not negotiate with their opponents. The

---

[107] Burnet, *Exposition of the thirty nine articles*, epistle dedicatory.   [108] *Ibid.* p. 125.

very fluidity of the personnel of royal government demonstrated the monarch's continuing ability to deal with both factions. Perhaps the only time
when a party became completely detached from the court was in the aftermath of a Jacobite assassination plot against the king in 1696. Then the whigs
succeeded in enforcing the principle that only those who swore to William's
rightful and lawful authority were eligible for public office.[109] However, even
this partisan exclusion proved brief. Within months, tories were creeping
back onto local commissions of the peace and town corporations, and within
a very few years, William was welcoming them back into national
government.

Quite how much Williamite rhetoric contributed to this continuing freedom of manoeuvre is, as ever, difficult to assess. Over constitutional issues, it
seems likely that it was not courtly reformation which kept all groups in play,
so much as the decision not to endorse a particular interpretation of the legal
basis of William's rule. In the field of faith, however, there is some evidence
that reformation propaganda may have prevented too serious a rupture
between the court and party politicians. It comes from the response to the
regime's language by the religious constituencies of the whig and tory parties.
In the 1690s, both the whiggish dissenters, and those members of the clergy
who co-operated with tory attempts to defeat comprehension, found the
Williamite position sufficiently attractive to adopt. Although the two groups
stressed rather different aspects of the royal ideology, courtly propaganda
proved flexible enough to be rehearsed by both nonconformists and anti-
comprehensionists in their own political and religious discourses. Thus,
despite their wide disagreements in other fields, men who supported the
different parties endorsed key points of William's rhetoric. This might suggest
that the polemic was having some success in keeping whigs and tories open to
the benefits of the king's rule.

The case of the dissenters is the clearer. There were at least three good
reasons why nonconformists in the 1690s might want to adopt courtly
reformation arguments. First, many dissenters saw themselves within a 'puritan' tradition, which had always placed great stress on personal and national
righteousness. The programme of purgation and renewal announced by
William's regime would have been reassuringly familiar to nonconformist
leaders such as Richard Baxter and John Howe, who had made their names in
the moral reform movements of the middle of the century.[110] Second, courtly
reformation could be used to argue for a generous ecclesiastical settlement. As
has been shown, the rhetoric's broad conception of the true church, and its

---

[109] Horwitz, *Parliament, policy and politics*, pp. 175–6.
[110] For the involvement of these men in both 1650s and 1690s movements see Lamont, *Richard
Baxter*; Rose, 'Providence, protestant union'.

reflections on the evils of protestant division, suggested that orthodoxy should not be too rigidly defined, and that nobody should be persecuted for minor disagreements over liturgy or church government.[111]

Third, the royal rhetoric could calm fears about the position of dissent after 1689. Although it was clear that nonconformists would be more secure under William than under the Restoration regimes, their exact place in society was still worryingly ambiguous. Particularly, it was uncertain how far they had been readmitted to full citizenship. On the negative side, the principle of free worship had not been explicitly endorsed in 1689. The measure of toleration granted had been worded so that it simply suspended the penalties for dissent, and the test acts remained to exclude non-anglicans from public office. On the positive side, indulgence permitted nonconformists a new economic and social prominence; whilst lax enforcement of the test, and the practice of occasional conformity, permitted some of them to behave as if fully emancipated. Dissenters were thus in a difficult position. They became prominent in society, gaining visible wealth and power; but they could be attacked by tories for assuming illegitimate and illegal influence.[112]

In this situation, courtly reformation could be extremely comforting. It stated that dissenters should not be marginalised because they were potential members of William's godly nation. The dissenters might thus exploit the court's language to integrate themselves with their fellow subjects. For instance, nonconformist sermons to the societies for reformation of manners repeatedly took up the Williamite equation of zeal for reformation with patriotism, and used it to suggest that godly dissenters were full members of the national community. Edmund Calamy used precisely this technique when preaching in 1698. He argued that sinners undermined their nation's security, but, by contrast, insisted that 'We' [his reformation society audience, including many nonconformists]

shall show our selves *Lovers of our King and Country*, by helping forward the Execution of those good Laws which are in force amongst us, against Prophaness and Debauchery; the general, common and un-opposed Breach whereof, would open a wide Gap for the most desolating Calamities to enter and over-flow us.[113]

John Shower similarly described men's national loyalty and treachery wholly in terms of their attitude to the societies' work. On the one hand the motives for supporting the bodies were 'the publick interest of the kingdom', 'the

---

[111] See above, pp. 161–2.

[112] See Gary Stuart de Kray, *A fractured society: the politics of London in the first age of party, 1688–1715* (Oxford, 1985), ch. 3; Michael R. Watts, *The dissenters: from the Reformation to the French revolution* (Oxford, 1978).

[113] Edmund Calamy, *A sermon preach'd before the societies for reformation of manners, February 20 1698/9* (1698), p. 33.

honour of our nation and city', and 'love and loyalty to the king's majesty'.[114]
On the other hand

They who are negligent in this, and other Instances of Publick Service, which their
Place and Station in this City call them to, they betray their Country, are unfaithful to
their Trust, and shall answer to God for their omissive Treachery.[115]

Given the attractions of the rhetoric, it was not surprising that nonconformists in the 1690s became enthusiastic advocates of courtly reformation.
The first hint of their attachment came on 2 January 1689. Then, a delegation
of around ninety dissenting ministers went to William to thank him for his
deliverance of the protestant religion, and to promise backing for his attempts
to secure it.[116] Later, as the new king's propagandists elaborated their case,
dissenters lent their support. Not only did they reinforce the courtly reformers' words, they even took the initiative in developing aspects of the rhetoric.
For instance, after the coronation of William and Mary in April, the dissenting ministers of London addressed the new monarchs to congratulate
them on the event. They expressed the same sort of near-millennial hopes for
the king's rule which had dominated Burnet's sermon at the service, and then
went on to provide one of the earliest portraits of the queen as the exemplary
powerhouse of national renewal.

'Tis an auspicious Sign of publick Felicity, when Supreme Virtue and Supreme Dignity
meet in the same Person. Your inviolable firmness in the profession of the Truth, and
exemplary Piety, are the most Radiant Jewels in your Crown. The lustre of your
Conversation, unstain'd in the midst of tempting Vanities, and adourn'd with every
Grace, recommends Religion as the most honourable and amiable Quality, even to
those who are averse from hearing Sermons, and apt to despise serious Instructions
and Excitations to be Religious.[117]

Dissenters were also careful to share the burden of propagating the royal
case. They observed the national fasts and thanksgivings called by the regime,
and ensured that their ministers both preached and published appropriate
sermons. One congregational divine, Timothy Cruso, was particularly active
from the beginning. He printed much of his pulpit oratory in 1689, including
his sermon on the 31 January thanksgiving for William's arrival, his address
on the 5 June fast day for the war, and his preaching in the autumn on
Gunpowder Day. All these echoed themes laid down by the established

---

[114] John Shower, *A sermon preach'd to the societies for reformation of manners in the cities of
London and Westminster ... November 15 1697* (1698), pp. 46, 64.

[115] *Ibid.* p. 65. See also Daniel Williams, *A sermon preached at Salters-Hall to the societies for
reformation of manners, May 16 1698* (1698), p. 53.

[116] *The address of the nonconformist ministers (in and around the city of London) to his
highness the prince of Orange* (1689).

[117] *An address of the dissenting ministers (in and about the city of London) to the king and
queen, upon their accession to the crown* (1689), pp. 6–7.

Williamite clergy.[118] Nonconformists also joined in on other occasions when the court encouraged the English to reflect on William's reformation. For example, they participated wholeheartedly in the national mourning for Queen Mary in 1694. Following the official line set by the bishops, they reviewed Mary's efforts for moral renewal, reminding their audiences of her personal virtues, and insisting that her death must signal renewed efforts for reformation under her grieving spouse.[119] The Peace of Ryswick in 1697 provided another opportunity for dissenters to spread the word. William Bates produced a speech to the king which congratulated him on his victories over popery, and insisted there were 'more noble victories' to be won against 'profaness in manners' on the domestic front.[120] Bates told William he hoped national sins

by Your Authority and Influence, may be Restrain'd, if not truly Reform'd; for whereas other Princes assume an Infamous Prerogative to Live as they List, to satisfie their Vicious Appetites without Controul; Your MAJESTY Exhibits such Excellent Vertues in Your Practice, as may be a Persuasive Pattern, and Commandingly Exemplary to Your Subjects.[121]

John Howe, the veteran presbyterian, echoed these sentiments, calling for the establishment of a true Israel now that peace allowed William to concentrate on righteousness at home.[122] Taken together, such nonconformist words supplied an important complement to the Williamite propaganda machine. In the 1690s dissenting ministers ensured that the reformation message reached those parts of the population which excused themselves from worship in the established church, and added their voices to the chorus of loyal calls for renewal which issued from contemporary pulpits and press.

At first sight, the tories' religious constituency – anti-comprehensionist anglicans – do not seem to have been as enamoured of courtly reformation as nonconformists. The case put by Nottingham's circle in 1689 to persuade churchmen of the merits of union was almost totally unsuccessful. Not only were many clerics unconvinced by the argument for an ecclesiastical

---

118 Timothy Cruso, *The mighty wonders of a merciful providence, in a sermon preached on January 31 1688, being the day of publick thanksgiving ... prince of Orange* (1689); Timothy Cruso, *The churches plea for the divine presence to prosper humane force, in a sermon preached June 5 1689, being the day appointed for a general fast* (1689); Timothy Cruso, *The excellency of the protestant faith as to its objects and supports, in a sermon preached November 5 1689* (1689).

119 See John Howe, *A discourse relating to the much-lamented death and solemn funeral of our incomparable and most gracious Queen Mary, of most blessed memory* (2nd ed, 1695), p. 38; William Bates, *A sermon preached upon the much lamented death of our late gracious sovereign Queen Mary* (1695).

120 William Bates, 'Dr Bates congratulatory speech to the king, Novemb. 22 1697, in the name of the dissenting ministers in and about London', printed as the preface to John Howe, *A sermon preach'd on the late day of thanksgiving, Decemb. 2 1697* (1698).

121 *Ibid.*

122 Howe, *Sermon ... December 2 1697.*

settlement, several actively countered it with a press campaign of their own. Jane's *Letter to a friend* was only the first shot in a barrage of pamphlets which lasted until 1690. Most of these were anonymous, but G. V. Bennett has connected some of them with Aldrich's group at Christ Church.[123] Taken together, the tracts reveal the existence of a body of writers who were prepared, not simply to oppose the conciliation of dissent, but to question the very logic of courtly reformation which had been used to promote it.

At the most basic level, the pamphleteers savaged the king's spokesmen themselves. They accused those who served on the 1689 ecclesiastical commission of having no firm convictions, and of being too prepared to bend to circumstance in pursuit of their own ambitions.[124] The attack was not merely personal, however. As they made their case against concession, anti-comprehensionists undercut some of the key assumptions of reformation rhetoric. Most damagingly, they questioned whether a corrupt catholicism was the most important enemy a true Christian had to face. In defending the old constitution of the English church, they used two arguments which suggested non-anglican protestants were the real adversary.

First, they reiterated an extreme version of the moral pathology of dissent which had been developed amongst Restoration clerics. In anti-comprehensionist rhetoric, dissenters were once again vilified as sinful schismatics who had abandoned all restraint in their worship of their own opinions. They were not just proud and obstinate; they were ungovernable, ambitious and hate-filled men, who sensed an opportunity to pull down the clergy who had tried to control them.[125] The pamphlets were thus full of images of the church as a fortress, with enemies at its walls, whose garrison must resist suicidal appeals to open the gates.[126] Second, the anti-comprehensionists made a case for the English hierarchy as the sole form of a true church. After the Restoration, some anglican writers had begun to stress the aspects of their establishment, particularly episcopacy, which set it apart from other protestant bodies. They had turned away from traditional ecclesiology, which had seen the English

---

[123] Sutherland and Mitchell, *History ... University of Oxford*, V, 27–8.

[124] [Henry Maurice], *Remarks from the country; upon the two letters relating to the convocation and alterations in the liturgy*, (1690), pp. 1–3; [Long], *Vox cleri*, p. 37.

[125] *The lay man's religion humbly offered as a help to a modest enquiry every man into his own heart* (1690), pp. 21–4; *The church of England and the continuation of the ceremonies thereof vindicated from the calumnies of several late pamphlets* (1690), pp. 2, 9, 30, 51–8; [Thomas Grice], *A short vindication of the constitution of the church of England endeavouring to prevent all future quarrels and protestations* (1689), pp. 16–17; *The danger of the church of England from a general assembly of the covenantors in Scotland* (1690); William Beveridge, *A sermon preach'd before the convocation of the bishops and clergy of the province of Canterbury at Westminster, Novemb. the 18th 1689* (1689), preface by J. G., the translator – the sermon was originally delivered and published in Latin; [Maurice], *Remarks from the country*, p. 11; Long, *Vox cleri*, pp. 1–10.

[126] Long, *Vox cleri*, pp. 10, 12; [Jane], *Letter to a friend*, p. 6.

church as a branch of a wider reformed Christendom, and had begun to deny full validity to communions which did not share the peculiar features of the English ecclesia.[127] In 1689, when the church was in danger of alteration to conciliate dissent, these tendencies emerged more stridently. The sense of immediate threat brought a more vivid insistence that the English hierarchy was the model which all other churches must follow. As one author put it, 'is it necessary to reform that church which is confessed to be the best reformed church in the world; that church to whose pattern all the rest do desire, and only want power and opportunity to conform their own?'.[128]

Between them, these arguments threatened to replace the notion of Antichristian popery (on which Williamite propaganda depended) with a different account of God's enemies, which might call into doubt the reformer's defence of the new regime. Instead of isolating popery as the great source of sin, against which all reformed Christians must unite, anti-comprehensionists perceived a true church besieged by a variety of adversaries, of whom some breeds of protestants were as dangerous as catholics. This exclusive view of godliness might, if developed further, threaten the whole Williamite position. It might make it difficult to sell a foreign Calvinist, who had not joined the anglican communion before 1688, as the leader of God's cause on earth, and as a providential deliverer of the English people.

Yet despite this potential threat to the Williamite case, it is important not to overplay the anti-comprehensionists' opposition to courtly reformation. Analysis of the pamphleteers' efforts makes it clear that the dangerous parts of their argument were developed with the narrow and specific purpose of defeating comprehension. There is no evidence that a systematic, wholesale refutation of Burnet's thought had been worked out within tory circles. Although some elements of the reformers' case were undermined, large parts of it, those which did not directly argue for anglican concessions, were left unmolested. The pamphleteers did not, for instance, cast any doubt on the belief that James's fall had been a providential act of God, or that moral renewal might follow the Revolution. Even the challenge to the more ecumenical aspects of Williamite argument was limited to the purpose of defeating Nottingham's ecclesiastical schemes. The aspersions cast on non-anglican protestants were restricted to *English* dissenters. The pamphleteers attacked the men they were being asked to conciliate, but left those in foreign reformed churches alone. Even though the protestants abroad did not adhere to the best ecclesiastical model, they were not vilified as intransigent schismatics, and their opinions were even respectfully quoted to prove the esteem in which the

---

[127] Spurr, *Restoration church*, pp. 132–64.
[128] Long, *Vox cleri*, p. 12. See also, *Church ... continuation of the ceremonies*, preface.

existing English establishment was held throughout the world.[129] The possibility that the anti-comprehensionists might unravel courtly reformation by questioning William's membership of the godly cause was thus not realised. The pamphleteers' criticism was highly focused, and left much of the essential fabric of Williamite ideology alone.

Moreover, the anti-comprehensionists adopted parts of their opponents' case. In a curious mirroring of dissenting practice, they absorbed reformation arguments into their own position. They found it particularly convenient to accept the image of William as a faithful guardian and godly governor of the church. This enabled them to counter the accusation that they were being disloyal to the monarch, and so allowed them to side-step the potentially damaging accusations of Jacobitism which were levelled by their pro-comprehensionist opponents. Thomas Long, a prebendary of Exeter, pursued exactly this strategy. His principal piece, *Vox cleri*, used the idea of William's concern for the establishment to suggest that the king would never support alterations which his clergy thought ill considered. In the preface to his work, Long answered the argument that William clearly wanted concessions, by pointing out that the king had left this issue for convocation to decide. In the main body of the text, the author reinforced this by interpreting William's statements in support of the church as royal confidence in the current, unaltered establishment.

Their Majesties desire may be best known by their living in the Communion of the Church as now established, and his former and late Declarations to favour and protect it; for which the Convocation have addressed their Thanks, and doubt not of it.[130]

Long later used the programme of ecclesiastical improvement contained in the September warrant to further refute the king's supposed encouragement of concession. Responding to the suggestion that comprehension was the 'design and intent' of William's policy in calling convocation, he stated (with somewhat garbled grammar)

First I believe, (whatever may be the design of some Men) is not the intent of the Convocation; they may intend the better Establishment of the present Constitution, the Reformation of the Lives and Manners of some of the Clergy, by new Canons and Censures, to be provided against the Ignorance and Idleness of some, and the Irregularity and scandalous Behaviour of others.[131]

---

[129] M. M., *Letter from the member of parliament, in answer to the letter of the divine, concerning the bill for uniting protestants* [1689], p. 7; Beveridge, *Sermon ... convocation ... 18 Novemb.*, p. 28; [Long], *Vox cleri*, p. 22; [John Willes], *The judgement of the foreign reformed churches concerning the rites and offices of the church of England shewing there is no need of alteration* (1690).

[130] [Long], *Vox cleri*, p. 21. See also [Thomas Long], *The case of persecution charg'd on the church of England consider'd and discharg'd in order to her justification and a desired union of protestant dissenters* (1689), epistle dedicatory.

[131] [Long], *Vox cleri*, p. 55.

Long's allies similarly employed the reformers' image of the king. *Vox laici*, an anonymous anti-comprehension pamphlet, cited William's public attachment to the church to suggest that he opposed the current plot to pull it down.[132] Henry Maurice, a member of Aldrich's Oxford circle, admitted that he had no direct answer to the suggestion that William wanted comprehension, but then asserted a belief in the king's faithful government of the church, which he thought made such a desire unlikely. He compared William to James I, recalling that the enemies of the establishment in 1603 had hoped that the new monarch would meet their demands, but had been disappointed to discover real royal concern to protect the church.[133] William Beveridge, whilst preaching extreme caution on comprehension to convocation, and lauding the current establishment, suggested that the new king had given the church a chance to rectify any shortcomings.

Since therefore God has committed such a Church to our care; and since his Vicegerent here has now given us an opportunity to prosecute all things, that may tend to the peace, and advantage of his Church, let us employ all our powers and faculties for its accomplishment.[134]

Even William Jane, whose *Letter to a friend* launched the bitter attacks against the courtly reformers, excused the king from complicity in their plans. He stated the royal name was being misused if it was employed in support of comprehension, and hoped that William's calling of convocation would defeat the schemes of wicked men.

Of course, such language was, at one level, a complete perversion of Williamite rhetoric. It turned an element of court ideology back on its creators to destroy their ecclesiastical policy. Yet, there was a sense in which this appropriation of reformation images was a victory for the propagandists. Their opponents had effectively accepted the reassurances about William's religious attitudes which his spokesmen had built into their case. Anti-comprehensionists had seized on those speeches and documents which the court had so carefully provided to establish the king's concern for the church. Ultimately, this rendered their arguments much less dangerous. If the reassurance contained in reformation had not saved the preferred ecclesiastical settlement, it had allowed opposition to the proposed concessions to be combined with support for William's kingship. It had avoided churchmen having to face a regime which appeared completely hostile to their interests, and so reduced the risk of their alienation.

The use anti-comprehensionists could make of Williamite argument opened the way for a more thoroughgoing endorsement once the threat of comprehension had gone. In the 1690s many who had opposed protestant

---

[132] *Vox laici*, p. 18.   [133] [Maurice], *Remarks from the country*, p. 18.
[134] Beveridge, *Sermon ... convocation ... 18 Novemb.*, p. 28.

union joined the courtly reformers in spreading their propaganda. In a sense they had little choice. The dissemination of Williamite rhetoric was so bound up with the church that anyone who wished to retain a position in the establishment had to become implicated. All clerics were required to officiate at fast and thanksgiving services, read out the royal proclamations against vice, and act on the injunctions and letters raining down from their king, queen, and metropolitan. However, there were also examples of more willing and enthusiastic action from anti-comprehensionists. The reformation case had considerable attractions for these people once it had ceased to be associated with pressure to admit dissenters to the church. It offered reassurance that ecclesiastical improvements might be made under the new regime; it suggested a key role for the clergy in national life; and it continued the churchmen's old concerns with national sin and repentance.

Some of the leaders of the 1689 agitation against comprehension helped William's cause by going to court and adding to the image of the godly royal household. William Beveridge had preached the opening sermon to convocation and warned that body against unnecessary concessions. Yet he was a court chaplain, and published addresses to the monarchs, adding his considerable spiritual reputation to the Chapel Royal. Others who went to palace pulpits in the 1690s included William Jane, Bishop Thomas Sprat (who had withdrawn in protest from the ecclesiastical commission in 1689), and Francis Atterbury, a young Oxford man who, whilst not taking a leading role over comprehension, had rapidly emerged as the star of Dean Aldrich's anti-unionist party.[135] Moreover, when such men preached after 1689, their message was often indistinguishable from that of Burnet, Tillotson, and their allies. For example, William Jane preached a thanksgiving sermon at St Margaret's Westminster in 1691, which followed all the fundamental court assumptions.[136] It accepted that the recent past had seen a threat from catholicism, linked to spreading vice and debauchery; it recognised that William's foreign wars had involved England in a godly struggle with these forces of evil; and it acknowledged that moral reformation at home was essential to this struggle.

---

[135] The court sermons were Thomas Sprat, *A sermon preached before the king and queen at Whitehall on Good Friday 1690* (1690); Thomas Sprat, *A sermon preached before the king and queen at Whitehall on Good Friday April 6 1694* (1694); Francis Atterbury, *A sermon before the queen at Whitehall, May 29 1692* (1692); Francis Atterbury, *The Christian religion encreased by miracle. A sermon preached before the queen at Whitehall, October 21 1694* (1694); Francis Atterbury, *The scorner uncapable of true wisdom. A sermon preached before the queen at Whitehall, October 28 1694* (1694); William Jane, *A sermon preached before the king and queen at Whitehall, in November 1692* (1693).

[136] William Jane, *A sermon preached before the honourable House of Commons at St Margaret Westminster on Thursday, 26 November 1691, being a day of publick thanksgiving* (Oxford, 1691).

If irreligion, and infidelity be rife in the earth, if atheism, heresy, and prophaness shall take root among us, and overspread the Land with a contemt of Virtue, and Religion, 'its not our Fleets and Armies, our Forts and Garrisons, that can secure us. These are the crying sins, that have heretofore threatened the return of *Popery* upon this kingdom, and if they are still suffered to continue, and encrease, 'twill be a very hard matter to keep it out.[137]

Jane's concluding passage was an even more powerful and orthodox expression of Burnet's position, which suggested that personal reformation would secure more than individual salvation. If pursued by the whole population it would unite England around her monarch, earn the blessing of God upon the nation, secure her future, and ultimately 'make our Sion to continue a praise in the earth'.

A Righteous God will protect, and defend a Righteous people ... *[N]othing but iniquity can be our ruin.* What then remains, but that we should resolve this day to pursue those things, which make both for our present, and eternal interest, that we express our gratitude to God, and love to our Country, by a practice suitable to that holy Religion we profess, that our rejoycings, and thanksgivings, may not be the work of one day only, but of our lives. This is the way to shew your selves good Subjects and good Patriots, and such as are really concerned for the good and welfare of your Country.[138]

The case of Bishop Sprat was similar. When he preached at Whitehall on Good Friday, 1690, he was excited by the feeling that these early years of William's reign offered an opportunity for moral renewal.[139] Whilst stressing the importance of the established church in this process, he recognised the court's role in leading the reformation and told William and Mary that they had been placed at the head of society in order to purge it of sin.

For You thus indefatigably to copy after this Blessed *Example* of our Lord *Christ*, were the certain means for You to prove the greatest Blessings to the whole Nation wherein you live; that is, to become Good, as well as Great *Examples* to it: You, I mean, whom GOD has placed in so high a rank of Dignity and Honour in this World.[140]

Again, Francis Atterbury supported the courtly reformation case. His father had greeted the Revolution with an apocalyptic sermon entitled *Babylon's downfall*.[141] On 29 May 1692, the son preached before the queen. Although this was the day of thanksgiving for the Restoration, Atterbury followed the usual courtly line of using 1660 for strictly Williamite ends. The return of Charles II was not the focus of the sermon, but was merely used as one incident in a pattern of providential history, which had culminated in God's

---

[137] *Ibid.* p. 28.   [138] *Ibid.* p. 34.
[139] Sprat, *Sermon ... king and queen ... Good Friday 1690.*   [140] *Ibid.* pp. 37–8.
[141] Lewis Atterbury, *Babylon's downfall, or England's happy deliverance from popery and slavery, being the substance of a sermon preached before the Lord Mayor ... June 28 1691* (1691).

blessings upon England under the present monarchs. Referring to recent military success, he stated there had been 'fresh instances of mercy and goodness, which God even now had been pleased to bestow on us'. Atterbury made his attachment to the court's propaganda clearer when he interpreted these divine blessings as rewards for the court's programme of reformation. In granting victory, God was

Answering at last the many *Prayers* and *Fastings*, by which we have besought him so long for the Establishment of Their Majesties Throne, and for the Success of their Arms: and giving us at length an Opportunity of appearing before him, in the more delightful part of our Duty; in the voice of *Praise* and *Thanksgiving*.[142]

Atterbury thus not only asserted William's legitimacy and the benefit the nation received from him, he did so in terms mapped out by the king's own propagandists.

None of this is to say that anti-comprehensionists lapsed into total acquiescence in Williamite arguments. The passionate fear for the church's safety, which had driven them in 1689, was still present under the surface, and was stirred by increasing evidence that, whatever the claims of the court, their establishment was not faring well in the 1690s. At the beginning of the decade many talented and experienced clerics had lost their positions in a general ejection of non-juring ministers. By contrast, dissenters seemed to be thriving under the new regime. As has been mentioned, toleration removed the need for nonconformist discretion, and made the size, wealth, and influence of their community graphically apparent. At the same time, many of the clergy suffered economically from high land taxes and agricultural depression; whilst a wave of anti-trinitarian and deist writing threatened the triumph of heresy. All this was deeply disturbing to men who, even in 1689, had seen their establishment as a fortress under siege.[143]

In 1696 Francis Atterbury gave these anxieties a voice. His *Letter to a convocation man* deplored the state of English religion, and demanded the recall of the church's legislative body so that the clergy could organise a response to the dangers they faced.[144] The pamphlet signalled a loss of faith in William's episcopacy and their ideology, as it accused the king's ecclesiastical government of failing the moral and spiritual challenges of the decade. The tract complained bitterly about the progress of heresy and immorality, and hinted that the monarch had left them unchecked.[145] The demand that convocation sit whenever parliament met implied that William's normal

---

[142] Atterbury, *Sermon ... Whitehall May 29 1692*, p. 5.
[143] A good summary of anglican fears after the Revolution can be found in Geoffrey Holmes, *The trial of Dr Sacheverell* (1982), ch. 3.
[144] [Francis Atterbury], *A letter to a convocation man concerning the rights, powers and privileges of that body* (1697).
[145] *Ibid.* especially pp. 9–14.

supervision of his church through his supremacy, and his bishops, was insufficient. It had not upheld the interests of the establishment, and had allowed threats to orthodox religion. Atterbury insisted that William's government of the church needed an ecclesiastical body to inspire, encourage, and supervise it. All this, of course, was a direct challenge to the doctrines of courtly reformation. Atterbury had not only suggested that William's much heralded protection of the church had proved a sham, he had also expressed deeper doubts about the central claim within royal ideology. He had questioned whether a secular ruler could legitimately lead a moral and religious renewal. As Mark Goldie has shown, Atterbury's thought owed much to an anti-Erastian discourse developed by non-jurors to protest against their deprivation by William. The pamphleteer had followed ejected ministers such as Henry Dodwell in suggesting that ethical and ecclesiastical matters belonged to a different sphere to temporal affairs, and that these two elements of human experience were subject to wholly separate authorities.[146] Whilst secular powers might supervise secular things, Atterbury argued that spiritual matters must be governed by the authority of clerics. This was an extremely dangerous doctrine for William because it threatened to exclude his temporal authority from the very arena of morality and godliness in which its claims to legitimacy had been built.

The courtly reformers responded with an energetic attack upon Atterbury's position. Tenison supervised Wake in a massively learned refutation of the *Letter*'s arguments for the power of convocation.[147] Burnet joined in.[148] Yet it was too late. Atterbury had caught a popular mood, and a full-scale campaign to secure the return of convocation began.[149] Worse still, this fed into party politics, when leading tories added it to the group's programme at Westminster.[150] Reformation thus ceased to be an ideology around which men of different principles could unite, as one of the two parties came to be characterised by an attack upon its logic.

Nevertheless, for much of William's reign the royal rhetoric had held the line. It had brought together diverse strands of English protestantism, which had formed cores of support for the two opposing parties. Although

---

146 Mark Goldie, 'The non-jurors, episcopacy, and the origins of the convocation controversy', in Eveline Cruickshanks, ed., *Ideology and conspiracy: aspects of Jacobitism 1689–1759* (Edinburgh, 1982), pp. 15–35.

147 William Wake, *The authority of Christian princes over their ecclesiastical synods asserted* (1697).

148 Gilbert Burnet, *Reflections on a book entitled [The rights, powers and privileges of an English convocation]* (1700).

149 A bitter pamphlet campaign erupted around the positions set out by Atterbury and Wake. See Bennett, *Tory crisis*, pp. 50–4; Every, *High church party*, pp. 86–9; G. R. Cragg, *Reason and authority in the eighteenth century* (Cambridge, 1964), pp. 181–93; G. V. Bennett, *White Kennett, 1660–1728, bishop of Peterborough* (1957), pp. 36–53.

150 Bennett, *Tory crisis*, p. 55.

dissenters and anti-comprehensionist churchmen had pursued conflicting aims, they had both taken up elements of Williamite propaganda, and so signalled that loyalty to the king was an integral part of their cause. Such mutual appropriation of the court's case does perhaps reveal why William was able to work with both whigs and tories for most of his time in England. It may account for the king's success in avoiding the trap of factional monarchy, and so provide part of the explanation for his success in dealing with parliamentary politics.

6

Courtly reformation and country politics

THE PROBLEM OF COUNTRY POLITICS

The pattern of conflict between court and country in the reign of William III was very similar to that between whigs and tories. In both instances, a short period of consensus during the prince of Orange's invasion rapidly collapsed back into divisions reminiscent of Charles II's time, and caused considerable difficulties for the new king in his dealings with parliament. In both cases, these difficulties were considerably ameliorated by the deployment of courtly reformation. Just as the rhetoric of moral renewal had allowed William to appeal to partisan politicians, it provided a way in which he could make himself attractive to those suspicious of executive power. By developing a sixth reformation strategy – the presentation of the new regime as the scourge of bureaucratic corruption and vice – William's propagandists were able to calm parliamentarians' fears of the court, and to secure enough support in the legislature to make government possible.

In the case of court and country, the brief consensus of 1688 resulted from the almost total estrangement of the political nation from James II's court. In the face of royal policy since 1685, the mistrust of the executive, which had characterised the country position in the 1670s, became very widespread indeed. By his attacks on the church, James had alienated the traditional supporters of the crown, without attracting any other significant sector of the English elite to his cause. Whilst most of the old opponents of Charles II's ministries had remained unimpressed with the new catholic monarch, old court stalwarts, such as Danby, Clarendon, and Musgrave, began to work against the government, or retired into a bewildered private life. By 1688, disgust had become so general that old distinctions between court and country had been largely dissolved. The wide popularity of William's *Declaration*, a thoroughgoing country document with its demand for a parliamentary check on court abuses, demonstrated an almost universal

191

willingness to see executive action controlled by an independent agency, and a desire to make the constitutional limitations of monarchical authority explicit.

The dissolution of this consensus began almost as soon as it had crystallised. The breakdown was precipitated by William's attempts to defend the prerogatives of the English crown. As has been shown, the prince wished to inherit the plenitude of royal power in 1688/9, and worked against attempts to limit it, even when those attempts took their cue from his own manifesto.[1] William thus forced English politicians to choose between two opposed positions at the very moment they had reached broad agreement. The prince's desire for full authority demanded that peers and MPs decide whether their new ruler could be trusted with the power which their displaced king had so recently abused. On the one hand, it was possible to believe that William's claim to unrestrained authority was acceptable. If it was assumed that the Revolution had swept away the source of executive excess, then it would be appropriate to invest William with all the influence traditionally enjoyed by English monarchs. On the other hand, any doubt that court corruption had been uprooted in 1688 led to the conclusion that it was not safe to leave the royal administration unharnessed. This basic dilemma had begun to divide the English by February 1689, and led to the rapid re-emergence of court and country mentalities. As early as the discussions over the declaration of rights in the convention, attempts to impose constitutional checks on executive power became controversial.[2] Similarly, in the first days of 1689, parliamentary attempts to sort out the new king's revenue sparked heated exchanges. Some MPs argued against the usual lifetime grant of customs and excise to the monarch. They suggested that such a denial would force William into dependence on his legislature, and so guarantee good royal behaviour.[3] Other MPs were horrified by this suggestion. Objecting that not granting the revenue was a churlish way to treat a national deliverer, they sparked a debate between the executive's supporters and opponents which was to become more bitter as William's reign wore on.[4] The process of polarisation occurred in two broad stages, most neatly divided by the peace of Ryswick in 1697. Since disputes between court and country before and after this date were characterised by different patterns of politics, it will be convenient to consider the two periods in turn.

---

[1] See above, pp. 27–8, and Claydon, 'William III's *Declaration of Reasons*'.
[2] Grey, IX, 32, 33–4, 37.
[3] See speeches by Sir Thomas Clarges and Sir Edward Seymour, Grey, IX, 123, 125.
[4] See speech by Sir Robert Howard, Grey, IX, 125–6.

COUNTRY POLITICS BEFORE RYSWICK

The years of the early and mid-decade were marked by disputes between 'country' and 'court' in three broad areas. The first of these was the capacity of parliament to scrutinise the king's administration. This controversy opened up in 1689, when the Commons launched an investigation into the disastrous and undersupplied campaign by the duke of Schomberg's army in Ireland. In the summer and autumn of William's first year, angry MPs demanded to see Privy Council minutes relating to the Irish war, and asked who had recommended a corrupt commissary, John Shales, for his post. The king, supported by his allies in parliament, refused to provide this information. During a series of bad-tempered exchanges, he claimed that the Commons' requests were an unwarranted trespass on the secrets of the state, and that they threatened his control of administrative servants.[5]

In the following years, arguments over parliamentary scrutiny continued. Escalating wartime taxation ensured that the Commons did not confine themselves to exposing corrupt bureaucrats, but also demanded the right to regulate public expenditure. In the early 1690s, royal servants found themselves under constant and unprecedented investigation, as the legislature constructed a new system for the examining of government finance. In 1689, demands by MPs for information about the court's monetary needs forced the executive to submit estimates of future expenditure.[6] From 1691, these estimates came to be examined in great depth, as the House used its committee system to subject them to head-by-head scrutiny.[7] In 1690, the threat of legislative intrusion intensified with the establishment of the commission for public accounts. This body, consisting of a small group of elected MPs, investigated all aspects of public expenditure, and compiled comprehensive, and often hostile, reports on what it discovered.[8] In 1694/5 the Commons went still further. With their demand that accounts be produced for the king's civil establishment, and with their instruction to their commissioners to examine the customs and excise, they cut to the heart of the monarch's private financial business.[9] Naturally, the court resented much of this parliamentary inquisitiveness. In the years before Ryswick, the executive struggled with the legislature, making various attempts to restrain the Commons' curiosity.

---

[5] Horwitz, *Parliament, policy and politics*, pp. 31–4; Cobbett, V, 280–4, 453–4, 458–61.
[6] See William Shaw, ed., *Calendar of Treasury books, Volume IX, 1689–1691* (5 parts, 1931), part 1, cxxviii–cxxix.
[7] See, for example, Luttrell, *Diary*, pp. 7–11, 17–20, 29–33, 51–4; *CJ*, 10, 552–3.
[8] J. A. Downie, 'The commission of public accounts and the formation of the country party', *EHR*, 91 (1976), 33–51.
[9] Shaw, *Calendar ... Treasury books*, IX, part 1, cxlv–cxlvi

Privy Councillors tried to bypass item-by-item examination of expenditure in the house; bureaucrats attempted to frustrate the investigations of the accounts commission; and, on at least one occasion, a minister denounced investigating MPs as malicious and ignorant.[10]

In the early 1690s, a second area of debate between court and country joined disagreements over parliamentary scrutiny. This was the issue of executive control over the legislature. From 1691, many parliamentarians campaigned to reduce court influence over the membership and actions of the House of Commons. A widespread fear that royal servants might try to emasculate the body which scrutinised their actions led to two legislative proposals designed to reduce this possibility. First, place bills attacked those MPs who risked their independence by taking posts in the king's service.[11] Second, a series of bills to shorten the duration of parliaments aimed to force members to face their constituents more often, and so guarantee that they would be more dependent on their electorate than the court.[12] Both these types of measure were opposed vigorously. The king and his allies claimed that the proposals would weaken the royal prerogative, and they used all available tactics, including the royal veto, to defeat them.[13] Tensions only eased in 1694, when the king, facing difficult political circumstances, gave way to the Commons' fourth attempt to pass a triennial bill.[14]

The war years witnessed the emergence of a third area of dispute. This was a legal debate about the rights of an English subject when accused of treachery. In the face of continual Jacobite plots, some parliamentarians became concerned that a worried regime might abuse its judicial power. In particular, they began to fear that when men were tried for treason, the desire to convict the king's enemies might override the rights of the accused. Acting on this anxiety, some MPs sponsored measures to regulate treason trials. In repeated sessions they promoted bills to ensure that no one would be prosecuted for crimes against the state unless there was watertight evidence against them. Court supporters opposed these measures, believing that they would place the king in danger. They argued against the country members' initiative, and manoeuvred to defeat it in four successive sessions before William gave way in 1696.[15]

---

[10] Luttrell, *Diary*, pp. 10, 29, 31, 58; Downie, 'Commission of public accounts'.
[11] Rubini, *Court and country*, pp. 100–3.
[12] The suggestion that parliaments should have shorter lifespans was first raised in November 1689. See *HMC Lords, 1689–90*, pp. 343–4. Bills to reduce the length of parliament were subsequently introduced in the same sessions as place bills – Rubini, *Court and country*, pp. 104–14.
[13] Luttrell, *Diary*, pp. 335–6, 390–1.
[14] Rubini, *Court and country*, pp. 113–14.
[15] *Ibid.* pp. 122–6; Brian W. Hill, *Robert Harley: Speaker, Secretary of State and premier minister* (New Haven, Connecticut, 1988), pp. 28, 30–1.

These tensions were obviously a serious problem for the court. They not only provided another source of distracting political division, they also posed the constant threat of rupture between king and parliament. With William's administration under so much suspicion, there was a danger that legislators might lose faith in their new monarch. The worst imaginable possibility was that the country mentality might lead to wholesale Jacobitism. Paul Monod has shown that several influential Jacobites had originally supported the Revolution, but had become disillusioned by perceived autocracy and corruption in the Williamite executive.[16] So hopeful was this development for the exiled court, that James himself made sporadic attempts to encourage country-minded Englishmen into his camp.[17] Almost as disturbing was the chance that an organised opposition might form in parliament. With the menu of suspicions lengthening through the early 1690s, there was a danger that shared mistrust of William might unite a group of politicians prepared to challenge him for control of the Lords or Commons. In such a scenario, the king would have to deal with a disciplined phalanx of men, dedicated to limiting his power, and would have to defeat them before securing the legislation or supply he desired.

At first, this threat was limited by the sporadic nature of country politics. Initially, the various expressions of country sentiment did not form a co-ordinated programme, and it was very common for legislators to agree with some attacks on the executive, whilst objecting to others. Moreover, those who were suspicious of the court were polarised between whig and tory camps. This meant that country alliances in parliament broke down when partisan issues were discussed; and it also meant that co-ordinated attacks on the ministry were difficult, since MPs and peers would not criticise royal servants belonging to their own faction.[18] Nevertheless, even in the early decade, a degree of political organisation could be perceived through the confusions of country action. A tight-knit group in the Commons, centred on Thomas Clarges, Paul Foley, Robert Harley, and Christopher Musgrave, stood behind many of the attempts to scrutinise, criticise, and regulate the executive. Despite being divided between whigs and tories, the members of this group were in contact, writing to one another frequently, and meeting through mutual service on the public accounts commission.[19] In the House of Commons their behaviour was sometimes so well choreographed that there

---

[16] Paul Monod, 'Jacobitism and country principles in the reign of William III', *HJ*, 30 (1987), 289–310.

[17] See, for example, James II, *His majesties most gracious declaration to all his loving subjects . . . given 17 April 1693* (St Germains, 1693). This promised frequent parliaments, and legislation to secure fair judicial trials if James was returned to power.

[18] Henry Horwitz, 'The structure of parliamentary politics', in Holmes, *Britain . . . Glorious Revolution*, pp. 96–115; Horwitz, *Parliament, policy and politics*, pp. 98, 317.

[19] Hill, *Robert Harley*, pp. 25–8.

must have been some degree of foreplanning. Not only did these men support each other in their verbal savaging of ministers, they staged ambushes on the administration's control of procedure.[20] Well before 1697, therefore, William faced a substantial problem. His propagandists had to cope with an organised body of opinion, which viewed his executive and servants as potential enemies in a battle for regulated and controlled government.

THE COURTLY REFORMATION RESPONSE:
THE COUNTRY COURT

Courtly reformation was to play an important role in calming suspicion of the executive before the peace of Ryswick. However, to appreciate this, a much better understanding of the country mentality in the early and mid-1690s is required. Whilst some of the logic behind attacks on the court has been described above, no real attempt has been made to unearth the underlying ideology which motivated these assaults. This intellectual excavation is necessary because without it, it is impossible to assess what purchase courtly reformation might have had upon country politicians. Historians need to know what motivated men to attack William's executive before they can say how official propaganda could have moderated such opposition.

Here, existing historiography has been rather disappointing. Because of an uneven distribution of evidence, most studies of country mentality under William have concentrated on the years after 1697. In this period, parliamentary attacks on the executive were accompanied by vastly more press polemic than had been the case before. Some scholarship, particularly an important article by Colin Brooks, has braved the period before Ryswick, for which there is far less printed material; but the patchiness of the sources, and the fluidity of politics, have prevented such work defining country philosophy too closely. Brooks himself complained that the ideals in which he was interested could not be easily discovered, but had to be 'pieced together, or rather distilled'.[21] As a result, he could not ascribe a tightly formed ideology to men like Clarges and Foley in the war years, but instead merely outlined a less structured country 'persuasion'. Brooks presented this as a set of prejudices and sentiments which influenced political behaviour; but he did not intend it as a rigid set of doctrines or a political programme which would have dictated fixed responses to each situation. Rather, the 'persuasion' was a 'broad judgement of public affairs', informed by somewhat vague notions such as pessimism, mistrust, a sense of political responsibility, and a model of England as a federation of gentry estates and localities.[22]

---

[20] See, for example, Luttrell, *Diary*, pp. 7–11, 17–20.
[21] Brooks, 'Country persuasion', p. 139. [22] *Ibid.* pp. 136–44.

At first sight, Brooks's work suggests that it is impossible to formulate a country ideology before 1697, and so implies that it would be difficult to assess what appeal courtly reformation might have had amongst back-benchers. At second glance, however, the idea of a country 'persuasion' looks rather more promising. Whilst it rules out a clearly defined political philosophy amongst Clarges, Harley, and their allies, it does suggest that there were less systematic habits of thought which united parliamentarians in their attacks on the court. If the evidence from the early 1690s is reviewed with this in mind, it becomes easier to discover aspects of country politics on which Williamite rhetoric might have worked. Whilst courtly reformation cannot be set up against a well-articulated and coherent anti-court position, careful attention to the pattern of criticism does reveal two broad concerns amongst the suspicious MPs which Burnet and his colleagues could address and turn to William's advantage.

First, it is clear that Clarges and his allies were motivated by a heightened moral sense. Their attempts to restrain the court were rooted in a deep concern about vice, which shaped both their analysis of England's ills and their proposed solutions. David Hayton has pioneered work on this moral sense with his study of MPs in the 1690s.[23] Looking at the personal histories of members of the House of Commons, Hayton noted a remarkable correlation between interest in restraining the court, and desire for moral reformation. He showed that those who supported attacks on court power were extremely likely to be involved in contemporary movements to amend the nation's manners, and then suggested a possible reason for this link. He argued that there was a natural affinity between the two enthusiasms, since the usual contemporary explanation of abuses at court was moral failing amongst courtiers. Since it was the greed, dishonesty, and ambition of the king's servants which led to miscarriages of government, moral reformation and restraint of the executive had to be pursued in tandem.[24]

Most of Hayton's evidence was drawn from the last years of William's reign, but the connection between moralism and parliamentary control also operated during the war. In the early 1690s the controlling figure in back bench rhetoric was the debauched courtier. When MPs analysed the danger from the executive, they pitched upon vicious individuals, 'knaves and villains' who, they assumed, infested the king's service.[25] This attitude ran through all the country campaigns. Particularly, investigation into government finance was driven by the conviction that the heavy demand for taxes, and the growing national debt, were caused by the dishonesty and financial

---

[23] Hayton, 'Moral reform and country politics'.
[24] *Ibid.* pp. 83–7.
[25] The quote is from the speech by John Smith on the Irish miscarriages, 16 November 1689, Cobbett, V, 455.

greed of evil courtiers. 'We are told that still there is a vast debt behind', said Sir Francis Winnington in 1693, 'but there are vast pensions and gifts.'[26] 'The money is not all spent', complained William Garroway when speaking in 1689 of army supply, 'I think it may be embezzled.'[27] 'Certainly there has been mismanagement', said Clarges in 1690 when demanding proper financial accounts.

It is the common talk of the town ... Men cannot know these things by inspiration – Land and Tide-Waiters brag what they can smuggle and cheat – Farmers were Managers, but after they had made up their own pack, they cared not what became of the rest.[28]

Similarly, attempts to reduce executive control over the legislature were sparked by moral considerations. In promoting place and triennial bills, MPs were at least as much exercised by the influence of individual debauchees, as worried by the executive's power as an impersonal institution. Although arguments for these measures could be made using constitutional language, this rhetoric was usually underpinned by another discourse, expressing disgust at the vice of ministers and courtiers. For example, in a debate of 28 February 1693 on a triennial bill, much appeal was made to the idea that frequent parliaments were guaranteed by England's existing laws. Yet the bill was also promoted by suggesting that a long parliament corrupted politicians' virtue. They made a Commons seat a valuable prize, and encouraged vicious courtiers to try to debauch members. The longer the House sat, the more it entered into an immoral economy of bribery and greed, which dishonest officials would dominate. Robert Harley contended that the bill was for the Commons' 'honour', whilst Foley opined 'it is necessary for us to have frequent parliaments, and to take care also that parliaments be not corrupted, which frequent and fresh are less subject to'.[29] After hearing that bribes had become ubiquitous in previous long parliaments, one backbencher explained 'when men continue here long they alter'.[30] The language supporting place bills echoed these themes. MPs on the government's payroll were held to have lost their independence, and so to threaten the proper constitutional balance between court and Commons. Yet they were also attacked as potentially immoral. As courtiers, who voted supply, they were seen as having an opportunity to increase the funds which they could embezzle, and lavish away on their lusts. Sir Charles Sedley once explained that

the King and the People always have the same Interest, and it is not the King's to take one Penny more from the People than will just carry on the Government; it is the

---

26 *Ibid*. col. 794.   27 Grey, IX, 389.   28 *Ibid*. X, 27.
29 Cobbett, V, 761.   30 *Ibid*. 760.

People's Interest to give him full as much: But it is the Courtiers Interest to get all they can for him here, that they may obtain their Request more easily at *Whitehall*.[31]

Given half a chance, such men would defraud the king of his income and 'devour' his revenue.[32]

If the country position rested on moralism in the early 1690s, it was also shaped by political memory. As Colin Brooks has pointed out, many of the men who tried to restrain the executive had had long public careers, and the attitudes of all of them had been influenced by the record of preceding reigns.[33] If not every country politician in the 1690s had been a persistent critic of the Caroline and Jacobean courts, the mounting evidence of abuse before 1688 had united all in the belief that they had witnessed the corruption of English government. Most had been vigorously anti-catholic in the decades before the Revolution, and had come to fear that a popishly affected court was the entry point for debauchery and arbitrary principles. After 1688 MPs felt they had seen the luxury and extravagance of Charles's administration lead into the naked ambition of his brother's. It was, therefore, inevitable that suspicion of William's executive would be shaped by the experience of what had happened before he arrived.

In the early and mid-1690s, this political memory revealed itself in almost every aspect of anti-court rhetoric. Limitations on William were usually presented as attempts to prevent a repetition of what had happened before. Back-bench language was soaked in recent historical allusion, with the mistakes of the past used as justification for parliamentary assertiveness now. This came out most clearly in the 1689–90 debates on the revenue. The chief reason given for forcing William to meet parliament by denying him a life-time grant was that permanent awards of customs and excise were believed to have caused the problems of the Restoration. A fortnight after William had gained the crown Clarges stated 'I think we ought to be cautious of the revenue, which is the life of the government, and consider the two last reigns'.[34] He was supported by Sir Edward Seymour who suggested

What you settle on the Crown, I would have so well done as to support the Crown, and not carry it to excess. We may date our misery from our bounty here. If King Charles II had not had that bounty from you, he had never attempted what he had done.[35]

This remained the basis of MPs' logic into the revenue debates of the following year. In 1690, Seymour repeated his argument, stating 'We are told of

---

[31] Charles Sedley, *The poetical works of the honourable Sir Charles Sedley, baronet, and his speeches in parliament* (1707), p. 217.
[32] *Ibid.* pp. 218–19.
[33] Brooks, 'Country persuasion', p. 137.　　　　[34] Grey, IX, 123.
[35] *Ibid.* p. 125.

former kings who had this revenue, that from such easy concessions came our miseries'.[36] Similarly, horror stories from the past were used to press for triennial and place legislation. Tales of Charles II and his 'pensioner' parliaments were endlessly retold to prove the dangers of inaction.

The back-benchers' historical sense was also revealed in the assumption that any shortcoming in William's government must be, in some sense, a survival from Charles and James's days. The Restoration court had become such a paradigm of corruption, that it seems to have been difficult for Clarges and his allies to imagine abuses unconnected with it. The corrupt methods of contemporary courtiers were usually traced back to the 1670s and 1680s, so that the charge against William's executive became the perpetuation of old evils rather than the invention of new. For instance, the first report of the commission for public accounts set many of the abuses it described in a historical context. As it berated the army for enlarging the number of commissions, so that more officers lived off the service without any increase in military strength, it observed, 'the first enlarging of establishments, as to numbers and pay, began in the time of the Lord Clifford's ministry, and was augmented in the reign of the late King James'.[37] The commission also complained that money was repaid to dishonest creditors of the pre-Revolution government, and highlighted the excessive pensions, gifts, and payments which were lost to James's dismissed servants.[38]

From tracing this survival of corrupt methods, it was a short step to imagining the survival of corrupt persons. Miscarriages under William were often attributed to debauched officials of the preceding regime who had not been purged in 1688. One of the charges brought against John Shales in 1689 was that he had worked for James II.[39] Similarly, Clarges suggested in 1693 that national misfortune stemmed from those 'arraigned in former times, now in offices'; whilst in 1691 Sedley portrayed William as surrounded by a band of established fraudsters who had learnt their trade before he arrived. 'He's a wise and virtuous prince', the MP asserted, 'but he is but a young king, encompassed and hemmed in among a company of crafty old courtiers, to say no more of them, with places, some of three thousand, some of six and some eleven thousand.'[40]

Of course, it is important to be wary of presenting all attacks on government personnel as examples of country sentiment. The most obvious reason for caution is that partisan rivalry, the hatred between whigs and tories, could adopt anti-executive rhetoric when these parties were trying to dislodge one another from office. The year 1695, for instance, saw the publication of

[36] *Ibid.* X, 13–14.   [37] *HMC Lords, 1690–1*, p. 407.
[38] *Ibid.* pp. 408–9, 420–2, 425–8.   [39] *CJ*, 10, 298.
[40] Sedley, *Speech*; Cobbett, V, 776.

proceedings in parliament against a number of officials caught misappropriating money and accepting bribes. The Commons debates were printed in pamphlet form, along with a preface explaining the need to guard against public corruption.[41] However, whilst this work reported the activities of the commissioners for public accounts, it did not originate from Harley and Clarges's circle. Rather, it sprang from a group of militant whigs, who wished to use the parliamentary enquiry to blacken the toryism of its chief targets.[42] Other pamphlets and speeches also used country language as cover for partisan attacks.[43] Yet although such rhetoric had party motives, and so cannot be used as direct evidence of country attitudes, it still illuminates the back-benchers' political memory. As they tried to pick up support from MPs for their sallies, whigs and tories accused their victims of having co-operated with pre-Revolution governments. In 1689, John Howe dressed his attack on tory ministers' mishandling of the Irish crisis as an attack on men who had served in James's Privy Council, and used their connection with the old regime as proof of their dishonesty.[44] The 1695 pamphlet on bribery similarly attacked tories as relics of a past dark age. Its preface warned

It is yet fresh in Memory, how our own Nation was brought to the very Brink of Destruction by the corrupt Practices of the Reign of Charles the Second. *Then was the time* when all Men of Vertue, untainted Probity, and Love to their Country ran the Hazard of being ruin'd.[45]

Tories replied by accusing leading whigs of being just as implicated in the mire of the Restoration regime. In 1695 they defended their men by pointing out their accusers were supported by the earl of Sunderland, the great unprincipled courtier of James's reign.[46] Both sides, therefore, knew that there was political capital to be made amongst back-benchers by associating enemies with the terrible memory of what had gone before.

Having outlined the moralism and historical sense of the country worldview before Ryswick, it is possible to show how courtly reformation placated the government's critics. Once suspicion of government after the Revolution is understood as an amalgam of ethical righteousness and vivid political

---

[41] *A collection of the debates and proceedings in parliament in 1694 and 1695 upon the inquiry into the late briberies and corrupt practices* (1695).

[42] See Horwitz, *Parliament, policy and politics*, pp. 146–52.

[43] In the early 1690s whigs especially used this device, accusing tories, as the old court party, of being addicted to the court life. See *Plain English: or an inquiry into the causes that have frustrated our expectations from the late happy Revolution* (1691); [John Hampden], *Some short considerations about the most proper way of raising money in the present conjuncture* (1691); [John Hampden], *Some short considerations concerning the state of the nation* [1692]; *An honest commoners speech* (1694).

[44] Cobbett, V, 281.

[45] *Collection of the debates*, preface, p. iii.

[46] *A letter from a gentleman in Yorkshire, to his countryman in London, concerning the duke of Leeds, with an answer* (1695), pp. 32–3.

memory, a parallel begins to emerge between the assumptions of country politicians and those of Williamite propagandists. Since men like Clarges and Harley saw personal debauchery as the root of public abuse, and since they viewed the Restoration court as the root of all evil, their rhetoric effectively echoed the denunciation of past sin which dominated courtly reformation. Both country politicians and the new government claimed to want to eradicate debauchery which had become ensconced during the late reigns. As a result, William's propagandists were given a chance to neutralise attacks upon the executive. If they took their usual line, and stressed the court's lead in eliminating the sins of the Restoration, they might hope to persuade men like Harley and Clarges into collaboration and consensus.

The appeal of Williamite moral reform to the country mentality was evident amongst some of the most active critics of the administration. In the 1690s, some of those most suspicious of the executive also became ardent advocates of the courtly reformation programme. The degree to which this occurred can be illustrated by the case of Robert Harley and Paul Foley. These two country stalwarts belonged to an intimate political connection, based on their two families, which left considerable evidence of its beliefs in the large number of letters which passed between clan members. In this correspondence, mistrust of William's executive was matched by a belief in the king's providential role as a reformer, and an enthusiasm for the moral crusade he launched. The two families were sufficiently convinced by the royal message of reformation that they were prepared to help broadcast it, both within their homelands on the Welsh borders, and nationally. In February 1689, they organised the thanksgiving for William's intervention in their locality. They thus helped to drive home the idea that England had been delivered from debauching rulers and that the new monarch was an arm of the Lord. Robert Harley reported to his father, Sir Edward, that the day had been 'solemnly observed here with a very great congregation and very excellent sermon'.[47] Later, the Harleys and Foleys gave enthusiastic support to the first concrete manifestation of courtly reformation, the attempt to renew the church as an instrument of godly righteousness. They campaigned for candidates for the 1689 convocation who would back Nottingham's ecclesiastical programme, and were bitterly disappointed that the earl's opponents triumphed in that body. 'We may as soon expect reformation from a convention of infernal spirits as from any of these', wrote Robert's brother, Edward.[48] In the years that followed, the convention also weighed in behind Queen Mary's attempts to reform manners through the law, and aided William's programme of national humiliation through fast days.[49] When a new day of repentance was

---

[47] *HMC Portland*, III, 428.   [48] *Ibid.* 41.   [49] *Ibid.* 470–1, 482–3, 485, 487.

announced, London-based members of the families rushed the news out to Herefordshire, so that the neighbourhood could be prepared.[50] Most significantly, support for reformation within the families' circles was explicitly recognised as a form of support for the new court. When John Boscowen wrote to Robert Harley on 27 September 1690, telling him of the success of fasting in London, he congratulated his friend on holding his locality to the linked causes of reform and the king.

I am glad your country is so firm to the Government when others deviate. . . . The King declared yesterday his intension was the fast should be observed while the war continued in Ireland. The London and adjacent ministers neglected it the last day without an order from his Majesty on pretence that it was 'outed' by the Thanksgiving.[51]

At first glance, it is harder to demonstrate the commitment of other country leaders to William's moral and religious programme. There is a particular problem with tories such as Clarges and Musgrave, since these men helped to wreck Nottingham's ecclesiastical plans in 1689, and so scotched William's early hopes for church-led reformation. However, as has been shown, opposition to Williamite schemes for protestant union ought not to be read as hostility to the whole idea of royal reform.[52] Musgrave was active in the movement for reformation of manners, and there are glimpses in Clarges's political rhetoric that he believed England had been delivered to a truly virtuous monarch in 1688.[53]

Consensus over moral reform was, of course, useful to William. It meant that in one area of policy, at least, the king was viewed as a friend by his fiercest critics. Yet courtly reformation did more than construct a narrow alliance between country members and the executive on the specific issue of morality. It also operated in some of the more controversial debates which divided the crown from its subjects. Since Williamite propaganda paralleled the assumptions of the country members, the regime's defenders could use it to deflect and manage criticism. Because official rhetoric shared MPs' horror of Restoration debauchery, William's spokesmen could construct his executive as a sort of *country* court. They could point out that a government founded on the principles outlined by Burnet actually shared many of the same concerns, and recognised the same enemies, as its back-bench critics.[54] The reformers could therefore hold up the king as an exponent of country

---

[50] *Ibid.* 462.   [51] *Ibid.* 450.

[52] See above, pp. 183–8.

[53] For Musgrave's interest in moral reform, see Hayton, 'Moral reform', p. 90. For Clarges's support for William and the new regime, see the qualifications in his criticism of the court in the speeches reported in Grey, IX, 123; Luttrell, *Diary*, p. 215; Cobbett, V, 624.

[54] For one example, see Tenison, *Sermon against self-love*, pp. 10–11, which criticised corrupt administrators who milked public funds.

principles, who wanted to rid his administration of its inherited debauchery, and who would welcome the help and encouragement of country members in this task. Using this technique, the royal propagandists could hope to corral potential criticism into relatively safe areas. They could try to persuade parliamentarians that any divisions between them and the court stemmed, not from ideological incompatibility, but merely from the practical problems of getting a programme of reform past a powerful and entrenched system of corruption.

Courtly reformation was most successfully applied to calm country fears in the discussions over parliamentary scrutiny of public finance. Although the court sometimes took a stand on its prerogative when faced with demands to investigate its expenditure, blank opposition was not its only response. More usually, it employed the ideal of a purging king to try to channel back-bench energies. The starting point for the strategy was the image of the court contained in reformation propaganda. It has been repeatedly stressed that the new monarchs were presented as a source of piety and virtue in contrast to the debauched excesses of the Restoration regimes. What must be emphasised here is that royal frugality formed a central part of this picture. William and Mary were portrayed as careful and honest husbands of government funds, who had broken with the financial extravagance and waste of Charles and James. For instance, Burnet and his allies made much of the queen's lead in restraining unnecessary expenditure at court; whilst the king was shown to prefer the hardships of the military camp to the costly ease of palaces.[55] Most importantly, royal propagandists defended this image of frugality in the face of the government's escalating requests for funds. They admitted that taxes had risen, but argued that this was solely due to the demands of war. Williamite pamphleteers pointed out that the king spent his money on necessary arms and fighting men, and did not dissipate them in courtly extravagance as his predecessors had done. One writer asserted that men were now 'satisfied that their money is employed for the uses intended, not lavishly and unaccountably thrown away on pensions, &c', and another stated

What we give his Majesty, he bestows ... in providing for our defence, not for his own pleasure or humour: He is none of those that are bewitched with the Charms of an opulent Fortune, or dazzled with the Lustre of a Crown, and thereupon fall to Luxury and glorious Ease, and progress their kingdoms round for an expensive Recreation. He delights not in stately and sumptuous Palaces, nor consumes his Revenues in erecting or adorning such.[56]

[55] Fowler, *Discourse of the great disingenuity*, preface, p. 12; Burnet, *Essay ... late Queen*, p. 82. Contemporary opinion of William was that, if anything, he spent too little on outward display, and was miserly with court hospitality. See Burnet, *History ... own times*, IV, 2–3.

[56] *The character of a bigotted prince; and what England may expect from the return of such a one* (1691), p. 19; *Short reflections upon the state of affairs in England: more especially, with relation to the taxes and contributions now necessary* (1691), pp. 24–5.

Spokesmen for the Treasury in parliament joined in this presentation, offering panegyrics on William's careful use of money. For instance, Sir George Treby, trying to head off doubts about the court's financial demands in the Commons late in 1689, reminded members that there had been a change in English government. 'I have seen a time', he claimed, 'when those who cheated the king were thought the best men. The money we are to pay now is our redemption money; for what we paid to beat our enemies formerly, was spent upon dissolute persons at court.'[57]

Here, court spokesmen were not simply elaborating their picture of a virtuous monarch. They were also developing the ideal of a country court. By incorporating frugality and fiscal probity into the royal programme of reformation, the court could signal that it recognised back-bench anxiety about financial mismanagement, and that it was taking action to settle their fears. When asking for money from parliament, the king usually accompanied his request with a pledge that any supply granted would not be misdirected. This tacitly acknowledged that past experience had given parliamentarians legitimate cause for concern, and promised that things would be different under the new reforming government. As early as 8 March 1689, William, recommending that troops be sent for the reduction of Ireland, stated 'I will engage my solemn word to you that whatever you shall give in order to these public ends shall be strictly applied to them'.[58] Opening the 1690–1 session of parliament, he assured the House 'I have asked no revenue for myself, but what I have readily subjected to be charged to the uses of the war'.[59] In his address to parliament on 25 November 1690, William reinforced this message, saying of the supplies the Commons was considering approving, 'I shall not be wanting on my part, to see them exactly applied to those uses for which you intend them'.[60]

This ideal of a frugal court, struggling to overcome the corrupt legacy of the past, opened the way for attempts to neutralise hostility from back-benchers. Since courtly reformation suggested monarch and legislators shared the same objectives, it permitted the executive to offer even the most suspicious MPs a role in the government's own programme of fiscal reform. Those concerned about possible waste and misappropriation within the administration might be recruited as *constructive* critics: men who would help the king by delving into his bureaucracy and unearthing any surviving corruption. William, therefore, welcomed much parliamentary enquiry. Although there were tensions between court and legislature over scrutiny in the early 1690s, this should not detract attention from repeated offers made by the king to open up the inner secrets of his administration.

[57] Grey, IX, 393.   [58] *CJ*, 10, 45.   [59] *Ibid.* 425.   [60] *Ibid.* 482.

The court's willingness to be investigated in the early 1690s can be observed in the construction of the system of financial scrutiny by the Commons in that decade. This system of legislative investigation of public expenditure was described above as a response to MPs' fears about the costs of government. However, whilst back-bench pressure to investigate public finance was responsible for much of the new mechanism, the court itself also took a lead. On its own initiative, it prepared public accounts, provided estimates, and gave access to the internal workings of its bureaucracy. On 28 June 1689 the king, warning that not enough had yet been granted to cover the cost of war, suggested that parliament might like to check how money was being spent in order to satisfy themselves that his need was genuine.

The necessary Expence of this Year will much exceed the sums you have yet provided for it. And, that you may make the truer judgment in that Matter, I am very willing you should see how all the Monies have been hitherto laid out: And to that End I have commanded those Accounts be speedily brought to you: By which you will see how very little of the Revenue has been applied to any other Use, than that of the Navy and Land forces.[61]

Despite the fact that the Commons did not respond to this offer, William persisted. Opening parliament in October he stated 'that you may be satisfied how the money has been laid out which you have already given, I have directed the accounts to be laid before you, when you think fit to call for them'.[62] This time the House took up the royal initiative and called for the accounts, which were presented on 1 November.[63] Next year, the king repeated his performance, again offering the Commons access to the hidden operations of his administration. Returning to Westminster from Ireland for the winter session, he told his legislators 'I did, at my departure, give order for all the public accounts to be made ready for me against my return, and I have commanded them to be laid before the House of Commons'.[64]

William was willing to allow scrutiny even when parliamentarians took the initiative. As was mentioned above, the practice of providing estimates for future expenditure originated in Commons demands for information in 1689. Yet, even though these requests were a novel intrustion into the mysteries of state, they were readily accepted by the court. On William's orders, his ministers responded with detailed 'states' of the army, navy, and ordnance, which, in 1691, became the basis for parliament's first systematic review of spending plans.[65] Even when the Commons asked for accounts from the king's civil administration in 1694–5, financial openness was maintained. William provided the required information quickly and efficiently,

---

[61] *Ibid.* 200.   [62] *Ibid.* 271.   [63] *Ibid.* 278.   [64] *Ibid.* 425.   [65] *Ibid.* 278.

and accepted a series of Commons resolutions controlling what he did with his own money – even though their position in law was extremely dubious.[66]

Scrutiny was even encouraged through the commission for public accounts. Despite the anger amongst some court politicians about the activities of this body, William's executive was not initially, or ever absolutely, hostile to it. Such a commission was, after all, a logical development at a time when the court had started to provide accounts, and would fit with the wider policy of trying to work with parliamentary investigators. Accordingly, William gave the commission much support. The idea for a body to investigate public accounts was first floated in the early months of 1690, when a bill was introduced to the Commons to empanel nine MPs.[67] Although this bill was lost at an adjournment in May, there is no evidence that William was hostile to the measure; and Burnet was later to claim that the whole scheme had been a royal initiative.[68] Burnet's view appears to be confirmed by events in the summer, when the king moved to rescue the commission. On his own authority, William attempted to set up a body which would have had the same functions, and the same membership, as that envisaged in the spring proposals. This royal design to establish an inquisition on finance was only frustrated by a factional dispute between whigs and tories.[69] When parliament met again in October, court politicians again appear to have offered no resistance to the reintroduced bill, and William gave the measure his assent that winter.[70]

It is true, as J. A. Downie has shown, that the commission's enquiries were systematically frustrated by certain ministers and bureaucrats once the body got down to work.[71] Yet again, this was not the full picture. Considering how hostile to the executive the commission's reports were, it is curious how much help these men obtained from the court in compiling their criticisms. As Harley and his team laboured through 1691, the executive fulfilled its statutory duty to pay them, and to meet all their expenses; and it ordered its officers to co-operate in their work.[72] To take one example: at the end of June 1691 viscount Sidney, the Secretary of State, wrote to the earl of Suffolk to warn against any attempts to frustrate the commissioners' enquiries into the cost of Dutch forces in England. Suffolk was told to muster his soldiers so he could

---

[66] Shaw, *Calendar ... Treasury books*, IX, part 1, cxlvi–cli
[67] For the empanelling process over the period 19–22 May 1690, see *CJ*, 10, 421–2.
[68] Burnet, *History ... own time*, IV, 116–17.
[69] *CSPD, 1690–1*, p. 29; Horwitz, *Parliament, policy and politics*, p. 59.
[70] The bill passed the Commons on 26 December 1690, *CJ*, 10, 538; and received the royal assent under two weeks later, *LJ*, 14, 618.
[71] Downie, 'Commission of public accounts'.
[72] For the statutory payments see Shaw, *Calendar ... Treasury books*, IX, part 3, 1080, 1149, 1151.

inform the commission how many he had, and was ordered to admit any person that body sent to witness the event.[73] Even after the first report was published, William still saw advantages in approving parliamentary scrutineers. Robert Harley, the rising star of the commission, reported in 1692 that the king had received him and his colleagues graciously and thanked them for their efforts.[74]

All this court effort gained a satisfying response. During the various campaigns of enquiry, country MPs avoided direct opposition to the court by taking up the offer of alliance. They were always careful to place their activities in the context of the *royal* programme of reform and presented themselves, not as wrathful and hostile avengers of the court's transgressions, but as exposers of administrative corruption which the king's own efforts had not yet succeeded in purging. This attitude was visible in the debates over access to Privy Council deliberations in 1689. In the Shales case, those MPs who requested information suggested that William was surrounded by debauchees from the last reign, and presented their demands as an attempt to remove these dangerous men. More sustained evidence that country MPs became recruits for a royal programme of purgation came from the commission of public accounts. Just as it is important not to overplay the hostility of the court to its parliamentary scrutineers, it is vital not to exaggerate the alienation of scrutineers from the court. Whilst the accounts commission did help to forge a country alignment in parliament, and listed a huge number of mismanagements under William, it always assumed the good faith of the king's government. The commission adopted the role of ally in administrative reformation, and provided vital information to the king as well as to the Commons. Thus, in the first report, William and his honest servants were portrayed as the victims, not the perpetrators, of miscarriages. The king was informed that he had paid back loans to people who had lent, not their own, but public money; and he was told that he was unwittingly paying his revenue officers' business expenses. He was also informed that excessive pensions were being unaccountably doled out to worthless individuals, and that his servants had increased their salaries 'upon slight pretences'.[75] Most importantly, William was informed that it was his own great project, the war, which was being most hampered by waste. For instance, the commissioners pointed out that the system of checking army payments had broken down, with the result that many warrants had been obtained to release money above the number of effective men. Consequently, funds were unaccountably filched

---

[73] Sidney to Suffolk, 29 June 1691, *CSPD, 1690–1*, p. 428.
[74] Robert Harley to Sir Edward Harley, 17 November 1692, *HMC Portland*, III, 507.
[75] *HMC Lords, 1690–1*, pp. 404–8.

away and officers complained that 'they had received very little money, although they find great sums charged by the Treasurer at War'.[76]

The Commons's response to the first report reinforced the sense of participation in a royal programme. The resolutions taken after consideration of the commission's document censured the king's administration only mildly, and were designed to provide more details of those who defrauded him. They asked for greater details of salaries and fees, and asked the commissioners to list those who charged William for their business expenses and had fraudulently lent him public money.[77] Speeches, too, presented the report as helpful to the monarch as it would allow him to know the full extent of the corruption with which he was still surrounded. Sir John Thompson stood 'amazed that, in the best times and governments, things should still be in such darkness'. He 'believed we are under the best of kings, but never was so much goodness so abused'. William was 'in hands that do not understand their business'; he was 'wholly ignorant of these matters, and therefore I think we ought to address the king to acquaint him therewith'.[78] Sir Charles Sedley agreed. He demanded 'that the king might be acquainted with these matters. He keeps at Kensington and the courtiers keep him there as in a box.'[79]

This underlying spirit of collaboration survived even manoeuvres by the supporters of the ministry to emasculate the commission. In 1692, the Lords made an attempt to alter the legislation renewing the commission's authority, so that MPs more sympathetic to the administration might sit on it. Country spokesmen objected, and bitter debate ensued when the Commons attempted to secure their original list of names by tacking it to a money bill.[80] However, even at this time of strain, Clarges and his friends still insisted they were the court's true allies. Christopher Musgrave used William's financial openness to justify the tack, and argued that the monarch himself demanded an independent and effective commission.

> It is also said the King desires an account may be taken of the moneys given; if so, it is no doubt the Lords will pass it. And this clause will tend much to satisfy the country whom you have loaded so much, and therefore I think it is for the service of the King to pass it.[81]

In the early 1690s William's propagandists had greater difficulty ameliorating country criticism of treason trials, and of executive influence over the legislature, than of financial waste. This was because, in these other areas, William flatly rejected Commons initiatives. As has been mentioned, the king

---

[76] *Ibid.* p. 408.   [77] *CJ*, 10, 572.
[78] Grey, X, 191; Luttrell, *Diary*, pp. 58, 55.
[79] *Ibid.* p. 55.
[80] *Ibid.* pp. 161–3, 166, 170–1, 179, 184, 186–8.
[81] *Ibid.* p. 188.

insisted that treason, place, and triennial bills aimed at the vital core of his prerogative, and was prepared to kill them off with a weapon as blunt as the veto. In this situation, there was limited scope for reformation discourse to operate. With William ensuring that the executive and back-benchers remained starkly opposed, it was difficult to present his regime as an ideal country court. It was, perhaps, a mark of the difficulties the courtly ideologists faced on these issues, that their usually close political cohesion broke down. When the bishops' loyalty to the executive could not be squared with their reforming approval for country campaigns, they were torn into opposing camps by contradictory principles. On the triennial bill, for instance, Burnet sided with the country initiative, whilst Sharp vigorously defended his royal master's prerogative.[82] By contrast, on the 1696 attainder of Sir John Fenwick – an incident which raised the arguments over treason trials – Sharp, Kidder, and Fowler attempted to defend the accused, whilst Burnet, Tenison, and Patrick voted to protect the government.[83] After one parliamentary debate over the Fenwick case, Sharp and Burnet even descended to verbal brawling in the lobby of the Lords.[84]

Yet, whilst the executive was in no position to promote itself as a country court in discussions over treason and legislative autonomy, this did not mean that the rhetoric of courtly reformation was of absolutely no use. The evidence from parliamentary debates is fragmentary, but it seems to suggest that royal propaganda had created a general political atmosphere which helped to contain criticism of the executive within relatively safe forms. Even in areas where William was openly obstructing them, back-bench politicians did not transgress the rhetorical parameters set by the country court. By and large, they portrayed the king as an ally in the reforming process, and continued to present their activities as a contribution to a *Williamite* campaign. Parliamentarians had either been genuinely convinced of William's virtue by the court's general propaganda campaign, or they found it difficult to construct arguments which rejected the royal image. If any country members had doubts about the king's purging zeal, they clearly judged it prudent to put them aside in public, and develop arguments for their favoured measures which incorporated the court's claims.

This was evident in the points used to promote place, triennial, and treason bills. One of the most popular ways to advance these measures in the early 1690s was to suggest that they must be passed *now* because William's reign offered a unique opportunity to establish virtuous government. The line is well exemplified by Sir Charles Sedley's intervention in a debate on a treason

---

[82] See Hart, *Life … Sharp*, pp. 208–9; Clarke and Foxcroft, *Life … Burnet*, p. 316.
[83] Horwitz, *Parliament, policy and politics*, p. 337.
[84] Hart, *Life … Sharp*, pp. 206–7.

bill in 1691. Advocating the measure, Sedley implored 'Let us not then here
... deprive his majesty of the glory of passing an act, which most men in all
ages desired, but could never hope to obtain, but from so gracious a prince'.[85]
This argument countered the arguments of Privy Councillors who opposed
the bill, but it also limited the back-bencher's assault. It flattered the king by
suggesting there was a sort of 'Williamite moment' in which beneficial and
virtuous legislation might be passed. Sedley's words therefore constructed his
own version of a country court. The MP presented William as a man prepared
to break with entrenched executive corruption, and co-operate with his
people to root it out.

Sedley was a peculiarly passionate supporter of the king, but his language
was typical of campaigners for treason bills and measures to ensure parliamentary autonomy. The idea of a Williamite moment became almost the chief
argument for the former type of reform in the early 1690s. In the same 1691
debate which saw Sedley defend his 'gracious' prince, John Howe warned the
House that if they did not obtain a treason trial bill 'in the time when we have
a king that will secure our liberties, we never shall'.[86] The following year, the
arguments for unique opportunity were reintroduced with the treason
measure. In a debate on 18 November, Robert Harley stated 'I think it is the
proper time to get good laws in a good reign, and therefore I am for this bill
now'.[87] A week later, John Granville summarised the mood with the following contribution. 'The best time to have this bill, is when we can get it. Now
we have a good prince on the throne, and no more seasonable time than
now.'[88] Similar points were made to promote place and triennial legislation.
On 28 January 1693, Robert Harley argued for a measure to exclude place-
men on the grounds that 'such remedies, to obtain good things, must be
obtained in good reigns', whilst on 9 February the same year, a bill for
frequent parliaments was pressed by Goodwin Wharton who explained 'I
have no distrust of the king, but would have it now to be gained against [a
future] bad prince'.[89]

The power of the country court was as well revealed when William rejected
Commons proposals, as when back-benchers advanced their measures. On
the face of it, royal vetoes of place, treason, and triennial bills ought to have
dissipated the mirage of a country king amongst back-benchers. Yet curiously, such actions merely strengthened calls for an alliance against the
common enemy. Historians are fortunate that they can study one such
reaction in detail. On 9 January 1694, when the House of Commons went
into a Grand Committee to discuss the royal veto of a place bill, Anchitell

[85] Cobbett, V, 685.
[86] *Ibid.* 686.
[87] *Ibid.* V, 713; Luttrell, *Diary*, p. 237.
[88] Cobbett, V, 740.
[89] *Ibid.* V, 760, 766–7.

Grey was present, and wrote an extensive account of the proceedings.[90] Grey's notes reveal that many MPs were extremely angry and reflected bitterly on the fact that they had granted vast sums to William before he repaid them with such scant regard. Some presumed to lecture their monarch on constitutional practice, and some hinted darkly that supply should be withheld in punishment for the court's actions.[91] Yet, despite their anger, most members were careful to preserve the image of William as an ally, who shared their fundamental objectives. The debate was dominated both by the search for an explanation of what had happened which did not question the king's virtue; and by appeals to the monarch to recognise the place bill as part of his own reformation programme.

The most common explanation of William's veto in the Commons discussions was corrupt advice. Clarges kicked off the debate with a ringing denunciation of vicious royal servants whom, he claimed, had prevailed upon the king.

I am sorry for the occasion of the Committee. I will not say any thing concerning his Majesty, only of the evil Counsellors that presumed so to advise the King … Formerly, just Bills and Grievances were first passed; and after that, the Money given. Now, in great respect to his Majesty, the order is inverted, and our Grievances denied redress. I cannot think the King to blame, since his Declaration hath been to concur with us in any thing, to make us happy. I should have been glad if the Counsellors, or some of them, would have given some reason for the Rejection of this Bill.[92]

Sir Thomas thus preserved the rhetoric of alliance between monarch and back-benchers by conjuring up a common enemy in evil advisers. Clarges's trick proved popular. As the debate proceeded, more members spoke of wicked counsellors, and these figures became the chief target of the address which the House sent to William when it had finished its deliberations. Charles Hutchinson complained that gifts of money by the House had gained it less interest at court than 'false' men, whilst Geoffrey Jeffreys demanded to know who exactly had recommended the rejection.[93] Although this latter suggestion was opposed because it threatened to stir up damaging partisan jealousies, members did resolve that whosoever had advised the king to veto was an enemy to the monarchs. Finally it addressed William to 'harken to the advice of your parliament, and not to the secret advices of particular persons, who may have private interests of their own, separate from the true interest of your majesty and your people'.[94]

As the Commons homed in on evil counsellors, they also tried to re-emphasise their common purpose with their prince by presenting the rejected

---

[90] Grey, X, 375–80.
[91] See especially Paul Foley and William Bromley's contributions, *Ibid.* X, 376, 378.
[92] *Ibid.* 375–6.   [93] *Ibid.* 376, 377.   [94] *Ibid.* 377; *CJ*, 11, 72.

bill as another effort to purge out sin. Member after member stressed that legislation was a 'remedy for corruption', a measure for 'clearing' parliamentary vice, a bill which tended 'immediately to keep ourselves uncorrupt'. Some MPs took the argument further and bluntly told William that his actions had undermined his whole case since coming to the throne. A deceived king was departing from his *own* reformation. 'The nature of the bill', Hutchinson reminded the House, 'was to take off scandal.' Its rejection only gave ammunition to Jacobites who could say 'we have only changed our prince, but not for the better, at so many millions expense'.[95] John Thompson similarly presented the royal veto as a betrayal of Williamite principles. 'When I gave my voice to make the prince of Orange king, I thought to have seen better times than these.'[96] Such arguments permitted sharp censure without irrevocably souring relations with William.

In fact, the ideal of a country court had so controlled the debate, that the executive was left with considerable scope for regaining support. When William replied to the Commons address, he played upon the evident faith in him as a reformer and accepted the offers of a renewed alliance which had been wrapped up in the back-bench criticisms. He acknowledged he may have been let down by advisers, and promised to work with parliament in future. He thanked the Commons for its 'zeal in the common interest' and concluded

I am persuaded, that nothing can so much conduce to the Happiness and Welfare of this Kingdom, as an entire Confidence between the King and People; which I shall, by all means endeavour to preserve: And I assure you, I shall look upon all such Persons to be my Enemies, who shall advise any thing that may lessen it.[97]

Whilst this reply was rejected as inadequate by some, it was effective enough to stall any further Commons action over the royal veto that session. In the debate on the king's answer, many MPs expressed delight that William had taken their side against his corrupt officials, and a motion to press him for more specific commitments was defeated by 229 votes to 88.[98]

Of course, it is possible to account for the behaviour just described without invoking courtly reformation propaganda. It is arguable that the language of country members in the early 1690s was entirely conventional, and does not, therefore, need a deliberately created image of a reforming king to explain it. Such a case would be based on the observation that claims to support a virtuous monarch against his corrupt servants were traditional gambits, wheeled out to attack royal policy without risking treasonous reflections on the head of state.

Since so much country language in the 1690s, especially the concentration

---

[95] Grey, X, 376.   [96] *Ibid.*   [97] *CJ*, 11, 74.
[98] Grey, X, 382–6; *CJ*, 11, 75.

on evil counsellors, did follow established patterns, such an objection has weight. However, although MPs in the 1690s were undoubtedly using conventions, the decade in which they lived was sufficiently different from preceding periods, that mere rhetorical tradition is probably not a strong enough explanation for their style of argument. In the first place, the terms of the Revolution settlement had begun to open up the possibility of criticising the king directly. During the debates in the 1689 convention, the attempt to define why it had been legitimate to displace a ruler had led to the recognition that monarchy was a trust.[99] The declaration of rights suggested that the king's title was no longer indefeasible, but portrayed it as conditional on his ruling under the constitution, and on his governing in the public interest.[100] Moreover, royal adherence to these conditions was held, at least *in extremis*, to be capable of being judged by subjects. Once this view of monarchy had been accepted, personal criticism of the monarch became thinkable. Since it was recognised that the king could transgress laws and contracts, men might warn their ruler that he was abusing his trust, and attach the blame for miscarriages to him.[101] The 1690s were also different from previous decades because William's position was challenged. Jacobite critics, not believing their target to be a legitimate ruler, were not constrained by the tradition of avoiding attacks on the head of state, and went for the kill. James's supporters produced a widely available series of attacks upon William's policies, which blamed him personally for miscarriages and disasters. The new theoretical ability to criticise the king directly was thus joined by a rhetoric which did not hesitate to do so.

In these circumstances, the country members' arguments over treason, place, and triennial bills may have been conventions, but they were not empty platitudes. Adopting a language which limited and contained criticism of the court was a positive choice. It meant rejecting Jacobitism, and the new possibility of laying blame at William's door. The country mode of discourse does, therefore, require some explanation. Courtly reformation, with its construction of a country court, provides a cogent one. It is arguable that country members, shocked by what had happened under the Restoration regimes, and bruised by their experience of administrative secrecy, waste, and ambition, could only have been persuaded to continue with old forms of criticism by an executive which demonstrated that it shared their analysis of

---

[99] See Henry Horwitz, '1689 (and all that)', *Parliamentary History*, 6 (1978), 23–32.
[100] Though for modern debate on this, see Schwoerer, *Declaration of rights*, p. 6.
[101] For the removal of the constitutional shield protecting the monarch in 1688, see Howard Nenner, 'The constitution in retrospect from 1689', in Jones, *Liberty secured?*, pp. 88–122, especially pp. 105–7; Janelle Greenburg, 'Our grand maxim of state, "the king can do no wrong"', *History of Political Thought*, 12 (1991), 209–28.

what had gone wrong, and which offered an alliance to combat the agreed source of evil.

COUNTRY POLITICS AFTER RYSWICK: THE COUNTRY COURT PRESERVED

Country activity after the peace of Ryswick must be considered separately from that before, because anti-court politics was largely restructured in the mid-1690s. Although many of the same people were involved in attacking the executive after 1697 as had always been, and although some of their demands were familiar, there was a transformation in the allegiances, causes, methods, and beliefs of country politicians.

The first aspect of this reconstruction was a change in the partisan configuration of country politics. In the late 1690s, the cross-party country action which had characterised the war years was largely replaced as suspicion of the executive became an overwhelmingly tory phenomenon. The realignment had begun in 1694. Then, a young and intransigent group of whigs (soon to be known as the 'junto') completed a take-over of the ministry which had begun the previous year with the overthrow of the earl of Nottingham.[102] During the resulting whig monopoly, tories had been pushed towards a country position, since the sight of their enemies in power had made them mistrustful of the executive. By 1695, those tories who had participated in earlier ministries, and had once defended the court, had begun to adopt the language of suspicion.[103] At the same time, country-minded whigs, who felt betrayed by the hunger for office amongst the junto, began to break their traditional allegiances, and were effectively absorbed into the tory block in the Commons as they attacked the ministry.[104] The tories thus reconstituted themselves as a country party and added demands for legislative autonomy, parliamentary scrutiny, and judicial independence to their old ecclesiastical and constitutional platforms.[105] With the junto whigs defending the prerogatives and influence of the executive, party politics no longer cut across court–country divisions, but tended to reinforce them, and bestowed a greater consistency and clarity on anti-ministerial action.

---

[102] The political processes which led to this whig domination are laid out in Horwitz, *Parliament, policy and politics*, ch. 6; Keith Feiling, *A history of the tory party, 1640–1714* (Oxford, 1924), pp. 294–8.

[103] On 25 January 1695, Nottingham gave a speech savaging ministers' behaviour over the Lancashire treason trials and attacking the Bank of England: Keith Feiling, *History ... tory party*, pp. 307–8.

[104] See Hill, *Robert Harley*, chs. 3–4; Horwitz, *Parliament, policy and politics*, pp. 317–18.

[105] J. R. Jones, *Country and court: England 1658–1714* (1978), pp. 268–78 and ch. 15; J. H. Plumb, *The growth of political stability in England, 1675–1725* (1967), pp. 140–52; David Hayton, 'The "country" interest and the party system 1689–c. 1720', in Clyve Jones, ed., *Party and management in parliament, 1660–1784* (Leicester, 1984), pp. 37–86.

Country politics was also changed after Ryswick by the emergence of new controversies between the executive and its critics. Some of these were disputes which had begun in the early decade, but which had only come to prominence once the war had ceased to dominate the political agenda. A prime example was the argument over Irish land grants. Following William's defeat of the Irish Jacobites at Limerick in 1691, the king had given many estates forfeited by his enemies to close friends and courtiers. Unease that these lands had been lost to private profit, rather than augmenting public resources, was expressed at the time; but it was only with the coming of peace that the tory country group of MPs made a full investigation of the matter, and demanded resumption of William's gifts.[106] Other novel issues were peculiar to the post-war years. The peace of Ryswick itself sparked off a new argument about the future of the English army. Once a large body of soldiers was no longer required to fight the French, a dispute broke out between the court and the tory country block over whether it should be retained as a standing force, or disbanded. Whilst William wished to keep an effective military as a bulwark against possible future French aggression, his opponents worried that such a force might become the tool of an ambitious executive. They argued that a large army would provide the court with an instrument with which it might coerce parliament; and they suggested that it would provide the government with a vast new source of patronage with which to corrupt its legislative scrutineers. The battle was played out in a series of parliamentary debates between 1697 and 1699 which resulted in the reduction of England's land forces to a rump.[107] In the late 1690s, the tory country block also broke new ground exploiting fears about public finance. Early in the reign, the decision not to meet the huge costs of William's war entirely out of current taxation had resulted in the creation of mechanisms to manage a national debt.[108] Although most politicians recognised the necessity of this deficit-financing, there was increasing anxiety about its political impact. Many MPs in the tory country camp began to worry that the new Bank of England and the novel market in securities was increasing the power of the court. They feared that personal wealth was being tied up in government stock, so that men were discouraged from criticism of the executive

---

[106] J. C. Simms, *The Williamite confiscations in Ireland, 1690–1703* (1956), chs. 8–10.

[107] Lois G. Schwoerer, *No standing armies!: the anti-army ideology in seventeenth-century England* (Baltimore, 1974); Childs, *The British army*, ch. 8; Angus McInnes, *Robert Harley, puritan politician* (1970), pp. 35–7; Horwitz, *Parliament, policy and politics*, pp. 222–31, 249–54.

[108] P. G. M. Dickson, *The financial revolution in England: a study in the development of public credit* (1967), pp. 39–89.

which might undermine public credit. As a result, attacks upon the new instruments of finance became an established part of the country canon.[109]

A new appeal to public opinion formed a third element in the restructuring of country politics. During the war, country politicians had made relatively little use of the press to bolster their parliamentary activities. Some tracts, such as John Hampden's *Some short considerations* (1692), had been written to support country causes; but such efforts had been rare, and were usually the work of individuals, rather than forming part of a co-ordinated campaign.[110] After 1697, the situation was transformed. In the last years of William's reign, tory country initiatives at Westminster were always accompanied by huge outpourings of supporting literature. Perhaps encouraged by the lapse of licensing legislation in 1695, and the greater vigour of the political press which resulted, writers churned out works blasting the court and its policies. Most significantly, the political leadership of the tory country block was heavily involved in the activity. J. A. Downie has shown that Robert Harley was in contact with a number of political writers, including John Trenchard, John Toland, and Charles Davenant, who were responsible for many of the most influential works. Harley employed the writers to produce specific polemics, provided them with information, and co-ordinated their efforts with his own parliamentary manoeuvres.[111]

J. G. A. Pocock has pointed to a fourth new feature of country politics in the late 1690s – its ideology. Pocock has shown that as the pamphleteers worked to advance tory country causes after Ryswick, they developed an innovatory set of discourses with which to argue. He has suggested that the core of this new ideology was a 'civic humanist' language, developed over previous decades, particularly by the Interregnum republican, James Harrington.[112] The key features of the language – which was extensively modified in the 1670s to support a monarchical polity – were belief in a balanced constitution, stress upon the importance of checks on executive power, and an idealisation of land-owning and arms-bearing citizens as independent bulwarks against government encroachment.[113] The discourse was also characterised by what might be called a 'sociological' view of politics. It interpreted transformations in the pattern of power in the context of economic and

---

[109] Brewer, *Sinews of power*, p. 206; Dickinson, *Liberty and property*, pp. 106–7; Dickson, *Financial revolution*, pp. 15–35.

[110] Downie, *Robert Harley*, pp. 19–27.

[111] *Ibid.* pp. 28–57.

[112] For Harrington's contribution, see J. G. A. Pocock, ed., *The political works of James Harrington* (Cambridge, 1977), historical introduction, pp. 1–154.

[113] J. G. A. Pocock, 'Civic humanism and its role in Anglo-American thought', and J. G. A. Pocock, 'Machiavelli, Harrington and English political ideologies in the eighteenth century', both in J. G. A. Pocock, *Politics, language and time: essays on political thought and history* (1971), pp. 80–103, 104–47, respectively.

cultural processes, paying particular attention to changing patterns of property holding.[114] Despite a lacuna in the appearance of 'civic humanism' in the early 1690s, Pocock argued that the discourse was taken up by the tory country block after 1697 and developed further to criticise the junto court. Adapted to address the huge growth of William's military state, it was applied to attack the standing army and financial system advocated by the whig-dominated executive.[115] Country ideology at the end of the seventeenth century was, therefore, remodelled on what Pocock called 'neo-Harringtonian' lines. In practice, this meant it was elaborated to include a detailed analysis of the decline of the independent and public-spirited English freeholder; and it was expanded to consider the cultural and economic forces which allowed the executive to extend its influence.[116]

The clear question raised by the general restructuring of country politics is whether it affected the ability of William's court to contain criticism. Obviously, there were several ominous features of the new situation, which reduced the possibility that suspicious parliamentarians might co-operate with the executive, and direct their attacks into safe channels. The assimilation of country sentiment within the tory party, for instance, increased the bitterness between the court and its critics, as it added the old partisan hatreds to back-bench mistrust of those in power. The realignment also improved the organisation of country members in parliament. It replaced the earlier temporary alliances with a permanent grouping, whose leaders, such as Harley, could plan coherent strategies against the ministry. Similarly, the increase in the range of issues debated, and the organised use of the press, raised the stakes by expanding the forum of disagreement. By the end of the reign, country pamphleteers had launched a systematic attack on the whole record of the junto court, and demanded that every Englishman take sides in the dispute. However, for the historian of courtly reformation, it was the threat from the ideological changes in country politics which demands most attention. This is because the sort of language which Pocock described emerging in the late 1690s endangered the parallels of thought between the executive and its critics which had made collaboration possible during the war.

The problem with 'neo-Harringtonianism' was that it abandoned the debauched Restoration court as the sole source and paradigm of corruption. Concerned with the decline of a landed and armed citizenry, the new country rhetoric did not confine itself to the evil influence of the men surrounding

---

[114] Pocock uses the term 'sociological' to describe his writers' works in *Political works ... Harrington*, p. 139.

[115] See Pocock, *Machiavellian moment*, pp. 423–8; Pocock, *Political works ... Harrington*, pp. 135–42.

[116] A tory country defence of the landed classes after the late 1690s is explored in Holmes, *British politics*, ch. 5; Isaac Kramnick, *Bolingbroke and his circle: the politics of nostalgia in the age of Walpole* (Cambridge, Massachusetts, 1968).

Charles and James. Rather it was more interested in wider social processes, many of which were perceived to operate beyond the period of the Restoration regimes. For instance, the leading critics of the army ranged far outside the thirty years after 1660 in their writings. Andrew Fletcher, one of Pocock's leading neo-Harringtonians, explored the whole of post-medieval European history in his 1697 pamphlet *A discourse concerning militias*.[117] Demonstrating how the armed and landed nobility had lost its social prominence across the continent, Fletcher began his story around 1500, when the invention of print, the compass needle, and gunpowder had initiated cultural and economic change.[118] At the other extreme, and more disturbingly, writers on the junto's financial system concentrated on the short period *since* 1688. They began to consider how the economic effects of William's war had weakened the ancient gentry in the face of the executive, and so threatened to corrode the basis of alliance between court and country. If Restoration debauchery were not to be blamed for everything, then the two sides might no longer recognise the same enemy, and court appeals for aid in purging a common foe might fall on deafer ears.

The danger of such an irreparable breach can be seen in the new bogeymen who emerged in the literature of the late decade. As they analysed the decline of England's ancient gentry, country writers became interested in new elites, which they believed had begun to usurp the position of public-spirited landowners. Their 'Pocockian' understanding of contemporary ills began to revolve around an emerging class, whose adherence to the junto court posed a threat to England's balanced government. For country writers, the new class – a 'monied interest' of government creditors and stock dealers – held considerable influence by virtue of their wealth and alliance with the executive. However, unlike the landed gentlemen, whom they displaced, they had no estates or influence independent of government, and so would never endanger their position by restraining the court.[119]

For our purposes, the most important point about the new elite was that it was portrayed as a product of *William's* reign and policies. Country rhetoric stressed that those who undermined virtuous landed men, and supported the junto, were very recent social upstarts. According to the pamphleteers, most members of the whig court camp had been nobodies before 1688. They were 'men shot up ... like mushrooms', 'worthless fellows [grown] rich', 'scoundrels [made] gentlemen of great estates', 'glittering meteor[s]' who had very recently gained great houses, equipages and incomes at the expense of older

---

[117] [Andrew Fletcher], *A discourse concerning militias and standing armies with relation to the past and present governments of Europe and of England in particular* (1697).

[118] *Ibid.* especially pp. 7–10.

[119] Pocock, *Political works ... Harrington*, pp. 137–8; Pocock, *Machiavellian moment*, pp. 450–1.

elites.[120] Moreover, these nobodies were shown to have scaled the social ladder by taking advantage of *post*-Revolutionary opportunities. They had been parasites on the bureaucracy, and on the system of public finance, which had emerged only in the last few years to service William's wars. The epitome of this dangerous class of person was Charles Davenant's Tom Double.[121] Introduced in two pamphlets which combined a civic-humanist account of gentry decline, with popular, knockabout satire, Davenant's character encapsulated all the qualities of the *arriviste*, pro-junto class.[122] His career had been shaped by a conscious determination to advance himself at the expense of the independent and 'ancient gentry'.[123] Like all his colleagues, he had risen over the backs of honest English citizens by exploiting circumstances *since* 1688. He had manipulated the new national debt to defraud the public and line his own pocket.[124] He had promoted new taxes, like those on malt and leather, to increase the money available for embezzlement.[125] He had been to Ireland after James's defeat to ensure he got a share of the spoils.[126] As a result he had risen from obscure origins to the top of society. Born of a London shoemaker, and sacked for fraud in James II's reign, he was living the life of a lord by the time Davenant first introduced him in 1701.[127] In the author's cleverly constructed dialogue, Double boasted of his country estate to his companion, Whiglove, and reminded him

how I am lodg'd in Town ... I have my *French* Cook, and Wax-Candles; no Butchers Meat comes on my Table; I drink nothing but *Hermitage, Champagne* and *Burgundy* ... my very Footmen scorn *French* Claret. I keep my Coach and six, and out of my fine

---

[120] [James Drake], *The history of the last parliament begun at Westminster the tenth day of February, in the twelfth year of the reign of King William* (1702), p. 6; *A short defence of the last parliament with a word of advice for all electors to the ensuing* (1699); *England's enemies exposed*, p. 33; [John Trenchard], *A letter from a souldier to the Commons of England, occasioned by an address now carrying on by the protestants in Ireland* (1702), p. 25.

[121] Davenant was to become one of the chief country pamphleteers of the late 1690s, working closely with Harley. He had come to notice with several attacks on junto deficit finance. See [Charles Davenant], *Discourses on the publick revenues and on the trade of England* (1698); [Charles Davenant], *An essay on the probable methods of making a people gainers in the ballance of trade* (1699). For Davenant's career, see D. Waddell, 'Charles Davenant, 1656–1714: a biographical sketch', *Economic History Review*, 2nd series 11 (1958–9), 279–88.

[122] [Charles Davenant], *The true picture of a modern whig, set forth in a dialogue between Mr. Whiglove and Mr. Double, two under-spur-leathers to the late ministry* (1701); [Charles Davenant], *Tom Double return'd out of the country: or the true picture of a modern whig set forth in a second dialogue between Mr. Whiglove and Mr. Double* (1702).

[123] Davenant uses the phrase 'ancient gentry' in *Tom Double return'd*, p. 32.

[124] This point is made repeatedly throughout the two Tom Double pamphlets, but see especially [Davenant], *Tom Double return'd*, pp. 38–9.

[125] [Davenant], *True picture*, p. 25.

[126] *Ibid.* p. 24.

[127] For Double's beggarly career before the Revolution, see *ibid.* pp. 15–16.

Chariot I loll and laugh to see gallant Fellows, Colonels and Admirals, trudging a-foot in the Dirt.[128]

All this, of course, reversed the image of corruption which had prevailed before Ryswick, and made the task of William's propagandists far more difficult. The old paradigm of government evil – the debauched Restoration courtier – had held court and country together. Now, however, figures like Tom Double began to undermine this consensus. The two sides had now only an eroded basis for alliance, because 'neo-Harringtonian' fears about the fate of the landed had redescribed William's reign in country rhetoric. No longer was it a period of hope, when the nation might come together under the court's reformation to tackle the sins of the past. It was a darkening age, when new, and very destructive, forces had been called into being.

Yet, despite all that has been said, it is well to be cautious before writing off courtly reformation after Ryswick. Whilst Pocock's work does point to important developments in country ideology, it is vital not to overplay the changes which occurred. Pocock directed attention to the most 'theoretical' pamphlets and passages of late decade literature: ones where the social analysis of gentry decline was carried on most explicitly and systematically. If the material is read less selectively, it is clear that, although Pocock's 'civic humanist' rhetoric was important, it was not the whole story. Vital elements of the pre-Ryswick country worldview survived to run in tandem with Pocockian discourse. Indeed, the new 'sociological' models of corruption often appear to be little more than new polemical bottles, into which some very familiar fears were poured.

In the first place, most country writers of the late 1690s were still deeply concerned about the effects of personal immorality on political behaviour. As David Hayton has pointed out, the literature of the period linked private and public misdemeanour, and, as he suggests, it is likely that the average MP continued to worry more about sinful individuals than complex social processes.[129] Certainly, accusations of vice still formed a central plank of the country position. If one examines the caricatures of court supporters offered in the literature, it is clear that whilst they were 'Pocockian' monsters who undermined the public-spirited landed class, they were also simply and conventionally vicious. For example, a pamphlet of 1701, probably penned by Robert Harley himself, denounced its whig enemies as 'robbers, adulterers and drunkards ... sodomites and bardashers' who lived in luxury.[130] A

---

[128] *Ibid.* p. 31.

[129] Hayton, 'Moral reform', pp. 84–6.

[130] [Robert Harley], *The Taunton-Dean letter from E. C. to J. F. at the Grecian Coffee House, London* (1701). For the authorship of this piece see J. A. Downie, 'Robert Harley, Charles Davenant and the authorship of the *Worcester Queries*', *Literature and History*, 3 (1976), 83–99, especially 89.

follow-up work spoke of 'perjury, ingratitude, adultery, lying and slander-ing'.[131] This was, of course, vulgar abuse, but it was typical of the sort of language used to describe the court whigs, and it did indicate that private vice was still seen as a valid index of public evil. Even Tom Double, the archetypal 'neo-Harringtonian' villain, was portrayed as a man possessed by avarice, who tried to influence others by feeding their lusts. Davenant tells the reader of Double's obsession with making money, of his whore in his country house, and of voluptuous evenings designed to convert nobles to their cause.[132] In the closing conversation of the second pamphlet, which occurred as Double and Whiglove prepared a debauching dinner, Double explained that his party used vice as their chief instrument of policy. Only by corrupting the nation's manners could they hope to succeed, since only vicious individuals would fall in with their plans.

I have known a great many deluded by Pleasures and Luxury to betray their Country, who were not to be wrought upon by any other Motives. Therefore you see one of our Noble Friends, who is still at the Head of our Designs, sets himself in good Earnest to corrupt the Manners of all our Youth, in order to subvert the Constitution: ... He is the Patron of Licence and Disorder; his House is the School of Intemperance: What Lust in any of his Followers does he not study to please? Women, Musical Entertain-ments, Riots and Debaucheries of all kinds, are ready at hand for such as will be drawn into his Party by those sort of Alurements.[133]

The continuing moral basis of country thought after Ryswick was also apparent in the use of classical history. The decline of the Roman polity was an important theme in the pamphlets of the late decade, because it could be used to demonstrate the deleterious effects of social change on balanced constitutions. Special emphasis was placed on imperial expansion, which had disrupted the early Roman society of armed and landed citizens, and led through inequality and rivalry to slavery.[134] Yet whilst the pamphleteers' classical scholarship pointed to sociological models of England's plight, the story they told could also be read as a simple moral tale. The pamphleteers made it clear that imperial expansion would not have been nearly as danger-ous to the Romans, had not cruelty, intemperance, avarice, and dishonesty been prevalent amongst them. One of the most sustained accounts of Roman decline was Davenant's history of imperial debt in his polemic against

---

[131] [Robert Harley], *A letter from the Grecian Coffee House in answer to the Taunton-Dean letter, to which is added a paper of queries sent from Worcester* (1701).

[132] For the whore, see [Davenant], *True picture*, p. 31; for the dinners, see *Tom Double return'd*, p. 6. The obsession with money is ubiquitous through both pamphlets.

[133] [Davenant], *Tom Double return'd*, p. 95.

[134] Walter Moyle, 'An essay on the constitution of the Roman government' [1699], in Caroline Robbins, ed., *Two English republican tracts* (Cambridge, 1969); [John Toland], *The militia reform'd, or an easy scheme of furnishing England with a constant land force ... without endangering the publick liberty* (1697); [John Trenchard and Walter Moyle], *An argument shewing that a standing army is inconsistent with a free government* (1697), pp. 7–9.

William's Irish grants, the *Discourse upon grants and resumptions* (1700). Despite the work's careful attention to social forces and the principles of sound financial management, it was ultimately the moral failings of individual emperors which drove the narrative forward. Roman decline resulted from rulers who raided the public purse to feed their private lusts. Davenant attributed the destruction of the state to Mark Antony, 'whose luxury alone was sufficient to impoverish many rich nations'; to Nero, who wasted resources to service his addiction to pleasure; to Caracalla, who robbed the imperial treasury to 'feed the licentious appetites' of his followers; and to Macrinus who 'could not avoid plunging himself into the voluptuous courses of his predecessor'.[135] Ultimately, therefore, the cause of Roman decline was an ethical collapse at the centre, leading to degeneration throughout the state. 'When countries are effeminated by luxury, and impoverished by riot and ill conduct, that is, when they have neither virtue nor strength remaining, they presently become a prey to the warlike nations that will invade them.'[136]

The survival of moralism as a pillar of country thought helped to preserve the other great support of the pre-Ryswick worldview – the belief that the Restoration regimes were the source of most miscarriages. Whilst the 'sociological' bent of late 1690s discourse pushed writers to examine forces operating outside the period 1660–88, their lingering moral sense attracted them back to that notoriously vicious period. They continued to see Charles and James's courts as the entry point for the debaucheries which still plagued the nation. For instance, in the work of John Trenchard, the leading anti-army polemicist, the executive itch for a standing force was traced back to the luxuries of the Caroline household. The idea of a large, professional soldiery was conceived in a court whose manners had been corrupted by popery, and which had consequently aimed at arbitrary power to satisfy its appetites. Charles II was a 'luxurious effeminate prince' who

debauched and ennervated the whole Kingdom: His court was a Scene of Adulteries, Drunkeness, and Irreligion, appearing more like Stews, or the Feasts of *Bacchus*, than the Family of a Chief Magistrate: And in a little time the Contagion spread thro the whole Nation, that it was out of fashion not to be Leud.[137]

The junto were, therefore, merely continuing the traditions of Caroline and Jacobite ministries.[138] Other pamphleteers painted similar pictures of the Restoration regimes. Although Davenant's Tom Double was a product of post-Revolutionary times, his creator stressed that Charles's reign had also seen a vicious class of men reliant upon a corrupt executive. 'Many of [th]em

---

135 Charles Davenant, *A discourse of grants and resumptions* (1700), pp. 56, 60–2, 72, 78, 79.
136 *Ibid.* p. 77.
137 [John Trenchard], *A short history of standing armies in England* (1698), pp. 10–11.
138 [John Trenchard], *A letter from the author of the argument against a standing army* (1697), p. 14, made this point explicitly.

were debauched by pomp and splendour, and in the heat of their youth, they liked the pleasures of a court, but the riots of it compelled many of [th]em, at last, to depend upon its favours.'[139] Other country pamphleteers joined the chorus. One spoke of 'that inundation of profaness, lewdness and immorality, introduced by K[ing] Charles II, and his atheistical wits, to fit the nation for the intended yoke of popery and slavery.'[140] John Toland saw the church, politics, judiciary, and above all, morals 'debauched ... by the pattern showed us at court' under kings corrupted by the Roman faith.[141]

This echo of the pre-Ryswick worldview in later country ideology was vitally important for William's propagandists. It meant that their old language could preserve its role. Whilst the vice of the Restoration regimes was still perceived as a problem, the courtly reformation campaign to purge it might still be seen as relevant by country politicians. It might continue to knit court and country together even in the difficult conditions of the late decade.

The winter of 1697–8 provided a fine instance of a successful application of reformation propaganda after the war. It has been mentioned that William opened parliament in 1697 with an appeal for moral renewal. What has not been fully explored is the way his speech was received by MPs. On 7 February 1698, Sir John Phillips, a member with ingrained country attitudes, rose to remind the House of the king's appeal, and to suggest the House address William for a proclamation to reform manners.[142] After an extended debate, in which MPs discussed the threats to the ethical health of the nation, the Commons unanimously agreed to Phillips's proposal. What is interesting about the address which followed was that, like Phillips's original speech, it presented the initiative for action as royal. By talking of 'the late gracious declaration your majesty has made to us from the throne', the House accepted William as its leader in this area, and so preserved that alliance in reformation which had marked the years before Ryswick.[143] When the king responded, this sense of shared purpose was again underlined, as the proclamation thanked the legislature for its interest in moral renewal.[144] William's initial speech to parliament had thus led to a symbolic statement of unity between crown and legislature, which embraced even the most country-minded MPs. This was a particularly valuable coup at this time, because it was achieved when a majority of the Commons was developing its angry critique of William's army. Courtly reformation, therefore, had continued to balance political tension over some issues with cooperation on moral reform.

[139] [Davenant], *Essay on the probable methods*, p. 237.
[140] *Considerations on the nature of parliaments; and our present elections* [1698], p. 3.
[141] [John Toland], *The art of governing by parties: particularly in religion, in politics, in parliament* (1701), pp. 8–10.
[142] PRO SP 32 9, fols. 194–5.
[143] *CJ*, 12, 102–3.
[144] William III, *By the king, a proclamation ... 24 February 1697*.

The king's speech in 1697 also used the continuing parallels between courtly reformation and country thought to revivify the ideal of the country court. William's precise words in promoting further reformation were

I esteem it one of the great Advantages of the Peace, that I shall now have Leisure to rectify such Corruptions and Abuses as may have crept into any Part of the Administration during the War, and effectually to discourage Profaness and Immorality.[145]

This was an extremely clever statement. In the first place, it attempted to neutralise the feeling that many of England's troubles stemmed from the period after the Revolution. It admitted that mistakes might have been made after 1688, but explained that this was the result of William not having been in the country to prevent them happening. Secondly, and more significantly, the royal speech exploited the surviving mental connection between private and public sin. It juxtaposed the two as targets of royal attention, and so attempted to cash in on William's personal righteousness in order to suggest he was still the best hope for a purge of government. Effectively, the speech persisted with courtly reformation language in the belief that it might renew the early 1690s collaboration against administrative corruption.

By and large, the king's skilfully worded invitation was accepted, at least by country pamphleteers. An underlying support for William and his perceived policies survived into the literature of the late 1690s. Whilst charging that government had gone badly astray during the monarch's whig captivity, country writers still insisted that the king was fundamentally a virtuous man and an ally. For example, John Trenchard was prepared to defend William in his pamphlets against the standing army, despite worrying that he was too easily influenced by evil courtiers; whilst one of Tom Double's odious allies had the revealing name of 'Mr Kingcheat'.[146] Thus, far from including William in their attacks upon recent ills, many country writers appealed for him to return to his principles and lead his people against their wicked governors.

One of the most sustained treatments of this theme came in Davenant's *Discourse of grants and resumptions*. Like other country tracts of the late decade this offered a damning account of executive vices sprung up since 1688. It complained bitterly of embezzlement, of the unwarranted elevation of court servants, and of new systems of corruption so vast that large sections of the nation depended upon them.[147] Yet, whilst the pamphlet recognised William's chosen ministers as the cause of the trouble, and the conditions created by his war as its opportunity, it was adamant that the king himself

---

[145] *LJ*, 16, 175.

[146] See [Trenchard], *Short history ... standing armies*, p. 46; [Walter Moyle and John Trenchard], *The second part of an argument shewing that a standing army is inconsistent with a free government* (1697), pp. 22–4; [Davenant], *True picture*, p. 64.

[147] [Davenant], *Discourse of grants*, pp. 8–11.

was blameless. The image of a purging monarch persisted, as Davenant reminded his readers how William had thrown out the horrors of the Restoration regime and subsequently fought against vice and corruption.

At his first coming over he sav'd that Religion which our mean Complyance under former Princes had put in danger. ... All the Good [which we have subsequently received has been] the Effects of his own Wisdom, and his Virtues will at last bear down and Master all our Vices.[148]

Such language, of course, sat ill with complaints of degeneration in the 1690s, but Davenant squared the circle in the way suggested by the king in 1697. He insisted that William had been held back from his true policy of reform by the demands of war, and that all the evil that had been done had been perpetrated in spite of his best efforts. For Davenant, William was a virtuous prince

But as not all Seasons are not proper for Physick, so all Times are not fit for purging the Body Politick; Times of Action and War are not so convenient for such Councils as tend to correct Abuses in the State. Perhaps, during the late War, some Things may have been done in *England*, which the king, in his high Wisdom, may think necessary to animadvert upon now when He is at leisure from His Business in the Field.[149]

Now that peace had come, the king would embark on a campaign against these miscarriages, in which all honest men could join. 'No doubt when he goes upon so good a work, he will be assisted by all the best men of all parties, and by the whole body of his people.'[150]

Thus the writer who had done most to develop and popularise the late decade description of government vice, also continued to promote the ideal of the country court. Even after the battles and tensions of the king's last years, the image of a reforming monarch still channelled and moderated criticism. Country ideology may have been restructured after Ryswick, but the fundamental fears behind it had not altered, and it remained confined within the parameters set for it by a powerful official propaganda. So long as Englishmen were transfixed by horror of private sin and the Restoration regimes, they warmed to a man who claimed to put their anxieties to rest.

[148] *Ibid.* p. 21.   [149] *Ibid.* pp. 40–1.   [150] *Ibid.* p. 41.

Conclusion

On 11 March 1702, only ten weeks after William had addressed parliament for the last time, Queen Anne delivered her first speech to the legislature. As a royal propagandist, the new ruler enjoyed substantial advantages over her predecessor. She was a direct heir of James II, had been brought up in England, and had been a lifelong member of the anglican church. She therefore possessed all the traditional qualifications for English monarchy which her brother-in-law had lacked. At Westminster she made the most of her assets. In one passage of her speech, Anne tacitly alluded to the difference between her own nationality and that of William, and so hinted that court polemic might now be organised around new themes. She stated

as I know My own Heart to be entirely *English*, I can very sincerely assure you, there is not any Thing you can expect, or desire of Me, which I shall not be ready to do for the Happiness and Prosperity of *England*.[1]

Yet, although some of the old king's closest supporters were shocked by these words, it soon became clear that Anne would not introduce a novel court ideology.[2] The very address which appeared to reflect upon William's foreignness also expressed deep regret at his demise, and promised no change in his policy of opposition to France. In the years which followed, the incoming regime adopted the central tenets of Williamite rhetoric and put them to similar purposes. Anne, like William, would pose as the sponsor of reformation in her speeches and proclamations, and would use a message of national righteousness to unite the country behind her rule.[3]

It would be interesting to pursue the language of renewal into the new reign, and examine its use in the changing circumstances of the early eight-

---

[1] *LJ*, 17, 68. [2] Gregg, *Queen Anne*, pp. 152–3.
[3] See, for example, *By the queen, a proclamation for the encouragement of piety and virtue ... given 6 March 1702* (1702); *LJ*, 19, 145 – queen's speech to parliament, 5 April 1710.

eenth century. However, rather than being pulled into the political vortices of the 1700s, this study should conclude with some reflections upon the significance of court rhetoric under William III. After the preceding survey of courtly reformation, it is necessary to ask what the chief consequences of this propaganda were, and why scholars should be concerned with the activities of Burnet's bishops.

To answer these questions, it is useful to return to the ambitions announced at the beginning of this book. In the introduction to this study, I aspired to four main achievements. I hoped that an examination of William's publicity would allow an assessment of the court's ideological power at the end of the seventeenth century; that it would challenge the belief in wholesale secularisation in the post-Restoration period; that it would allow reflection upon the constitutional significance of 1688; and that it would help explain some of the long-term changes affecting the British polity between the Tudor and late Georgian eras. Now that the detailed survey of Burnet's activities is complete, these wider issues can be considered. In each area, study of courtly reformation suggests new interpretations, debates, and enquiries for scholars of the late Stuart period.

First, there is the question of the court's ideological power. In this field, the main result of studying royal reformation in the 1690s should be to rebalance the historiography of monarchical publicity. Hitherto, study of royal ideology has been distorted because the great interest in the propaganda strategies of Tudor and early Stuart monarchs has not been matched by similar attention to rulers after the Civil War. Whilst there have been numerous studies of courtly pageantry, etiquette, and display before 1640, much less has appeared on the ideological techniques of later kings and queens.[4] After the Restoration, the attention of historians of propaganda has tended to shift away from monarchs and their immediate entourages, towards groups which were independent of the court, and which, in many ways, competed with it for power. Thus after 1660, most study has been devoted to the development of propaganda machines by whig and tory parties, and to the methods used by country critics of government to bring their messages to the nation. These groups, with their extensive pamphleteering and electioneering, have been seen as the most innovative, active, and effective propagandists of the period, and their activities have consequently been found more interesting than those

---

[4] For a small selection of such work, see the works cited in chapter 2, footnote 33, and Roy Strong, *Holbein and Henry VIII* (1967); David Starkey, ed., *Henry VIII: a European court in England* (1991); S. J. Gunn and P. G. Lindley, eds., *Cardinal Wolsey: church, state and art* (Cambridge, 1991); Roy Strong, *Cult of Elizabeth*; Yates, *Astraea*; Roy Strong, *Britannia triumphans: Inigo Jones, Rubens and Whitehall Palace* (1980).

of the monarch.[5]

To an extent, of course, the decline of the royal household within the polity does provide some justification for this change of emphasis. It does make sense to devote less attention to the sort of court-based display which dominates accounts of earlier royal propaganda once the forum for this kind of message had lost its importance and influence. Yet, as this study has made clear, the decline of the household did not cause royal publicists to despair. When energised by the vision and enthusiasm of such people as Gilbert Burnet and Queen Mary, the court could run an impressive ideological campaign which utilised engines of mass communication, and broadcast ideas through an imaginative range of media. In fact, it could be argued that the abandonment of traditional, court-based propaganda enabled William's allies to stage a publicity programme which was more innovative and penetrative than their party or country rivals. A campaign which made extensive use of the popular press, which adapted the administrative organs of the state to spread its ideals, and which encouraged mass participation through fasting or reformation societies was both remarkably modern and potentially effective. The first result of courtly reformation studies, therefore, should be to revive interest in royal ideology after the Restoration. It should stimulate more thought about the monarch's ideological power in the later seventeenth century, and raise the question whether the court's ability to influence public debate survived rather longer than the shift of attention to party and country campaigns would imply.

The second issue to be considered was seventeenth-century secularisation. Much has already been said to rebut the idea that protestant and biblical thought-forms lost their hold after 1660, and little need be done to repeat these arguments here. From an examination of Burnet and his circle, it is clear that a leading group of Englishmen in the 1690s were enmeshed in ideals of true and false churches, of godly magistracy and moral reform. However, whilst this basic point needs no re-emphasis, this study's questioning of secularisation must still be stressed, since it demands that historians go further to explore the persisting influence of the early protestant worldview. Whilst several scholars have already argued that notions such as

---

[5] See, for example, J. O. Richards, *Party propaganda under Queen Anne* (Athens, Georgia, 1972); Downie, *Robert Harley*; Harris, *London crowds*, chs. 5–6; Kenyon, *Revolution principles*; Dickinson, *Liberty and property*; Goldie, 'Tory political thought'. The main exceptions to this trend have been studies of individual writers who supported late Stuart monarchs. See for example, Schonhorn, *Defoe's politics*; McKeon, *Politics and poetry*; Philip Harth, *Pen for a party: Dryden's tory propaganda in its contexts* (Princeton, New Jersey, 1993).

millenarianism and godly rule were central to aspects of late Stuart England (particularly the sense of national identity, and various campaigns for social renewal) this analysis has not been extended to other areas in which this study suggests it would be applicable.[6] Particularly, little work has been done on the influence of the protestant ideals on certain forms of political discourse. For example, country ideology in the late 1690s has overwhelmingly been discussed in secular terms. Scholarship in this area has been dominated by Pocock's account of 'neo-Harringtonianism' – a set of ideas which have been seen as resting on a 'sociological' rather than a theological understanding of politics. Consequently, historians have concentrated upon passages by such pamphleteers as Davenant and Trenchard in which corruptions of government were explained in terms of economics, advancing technology, and changes in the patterns of property-holding.[7] Yet the evidence from the response of country opinion to courtly reformation suggests that this creed was more eclectic than Pocock supposed. Even at the end of William's reign, those suspicious of executive power entertained many traditional protestant ideas along with the shibboleths of civic humanism. They still felt threatened by the debauching influence of the false, popish church, and could be moved by the image of a godly ruler.

Similarly, tory ideology in the 1690s has been discussed in largely secular terms. More interest has been shown in tory constitutionalism than tory theology, and even those scholars who have described the tories' vehement defence of the anglican communion have tended to explain their subjects' position by citing social, rather than spiritual, anxieties. In most works on the late Stuart toryism, the creed's rigid and defensive ecclesiology is shown to have stemmed from a fear that established clerics would lose influence, position, and wealth as heavy taxation, the toleration of dissent, and the weakening of church courts took their toll.[8] Yet again, the response of late Stuart Englishmen to courtly reformation suggests that there was more to tory ideology than these largely social concerns. The participation by tories in the promotion of William's ideology demonstrates that visions of the two churches, of godly magistracy, and of moral reform, were important to these men; and it suggests that links between reformation principles and core tory ideals should be explored further. The interaction between Williamite

---

[6] For such sensitivities, see Colley 'Britishness and otherness'; and the contributions to Davison et al., *Stilling the grumbling hive*.

[7] See the works by Pocock listed in the bibliography; Dickinson, *Liberty and property*, ch. 3; Downie, *Robert Harley*, pp. 19–23. Also, however, see David Hayton's work on the tory, and 'puritan', elements of country ideology in Hayton, 'The "country" interest'; Hayton, 'Moral reform'.

[8] This is the line broadly adopted in Bennett, *Tory crisis*, and Holmes, *Trial of Dr Sacheverell*. J. C. D. Clark, *English society* described a tory anglicanism which insisted on maintaining the social and political power of the clergy.

ideology and other political faiths thus demands that historians should show still greater sensitivity to 'early protestant' ideas in the late seventeenth century. Far from declining, these notions appear to have run through very many of the movements and philosophies of the period.

· After the examination of the court's ideological power, and the challenge to secularisation, this volume's third ambition was to cast light on the constitutional significance of 1688. After the arguments of chapter one and chapter five, this may seem an unobtainable objective, since these chapters demonstrated that courtly reformation was essentially non-constitutional. Burnet's case displaced the legal arguments of the Orange *Declaration* during the revolutionary period, and thereafter avoided detailed analysis of English fundamental law. Yet whilst courtly reformation had little direct to say about the precise extent of the king's power, it nevertheless had important implications for contemporary perceptions of this issue which do deserve some consideration.

Initially, it might appear that this study supports the case for the survival of high monarchical principles after 1688. The propaganda which it has examined magnified the glory and authority of William, and so exhibited no retreat from claims for the king's power on the part of the court. In particular, this study might seem to support the arguments of such scholars as Gerald Straka and J. C. D. Clark, who have asserted that the use of providence by royalist writers strengthened monarchical absolutism. It appears to confirm these scholars' contention that post-Revolutionary stress upon the heavenly origin of kingship implied that monarchs should not be challenged since they ruled by divine commission.[9] We have seen, for example, that providential discourse was adopted by the Orange party in 1688/9 to escape from the limitations upon the court which their earlier *Declaration* had seemed to threaten; and we have similarly seen how Burnet used the notion of William's providential mission to buttress royal authority at the 1689 coronation.[10]

Yet despite this aspect of courtly reformation, the Williamite message was more ambiguous than has been suggested. Although its providential elements could ally with extensive claims for royal power, there were other strands of thought within the propaganda which were far less supportive of pure monarchical authority, and which may even have involved an admission by the court that it should be restrained by other parts of the English polity. For example, the courtly reformers' historical analysis casts serious doubt upon the trustworthiness of the royal executive. Their picture of an England corrupted by a popishly affected court under Charles II did not flatter monarchical influence, and, as was demonstrated in chapter six, could be

---

[9] Clark, *English society, passim*, but especially pp. 125–6; Straka, *Anglican reaction*.
[10] See above, pp. 24–8, 61–3.

used to align William's regime with country principles. The propaganda
conceded that the court should have been supervised and controlled in the
past, and so allowed William to accept parliamentary scrutiny in his present.[11] As significantly, perhaps, the court's case after the Revolution involved the novel and potentially damaging admission that mere heredity was
an insufficient claim for holding the English throne. Within reformation
polemic, William's right to his position came not from his birth (such a case
would have led straight back to James's legitimacy), but from his actions in
upholding the true faith and from the marks of divine favour these elicited.
Such language may have been useful in publicising the heroism and zeal of
William, but it also tacitly accepted that tenure of the throne was *conditional*.
In the world created by Burnet and his allies, kingship depended on the ruler's
active promotion of godliness; and it was only fully legitimate when the
monarch fought for protestantism on the battlefield, purged popery out of the
nation, and worked to return England to its old piety and virtue.[12] From here,
it may have been a short step to seeing kingship as an ordinary political office.
Courtly reformation may have encouraged a view of monarchy as a post with
clear duties attached, whose occupant might be judged (as James II had been
judged) for not fulfilling these.[13] Thus although William's regime had abandoned its 1688 *Declaration* – a document whose case restricted royal action –
it is not absolutely clear that their adoption of a providential language
permitted a stronger assertion of royal power. Courtly reformation allowed
propagandists to preach up the king's beneficial influence, but did so on
grounds which encouraged questioning of the limits of his authority, and so
may have weakened high monarchism after 1688.

This volume's final aspiration was to help explain some of the long-term
changes which occurred in Britain between 1600 and 1800. Amongst the
mass of developments in these decades, two particular trends were picked out
for special consideration, because the 1690s were crucial for them. The first
was the emergence of England as a world power; and the second was the
stabilisation of a viable parliamentary system of government. In the remain-
der of this conclusion, I want to outline the importance of William's reign for
these two achievements, and reflect upon the influence which courtly reformation may have had in bringing them about.

[11] See above, pp. 203–4.
[12] See above, pp. 46–52.
[13] There is some evidence that the monarchy was seen as having definable and enforceable duties
in the period of William's reign. On 29 January 1689, parliament resolved that it was
'inconsistent and ruinous to a protestant state to be governed by a popish prince' – a
resolution which suggested that the English could demand a particular religious stance on the
part of its ruler. Similarly the clauses in the 1701 act of settlement relating to the monarchs'
overseas possessions suggested that the nation could require kings and queens to prioritise
England's interests over their own dynastic ambitions. (For these clauses, see above
pp. 124–5.)

The 1690s were crucial for England's rise to world status because they saw her first sustained commitment to a European war in the early modern era. The decade thus represented the first period in which the English state had . had to develop the sort of fiscal, military, and administrative bodies necessary to sustain the position of a major power. England had been to war before in the sixteenth and seventeenth centuries, but her conflicts had never lasted long enough, or involved her deeply enough, to stimulate the kind of infrastructural changes seen under William III. No foreign war conducted by the Stuarts had lasted longer than five years; Elizabeth's struggle with Spain had relied mostly upon Dutch and French troops; and the civil wars of 1640–52 had largely been too disruptive and chaotic to allow the construction of a powerful state machine. By contrast, the struggle with France in the 1690s forced the permanent recasting of English government so that it could sustain extended conflict. Despite considerable initial difficulties, institutions were developed to manage the mass mobilisation of society, and long-term solutions were discovered to the problems which this mobilisation produced. Thus, for the first time, English ministers and military officers gained experience of raising huge armed forces. In the years 1689–97, William employed an average of 117,000 Englishmen in his summer campaigns. This was a unprecedented figure – well over 2 per cent of his realm's *entire* population. Even more impressively, perhaps, this massive fighting force was kept in its fields of operation, and supplied with the materials it needed, for months and years at a stretch. In response to the logistical problems this presented, government departments charged with provisioning the king's forces grew in size and expertise as they transported huge quantities of weapons, clothes, horses, and food. At the same time, the need for money to pay for the war stimulated further innovations. Parliament developed routines for assessing and scrutinising the war's fiscal needs; new taxes were imposed, and new bureaucrats employed to collect them; and a new financial world, including the Bank of England and a vigorous stock market, emerged to service the government's debts.[14]

The role of courtly reformation within these processes was to keep the English committed to their transforming war with France. If the argument of chapter four of this volume is correct, then the promotion of William as a righteous instrument of God was a vital factor in sustaining the national struggle. Orange propaganda explained the king's battle to his subjects; it gave them enthusiasm for the fight; and it thus avoided the problems faced by earlier Stuart monarchs who had not engaged in prolonged warfare because they had failed to allay suspicions about their military policies. Repeatedly (in

[14] Dickson, *Financial revolution*; Childs, *British army*; Jones, *War and economy*; Geoffrey Holmes, *Augustan England: professions, state and society, 1680–1730* (1982), part 3.

the 1620s, in 1640, in 1666, and in 1674) William's predecessors had had to curtail conflicts because of parliamentary reluctance to pay for the military, or because of local resistance to mobilisation. In the 1690s, in contrast, popular and legislative support for the war held up because courtly reformation committed the English to the defeat of Louis XIV. Royal propaganda therefore ensured that the nation would fight a new kind of war, and so forced it to gear itself for massive and sustainable military activity.

Williamite propaganda may also have influenced the nature, as well as the fact, of England's transformation into a world power. As scholars such as John Brewer and Michael Mann have pointed out, England after the 1690s was remarkable, not so much for the scale of her military forces and infrastructure, but for their peculiar efficiency. Unlike the French, and other continental powers, the English developed a state which had access to most national resources, and which could direct these to the armed forces without dissipating them within its own machinery. In England there were no extensive tax exemptions, and the bureaucracy did not suffer from the sort of venality, and downright corruption, which crippled Bourbon government.[15] In explaining this difference, Brewer, at least, has placed considerable emphasis on the role of the English parliament. He has argued that whilst the legislature at Westminster empowered the king's government to collect revenue from all those it represented, its persistent strand of country suspicion ensured that it also acted as a steward for this money. Aware of its responsibilities to its constituency, parliament was vigorous in investigating rumours of waste, misappropriation, or corruption within the civil service, and so helped to eliminate the inefficiencies which plagued other governments. As a result, the English state could convert a higher proportion of its available resources into military power, and was consequently able to compete with nations such as France, whose raw population and economies were larger (at least until the later eighteenth century).[16]

If this explanation of England's success is correct, then it can be suggested that courtly reformation played a second role in her transformation to a world power. Chapter six of this book argued that Williamite ideology encouraged a constructively critical attitude on the part of parliamentarians. It invited them in to the most secret recesses of the king's administration so that they might help the monarch destroy the remaining traces of popish luxury and debauchery. Suggesting a role for parliament in which it could reform government without precipitating political crises, it channelled country sentiments into safe courses, and encouraged legislators to see themselves as regular inquisitors of the civil service. Such a role was, of course, precisely

---

[15] Brewer, *Sinews of power*; Michael Mann, *The sources of social power* (Cambridge, 1986), I, 478–80.

[16] Brewer, *Sinews of power*, ch. 5.

the one demanded by Brewer's explanation of English efficiency. It therefore seems probable that courtly reformation was instrumental in the development of England's efficient state, and can claim yet further credit for her rise to military eminence.

Analysis of the legislature as an explanation for England's great-power status naturally leads to discussion of the other long-term change for which the 1690s seem to have been crucial. This was the development of a viable parliamentary system. However whiggish such a statement may sound, England did make substantial constitutional progress between the middle of the seventeenth and the late eighteenth centuries. She passed from a series of crises, in which the role of the legislature was bitterly, even bloodily, debated, to a far more stable system under the Hanoverians, in which parliament met regularly without descending into debilitating disputes about its status. Within this extended transformation, William's reign does appear to have been crucial. The 1690s represented the first sustained period in English history when a king had called a parliament annually, and managed to avoid the sort of deadlock and strife which had plagued his predecessors' relations with that body. Despite tensions both within the two houses, and between Westminster and Whitehall, parties in the various disputes continued to look within the parliamentary system for solutions and resolutions. There was no appeal to arms by disgruntled courtiers, Lords, or Commons; the monarch's business was not interrupted by prolonged denial of revenue, or by endless impeachment of his ministers; and despite irritations which brought occasional talk of abdication, William was never forced into ruling without his legislature. As a result, the essential framework of a peaceful politics began to be constructed. Faction leaders came to concentrate upon parliamentary means of pursuing their objectives; and their attempts to establish electoral machines to win over voting opinion, and to build alliances in the House of Commons, began to crystallise new assumptions about the conduct of politics. Given the history of the earlier seventeenth century, this achievement was remarkable. Against the accumulated evidence of inevitable log-jam and breakdown, William showed that the nation's parliamentary representatives could be integrated into a stable polity.

From what has been said about the impact of courtly reformation on 1690s politics, it should be clear what role it might claim in the birth of the new parliamentary order. By moderating the forces which had formerly disrupted co-operation between king, Lords, and Commons, Williamite ideology did much to ensure the success of the royal political experiment. By convincing both whigs and tories that they might work with the monarch, and by redirecting country suspicions away from direct attacks upon the court, royal propaganda encouraged peers and MPs to work within Westminster, and forestalled the sort of disillusionment with parliamentary politics which had so frequently led to its suspension in the past. In the 1690s, the political nation may have been content to pursue its aims through the legislature because it was convinced that a godly magistrate was not a threat to its privileges and interests, and because it believed that that monarch's reforming mission could include both of the parties into which it had divided.

This last assertion raises a final, and overarching, point about William III and his publicity. It suggests that royal action in the 1690s should be accorded a much greater part than has been realised in the shaping of modern Britain. Previously, descriptions of the vital political developments which occurred in the late Stuart period have tended to leave the monarchy out of account. They have either discussed changes with reference to factors outside the royal court, or, at the very least, have attributed them to the crown's loss of influence. For example, current explanations for the stabilisation of party politics have looked well beyond the king and his circle. They have concentrated upon the need for political factions to build peaceful parliamentary machines once the legislature was the true site of power; they have cited underlying social trends which reduced the violence of political disagreements; they have stressed the growing public horror of seventeenth-century turmoil; or, famously, they have credited the personal dominance of Sir Robert Walpole.[17] Similarly, accounts of the accommodation between crown and parliament have tended to stress the strategic withdrawal of the former on contentious issues. Traditional accounts of the late Stuart period stressed the triumph of the legislature in 1688, and later historians have shown how members of the House of Commons came to dominate politics in the decades of war following that year.[18] Yet whilst existing historiography has much that is useful to say about the developments of the late Stuart era, its blindness to Williamite ideology has deprived it of vital parts of the picture. In contrast to many interpretations of Augustan England, this volume has suggested that it was the royal court, acting through an impressive publicity campaign, which shaped the events of the 1690s. By presenting himself as a Christian magistrate, the instrument and beneficiary of a godly revolution, William III himself may have done most to reconcile his subjects to a new world of parliamentary politics, and of legislative supervision of a growing state. In so

[17] Brian W. Hill, *The growth of parliamentary parties, 1689–1742* (1976), *passim*, but especially pp. 38, 231; Geoffrey Holmes, 'The achievement of stability: the social context of politics from the 1680s to the age of Walpole', in Geoffrey Holmes, *Politics, religion, and society in England, 1679–1742* (1986), pp. 249–80; J. V. Beckett, 'Introduction: stability in politics and society', in Jones, *Britain in the first age of party*, pp. 1–18, especially p. 17; Plumb, *Growth of political stability*.

[18] The classic statement of legislative victory in 1688 can be found in Macaulay, *History of England*, II, 392–8. The most vigorous account of stability through legislative victory in the 1690s can be found in Rubini, *Country and court*. Brewer, *Sinews of power*, ch. 5, suggests that parliamentarians suspicious of the court were reconciled with it under William as they began to participate in, and control, executive power.

far as the English could claim a unique and uniquely successful system of government in the centuries after 1688, it is possible that they owed it to one of the most remarkable campaigns of royal propaganda ever staged in their country.

Bibliography

MANUSCRIPT SOURCES

UNPUBLISHED

Bodleian Library

Additional Ms.
A 191
D 23
D 24

Ballard Ms.
45

Eng. hist. Ms.
B 209–10

Rawlinson Ms.
D 1396

Tanner Ms.
25

British Library

Additional Ms.
4292
4236
4239
34,510
70,015

Egerton Ms.
2621

Harley Ms.
6798

Loan Ms.
29/186
29/189

City of London Record Office
PD 10.91
Rep. 95
Rep. 97
Rep. 98

Dr Williams' Library
Morrice Ms. Q

Lambeth Palace Library
1743

Public Record Office
PC2 74/149
SP 32 9
SP 32 10
SP 32 11

LATER PUBLICATIONS OF MANUSCRIPT MATERIAL

Blencowe, R. W., ed., _Diary of the times of Charles the Second by the honourable Henry Sidney_ (2 vols., 1843)
Browning, Andrew, ed., _The memoirs of Sir John Reresby_ (2nd edn, 1991)
Calendar of state papers domestic, 1689–90 (1895)
Calendar of state papers domestic, 1690–1 (1898)
Cameron, W. J., ed., _Poems on affairs of state: Augustan satirical verse, 1660–1714_ (9 vols., New Haven, Connecticut, 1971)
Doebner, R., ed., _Memoirs of Mary, queen of England, 1689–1693_ (1886)
The Ellis correspondence (2 vols., 1829)
Foxcroft, H. C., ed., _The life and letters of Sir George Savile_ (2 vols., 1898)
    ed., _A supplement to the 'History of my own times'_ (Oxford, 1902)
Grey, Anchitel, _Debates of the House of Commons from ... 1667 to ... 1694, collected by A. Grey_ (10 vols., 1769)
Historical Manuscripts Commission, _Manuscripts of the House of Lords 1690–1_ (1892)
    Report on the manuscripts of his grace the duke of Portland, preserved at Wellbeck Abbey (5 vols., 1894)
    Report on the manuscripts of the late Allan George Finch (4 vols., 1922)
Horwitz, Henry, ed., _The parliamentary diary of Narcissus Luttrell, 1691–1693_ (Oxford, 1972)
James, G. P. R., ed., _Letters illustrative of the reign of William III from 1696 to 1708 addressed to the duke of Shrewsbury by James Vernon esq._ (3 vols., 1814)

Japikse, N., ed., *Correspondentie van Willem III en van Hans Willem Bentinck* (5 vols., Hague, 1927)

Journals of the House of Commons

Journals of the House of Lords

Kerr, Russell J., and Coffin Duncan, Ida, eds., *The Routledge papers: being extracts from the letters of Richard Lapthorne, gent, of Hatton Garden, London, to Richard Coffin, esq., of Routledge, Bideford, Devon* (1928)

The letters of Lady Russell (7th edn, 1809)

Luttrell, Narcissus, *A brief historical relation of state affairs from September 1678 to April 1714* (6 vols., Oxford, 1857)

Notes and Queries 2nd series 2 (1856), 245–7

Robinson, Amy Edith, ed., *The life of Richard Kidder, DD bishop of Bath and Wells, written by himself* (Frome, 1924)

Shaw, William, ed., *Calendar of Treasury books, volume IX, 1689–1691* (5 parts, 1931)

Singer, S. W., ed., *The correspondence of Henry Hyde, earl of Clarendon* (2 vols., 1828)

PRINTED PRIMARY SOURCES

MODERN CATALOGUES OF CONTEMPORARY MATERIAL

Arber, Edward, ed., *The term catalogues 1688–1709* (3 vols., 1905)

George, Mary Dorothy, ed., *Catalogue of prints and drawings in the British Museum. Division 1: personal and political satires* (11 vols., 1870)

Steele, Robert, ed., *Tudor and Stuart proclamations 1485–1714* (2 vols., Oxford, 1910)

Wing, Donald, ed., *Short title catalogue of books printed in England ... 1641–1700* (2nd edn revised, 3 vols., New York, 1972)

NEWSPAPERS AND PERIODICALS

The Athenian Gazette, or Casuistical Mercury

The London Gazette

PROCLAMATIONS (in chronological order)

By the king, a proclamation for the observation of the thirtieth day of January as a day of fast, ... given 25 January 1660 (1661)

By the king, a proclamation for the suppressing of disorderly and unseasonable meetings, ... given 20 September 1660 (1660)

By the king, a proclamation for the observation of the nine and twentieth day of May instant, as a day of publick thanksgiving ... given 20 May 1661 (1661)

By the king, a proclamation, ... given 29 June 1688 (1688)

By the king and queen, a proclamation for a general fast, ... given 23 May 1689 (1689)

By the king and queen, a proclamation for a general fast, ... given 20 February 1689 (1689)

By the king and queen's most excellent majesties, a proclamation for a fast, ... given 1 August 1690 (Dublin, 1690)

By the king and queen, a proclamation, ... given 1 October 1690 (1690)

By the king and queen, a proclamation for a general fast, ... given 9 April 1691 (1691)

By the king and queen, a proclamation for a publick thanksgiving, ... *given 22 October 1691* (1691)

By the king and queen, a proclamation against vitious, debauched and profane persons, ... *given 21 January 1691/2* (1691/2)

By the king and queen, a proclamation for a general fast, ... *given 24 March 1692* (1692)

By the king and queen, a proclamation for a publick thanksgiving, ... *given the 22 October 1692* (1692)

By the king and queen, a proclamation for a general fast, ... *given 13 April 1693* (1693)

By the king and queen, a proclamation for a publick thanksgiving, ... *given 2 November 1693* (1693)

By the king and queen, a proclamation for a general fast, ... *given 10 May 1694* (1694)

By the king and queen, a proclamation for a general fast, ... *given 16 August 1694* (1694)

By the king, a proclamation for a general fast, ... *given 18 March 1696/7* (1697)

By the king, a proclamation for preventing and punishing immorality and prophaness. ... *given 24 February 1697* (1697)

By the king, a proclamation for a publick thanksgiving, ... *given 12 March 1696* (1697)

By the king, a proclamation for a publick thanksgiving, ... *given 11 November 1697* (1697)

By the king, a proclamation for preventing and punishing immorality and prophaness, ... *given 9 December 1699* (1699)

By the queen, a proclamation for the encouragement of piety and virtue ... *given 6 March 1702* (1702)

BOOKS, PAMPHLETS, BROADSIDES, ETC.

An account of the ceremonial at the coronation of their excellent majesties King William and Queen Mary (1689)

An account of the progress of the reformation of manners in England and Ireland (1701)

An address of the dissenting ministers (in and about the city of London) to the king and queen, upon their accession to the crown (1689)

The address of the Lords and Commons, to the king's most excellent majesty, for maintaining the church of England as by law established, with his majesty's most gracious answer thereunto (1689)

The address of the nonconformist ministers (in and around the city of London) to his highness the prince of Orange (1689)

Animadversions upon the declaration of his highness the prince of Orange (1688)

Antimoixeia: or the honest and joynt-design of the Tower-Hamlets for the general suppression of bawdy houses, as incouraged thereto by the publick magistrates (1691)

Atterbury, Francis, *The Christian religion encreased by miracle. A sermon preached before the queen at Whitehall, October 21 1694* (1694)

   The scorner uncapable of true wisdom. A sermon preached before the queen at Whitehall, October 28 1694 (1694)

   A sermon before the queen at Whitehall, May 29 1692 (1692)

[Atterbury, Francis], *A letter to a convocation man concerning the rights, powers and privileges of that body* (1697)

Atterbury, Lewis, *Babylon's downfall, or England's happy deliverance from popery and slavery, being the substance of a sermon preached before the Lord Mayor . . . June 28 1691* (1691)

Augustine, *Concerning the city of God against the pagans* (Penguin classics edn, Harmondsworth, 1984)

Bale, John, *The image of both churches after the 'Reuelacion' of Sainct Iojn the evangelist* [1648?]

The ballance adjusted: or the interest of church and state weighed and considered upon this revolution [1689?]

Barker, Ralph, *A sermon preached at St Mary le Bow on Whitsunday, May 31 1691, at the consecration of . . . John, lord archbishop of Canterbury* (1691)

Bates, William, 'Dr Bates congratulatory speech to the king, Novemb. 22 1697, in the name of the dissenting ministers in and about London', in Howe, *Sermon . . . Decemb. 2 1697*

A sermon preached upon the much lamented death of our late gracious sovereign Queen Mary (1695)

Beveridge, William, *Of the happiness of the saints in heaven: a sermon preach'd before the queen at Whitehall, October 12 1690* (1690)

A sermon preach'd before the convocation of the bishops and clergy of the province of Canterbury at Westminster, Novemb. 18 1689 (1689)

[Bohun, Edmund], *The history of the desertion* (1689)

Burnet, Gilbert, *Charitable reproof: a sermon preached at St Mary-le-Bow to the societies for reformation of manners, 25 March 1700* (1700)

A discourse of the pastoral care (1692)

An essay on the memory of the late queen (1695)

An exhortation to peace and union in a sermon preached at St Lawrence-Jury on Tuesday 26 November 1689 (1689)

An exposition of the thirty nine articles of the church of England (1699)

Four discourses delivered to the clergy of the diocese of Sarum (1694)

The history of his own times (2nd edn, 6 vols., Oxford, 1833)

The history of the Reformation of the church of England (6 vols., Oxford, 1865)

Injunctions to the arch-deacons of the diocese of Sarum (1690)

A letter writ by the lord bishop of Salisbury, to the lord bishop of Coventry and Litchfield (1693)

Reflections on a book entitled [The rights, powers and privileges of an English convocation] (1700)

A sermon preached at Bow church before the court of aldermen on March 12 1689/90, being the fast day (1690)

A sermon preached at the coronation of William III and Mary II, king and queen . . . in the abby-church of Westminster, April 11 1689 (1689)

A sermon preached at the funeral of the most reverend father in God, John . . . lord archbishop of Canterbury (1694)

A sermon preached at Whitehall on 26 Novemb. 1691, being the thanksgiving day (1691)

A sermon preached before the House of Commons on 31 January 1688, being the thanksgiving-day for the deliverance of this kingdom from popery and arbitrary power (1689)

A sermon preached before the house of peers in the abby of Westminster on 5

November, being the gunpowder treason day, as likewise the day of his majesties landing in England (1689)

A sermon preached before the king and queen at Whitehall on 19 October 1690, being the day of thanksgiving for his majesties preservation and success in Ireland (1690)

A sermon preached before the queen at Whitehall on 16 July 1690, being the monthly fast (1690)

A sermon preached in the chappel of St James' before his highness the prince of Orange, 23 December (1689)

Some letters: containing an account of what seemed most remarkable in Switzerland, Italy etc. (Amsterdam, 1686)

Some sermons preached on several occasions (1713)

[Burnet, Gilbert], An enquiry into the present state of affairs, and in particular, whether we owe allegiance to the king in these circumstances (1688)

An enquiry into the reasons for abrogation of the test ([Amsterdam], 1688)

A letter containing some reflections on his majesty's declaration for liberty of conscience dated the fourth of April 1687 (1687)

The mystery of iniquity unvailed [1673]

Reasons against the repealing the acts of parliament concerning the test (1687)

Reflections on a paper entitled his majesty's reasons for withdrawing himself from Rochester (1689)

A review of the reflections on the prince of Orange's declaration (1688)

Three letters concerning the present state of Italy (1688)

Calamy, Edmund, A sermon preach'd before the societies for reformation of manners, February 20 1698/9 (1698)

The character of a bigotted prince; and what England may expect from the return of such a one (1691)

Character of his royal highness, William Henry, prince of Orange (1689)

Character [of William, prince of Orange] (Hague, 1688)

The church of England and the continuation of the ceremonies thereof vindicated from the calumnies of several late pamphlets (1690)

Churchill, Sarah, An account of the conduct of the dowager duchess of Marlborough (1742)

Clarke, Joshua, A sermon preached at St. Mary le Bow on Sunday 5 July 1691, at the consecration of ... John, lord archbishop of York, and ... Edward, lord bishop of Gloucester (1691)

Cobbett, William, ed., The parliamentary history of England (36 vols., 1806–20)

A collection of the debates and proceedings in parliament in 1694 and 1695 upon the inquiry into the late briberies and corrupt practices (1695)

The commissioner's proposals to his royal highness the prince of Orange, with his highness's answer (1688)

A complete collection of papers, in twelve parts: relating to the great revolution (1689)

Considerations on the nature of parliaments, and our present elections [1698]

The couragious souldiers of the west [1690]

Cox, Richard, ed., John Locke's 'Second treatise of government' (Arlington Heights, Illinois, 1982)

Cruso, Timothy, The churches plea for the divine presence to prosper humane force, in a sermon preached June 5 1689, being the day appointed for a general fast (1689)

The excellency of the protestant faith as to its objects and supports in a sermon preached November 5 1689 (1689)

The mighty wonders of a merciful providence, in a sermon preached on January 31 1688, being the day of publick thanksgiving ... prince of Orange (1690)

The danger of the church of England from a general assembly of the covenantors in Scotland (1690)

[Davenant, Charles], *A discourse of grants and resumptions* (1700)

Discourses on the publick revenues and on the trade of England (1698)

An essay on the probable methods of making a people gainers in the ballance of trade (1699)

Tom Double return'd out of the country: or the true picture of modern whig set forth in a second dialogue between Mr Whiglove and Mr Double (1702)

The true picture of a modern whig, set forth in a dialogue between Mr Whiglove and Mr Double, two under-spur-leathers to the late ministry (1701)

A defence of the archbishop's sermon on the death of her late majesty of blessed memory (1695)

[Defoe, Daniel], 'The legion memorial', in Scott, *Collection of scarce and valuable tracts*, XI, 255–9

[Drake, James], *The history of the last parliament begun at Westminster the tenth day of February, in the twelfth year of the reign of King William* (1702)

Dunton, John, *The life and errors of John Dunton esq., late citizen of London* (1705)

The Dutch design anatomised, or a discovery of the wickedness and unjustice of the intended invasion (1688)

England's crisis: or the world well mended (1689)

England's enemies exposed and its true friends and patriots defended (1701)

England's great deliverance (1689)

The expedition of the prince of Orange for England; giving an account of the most remarkable passages thereof, in *Complete collection of papers*, part 3, 1–8

[Flavell, John], *Mount Pisgah: a sermon preached at the publick thanksgiving, Febr. 14 1688/9* (1689)

[Fletcher, Andrew], *A discourse concerning militias and standing armies with relation to the past and present governments of Europe and of England in particular* (1697)

A form of prayer and thanksgiving to almighty God for having made his highness the prince of Orange the glorious instrument of the great deliverance of the kingdom from popery and arbitrary power (1688)

A form of prayer to be used on 5th June coming, being the fast day (1689)

A form of prayer to be used on Friday the eighth day of April next ... being the fast day (1692)

The form of the proceeding to the funeral of her late majesty Queen Mary II, (1695)

Fowler, Edward, *A discourse of the great disingenuity and unreasonableness of repining at afflicting providences* (1695)

A sermon preached at Bow-church, April 16 1690; before the Lord Maior and court of aldermen, and citizens of London being the fast day (1690)

A sermon preached at St Mary le Bow to the societies for reformation of manners, June 26 1699 (1699)

A sermon preached before the House of Lords in the abbey-church at Westminster upon Thursday the Sixteenth of April 1696 (1696)

[Fowler, Edward], *A vindication of an undertaking of certain gentlemen, in order to the suppressing of debauchery and profaness* (1692)

A full account of King William's royal voyage and safe arrival at the castle of Belfast in Ireland (1690)

A *full account of the two great victories lately obtained before Limerick by K. William's forces over the French and Irish rebels* (1690)

A *further account of the prince's army, in a letter from Exon. Novemb.* 24, in *Complete collection of papers*, part 3, 8–9

Gardiner, James, *A sermon preach'd before the House of Lords at the abbey church of St Peter's Westminster on Wednesday 11 December 1695, being the day appointed for a solemn fast and humiliation* (1695)

Great news from Limerick giving an account of the successful victory over the Irish rebels (1690)

Great news from Salisbury (1688)

Grice, Thomas, *A short vindication of the constitution of the church of England endeavouring to prevent all future quarrels and protestations* (1689)

[Hampden, John], *Some short considerations about the most proper way of raising money in the present conjuncture* (1691)

Some short considerations concerning the state of the nation [1692]

[Harley, Robert], *A letter from the Grecian Coffee House in answer to the Taunton-Dean letter, to which is added a paper of queries sent from Worcester* (1701)

The Taunton-Dean letter from E. C. to J. F. at the Grecian Coffee House, London (1701)

Hartcliffe, John, *A treatise of the moral and intellectual virtues* (1691)

Hayley, William, *A sermon preach'd at the church of St Mary le Bow before the societies for reformation of manners upon Monday October 3 1698* (1699)

An heroic poem upon his majesties most gracious releasing the chimney-money (1689)

His grace the duke of Schomberg's character ... together with some old prophecies, foretelling the conquest of that kingdom by the protestant army under his grace's command [1689]

An historical account of the memorable actions of the most glorious monarch, William III (1689)

The history of the most illustrious William, prince of Orange: deduced from the first founders of the ancient house of Nassau, together with the most considerable actions of this present prince (1688)

An honest commoners speech (1694)

Horneck, Anthony, *A sermon preached at Fulham, in the chappel of the palace, upon Easter-day 1689, at the consecration of the right reverend father in God, Gilbert, lord bishop of Sarum* (1689)

Several sermons on the fifth of St Matthew (2nd edn, 1706)

The true nature of righteousness in a sermon preached before the king and queen at Whitehall, 17 November 1689 (1689)

Howe, John, *A discourse relating to the much-lamented death and solemn funeral of our incomparable and most gracious Queen Mary, of most blessed memory* (2nd edn, 1695)

A sermon preach'd on the late day of thanksgiving, Decemb. 2 1697 (1698)

James II, *His majesties most gracious declaration to all his loving subjects ... given 17 April 1693* (St Germains, 1693)

Jane, William, *A sermon preached before the honourable House of Commons at St Margaret Westminster on Thursday 26 November 1691, being a day of publick thanksgiving* (Oxford, 1691)

A sermon preached before the king and queen at Whitehall in November 1692 (1693)

[Jane, William], *A letter to a friend, containing some quearies about the new com-*

mission for making alterations in the liturgy, canons &c of the church of England [1689]

[Johnston, Nathaniel], *The dear bargain; or, a true representation of the state of the English nation under the Dutch*, [1689?]

A justification of the proceedings of the … House of Commons in the last sessions of parliament (1701)

Kidder, Richard, *The charge of Richard, lord bishop of Bath and Wells to the clergy of his diocese at his primary visitation begun at Axebridge, June 2 1692* (1693)

'The life of Anthony Horneck', preface to Horneck, *Several sermons*

Knight, John, *The speech of Sir John Knight of Bristol, against the bill for a general naturalisation* [1694]

[Lawton, Charlwood], *A short state of our condition with relation to the present parliament* (1693)

The lay man's religion humbly offered as a help to a modest enquiry every man into his own heart (1690)

[Leslie, Charles], *Remarks on some late sermons: and in particular, on Dr Sherlock's sermon at the Temple, Dec. 30 1694* (1695)

A letter from a gentleman in Yorkshire, to his countryman in London concerning the duke of Leeds, with an answer (1695)

A letter to a member of the committee of grievances, containing some seasonable reflections on the present administration of affairs, since managed by Dutch councils [1690]

Lloyd, William, *A discourse of God's ways in dispensing of kingdoms* (1691)

A sermon preached before her majesty on May 29, being the anniversary of the restoration of the king and royal family (1692)

A sermon preach'd before the House of Lords, at the abbey-church of St Peter's Westminster on Saturday 30 January 1696/7 (1697)

A sermon preached before the king and queen at Whitehall, March the twelfth 1689/90, being the fast day (1690)

A sermon preached before their majesties at Whitehall, on the fifth day of November 1689 (1689)

A sermon preached before the queen at Whitehall, January 30, being the day of the martyrdom of King Charles the First (1691)

[Long, Thomas], *The case of persecution charg'd on the church of England consider'd and discharg'd in order to her justification and a desired union of protestant dissenters* (1689)

Vox cleri: or the sense of the clergy concerning making alterations in the established liturgy (1690)

M. M., *Letter from the member of parliament, in answer to the letter of the divine, concerning the bill for uniting protestants* [1689]

Manningham, Thomas, *A sermon preach'd at the parish church of St Andrews, Holborn, 30 December 1694. On the most lamented death of our most gracious soveraign Queen Mary* (3rd edn, 1695)

Mary II, *Her majesties gracious letter to the justices of the peace in the county of Middlesex, July 9 1691, for the suppressing of prophaness and debauchery* (1691)

[Maurice, Henry], *Remarks from the country; upon the two letters relating to the convocation and alterations in the liturgy* (1690)

Middlesex Quarter Sessions, *Mid. ss. Ad. General. Quateral session [Public order respecting vice and immorality]* (1691)

Min Heer T. Van C.'s answer to Min Heer H. Van L.'s letter of 15 March 1689;
   representing the true interests of Holland and what they have already gained by
   our losses [1689]
The modern fanatical reformer, or the religious state tinker (1693)
[Montgomery, James], *Great Britain's just complaint for her late measures, present*
   sufferings and the future miseries she is exposed to (1692)
Morgan, Matthew, *A poem to the queen, upon the king's victory in Ireland, and his*
   voyage to Holland (Oxford, 1691)
Moyle, Walter, 'An essay on the constitution of the Roman government' [1699], in
   Robbins, *Two English republican tracts*
[Moyle, Walter], *An essay on the Lacedeamonian government* (1698)
The muses farewell to popery and slavery, or a collection of miscellaneous poems,
   satyrs, songs &c (1689)
The mystery of phanaticism, or the artifices of the dissenters to support their schism
   (1698)
Ollyffe, John, *England's call to thankfulness for her great deliverance ... in a sermon*
   preach'd in the church of Almer in Dorsetshire on Feb 14 1688/9 (1689)
An order of the Lords spiritual and temporal and Commons assembled at West-
   minster in this present convention for a publick thanksgiving (1688)
Patrick, Simon, *Angliae speculum, a glass that flatters not: presented to a country*
   congregation at the late solemn fast, April 24 1678 (1678)
   The autobiography of Symon Patrick, bishop of Ely (Oxford, 1839)
   The bishop of Ely's letter to the clergy of his diocese (1692)
   A letter of the bishop of Chichester to his clergy (1690)
   A sermon against murmuring preached at St Paul's Covent-Garden on the fifth
   Sunday in Lent, March 17 1688/9 (1689)
   A sermon preach'd at St Paul's Covent Garden on 31 January 1688, being the
   thanksgiving day for the deliverance of the kingdom (1689)
   A sermon preach'd at St Paul's Covent Garden, on the day of fasting and prayer,
   Novemb. 13 1678 (1678)
   A sermon preached at St Paul's Covent Garden, on the first Sunday in Lent; being a
   second part of the sermon preached before the prince of Orange (1689)
   A sermon preached before the king and queen at Whitehall, April 16 1690, being the
   fast day (1690)
   A sermon preached before the king and queen at Whitehall, March 1 1688/9 (1689)
   A sermon preach'd before the queen at Whitehall, 8 April 1692, being the fast day
   appointed to implore God's blessing on their majesties persons (1692)
   A sermon preached in the chappel of St James' before his highness, the prince of
   Orange, 20 January 1688 (1689)
The people of England's grievances inquired into [1693?]
Plain English: or an inquiry into the causes that have frustrated our expectations from
   the late happy revolution (1691)
The poor man's plea, in relation to all the proclamations, declarations, acts of
   parliament &c, which have been ... for a reformation of manners (1698)
A praier for the present expedition ([Hague], 1688)
The price of the abdication [1693]
The prince of Orange his declaration, shewing the reasons why he invades England,
   with a short preface, and some modest remarks on it (1688)
Proposals for a national reformation of manners, humbly offered to the consideration
   of our magistrates and clergy (1694)

The protestant commander; or a dialogue betwixt him and his loving lady [1690]

The puritanical justice: or the beggars turn'd thieves. A farce as it was late acted about the city of London (1698)

Reformation of manners: a satyr (1702)

A relation from the city of Orange of a crown of light that was there seen in the air, 6 May 1688, in *Complete collection of papers, part 1, p. 22.*

Remarks on the present confederacy and late revolution in England (1693)

A remonstrance and protestation of all the good protestants of this kingdom, against deposing their lawful sovereign, King James II (1689)

Robbins, Caroline, ed., *Two English republican tracts* (Cambridge, 1969)

The royal flight, or the conquest of Ireland (1690)

The royal voyage, or the Irish expedition (1690)

Royse, George, *A sermon preached before the king at Belfast on 14th day of June 1690* (1691)

The sad estate of the kingdom [1690]

Sanders, Nicholas, *De origine ac progressu schmatis anglicani liber* (Rome, 1586)

Scott, John, *A sermon preached at Fulham on Sunday Oct. 13 1689 at the consecration of ... Edward, lord bishop of Worcester, Simon, lord bishop of Chichester* (1689)

Scott, Walter, ed., *A collection of scarce and valuable tracts, on the most interesting and entertaining subjects* (13 vols., 1809–15)

Sedley, Charles, *The poetical works of the honourable Sir Charles Sedley, baronet, and his speeches in parliament* (1707)

The speech of Sir Charles Sidley in the House of Commons (1691)

Sharp, John, *A sermon about the government of the thoughts preach'd before the king and queen at Whitehall, 4 March ... 1693/4* (1694)

A sermon preached before the honourable House of Commons at St Margaret's Westminster, Wednesday 21 May 1690 being the day of the monthly-fast (1690)

A sermon preach'd before the king and queen at Whitehall, 12 Nov. 1693, being the day appointed for a publick thanksgiving (1693)

A sermon preached before the Lords spiritual and temporal in parliament assembled in the abbey-church at Westminster, on the fifth of November 1691 (1691)

A sermon preached on 28 June at St Giles in the Fields ... at his leaving the parish (1691)

A sermon preached on the day of the publick fast, April 11 1679, at St Margaret's Westminster, before the honourable House of Commons (1679)

To the reverend clergy of the diocese of York (1699)

Sherlock, William, *The case of allegience due to sovereign powers, stated and resolved* (1691)

A short defence of the last parliament with a word of advice for all electors to the ensuing (1699)

Short reflections upon the state of affairs in England: more especially, with relation to the taxes and contributions now necessary, (1691)

Shower, John, *A sermon preach'd to the societies for reformation of manners in the cities of London and Westminster ... November 15 1697* (1698)

The soldiers return, or his promise to his country-men perform'd [1690]

Some observations upon keeping the thirtieth of January (1694)

Some reflections upon his highness the prince of Orange's declaration (Edinburgh, 1688)

Sprat, Thomas, *A sermon preached before the king and queen at Whitehall on Good Friday 1690* (1690)

A sermon preached before the king and queen at Whitehall on Good Friday April 6 1694 (1694)

[Stephens, Edward], *An admonition concerning a publick fast* (1691)

An appeal to earth and heaven against the Christian Epicureans, who have betrayed their king and countrey (1691)

The beginnings and progress of a needful and hopeful reformation in England (1691)

A plain relation of the late action at sea, between the English and the Dutch, and the French fleets from June 22 to July 5 last (1689)

A specimin of a declaration against debauchery, tendered to the consideration of his highness, the prince of Orange (1688)

Stillingfleet, Edward, *The bishop of Worcester's charge to the clergy of his diocese in his primary visitation, begun at Worcester, Sept 11 1690* (1691)

Reformation of manners, the true way of honouring God. With the necessity of putting the laws in execution against vice and profaness. In a sermon preach'd at Whitehall [1709?]

A sermon preach'd before the queen at Whitehall February 22 1688/9 (1689)

A sermon preached on the fast day, November 13 1678, at St Margaret's, Westminster before the honourable House of Commons (2nd edn, 1678)

Talbot, William, *A sermon preached at the cathedral church of Worcester upon the monthly fast day, September 16 1691* (1691)

Tenison, Thomas, *His Grace the lord archbishop of Canterbury's letter to the right reverend the lords bishops of his province* (1699)

A sermon against self-love &c preached before the honourable House of Commons on 5 June 1689, being the fast day (1689)

A sermon concerning the coelestial body of a Christian, after the resurrection: preached before the king and queen at Whitehall, April 8 1694, being Easter day (1694)

A sermon concerning the folly of atheism preached before the queen at Whitehall, February 22 1690/1 (1691)

A sermon concerning holy resolution preached before the king at Kensington December 30 1694 (1695)

A sermon preached at the funeral of her late majesty Queen Mary of ever blessed memory in the abbey church in Westminster upon March 5 1694/5 (1695)

[Tenison, Thomas], *A discourse concerning the ecclesiastical commission open'd in the Jerusalem-Chamber, October 10 1689* (1689)

Tillotson, John, *A sermon preach'd at Lincoln's Inn chappel on 31 January 1688, being the day appointed for a public thanksgiving* (1689)

A sermon preach'd at St Mary le Bow before the Lord Mayor ... of London on Wed. 18 June, a day appointed by their majesties for a solemn monthly fast (1690)

A sermon preach'd at Whitehall before the queen on the monthly fast day, Sept. 16 1691 (1690)

A sermon preached before the honourable House of Commons on Wednesday 16 April. A day appointed by their majesties for a solemn monthly fast (1690)

A sermon preach'd before the king and queen at Hampton-Court April 14 1689 (1689)

A sermon preached before the king and queen at Whitehall, October 27, being the day appointed for the publick thanksgiving (1692)

[Tillotson, John], *A form of prayers used by his late majesty K. William III when he received the holy sacrament* (1704)

[Toland, John], *The 'art of governing by parties: particularly in religion, in politics, in parliament* (1701)

The militia reform'd, or an easy scheme of furnishing England with a constant land force ... without endangering the publick liberty (1697)

[Traubman, Matthew], *London's great jubilee, restor'd and perform'd on Tuesday October 29 1689* (1689)

[Trenchard, John], *A letter from a souldier to the Commons of England, occasioned by an address now carrying on by the protestants in Ireland* (1702)

A letter from the author of the argument against a standing army (1697)

A short history of standing armies in England (1698)

[Trenchard, John, and Moyle, Walter], *An argument shewing that a standing army is inconsistent with a free government* (1697)

The second part of an argument shewing that a standing army is inconsistent with a free government (1697)

A true account of the prince of Orange's coming to St James, on Tuesday the 18 of December 1688, about three of the clock in the afternoon (1688)

A true and exact relation of the prince of Orange his public entrance into Exeter ([Exeter], 1688)

A true and faithful account of the present condition of the kingdom of Ireland (1690)

A true and perfect journal of the affairs in Ireland since his majesties arrival in the kingdom (1690)

A true copy of the paper delivered to the sheriffs of London and Middlesex by William Anderton, at the place of execution [1693]

The valiant souldiers misfortune: or his grace the duke of Schomberg's last farewell [1690]

Vox laici: or the laymen's opinion touching the making alterations in our establish'd liturgy (1689)

Wake, William, *The authority of Christian princes over their ecclesiastical synods asserted* (1697)

An exhortation to mutual charity and union among protestants in a sermon preach'd before the king and queen at Hampton Court, May 21 1689 (1689)

Of our obligation to put our trust in God rather than in men ... a sermon preached before ... Gray's-Inn, upon the occasion of the death of our late royal sovereign, Queen Mary (1695)

A sermon preach'd before the honourable House of Commons at St Margaret's Westminster, June 5 1689, being the fast day (1689)

A sermon preach'd before the Lord-Mayor ... on Thursday 26 November, being the day of the publick thanksgiving (1691)

A sermon preached in the parish church of St James Westminster, April 26 1696, being the day of thanksgiving (1696)

Waterhall, Edward, *A sermon preached at Whitehall, before the queen, on the fourth Sunday in Lent, March 22 1690, reflecting on the late sufferings and deliverances of the protestants in the city and county of Cork* (Cork, 1691)

[Whittel, John], *An exact diary of the late expedition of his illustrious highness, the prince of Orange* (1689)

[Willes, John], *The judgement of the foreign reformed churches concerning the rites and offices of the church of England shewing there is no need of alteration* (1690)

William III, *The declaration of his highness William Henry, prince of Orange, of the reasons inducing him to appear in armes in the kingdom of England* (Hague, 1688)

His majesties gracious message to the convocation sent by the earl of Nottingham (1689)

His majesties letter to the lord bishop of London, to be communicated to the two provinces of Canterbury and York (1689)

His majesties most gracious speech to both houses of parliament, 19 October 1689 (1689)

The prince of Orange his speech in defence of the protestant religion (1688)

William III and Mary II, *A copy of the king and queen's commission sent to the convocation now assembled at Westminster* [1689]

Their majesties declaration against the French king (1689)

Williams, Daniel, *A sermon preached at Salters-Hall to the societies for reformation of manners, May 16 1698* (1698)

Woodhouse, John, *A sermon preach'd at Salters Hall to the societies for reformation of manners, May 31 1697* (1697)

Woodward, Josiah, *An account of the rise and progress of the religious societies* (1701)

An account of the progress of the reformation of manners in England, Scotland and Ireland (1701)

[Woodward, Josiah], *An account of the societies for the reformation of manners, in London and Westminster, and other parts of the kingdom* (1699)

SECONDARY SOURCES

Adamson, J. S. A., 'Oliver Cromwell and the Long Parliament', in Morrill, *Oliver Cromwell*, pp. 49–92

Allison, C. F., *The rise of moralism* (1966)

Anglo, Sydney, *Images of Tudor kingship* (1992)

Ashcraft, Richard, 'Latitudinarianism and toleration: historical myth versus political history', in Kroll *et al.*, *Philosophy, science and religion*, pp. 151–77

Revolutionary politics and Locke's 'Two treatises of government' (Princeton, 1986)

Ashcraft, Richard, and Goldsmith, M. M., 'John Locke, revolution principles and the formation of whig ideology', *HJ*, 26 (1983), 773–800

Aubrey, Philip, *The defeat of James Stuart's armada, 1692* (Leicester, 1979)

Bahlmann, Dudley W. R., *The moral revolution of 1688* (New Haven, Connecticut, 1957)

Baker, Derek, ed., *Renaissance and renewal in Christian history* (Oxford, 1977)

Barclay, Andrew, 'The impact of King James II on the departments of the royal household' (unpublished PhD dissertation, University of Cambridge, 1994)

Barry, Jonathan, 'Cultural patronage and the anglican crisis in Bristol, *c.* 1689–1775' in Walsh *et al.*, *The church of England*, pp. 191–208

Bartel, Roland, 'The story of public fast days in England', *Anglican Theological Review*, 37 (1955), pp. 190–220

Bauckham, Richard, *Tudor apocalypse* (Oxford, 1978)

Baxter, Stephen B., *William III* (1966)

'William III as Hercules: the political implications of court culture', in Schwoerer, *Revolution of 1688/9*, pp. 95–106

ed., *England's rise to greatness, 1660–1763* (Los Angeles, 1983)

Beales, Derek, and Best, Geoffrey, eds., *History, society and the churches* (Cambridge, 1985)

Beckett, J. V., 'Introduction: stability in politics and society', in Jones, *Britain in the first age of party*, pp. 1–18

Beddard, Robert, 'The Guildhall declaration of the 11th December, 1688, and the counter revolution of the loyalists' *HJ*, 11 (1968), 403–20

A kingdom without a king: the journal of the provisional government in the revolution of 1688 (Oxford, 1988)

'The Restoration church', in Jones, *Restored monarchy*, pp. 155–76

'The unexpected whig revolution of 1688', in Beddard, *Revolutions of 1688*, pp. 11–101

ed., *The revolutions of 1688* (Oxford, 1991)

Bennett, G. V., 'Archbishop Tenison and the reshaping of the church of England', *Friends of Lambeth Palace Library, Annual Report* (1981), pp. 10–17

'Conflict in the church', in Holmes, *Britain ... Glorious Revolution*, pp. 155–75

'King William III and the episcopate', in Bennett and Walsh, *Essays ... church history* (1966), pp. 104–32

Tory crisis in church and state: the career of Francis Atterbury (Oxford, 1975)

White Kennett, 1660–1728, bishop of Peterborough (1957)

Bennett, G. V., and Walsh, J. D., eds., *Essays in modern English church history* (1966)

Bergeron, D., *English civic pageantry, 1558–1642* (Columbia, South Carolina, 1971)

Bickersteth, John, *The Clerks of the Closet in the royal household: five hundred years of service of the crown* (Stroud, 1991)

Birch, Thomas, *The life of the most reverend Dr John Tillotson, lord archbishop of Canterbury, copied chiefly from his original papers and letters* (1752)

Brewer, John, *The sinews of power: war, money and the English state* (1989)

Brooks, Colin, 'The country persuasion and political responsibility in England in the 1690s', *Parliaments, Estates and Representations*, 4 (1984), 135–46

Browning, Andrew, *Thomas Osbourne: earl of Danby and duke of Leeds, 1632–1712* (3 vols., Glasgow, 1951)

Bucholz, R. O., *The Augustan court: Queen Anne and the decline of court culture* (Stanford, 1993)

Burtt, Shelley, *Virtue transformed: political argument in England, 1688–1740* (Cambridge, 1992)

Capp, B. S., *The fifth monarchy men: a study in seventeenth-century English millenarianism* (1972)

Carpenter, Edward, *The protestant bishop: the life of Henry Compton, bishop of London* (1956)

Thomas Tenison, archbishop of Canterbury, his life and times (1948)

Carswell, John, *The descent on England: a study of the English revolution of 1688 and its European background* (1969)

Carter, Jennifer, 'The Revolution and the constitution' in Holmes, *Britain ... Glorious Revolution*, pp. 39–58

Chapman, Hester W., *Mary II, queen of England* (Bath, 1972)

Childs, John, *The British army of William III, 1689–1702* (Manchester, 1987)

Christianson, Paul, 'From expectation to militance: reformers and Babylon in the first two years of the Long Parliament', *JEH*, 24 (1973), 225–44

The reformers and Babylon: English apocalyptic visions from the Reformation to the eve of the Civil War (Toronto, 1978)

Christmas, Henry, ed., *Select works of John Bale DD, bishop of Ossory* (Cambridge, 1849)

Clark, J. C. D., *English society, 1688–1832* (Cambridge, 1985)

Clarke, T. E. S., and Foxcroft, H. C., *A life of Gilbert Burnet, bishop of Salisbury* (Cambridge, 1907)

Claydon, Tony, 'William III's *Declaration of reasons*, and the revolution of 1688/9', *HJ* (forthcoming)

Colley, Linda, 'Britishness and otherness. An argument', *JBS*, 31 (1992), 309–29
Britons: forging the nation, 1707–1837 (1992)

Collinson, Patrick, *The birthpangs of protestant England: religious and cultural change in the sixteenth and seventeenth centuries* (Basingstoke, 1988)
The religion of the protestants (Oxford, 1982)

Cragg, G. R., *From puritanism to the age of reason* (Cambridge, 1966)
Reason and authority in the eighteenth century (Cambridge, 1964)

Craig, A. G., 'The movement for the reformation of manners 1690–1715' (unpublished PhD dissertation, University of Edinburgh, 1980)

Cressy, David, *Bonfires and bells: national memory and the protestant calendar in Elizabethan and Stuart England* (1989)
Literacy and the social order: reading and writing in Tudor and Stuart England (Cambridge, 1980)

Cross, Clare, 'Churchmen and the royal supremacy', in Heal and O'Day, *Church and society*, pp. 15–35
The royal supremacy in the Elizabethan church (1969)

Cruickshanks, Eveline, ed., *Ideology and conspiracy: aspects of Jacobitism 1689–1759* (Edinburgh, 1982)

Curtis, T. C., and Speck, W. A., 'The societies for reformation of manners: a case study in the theory and practice of moral reform', *Literature and History*, 3 (1976), 45–64

Cust, Richard, 'Politics and the electorate in the 1620s', in Cust and Hughes, *Conflict in early Stuart England*, pp. 134–67

Cust, Richard, and Hughes, Anne, eds., *Conflict in early Stuart England* (Harlow, 1989)

Cust, Richard, and Lake, Peter, 'Sir Richard Grosvenor and the rhetoric of magistracy', *BIHR*, 54 (1981), 40–53

Davies, C. E., 'The enforcement of religious uniformity in England, 1668–1700, with special reference to the dioceses of Chichester and Worcester' (unpublished DPhil dissertation, University of Oxford, 1982)

Davies, Catherine, ' "Poor persecuted little flock" or "commonwealth of Christians": Edwardian protestant concepts of the true church', in Lake and Dowling, *Protestantism and the national church*, pp. 78–102

Davison, Lee, Hitchcock, Tim, Kearns, Tim, and Shoemaker, Robert, eds., *Stilling the grumbling hive: the response to social and economic problems in England* (1992)

de Krey, Gary S., *A fractured society: the politics of London in the first age of party* (Oxford, 1985)

Dickens, A. G., ed., *The courts of Europe: politics, patronage and royalty, 1400–1800* (1977)

Dickinson, H. T., *Liberty and property: political ideology in eighteenth-century Britain* (1977)

Dickson, P. G. M., *The financial revolution in England: a study in the development of public credit* (1967)

Dictionary of national biography, (63 vols., 1865–1900)

Downie, J. A., 'The commission of public accounts and the formation of the country party', *EHR*, 91 (1976), 33–51
'The development of the political press', in Jones, *Britain in the first age of party*, pp. 111–28

Robert Harley and the press: propaganda and public opinion in the age of Swift and Defoe, (Cambridge, 1979)

'Robert Harley, Charles Davenant and the authorship of the *Worcester Queries*', *Literature and History*, 3 (1976), 83–99

Duffy, Eamon, 'Primitive Christianity revived: religious renewal in Augustan England', in Baker, *Renaissance and renewal*, pp. 287–300

Ede, Mary, *Arts and society in England under William and Mary* (1979)

Edie, Carolyn A., 'The public face of royal ritual: sermons, medals and civic ceremony in later Stuart coronations', *Huntington Library Quarterly*, 53 (1990), 311–36

Ellis, E. L., 'William III and the politicians', in Holmes, *Britain ... Glorious Revolution*, pp. 113–34

Elton, G. R., *Policy and police: the enforcement of the Reformation in the age of Cromwell* (Cambridge, 1972)

Every, George, *The high church party, 1688–1715* (1956)

Facey, Jane, 'John Foxe and the defence of the English church', in Lake and Dowling, *Protestantism and the national church*, pp. 162–92

Fairfield, Leslie P., *John Bale: mythmaker for the English Reformation* (West Lafayette, Indiana, 1976)

Feather, John, *A history of British publishing* (1988)

Feiling, Keith, *A history of the tory party, 1640–1714* (Oxford, 1924)

Fincham, Kenneth, ed., *The early Stuart church, 1603–1642* (Basingstoke, 1993)

Findon, J. C., 'The non-jurors and the church of England, 1689–1716' (unpublished DPhil dissertation, University of Oxford, 1979)

Finlayson, Michael, *Historians, puritanism and the English revolution: the religious factor in English politics before and after the Interregnum* (Toronto, 1983)

Firth, Katherine R., *The apocalyptic tradition in Reformation Britain, 1530–1645* (Oxford, 1979)

Fletcher, Anthony J., 'The first century of English protestantism and the growth of national identity', in Mews, *Religion and national identity*, pp. 309–19

The outbreak of the English Civil War (1981)

Reform in the provinces: the government of Stuart England (New Haven, Connecticut, 1986)

Forster, C. G. F., 'Government in provincial England under the later Stuarts', *TRHS*, 5th series 33 (1983), 29–48

Fritz, Paul S., 'From "public" to "private": the royal funerals in England, 1500–1830', in Whaley, *Mirrors of mortality* (1981), pp. 61–99

'The trade in death: the royal funerals in England', *Eighteenth Century Studies*, 5 (1985), 291–316

Gascoigne, J., 'Politics, patronage and Newtonianism: the Cambridge example', *HJ*, 27 (1984), 1–24

Gibbs, G. C., 'Press and public opinion: prospective', in Jones, *Liberty secured?*, pp. 231–65

Gidley, Mick, and Bowlen, Kate, eds., *Locating the shakers: cultural origins and legacies of an American religious movement* (Exeter, 1990)

Gilbert, A. D., *Religion and society in industrial England* (1976)

Goldie, Mark, 'John Locke, Jonas Proast and the politics of toleration', in Walsh *et al.*, *Church of England*, pp. 143–71

'The non-jurors, episcopacy, and the origins of the convocation controversy', in Cruickshanks, *Ideology and conspiracy*, pp. 15–35

'The political thought of the anglican revolution', in Beddard, *Revolutions of 1688*, pp. 102–36

'The revolution of 1689 and the structure of political argument: an essay and an annotated bibliography of pamphlets in the allegiance controversy', *Bulletin of Research in the Humanities*, 83 (1980), 473–564

'The roots of true whiggism, 1688–94', *History of Political thought*, 1 (1980), 195–236.

'Tory political thought, 1689–1714' (unpublished PhD dissertation, University of Cambridge, 1977)

Goldie, Mark, Harris, Tim, and Seaward, Paul, eds., *The politics of religion in Restoration England* (Oxford, 1990)

Greenburg, Janelle, 'Our grand maxim of state, "the king can do no wrong"', *History of Political Thought*, 12 (1991), 209–28

Gregg, Edward, *Queen Anne* (1980)

Gregory, W. Jeremy, 'Archbishop, cathedral and parish: the diocese of Canterbury, 1660–1805' (unpublished DPhil dissertation, University of Oxford, 1993)

'The eighteenth century reformation: the pastoral task of the clergy after 1689', in Walsh *et al.*, *Church of England*, pp. 67–85

Greig, Martin, 'The thought and polemic of Gilbert Burnet, *c*. 1673–1705' (unpublished PhD thesis, University of Cambridge, 1991)

Grell, Ole Peter, Israel, Jonathan I., and Tyacke, Nicholas, eds., *From persecution to toleration: the Glorious Revolution in England* (Oxford, 1991)

Gunn, S. J., and Lindley, P. G., eds., *Cardinal Wolsey: church, state and art* (Cambridge, 1991)

Habermas, Jurgen, *The structural transformation of the public sphere*, translated by Thomas Burger (Boston, 1989)

Haley, K. H. D., *The first earl of Shaftesbury* (Oxford, 1968)

Haller, William, *Foxe's 'Book of martyrs' and the elect nation* (1963)

Harris, John, 'The architecture of the Williamite court', in Maccubin and Hamilton-Phillips, *The age of William III*, pp. 225–33

Harris, Tim, *London crowds in the reign of Charles II* (Cambridge, 1987)

Politics under the later Stuarts: party conflict in a divided society (Harlow, 1993)

Hart, Arthur Tindal, *The life and times of John Sharp, archbishop of York* (1956)

William Lloyd, 1627–1717 (1952)

Harth, Phillip, *Pen for a party: Dryden's tory propaganda in its contexts* (Princeton, New Jersey, 1993)

Hayton, David, 'The "country" interest and the party system 1689–*c*.1720', in Jones, *Party and management*, pp. 37–86

'Moral reform and country politics in the late seventeenth-century House of Commons', *PP*, 128 (1990), 48–91

'Sir Richard Cocks: the anatomy of a country whig', *Albion*, 20 (1988), 221–46

'The propaganda war', in Maguire, *Kings in conflict*, pp. 106–21

'The Williamite revolution in Ireland, 1689–91', in Israel, *Anglo-Dutch moment*, pp. 185–214

Heal, Felicity, and O'Day, Rosemary, eds., *Church and society in England: Henry VIII to James I* (1977)

Hill, Brian W., *The growth of parliamentary parties, 1689–1742* (1976)

Robert Harley: Speaker, Secretary of State and premier minister (New Haven, Connecticut, 1988)

Hill, Christopher, *Antichrist in seventeenth-century England* (1971)

The English bible in the seventeenth-century revolution (1993)

God's Englishman (Harmondsworth, 1970)

Some intellectual consequences of the English revolution (1980)

A turbulent, seditious and factious people: John Bunyan and his church, 1628–1688 (Oxford, 1988)

The world turned upside down: radical ideas during the English revolution (1972)

Hitchcock, Tim, '"In true imitation of Christ": the tradition of mystical communitarianism in early eighteenth century England', in Gidley and Bowlen, *Locating the shakers*, pp. 12–25

Holmes, Clive, 'The country community in Stuart historiography', *JBS*, 12 (1980), 54–73

Holmes, Geoffrey, 'The achievement of stability: the social context of politics from the 1680s to the age of Walpole', in Holmes, *Politics, religion, and society*, pp. 249–80

Augustan England: professions, state and society, 1680–1730 (1982)

British politics in the age of Anne (revised edn, 1987)

Politics, religion, and society in England, 1679–1742 (1986)

The trial of Dr Sacheverell (1982)

ed., *Britain after the Glorious Revolution* (1979)

Holmes, Geoffrey, and Speck, W. A., eds., *The divided society: parties and politics in England, 1694–1716* (1967)

Hopkins, Paul, 'Aspects of Jacobite conspiracy in England in the age of William III' (unpublished PhD dissertation, University of Cambridge, 1981)

'Sham plots and real plots in the 1690s', in Cruickshanks, *Ideology and conspiracy*, pp. 98–110

Horwitz, Henry, '1689 (and all that)', *Parliamentary History*, 6 (1978), 23–32

Parliament, policy and politics in the reign of William III (Manchester, 1977)

'Parliament and the Glorious Revolution', *BIHR*, 47 (1974), 36–52

Revolution politicks: the career of Daniel Finch, second earl of Nottingham, 1647–1730 (Cambridge, 1968)

'The structure of parliamentary politics', in Holmes, *Britain ... Glorious Revolution*, pp. 96–115

Hudson, W. S., 'Fast days and civil religion', in Hudson and Trinterud, *Theology ... England*, pp. 1–24.

Hudson, W. S., and Trinterud, L. J., eds., *Theology in sixteenth- and seventeenth-century England* (Los Angeles, 1971)

Hughes, Anne, 'Local history and the origins of civil war', in Cust and Hughes, *Conflict in early Stuart England*, pp. 224–53

Isaacs, Tina, 'The anglican hierarchy and the reformation of manners', *JEH*, 33 (1982), 391–411

'Moral crime, moral reform and the state: a study in piety and politics in early eighteenth-century England' (unpublished PhD dissertation, University of Rochester, New York, 1979)

Israel, Jonathan I., ed., *The Anglo-Dutch moment: essays on the Glorious Revolution and its world impact* (Cambridge, 1991)

'The Dutch role in the Glorious Revolution', in Israel, *Anglo-Dutch moment*, pp. 105–62

'William III and toleration', in Grell *et al.*, *From persecution to toleration*, pp. 129–70

Israel, Jonathan, and Parker, Geoffrey, 'Of providence and protestant winds: the Spanish armada of 1588 and the Dutch armada of 1688', in Israel, *Anglo-Dutch moment*, pp. 335–64

Jacob, M. C., *The Newtonians and the English revolution, 1689–1720* (Hassocks, Sussex, 1976)

Jacob, M. C., and Lockwood, W. A., 'Political millenarianism and Burnet's *Sacred theory*', *Science Studies*, 2 (1972), 265–79

Jones, Clyve, ed., *Britain in the first age of party* (1987)
    ed., *Party and management in parliament, 1660–1784* (Leicester, 1984)

Jones, D. L., *War and economy in the age of William III and Marlborough* (Oxford, 1988)

Jones, D. W., *A parliamentary history of the Glorious Revolution* (1988)

Jones, J. R., *Charles II: royal politician* (1987)
    Country and court: England 1658–1714 (1978)
    The revolution of 1688 in England (1972)
    ed., *Liberty secured? Britain before and after 1688* (Stanford, California, 1992)
    ed., *The restored monarchy, 1660–1688* (1979)

Kenyon, J. P., *Revolution principles: the politics of party 1689–1720* (Cambridge, 1977)
    The Stuart constitution: documents and commentary (Cambridge, 1966)

King, John N., *English Reformation literature: the Tudor origins of the protestant tradition* (Princeton, 1982)

Knights, Mark, *Politics and opinion in crisis, 1678–81* (Cambridge, 1994)

Kramnick, Isaac, *Bolingbroke and his circle: the politics of nostalgia in the age of Walpole* (Cambridge, Massachusetts, 1968)

Kroll, Richard, Ashcraft, Richard, and Zagorin, Perez, eds., *Philosophy, science and religion in England, 1640–1700* (Cambridge, 1991)

Lake, Peter, *Anglicans and puritans?: presbyterianism and English conformist thought from Whitgift to Hooker* (1988)
    'Anti-popery: the structure of a prejudice', in Cust and Hughes, *Conflict in early Stuart England*, pp. 72–106

Lake, Peter, and Dowling, Maria, eds., *Protestantism and the national church in sixteenth-century England* (1987)

Lamont, William M., *Godly rule: politics and religion 1603–59* (1969)
    Richard Baxter and the millennium: protestant imperialism and the English revolution (1979)
    'Richard Baxter, the apocalypse and the mad major', *PP*, 55 (1972), 68–90

Laquer, Thomas, 'The cultural origins of popular literacy in England', *Oxford Review of Education*, 2 (1976), 255–75

Levy, F. J., *Tudor historical thought* (San Marino, c.1967)

Lewis, Ioan, ed., *Symbols and sentiments: cross cultural studies in symbolism* (1977)

Loach, Jennifer, 'The function of ceremonial in the reign of Henry VIII', *PP*, 142 (1994), 43–68

Loades, David, 'The origins of English protestant nationalism', in Mews, *Religion and national identity*, pp. 297–308

Macaulay, T. B., *The history of England to the death of William III* (Heron books edn, 4 vols., 1984)

Maccubin, Robert P., and Hamilton-Phillips, Martha, eds., *The age of William III and Mary II: power, politics and patronage, 1688–1702* (Williamsburg, 1989)

MacCulloch, Diarmaid, *The later Reformation in England, 1547–1603* (Basingstoke, 1990)

McGifford, Michael, 'God's controversy with Jacobean England', *AHR*, 88 (1983), 1151–74

McInnes, Angus, *Robert Harley, puritan politician* (1970)
  'When was the English revolution?', *History*, 67 (1982), 377–92
McJimsey, Robert D., 'A country divided? English politics and the Nine Years War',
  Albion, 23 (1991), 61–74
McKeon, Michael, *Politics and poetry in Restoration England: the case of Dryden's
  'Annus mirabilis'* (1975)
Maguire, W. A., ed., *Kings in conflict: the revolutionary war in Ireland and its
  aftermath, 1689–1750* (Belfast, 1990)
Mann, Michael, *The sources of social power* (Cambridge, 1986)
Marshall, John, 'John Locke and latitudinarianism', in Kroll *et al.*, *Philosophy,
  science and religion*, pp. 253–82
Marshall, William M., 'Episcopal activity in the Hereford and Oxford dioceses,
  1660–1760', *Midland History*, 8 (1983), 106–120
Mews, Stuart, ed., *Religion and national identity* (Oxford, 1982)
Miller, John, *James II: a study in kingship* (1989)
  Popery and politics in England, 1660–1688 (Cambridge, 1973)
Monod, Paul, 'Jacobitism and country principles in the reign of William III', *HJ*, 30
  (1987), 289–310
  Jacobitism and the English people, 1688–1788 (Cambridge, 1989)
Morrill, John, 'The Britannic revolution, 1640–60' (Unpublished seminar paper read
  at the Cambridge seventeenth-century seminar, autumn term, 1992)
  ed., *Oliver Cromwell and the English revolution* (1990)
Nelson, Carolyn, 'English newspapers and periodicals', in Maccubin and Hamilton-
  Phillips, *Age of William III*, pp. 366–72
Nenner, Howard, 'The constitution in retrospect from 1689' in Jones, *Liberty
  secured?*, pp. 88–122
Parker, Geoffrey, *The military revolution: military innovation and the rise of the West*
  (Cambridge, 1988)
Pincus, Steven C. A., 'Popery, trade and universal monarchy: the ideological context
  of the outbreak of the second Anglo-Dutch war', *EHR*, 107 (1992), 1–29
Plant, Marjorie, *The English book trade: an economic history of the making and sale
  of books* (2nd edn, 1965)
Plomer, Henry R., *A dictionary of the printers and booksellers who were working in
  England, Scotland and Ireland, 1686–1725* (Oxford, 1922)
Plumb, J. H., *The growth of political stability in England, 1675–1725* (1967)
Pocock, J. G. A., *The ancient constitution and the feudal law: a study of English
  historical thought in the seventeenth century* (reissue with retrospect, Cambridge,
  1987)
  'Civic humanism and its role in Anglo-American thought', in Pocock, *Politics,
  language and time*, pp. 80–103
  'Machiavelli, Harrington and English political ideologies in the eighteenth century',
  in Pocock, *Politics, language and time*, pp. 104–47
  *The Machiavellian moment: Florentine political thought and the Atlantic repub-
  lican tradition* (Princeton, 1975)
  Politics, language and time: essays on political thought and history (1971)
  ed., *The political works of James Harrington* (Cambridge, 1977)
Pollard, Graham, 'The English market for printed books', *Publishing History*, 4
  (1978), 9–48
Popkin, Richard M., ed., *Millenarianism and messianism in English literature and
  thought, 1650–1800* (Leiden, 1988)

Pruett, J. H., *The parish clergy under the later Stuarts* (Urbana, Illinois, 1978)

Ray, Anthony, 'Delftware in England' in Maccubin and Hamilton-Phillips, *Age of William III*, pp. 301–7

Rex, Richard, *Henry VIII and the English Reformation* (Basingstoke, 1993)

Richards, J. O., *Party propaganda under Queen Anne* (Athens, Georgia, 1972)

Riley, P. W. J., *King William and the Scottish politicians* (Manchester, 1979)

Rivers, Isabel, *Reason, grace and sentiment: a study of the language of religion and ethics in England, 1660–1780* (Cambridge, 1991)

Roberts, Clayton, 'The constitutional significance of the financial settlement of 1690', *HJ*, 20 (1977), 59–76

Rose, Craig, 'Providence, protestant union and godly reformation in the 1690s', *TRHS* 6th series 3 (1993), 151–70

Rubini, Dennis, *Court and country, 1688–1702* (1967)

Rupp, Gordon, *Religion in England 1688–1791* (Oxford, 1985)

[Salmon, Nathaniel], *The lives of the English bishops from the Restauration to the Revolution* (1731)

Sandford, Francis, and Stebbino, Samuel, *A genealogical history of the kings and queens of England and monarchs of Great Britain* (1707)

Schama, Simon, *The embarrassment of riches: an interpretation of Dutch culture in the golden age* (1987)

Schonhorn, Manuel, *Defoe's politics: parliament, power, kingship and Robinson Crusoe* (Cambridge, 1991)

Schwartz, Hillel, *The French prophets: the history of a millenarian group in eighteenth-century England* (Los Angeles 1980)

Schuckman, Christiaan, 'Dutch printing and printmaking' in Maccubin and Hamilton-Phillips, *Age of William III*, pp. 281–92

Schwoerer, Lois G., 'The coronation of William and Mary, April 11th, 1689', in Schwoerer, *Revolution of 1688/9*, pp. 107–30

　　The declaration of rights, 1689 (Baltimore, 1981)

　　'The Glorious Revolution as spectacle: a new perspective', in Baxter, *England's rise*, pp. 109–49

　　'Images of Queen Mary II, 1689–95', *Renaissance Quarterly*, 42 (1989), 717–48

　　'A jornall of the convention at Westminster begun 22 January 1688/9', *BIHR*, 49 (1976), 242–63

　　No standing armies! the anti-army ideology in seventeenth-century England (Baltimore, 1974)

　　'Propaganda in the revolution of 1688–9', *AHR*, 82 (1977), pp. 843–74

　　ed., *The revolution of 1688/9: changing perspectives* (Cambridge, 1991)

Scott, Jonathan, *Algernon Sidney and the Restoration crisis, 1677–1683* (Cambridge, 1991)

Seaward, Paul, *The Cavalier Parliament and the reconstruction of the old regime, 1661–7* (Cambridge, 1989)

　　'Gilbert Sheldon and the London vestries', in Goldie *et al.*, *Politics of religion*, pp. 49–75

　　The Restoration, 1660–1688 (1991)

Shapiro, B. J., *Probability and certainty in seventeenth century England* (Princeton, 1983)

Sharp, Thomas, *A life of John Sharp, DD, lord archbishop of York* (2 vols., 1825)

Sharpe, Kevin, *Criticism and compliment: the politics of literature in the England of Charles I* (Cambridge, 1987)

The personal rule of Charles I (New Haven, Connecticut, 1992)

Sharpe, Kevin, and Lake, Peter, eds., *Culture and politics in early Stuart England* (Basingstoke, 1994).

Sherwood, Roy, *The court of Oliver Cromwell* (Cambridge, 1977)

Shoemaker, Robert B., 'Reforming the city: the reformation of manners campaign in London, 1690–1738', in Davison *et al.*, *Stilling the grumbling hive*, pp. 99–120

Prosecution and punishment: petty crime in London and rural Middlesex c. 1660–1725 (Cambridge, 1991)

Siebert, F. S., *The freedom of the press in England, 1476–1776* (Urbana, Illinois, 1952)

Simms, J. C., 'Schomberg at Dundalk', in Simms, *War and politics*, pp. 91–104

War and politics in Ireland 1649–1730 (1986)

The Williamite confiscations in Ireland, 1690–1703 (1956)

Somerville, C. J., *Popular religion in Restoration England* (Gainesville, Florida, 1977)

The secularization of early modern England: from religious culture to religious faith (Oxford, 1992)

Spaeth, Donald A., 'Common prayer? popular observance of the anglican liturgy in Restoration Wiltshire', in Wright, *Parish, church and people*, pp. 121–51

Speck, W. A., *Reluctant revolutionaries: Englishmen and the revolution of 1688* (Oxford, 1988)

'William – and Mary?', in Schwoerer, *Revolution of 1688/9*, pp. 131–46

Spufford, Margaret, 'First steps in literacy: the reading and writing experiences of the humblest seventeenth-century spiritual autobiographers', *Social History*, 4 (1979), 407–35

Small books and pleasant histories: popular fiction and its readership in seventeenth-century England (1982)

Spurr, John, 'The church of England, comprehension and the toleration act of 1689', *EHR*, 104 (1989), 927–46

' "Latitudinarianism" and the Restoration church', *HJ*, 31 (1988), 61–82

The Restoration church of England, 1646–1689 (New Haven, 1991)

'The Restoration church of England and the moral revolution of 1688', in Walsh *et al.*, *Church of England*, pp. 127–42

'Virtue, religion and government: the anglican uses of providence', in Goldie *et al.*, *Politics of religion*, pp. 29–47

Starkey, David, 'Representation through intimacy: a study in the symbolism of monarchy and court office in early modern England', in Lewis, *Symbols and sentiments*, pp. 187–224

ed., *The English court from the Wars of the Roses to the Civil War* (1987)

ed., *Henry VIII: a European court in England* (1991)

Stone, Lawrence, 'Literacy and education in England 1640–1900', *PP*, 42 (1969), 69–139

Straka, Gerald, *Anglican reaction to the Revolution of 1688*, (Madison, Wisconsin, 1962)

Strong, Roy, *Britannia triumphans: Inigo Jones, Rubens and Whitehall Palace* (1980)

The cult of Elizabeth: Elizabethan portraiture and pageantry (1977)

Holbein and Henry VIII (1967)

Royal gardens (1992)

Splendour at court: renaissance spectacle and illusion (1973)

Sutherland, L. S., and Mitchell, L. G., eds., *The history of the University of Oxford* (Oxford, 1986)

Swedenberg, H. T., ed., *The works of John Dryden*, (20 vols., Los Angeles, 1969)

Sykes, Norman, *From Sheldon to Secker: aspects of English church history, 1660–1768* (Cambridge, 1959)

William Wake, archbishop of Canterbury, 1657–1737 (2 vols., Cambridge, 1957)

Thompson, Martyn P., 'The reception of Locke's *Two treatises of government*, 1690–1705', *Political Studies*, 24 (1976), 184–91

Thomson, M. A., *A constitutional history of England, 1642–1801* (London, 1938)

Tyacke, Nicholas, *Anti-Calvinists: the rise of English Arminianism, 1590–1640* (Oxford, 1987)

Waddell, D., 'Charles Davenant, 1656–1714: a biographical sketch', *Economic History Review*, 2nd series 11 (1958–9), 279–88

Walsh, John, Haydon, Colin, and Taylor, Stephen, eds., *The church of England c.1689–c.1833: from toleration to tractarianism* (Cambridge, 1993)

Watts, Michael R., *The dissenters: from the Reformation to the French revolution* (Oxford, 1978)

Western, J. R., *Monarchy and revolution: the English state in the 1680s* (1972)

Weston, Corinne Comstock, and Greenburg, Janelle Renfrew, *Subjects and sovereigns: the grand controversy over legal sovereignty in Stuart England* (Cambridge, 1981)

Whaley, Joachim, ed., *Mirrors of mortality: studies in the social history of death* (1981)

Whiteman, E. A. O., 'The episcopate of Dr Seth Ward, bishop of Exeter (1662–1667) and Salisbury (1667–1688/9), with special reference to the ecclesiastical problems of his time' (Unpublished DPhil dissertation, University of Oxford, 1951)

Williams, Neville, 'The Tudors', in Dickens, *The courts of Europe*, pp. 147–68

Williams, Penry, *The Tudor regime* (Oxford, 1979)

Willman, Robert, 'The origins of "whig" and "tory" in English political language', *HJ*, 17 (1974), 247–64

Worden, Blair, 'Oliver Cromwell and the sin of Achan', in Beales and Best, *History, society and the churches*, pp. 125–45.

Wright, S. J., ed., *Parish, church and people: local studies in religion, 1350–1750* (1988)

Yates, Frances A., *Astraea: the imperial theme in the sixteenth century* (1975)

Zagorin, Perez, *The court and the country: the beginning of the English revolution* (New York, 1969)

Zimmerman, Franklin B., 'The court music of Henry Purcell' in Maccubin and Hamilton-Phillips, *Age of William III*, pp. 311–18

Zwicker, Stephen, 'England, Israel and the triumph of Roman virtue', in Popkin, *Millenarianism*, pp. 37–64

INDEX

Cambridge Studies in Early Modern British History

Titles in the series

DATE DUE
